Lecture Notes in Computer Science 7760

Commenced Publication in 1973
Founding and Former Series Editors:
Gerhard Goos, Juris Hartmanis, and Jan van Leeuwen

W0235162

Hironori Kasahara   Keiji Kimura (Eds.)

Languages and Compilers for Parallel Computing

25th International Workshop, LCPC 2012
Tokyo, Japan, September 11-13, 2012
Revised Selected Papers

 Springer

Volume Editors

Hironori Kasahara
Keiji Kimura
Waseda University
Faculty of Science and Engineering
Department of Computer Science and Engineering
27 Waseda-machi, Shinjuku-ku
Tokyo, 162-0042, Japan
E-mail: kasahara@waseda.jp
E-mail: kimura@apal.cs.waseda.ac.jp

ISSN 0302-9743   e-ISSN 1611-3349
ISBN 978-3-642-37657-3   e-ISBN 978-3-642-37658-0
DOI 10.1007/978-3-642-37658-0
Springer Heidelberg Dordrecht London New York

Library of Congress Control Number: 2013934838

CR Subject Classification (1998): D.1.3, D.3.2-4, D.2.4-5, D.2.11, D.4.1-2, C.2.4, C.4, F.2.2

LNCS Sublibrary: SL 1 – Theoretical Computer Science and General Issues

Typesetting: Camera-ready by author, data conversion by Scientific Publishing Services, Chennai, India

Printed on acid-free paper

Springer is part of Springer Science+Business Media (www.springer.com)

Preface

It is our pleasure to present the papers accepted for the 25th Anniversary International Workshop on Languages and Compilers for Parallel Computing (LCPC) held during September 11-13, 2012, at Waseda University in Tokyo, Japan, as the first workshop held outside the North American continent. Since 1988, the LCPC has been an established workshop that provides opportunities to share state-of-the-art research on all aspects of parallel computing, including parallel languages, compilers, runtime systems, tools, and computer architectures. This year's LCPC workshop marked its 25th anniversary and continued this tradition. The scope of the workshop spans parallel programming models, compiler and runtime optimizations, practical applications, and heterogeneous computing. This year's LCPC was attended by 89 registrants from across the globe. The conference tour to K Supercomputer Center located in Kobe was held on September 14, 2012.

This year, the workshop received 39 submissions from all over the world – 17 from Europe, 16 from North America, 4 from Asia, and 2 from Africa. Of these submissions, the Program Committee (PC) selected 16 papers for presentation at the workshop, representing an acceptance rate of 41%. Each selected paper was presented in a 30-minute slot during the workshop. In addition, six submissions were selected for presentation as posters during a 90-minute poster session. Each submission received at least three reviews. The PC held an all-day meeting on July 19, 2012, to discuss the papers. When each paper was discussed, PC members who had a conflict of interest with the paper were asked to temporarily leave the meeting. Decisions for all PC-authored submissions were made by PC members who were not coauthors of any submissions.

We were fortunate to have three superior keynote speakers at this 25th Anniversary LCPC Workshop. Arvind, Professor of Computer Science and Engineering at the Massachusetts Institute of Technology, gave a keynote talk titled "Programming in the Brave New World of Systems-on-a-Chip." The second keynote talk titled "Modeling Computation for HW/SW Codesign" was given by David Kuck, Intel Fellow and Professor Emeritus of the University of Illinois at Urbana-Champaign. The third keynote talk, "To Err Is Human; To Forgive, Divine," was given by Yoichi Muraoka, Professor of Computer Science at Waseda University.

We were also fortunate to be able to invite six distinguished speakers for technical sessions: David Padua from the University of Illinois at Urbana-Champaign, Lawrence Rauchwerger from Texas A&M University, Alex Nicolau from the University of California, Irvine, Professor Monica Lam from Stanford University, Professor Rudolf Eigenmann from Purdue University, and Utpal Banerjee from the University of California, Irvine. The presentation slides of these keynote and invited talks are available at the LCPC 2012 workshop website, http://www.kasahara.cs.waseda.ac.jp/lcpc2012.

We would like to conclude by thanking the many people whose dedicated time and effort helped make LCPC 2012 a success. We first want to thank all authors who contributed papers to the workshop. The hard work invested by the PC members and external reviewers in reviewing the submissions helped ensure a high-quality technical program for the workshop. The founding members, the Steering Committee members, and the LCPC 2011 Organizing Committee provided valuable guidance that greatly helped the preparation of the 25th commemorable LCPC. All participants in the workshop contributed directly to the technical vitality of the event either as presenters or as audience members. We would also like to thank the workshop sponsor Multicore Processor Research Institute. Finally, the workshop would not have been possible without the tireless efforts of the local arrangements staff at the Green Computing Systems Research & Development Center at Waseda University.

September 2012   Hironori Kasahara
                                                                  Keiji Kimura

Organization

LCPC 2012 was organized by the Department of Computer Science at Waseda University.

Steering Committee

Rudolf Eigenmann	Purdue University, USA
Alex Nicolau	University of California at Irvine, USA
David Padua	University of Illinois at Urbana-Champaign, USA
Lawrence Rauchwerger	Texas A&M University, USA

General Chair

Hironori Kasahara	Waseda University, Japan

Program Chair

Keiji Kimura	Waseda University, Japan

Program Committee

Calin Cascaval	Qualcomm, USA
Keith Cooper	Rice University, USA
Masato Edahiro	Nagoya University, Japan
Hiroki Honda	The University of Electro-Communications, Japan
Keiji Kimura	Waseda University, Japan
Pablo Montesinos-Ortego	Qualcomm, USA
Sanjay Rajopadhye	Colorado State University, USA
Vivek Sarkar	Rice University, USA
Jun Shirako	Rice University, USA
Michelle Strout	Colorado State University, USA
Kazunori Ueda	Waseda University, Japan

Proceedings Chairs

Jun Shirako	Rice University, USA
Mamoru Shimaoka (Vice Chair)	Waseda University, Japan

Local Arrangements Co-chairs

Akihiro Hayashi   Waseda University, Japan
Hiroki Mikami   Waseda University, Japan

External Reviewers

Vincent Cavé   Rice University, USA
Toshio Endo   Tokyo Institute of Technology, Japan
Nima Honarmand   University of Illinois at Urbana-Champaign,
                                 USA
Guillaume Iooss   Colorado State University, USA
Masaaki Kondo   The University of Electro-Communications,
                                 Japan
Christopher Krieger   Colorado State University, USA
Masayoshi Mase   Hitachi, Ltd., Japan
Kazuyuki Shudo   Tokyo Institute of Technology, Japan
Daisuke Takahashi   University of Tsukuba, Japan
Nozomu Togawa   Waseda University, Japan
Tomofumi Yuki   Colorado State University, USA
Yasutaka Wada   The University of Electro-Communications,
                                 Japan
Yun Zou   Colorado State University, USA

Sponsoring Institution

Advanced Multicore Processor Research Institute, Waseda University

Table of Contents

Workshop Posters

Just in Time Load Balancing

Rosario Cammarota, Alexandru Nicolau, and Alexander V. Veidenbaum

University of California Irvine

Abstract. Leveraging Loop Level Parallelism (LLP) is one of the most attractive techniques for improving program performance on emerging multi-cores. Ordinary programs contain a large amount of parallel and DOALL loops, however emerging multi-core designs feature a rapid increase in the number of on-chip cores and the ways such cores share on-chip resources - such as pipeline and memory hierarchy, leads to an increase in the number of possible high-performance configurations. This trend in emerging multi-core design makes attaining peak performance through the exploitation of LLP an increasingly complex problem.

In this paper, we propose a new iteration scheduling technique to speedup the execution of DOALL loops on complex multi-core systems. Our technique targets the execution of DOALL loops with a variable cost per iteration and exhibiting *either a predictable or an unpredictable behavior* across multiple instances of a DOALL loop. In the former case our technique implements a quick run-time pass - to identify chunks of iterations containing the same amount of work - followed by a static assignment of such chunks to cores. If the static parallel execution is not profitable, our technique can decide to run such a loop either sequentially or in parallel, but using dynamic scheduling and an appropriate selection of the chunk size to optimize performance.

We implemented our technique in GNU GCC/OpenMP and demonstrate promising results on three important linear algebra kernels - matrix multiply, Gauss-Jordan elimination and adjoint convolution - for which near-optimal speedup against existing scheduling techniques is attained. Furthermore, we demonstrate the impact of our approach on the already parallelized program `470.lbm` from SPEC CPU2006, implementing the Lattice Boltzman Method. On `470.lbm`, our technique attains a speedup up to 65% on the state-of-the-art 4-cores, 2-way Symmetric Multi-Threading Intel Sandy Bridge architecture.

1   Introduction

Parallel loops are the largest source of parallelism in ordinary programs - the coverage of parallel loops in SPEC CFP2000 and CFP2006[1, 2] is high ($\approx 90\%$) and many of these loops are inherently parallel or DOALL [3].The execution of DOALL loops in parallel can significantly speedup ordinary programs. Several dynamic [4–9] and static [10] techniques have been proposed for scheduling iterations of DOALL loops on parallel machines. However, scheduling DOALL loops on modern multi-cores - with complex memory hierarchy organizations and multiple levels of parallelism, such as instructions level parallelism, vector

H. Kasahara and K. Kimura (Eds.): LCPC 2012, LNCS 7760, pp. 1–16, 2013.

units, symmetric multi-threading etc. - may not deliver peak performance [11]. On one hand, while free of run-time overheads, static techniques are either too simple (e.g., the OpenMP [12] implementations in GNU GCC [13] and Intel ICC [14]) to cope with cases where the cost per iteration is variable, or too complex, e.g., profile-based techniques [10], to be implemented as part of run-time systems. Dynamic techniques, on the other hand, may reduce the benefit of the parallel execution when, for example, the run-time synchronization overhead is relatively large compared with the execution time (cost) of the serial loop, but can attain better load balancing with an appropriate selection of the chunk size.

This paper proposes a new scheduling technique to speedup the execution of DOALL loops on modern complex multi-core systems. Our technique targets the execution of DOALL loops with a variable cost per iteration - e.g., loops performing triangularization, that constitutes a fundamental step for many linear algebra solvers. The proposed technique relies on the assumption that parallel loops are invoked multiple times during the execution of an ordinary program, as exemplified by the number of instances of hot loops in SPEC OMP2001 [15, 16] (> 50 per hot loop) and NAS parallel benchmarks (from 100 to > 1000 times per hot loop). At run-time, our technique first attempts to find a static schedule such that the work is "optimally" distributed among cores. If such a schedule is not profitable and/or unattainable - because the behavior of present instances of the loop is not predictive of the behavior of future instances - our technique can decide to run such a loop either sequentially or in parallel, but using dynamic scheduling techniques with an appropriate selection of the number of iterations to schedule at once - referred to as a chunk size.

Specifically, our technique implements a quick pass at run-time, which attempts to determine chunks of iterations - that are expressed as a percentage of the total number of iterations - such that each chunk contains an equal part of the total cost of the loop. Such chunks are subsequently statically assigned to the p cores. Given that the assignment of chunks of iterations to cores is static, once the schedule is ready the proposed technique does not suffer of additional run-time overheads. Performance improves when the behavior of previous instances of the loops is predictive of the behavior of subsequent instances and the outermost loop is performs many iterations.

When a parallel loop does not exhibit a variable cost per iteration, our technique outputs chunks of equal size. For example, while scheduling a parallel loop with constant cost per iteration - such as the case of a basic implementation of matrix multiply - on two cores, our technique determines that 50% of the iterations must be assigned to one core and the remaining 50% must be assigned to the another core. On the contrary, in the case of a loop with a decreasing/increasing or exhibiting arbitrary variations in the cost per iteration, our technique will determine the percentage of iterations to assign to each cores such that each core will execute the same amount of work.

When the behavior of previous instances of a parallel loop is not predictive of the behavior of future instances, our technique can decide to execute the instances of such a loop in parallel, but opting for a dynamic scheduling strategy.

In this case, an estimation of the number of iterations to schedule at once, i.e., the chunk size is attempted. The determination of the chunk size uses an heuristic based on the average cost per iteration and the cost of synchronization overhead. The average cost per iteration is determined at run-time, whereas the cost of synchronization overhead is estimated offline using micro-benchmarking [17] on the architecture in use. The chunk size is determined dividing the cost of synchronization overhead by the average cost per iteration - refer to Section 2.2. Alternatively, if dynamic scheduling is not profitable, our technique opts to run the loop sequentially.

We implemented our technique in GNU GCC OpenMP and show promising results on three important linear algebra kernels - matrix multiply, Gauss-Jordan elimination and adjoint convolution implemented as in [5] - and 470.1bm from SPEC CPU2006 on 4-cores, 2-way Symmetric Multi-Threading (SMT) cores Intel Sandy Bridge architecture. Specifically, our technique attains nearly optimal speedup for the three kernels above and up to 65% performance improvement for 470.1bm against the use of prior scheduling techniques.

The rest of the paper is organized as follows: our technique is detailed in Section 2; Experimental results are presented in Section 3; Prior and related work are discussed in Section 4; The conclusion is presented in Section 5.

2   Just in Time Load Balancing

The technique proposed in this paper is motivated by the observation that in ordinary programs many instances of a parallel DOALL loop are usually executed within a serial loop [16]. Therefore, a few of these instances can be leveraged to learn properties of the parallel loop and prepare a schedule that optimizes program performance. Our initial goal is to prepare a schedule that distributes uniform chunks of iterations to the available cores. When the threads involved in the parallel execution start nearly at the same time (this situation typically occur for program executing parallel loops according to a fork-join execution model) such threads are also likely to complete their executions nearly at the same time and overall the number of elapsed cycles of the parallel execution is minimized.

The typical scenario considered in this paper is shown in Listing 1.1, where a sequence of many instances of a DOALL loop - the inner loop - are executed. The assumption made on Listing 1.1 about the body of the parallel loop are: (a) the body of the loop must contain re-entrant/thread-safe code; (b) the statements in the body of the loop are at most a function of the indexes of the loops surrounding it - in the example the body of the loop depends on the indexes xx and tt; (c) the loop bounds and the stride are constant (a relaxation of such an assumption is discussed later on in this section). [1]

The basic idea of our technique is to transform - at compile-time - the loop of Listing 1.1 into that of Listing 1.2. The outermost serial loop is "distributed" in

---

[1] Note that, the assumptions made on the body of the loop admit the presence of nested (parallel/serial) perfect or multi-way loops with conditional, functions calls, indirect references, etc.

three consecutive passes, as shown in Listing 1.2. [2] The first two instances of the parallel loop are executed sequentially whereas the subsequent instances are executed with a schedule determined by our technique. Overall, performance improves when the behavior of previous instances of the loops is predictive of the behavior of subsequent instances and the outermost loop performs many iterations.

Listing 1.1. Loop model

```
/* Serial loop iterating over time steps */
for (tt=0; tt<time_max; tt++)
{
  /* Parallel loop automatically parallelized with OpenMP */
  #pragma omp parallel for
  for (xx=start; xx<end; x+=stride)
  {
    /* Body of the loop */
    Body(xx, tt);
  }
}
```

Listing 1.2. Transformed, adaptive instrumented loop

```
...
/* parameters of the scheduling algorithm
   where p is the number of threads     */
int *parts;
int ii;
long long d, C;
...

/* Serial loop iterating over time steps */

/* Pass 1 - Compute the total cost per iteration  */
start_probe_cost(&C);
for (xx=start; xx<end; x+=stride)
{
  Body(xx, 0);
}
get_probe_cost(&C);

/* Pass 2.a - Compute the schedule */
start_diff_probe_cost(&d, &ii, p, C, parts);
for (xx=start; xx<end; x+=stride)
{
  Body(xx, 1);
  get_diff_probe_cost(&d, &ii, parts);
}

/* Pass 2.b - Configure the scheduler */
omp_set_scheduler(p, parts);

/* Pass 3 - execute the remaining instances of the
   parallel loop in parallel */
for (tt=2; tt<time_max; tt++)
{
  /* Parallel loop automatically parallelized with OpenMP */
  #pragma omp parallel for
  for (xx=start; xx<end; x+=stride)
  {
    /* Body of the loop */
    Body(xx, tt);
  }
}
```

---

[2] That the code in Listing 1.2 illustrates a principle implementation.

The first instance of the parallel loop is instrumented to compute the overall cost of the parallel loop - expressed in terms of the total number of elapsed cycles. The function start_probe_cost($\cdot$) initializes the variable C that will contain the total cost of executing the serial loop, whereas the function get_probe_cost($\cdot$) reads the elapsed cycles after the execution of the loop and assigns the number of cycles to C. This pass also counts the total number of iterations - referred to as # iterations and derives the average cost per iteration as the total cost divided by the number of iterations.

The second instance of the loop is instrumented to profile the cost per iteration and determine the percentages of iterations - taken in lexicographic order - that contain $\frac{1}{p}$ of the total cost of the loop. p is the number of available cores. In particular, the function start_diff_probe_cost($\cdot$,$\cdot$,$\cdot$,$\cdot$) initializes the following counters: (a) d - for each iteration, it will contain the cost per iteration; (b) the iteration number ii; and (c) the vector parts - which contains as many entries as the number of threads/cores. For example, in the case of four threads, the vector parts will be initialized as parts={0, 0, 0, 0} . During the execution of the second instance of the loop, the cost per iteration d is computed by subtracting the current cycles count from the count of cycles annotated at the previous iteration - such cycles counts are taken from the beginning of the loop. For example, let c_{ii-1} be the elapsed cycles from the beginning of the loop until the iteration $ii-1$ and c_{ii} be the cost accumulated from the beginning of the loop until iteration ii. The value of the counter d is defined according to Equation 1.

$$\text{d} = c_{ii} - c_{ii-1} \tag{1}$$

The function get_diff_probe_cost($\cdot$,$\cdot$,$\cdot$) implements the steps in Equations 2 and 3. In particular, for each $s = 1, 2, \cdots, p$ such a function finds the percentage of the iteration space containing $\frac{1}{p}$ of the total elapsed cycles and assign such percentage to the position s of the array parts (to compensate for the ceiling operation, for $s = p$, parts[p] = $100 - \sum_{s=1}^{p-1}$ parts[s]):

$$\forall s = 1, 2, \cdots, p \text{ find ii}_s : \sum_{ii=ii_{s-1}}^{ii_s} \text{d}_{ii} < s \times \frac{C}{p} < \sum_{ii=ii_{s-1}}^{ii_s} \text{d}_{ii} + \text{d}_{ii_s+1} \tag{2}$$

$$\text{parts[s]} = \lceil \frac{\text{ii}_s}{\#iterations} \rceil \times 100 \tag{3}$$

When a parallel loop exhibits a variable cost per iteration, the fraction of iterations containing a certain percentage, $x\%$, of the overall cost of the loop is no longer proportional to x, as it would be in the case of a loop with uniform cost per iteration. Furthermore, in the case of a loop with an uniform cost per iteration, the passes in Equations 2 and 3 provide parts to contain the equal elements. For example, let $p = 2$ and let us assume that the parallel loop have nearly-equal cost per iteration, then the array parts will be equal to parts={50, 50}. Likewise, for $p = 4$, parts={25,25,25,25} etc.

The next step in our run-time technique is the deployment of the schedule. If the number of operating threads are allocated to individual cores and nearly start at the same time, the run-time partitioning technique described above results in the minimum completion time - e.g., in the case of the OpenMP construct `parallel for`.

2.1 Instrumentation and Profiling Overhead

The definition of d given in Equation 1 is useful in practice. Such a definition allows (a) measuring the cost per iteration accurately and (b) estimating the accuracy with which the cost per iteration is measured - refer to Equation 4.

The sum of the costs per iteration, that is measured using the procedure `get_diff_probe_cost`$(\cdot,\cdot,\cdot)$, is an estimator of the whole cost of the serial loop. Therefore, at run-time the total count of elapsed cycles C can be compared with the quantity $\sum_{ii=1}^{\#iterations}$ d$_{ii}$ to estimate the accuracy of our profiling technique. Likewise, for such a comparison, the total number of instructions executed (instructions retired in the case of speculative out-of-order cores) can be used. We define the accuracy of the profiling as in Equation 4. The lower is $\epsilon\%$, the lower is the contribution of the instrumentation overhead to the run-time behavior of the parallel loop and the more the partitions of the iteration space convey the same amount of work to each core.

$$\epsilon\% = \frac{\left| C - \sum_{ii=1}^{\#iterations} d_{ii} \right|}{C} \times 100 \tag{4}$$

2.2 Extension to More Variable and Non Profitable Cases

There exist cases violating the assumptions that we made at the beginning of this section. For example, the bounds and the stride of the parallel loop can be functions of the outermost serial loop and/or functions of the input data. A typical illustration is provided by multi-grid kernels, that improve the resolution of raster images by varying the size of the image grid. In such a case, we relax our assumptions of constant bounds and strides and admit the possibility that the parallel loop bounds and/or stride can vary across instances of the parallel loop. However, our technique requires such a variation to be slow. That is, a given value of the loop bounds and/or stride spans for (i.e., is the same or similar) several subsequent instances of the parallel loop. We refer to such instances with similar behavior as phases. Such phases can either occur systematically, such as in the case of multi-grid kernels - where phase changes are triggered by the outermost loop, or in an unpredictable way - e.g., the behavior of the body of the loop depends on the input data. In the former case, our technique can be programmed to be triggered by phase changes, as the occurrence of a phase change can be predicted. In the latter case our technique can be re-invoked periodically and attempt to optimize performance.

Either way, admitting a slow variation of the bounds and/or stride of the parallel loop implies that the elapsed time of the parallel loop vary across phases.

This means that there can be instances of the parallel loop where the parallel execution is not profitable (e.g., when the body of the parallel loop is too small compared with the parallelization overhead) and instances of the parallel loop with a large number of iterations and a small uniform cost per iteration, where a dynamic iteration scheduling technique may perform better than a static technique when the chunk size is selected properly. Furthermore, dynamic scheduling techniques are important as they can cope with adversary conditions of the system underneath - multi-programming conflicts or over/bad utilization of architectural resource, including under utilization of the memory hierarchy.

Arbitrary variable and unprofitable cases mentioned above are taken into account in the following extension of our technique, where the source code of Listing 1.1 is transformed in that of Listing 1.3. Such code extends our technique with a set of conditions to enable/disable its passes in order to trigger the exploration of static and dynamic iteration scheduling techniques. The code in Listing 1.3 has the ability to adapt to different phases in which instances of the parallel loop can execute. Such an extension allows for the possibility to switch from the proposed static iteration scheduling schema to a dynamic scheduling schema, where the determination of the chunk size is fundamental to optimize performance.

Listing 1.3. Transformed, instrumented loop

```
/* Serial loop iterating over time steps */
for (tt=0; tt<time_max; tt++)
{
    if (condition_pass1(tt) or switch_scheduling) {
        /* Pass 1 — Compute the total and the average
           cost per iteration */
        ...
    }
    if (condition_pass2(tt) or switch_scheduling) {
        /* Pass 2.a — Compute the schedule */
        ...
        /* Evaluate when to switch or to keep the schedule to:
           sequential, parallel static or dynamic */
        ...
        /* Pass 2.b — Compute chunk size and configure the scheduler */
        ...
    }
    if (condition_pass3(tt) or switch_scheduling) {
        /* Pass 3 — execute the remaining instances of the
           parallel loop in parallel */
        ...
    }
}
```

In this work, the determination of the chunk size is performed in the following steps. Micro-benchmarks are used offline [17] to measure synchronization overheads - that are subsequently factored into our technique.[3] The chunk size is determined such that the average cost per iteration (which is computed in pass 1 of Listing 1.3) times the chunk size is greater than the synchronization overhead. Such a rule for selecting the chunk size guarantees that the resulting synchronization overhead is lower than the cost of the serial loop. Therefore the parallel execution on a number of cores $p > 2$ is profitable. Let n be the number

---

[3] Note that, run-time overheads are tightly coupled to the architecture underneath.

Table 1. System level setup

Model	Intel(R) Core(TM) i7-2600 CPU @ 3.40GHz
L1 I/D cache [KB]	32
L2 cache [kB]	256
LLC [MB]	8
Memory [GB]	8
Compilers/linker, options	GNU GCC 4.6.2, -O3 -fopenmp
Operating system	Linux kernel 3.0.0

of iterations and $a = \frac{C}{n}$ the average cost per iteration. Let δ be the cost of synchronization. The total cost of executing the parallel version of the loop on a single core, with a certain chunk size will be equal to $C + \delta \times \frac{n}{\texttt{chunk\_size}}$ - as the threads will be executed in a serial fashion. Imposing $\delta \times \frac{n}{\texttt{chunk\_size}} < C$, provides the total cost of execution on one core being less than $2C$. Therefore, the total cost of execution on p cores will be less than $\frac{2}{p} \times C$, which guarantees a speedup larger than one when $p > 2$. Eventually, $\delta \times \frac{n}{\texttt{chunk\_size}} < C$ is equivalent to $\frac{C}{n} \times \texttt{chunk\_size} > \delta$, which is equivalent to $a \times \texttt{chunk\_size} > \delta$, or otherwise $\texttt{chunk\_size} > \frac{\delta}{a}$. In this work we select the chunk size such as $\texttt{chunk\_size} = \lceil \frac{\delta}{a} \rceil$.

Finally, during a phase when the total cost of the loop is small compared to the parallelization overhead - for example because the number of iterations and the cost of the body of the parallel loop are relatively small, our extended technique can decide to run the serial version of the loop - refer to the pass 1 in Listing 1.2.

3   Experiments

We implemented our technique in the GNU GCC compiler as an extension of its OpenMP implementation [12, 18] - referred to as GOMP. GOMP includes a static scheduler that distributes equal chunks of iterations to the available cores, and two dynamic schedulers in each of which an idle core gains exclusive access to the queue of iterations and fetches the next available chunk of iterations. Fixed chunk size scheduling and Guided [4] are the two dynamic scheduling strategies implemented in GOMP. In addition, we implemented two other popular dynamic scheduling strategies: Factoring [5] and Trapezoid [7].

We use PAPI [19] to access the hardware performance counters and measure elapsed cycles. Our experiments are conducted on the state-of-the art Intel Sandy Bridge architecture - the system level configuration illustrated in Table 1. The dynamic frequency scaling was disabled to provide dependable time and counters measurements.

As benchmarks, we use OpenMP implementations in C [20] of three linear algebra kernels: Matrix Multiply; Gauss-Jordan elimination; and Adjoint Convolution [4] - and the program 470.lbm from SPEC CPU2006 [2], which implements

---

[4] Our implementation resembles the parallel form of such kernels as illustrated in [5].

the Lattice Boltzman Method as illustrated in [21]. Fifty instances of matrix multiply and adjoint convolution were executed for each experiment. The number of times the parallel loop in Gauss-Jordan elimination is iterated is a function of its outermost serial loop [5]. The first few - up to 5 - instances are leveraged by our technique to find a profitable schedule.

We selected the three kernels above to verify that the profiling method included in our technique effectively provides accurate estimates of the cost per iteration and thus that our technique can accurately compute partitions of iterations with equal costs during the training phase. A more in depth description of the run-time properties per iteration of these kernels is discussed below. Such kernels are also utilized to verify basic scalability properties in the performance results attained with our technique against the use of prior scheduling techniques, when the number of threads increases. Eventually, the program 470.1bm is used as a real world example to test our technique.

Table 2. Average cost per iteration and standard deviation

	Matrix Multiply	Gauss-Jordan elimination	Adjoint convolution
Average # cycles per iteration	26786087	1936474	9346
Standard deviation	22683	860399	5337

A summary of the variability of the cost per iteration for the kernels matrix multiply, Gauss-Jordan elimination and adjoint convolution is shown in Table 2 - each column reports the average cost per iteration of one instance of each kernel and the corresponding standard deviation.

For matrix multiply and Gauss-Jordan elimination, we adopted matrices of type double whose size is 1024×1024 - a single matrix has the same size as the last level of cache in our architecture. Matrix multiply exhibits a constant cost per iteration. The small variability in the cost per iteration is due to the variable latency in the accesses to memory compared with the larger iteration cost. Gauss-Jordan elimination exhibits a cost per iteration that is slightly variable because of a conditional in the body of the parallel loop. This kernel executes multiple instance of its innermost parallel loop. The cost per iteration within each instance of the parallel loop has a trapezoidal shape, which vary slowly - from nearly rectangular to nearly triangular - across subsequent instances of the parallel loop. For adjoint convolution, we adopted vectors of type double whose size of 102400. The cost per iteration decreases with a constant rate and falls in a large range of costs. More importantly, iterations with larger cost are not uniformly distributed across the iteration space. Most of the whole cost of the loop is concentrated within the first few iterations. As we will see in this section, such a biased distribution of the cost per iteration is a limiting factor for dynamic schedulers.

The program 470.1bm, using the reference dataset in SPEC CPU2006, calls frequently (> 100 times) the function LBM_performStreamCollide, that accounts for most of the execution time of the program. Such a function includes a singly nested parallel loop with conditionals - the loop is hand-optimized as illustrated in [21]. The cost per iteration is constant although very small (each iteration executes in ≈ 3 ns). The number of iterations in the corresponding reference input data set [2] is very large (it amounts to 26,000,000 iterations).

3.1 Profiling Accuracy and Micro-benchmarking Summary

The iteration cost profiling method employed in the pass 2 of our technique (refer to Listing 1.2) provides accurate estimates of the cost per iteration - refer to Table 3. For each benchmark $\epsilon\%$ is very small - negligible in the case of matrix multiply and adjoint convolution. The worse case estimation happens in the case of the kernel adjoint convolution, because of the presence of a few iterations with large costs followed by plenty of iterations with progressively small costs. Profiling of the former type of iterations is more accurate than that of the latter type of iterations, nevertheless $\epsilon\% < 2\%$ is fairly small.

Table 3. Relative estimation error - refer to Equation 4

	Matrix Multiply	Gauss-Jordan elimination	Adjoint convolution
$\epsilon\%$	0.04	0.03	1.9

On the architecture in use - refer to Table 1 - we characterize the overhead costs involved with the use of the OpenMP constructs for scheduling and synchronization using the suite of Open MP micro-benchmarks proposed in [17]. The overhead involved in the parallel execution of a parallel loop on p cores is empirically defined as $O(p) = T_p - \frac{T_s}{p}$, where T_s is the number of cycles needed for the sequential execution and T_p is the number of cycles need for the parallel execution. Our experimental results - conducted for $p = 2, 4, 6, 8$ can be summarized as follows: (a) the overhead involved with static scheduling is $\approx 0.25\mu s$ for up to four threads and bumps up to $\approx 3\mu s$ for more than four threads - because of the presence of two hardware threads sharing the same core in a symmetric multi-threading fashion. Such an overhead is independent from the number and the sizes of the chunks; (b) the overhead involved with dynamic fixed chunk scheduling increases with the number of threads - it raises from ≈ 0.25 to $17\mu s$. However, this overhead drops significantly when the chunk size increases - the trend is that the overhead decreases as $\approx \frac{1}{\text{chunk\_size}}$; (c) the overhead involved with guided scheduling increases with the number of threads - it raises from ≈ 0.25 to $4.5\mu s$, and decreases nearly linearly when the chunk size increases.

3.2 Experimental Results

We present a first set of results aimed to compare static and dynamic iteration scheduling schemes, including the one proposed as a part of our technique - which we refer as nuStatic. nuStatic schedules statically chunks of itera- tions with equal cost - in terms of elapsed cycles - to cores. We recall that in nuStatic chunks contains the same number of iterations in the case of loops with constant cost per

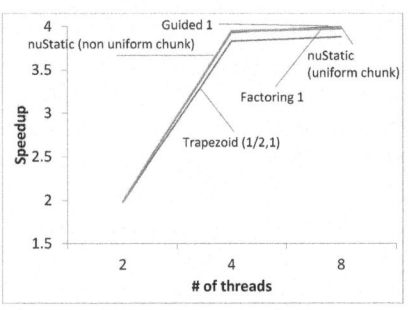
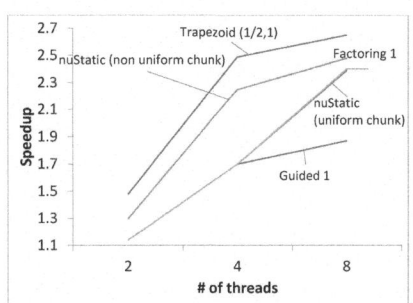

(a) Matrix multiply   (b) Gauss-Jordan elimination

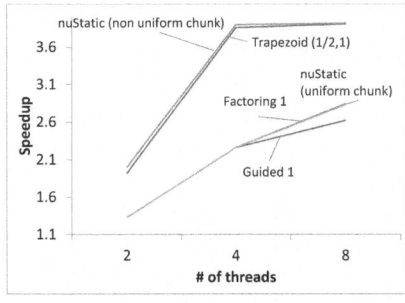
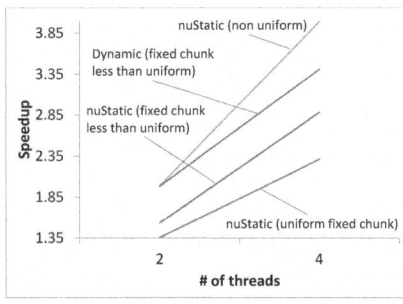

(c) Adjoint convolution   (d) Adjoint convolution analysis

Fig. 1. Performance evaluation/analysis of individual scheduling techniques for multiple threads

iterations, whereas chunks contain different numbers of iterations when the cost per iteration vary. In the case of constant cost per iteration nuStatic is equivalent to the classic scheduler implemented in conven- tional OpenMP implementations. We refer to the case of classic static scheduling as nuStatic uniform chunk, whereas we use the term nuStatic non uniform chunk to refer the case of static scheduling when non uniform chunks are determined at run-time by our technique.

For matrix multiply all the iteration scheduling techniques attain nearly the same cost. Performance is shown in Figure 1(a). nuStatic uniform chunk and nuStatic non uniform chunk determine the same vectors of parts and the parts are equal. For example, $p = 2$ implies that parts={50, 50}.

For Gauss-Jordan elimination - refer to Figure 1(b), we re-execute the determination of the vector parts three times - at the beginning, at $\frac{1}{3}$ and at $\frac{2}{3}$ of the iterations of the outer-most loop. For example, when $p = 4$ and during each training phase, the following vectors of parts are learned by our technique: first parts $= \{25, 25, 25, 25\}$; subsequently parts $= \{15, 20, 25, 40\}$; and finally parts $= \{10, 15, 25, 45\}$. While performance attained by nuStatic non uniform chunk is slightly lower than that attained with Trapezoid, the former significantly outperforms the other schedulers, because of its relatively low synchronization overhead. Performance of nuStatic non uniform chunk size can conceivably approach performance of Trapezoid by providing the former with more re-invocations of the pass 1 in our technique.

Among the three kernels considered in this paper, the most interesting is adjoint convolution. For adjoint convolution, neither static nor dynamic scheduling strategies are able to deliver good performance - refer to Figure 1(c). The issue with dynamic scheduling is either that synchronization costs are large compared with the cost per iteration and/or severe load imbalance occurs because iterations with large cost fall in large initial chunks - see the cases of Factoring and Guided. Unfortunately, an increase of the chunk size does not help reduce the size of the first few chunks for both Factoring and Guided. On the contrary, the fact that the first few chunk sizes are smaller in the case Trapezoid determines its success when compared with the other techniques. Nevertheless, to learn at runtime the parameters of Trapezoid for any kind of loop would be expensive. On the contrary, nuStatic provides equal or better performance than Trapezoid and the training phase of nuStatic is simple and efficient. Note that on an alternative implementation of adjoint convolution, when the cost per iteration increases, Trapezoid would have been unable to deliver best performance.

For adjoint convolution, an analysis of the capabilities of nuStatic compared with classic static and dynamic scheduling is presented in Figure 1(d). In the case of static scheduling, when equal chunks of iterations are distributed among the cores, performance is reduced because of load imbalance. For example, when $p = 2$, the thread assigned with the first chunk of iterations executes much more work than the other thread - because 50% of the whole cost of the loop is contained in the first 30% of the iterations. Likewise, when a smaller chunk size is used, threads are assigned multiple chunks of iterations in a round robin fashion. For example, the first threads will execute 60% of the iterations in two chunks, whereas the second thread will execute 40% in two chunks. However, independently from the cost associated with re-scheduling chunks on threads, 60% of the iterations containing much more than 50% of the total cost of the loop. The issue with dynamic fixed chunk scheduling is that the synchronization overhead becomes large when the number of threads increases - refer to Figure 1(d). While performance of dynamic fixed chunk scheduling is comparable with that of nuStatic on two threads - giving the appearance that dynamic scheduling could cope with all the cases nuStatic can, nuStatic significantly outperforms dynamic on four threads.

Overall, 1(c) shows that nuStatic performs as well as Trapezoid and outperforms other iteration schedulers. For different number of threads nuStatic determines the following parts of the iterations space: $\{30, 70\}$ when $p = 2$; $\{13, 16, 21, 50\}$ when $p = 4$ and $\{6, 7, 8, 9, 11, 15, 36\}$ when $p = 8$.

Finally, we present an analysis of the program 470.lbm - Figure 2. We focus our attention on the performance of the parallel section in the function

LBM_performStreamCollide - within which the program spends a significant percentage of its execution cycles ($> 90\%$). Our technique selects dynamic scheduling with a chunk size of 40, which is determined as follows. From the micro-benchmarking experiments, the minimum synchronization overhead is attained for 8 threads - this overhead is $\approx 0.12\mu s$. $3 \times 10^{-9} \times$ chunk_size $= 0.12 \times 10^{-6}$, which corresponds to a chunk_size=40. Such a chunk size represents a conservative choice for a lower number of threads. In the case of two threads, Guided 40 is selected, whereas when the number of threads increases to four and eight, our technique switches to Fixed chunk, with a chunk size equal to 40, and attains significant speedups over the baseline. Note that, in the case of Fixed chunk, a chunk size equal to 40 means that idle threads attempt to fetch 40 iterations at a time. In the case of Guided, a chunk size equal to 40 indicates the minimum number of iterations that can be fetched. Figure 2 shows performance improvements up to 65% for 470.1bm. In Figure 2, the baseline is the sequential execution time. When $p = 2$, Guided 40 is selected by our technique as it outperforms both Dynamic 40 and nuStatic [5], whereas, for $p > 2$, Dynamic 40 is selected by our technique. For $p > 2$, Dynamic 40 significantly outperforms the other techniques.

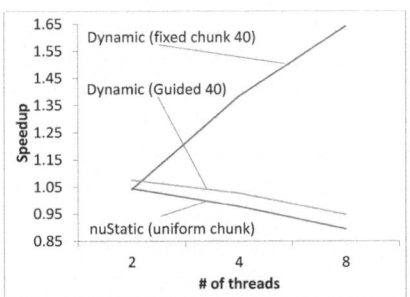

Fig. 2. Speedup 470.1bm

3.3 Future Work on the Determination of the Number of Threads

The determination of the number of threads/cores to use is also a fundamental point for balancing performance versus load imbalance versus power consumption during the execution of a DOALL loop. While the determination of the number of threads can be attempted using corollaries of Amdahl's law, e.g., [22], such corollaries do not account for the complex system/software interactions happening on real systems - an example is provided by the case of 470.1bm explained above, where a combination of the number of threads, the scheduling technique and an appropriate selection of the chunk size are both necessary to attain a significant speedup. We plan to extend the technique proposed in this paper to select at run-time both the number of threads and the iteration schedule for speeding up the performance of parallel loops.

---

[5] In this particular case, where the cost per iteration is constant, we remark that nuStatic is equivalent to classic static scheduling.

4   Related Work

Parallel loops and in particular DOALL loops are pervasive in ordinary programs, e.g., $\approx 90\%$ [10] of the loops present in SPEC CPU2000 [1] are parallel and DOALL loops or can be restructured to expose parallelism [23, 24]. As implemented in the OpenMP pass of modern compilers, scheduling techniques for executing DOALL loops can be roughly divided in two categories: static - where the scheduler is responsible to assign chunks of iterations to the available cores; dynamic (fixed chunk or self-scheduling) - where idle cores first use synchronization (mutex/locks) to earn an exclusive access to the queue of iterations and second fetch a chunk of iteration to execute [4, 5, 7]. The time spent by idle threads to acquire/release the queue of iterations multiplied by the number of exclusive accesses and times the average number of cores attempting to fetch iterations concurrently constitutes the synchronization overhead for dynamic scheduling strategies. Such an overhead can either reduce significantly or annihilate the benefits of a parallel execution. Several dynamic scheduling techniques allow the cores to fetch chunks with a progressively small chunk size [4, 5, 7, 25] to reduce scheduling overhead and improve load balancing. Yue and Liljia in [8] proposed the generation of chunking heuristics using genetic algorithms and show performance improvements against guided [4], factoring [5] and trapezoid [7] self-scheduling. However, performance attained using dynamic and in particular self-scheduling techniques is shown to be negatively impacted by the presence of a relatively large standard deviation in the cost per iterations [8]. Under the assumption that iterations with large cost are distributed according to well known statistical distributions, e.g., normal distribution, there exist dynamic scheduling techniques [6, 9] aimed to improve performance of parallel loops. The technique proposed in this paper addresses the case of variability of the cost per iteration independently from the distribution of such costs. This is especially important for such cases when iterations with large cost occur in bursts.

Kejariwal et al. in [10] proposed an offline profile-based iteration space partitioning technique, where the profile is based on cache miss count. Such a profile-based technique is rigorous, but fairly expensive. Partitioning requires: storing the sequence of cost per iterations - which can be arbitrarily large depending on the input size; numerical interpolation of such a sequence; numerical integration to compute parts of the iteration space convey nearly-equal costs. The technique proposed in this work is fairly simple to implement and execute at run-time. Furthermore, expressing the partitions in terms of percentages of the iteration space releases the partitions from the particular instance of a parallel loop. This is particularly useful in the case of parallel loops with a fixed geometry of the iteration space, such as the case of the kernel adjoint convolution. The partitioning found for a given input size can be applied for any input size and still provides nearly-optimal work sharing. Similarly to Just-in-Time compilation [26], our technique attempts to optimize code execution from past observations. Differently from such techniques, past observations are utilized to determine a schedule able to optimize performance of DOALL loops. Rauchwerger et al. [27] proposed a technique for finding an optimal schedule to execute partially parallel loops. That is, loops whose parallel execution requires synchronization to ensure the correct execution order of the iterations of the loop. In this work we focus on DOALL loops. While iterations of DOALL loops can be executed in any order, different schedules can attain significantly different performance on modern multi-core systems. In particular, we acknowledge the importance of both static and dynamic scheduling techniques, and propose a new run-time technique that (a) accurately profiles the iteration space; (b) partitions the iteration space in non uniform chunks of iterations containing equal portions of the execution time; (c) attempts to schedule such chunks of iterations or to find the dynamic schedule that is more suitable for the particular instances of the loop on a given architecture.

5   Conclusion

We proposed a new scheduling technique to speedup DOALL loops in ordinary programs on modern complex multi-core systems. Our technique targets the execution of DOALL loops with variable cost per iterations and exhibiting either a predictable or an unpredictable behavior across multiple instances of a loop. In the former case our technique implements a quick run-time pass to determine chunks of iterations containing the same amount of work to cores, which is followed by a static assignment of such chunks to core. At run-time, the performance of such a static schedule is compared with the performance of both the sequential execution and the parallel execution using dynamic scheduling techniques - with an appropriate selection of the chunk size to optimize performance. The best scheduling technique is subsequently employed for executing subsequent instances of the parallel loop.

We implemented our technique in GNU GCC OpenMP and show promising results on the linear algebra kernel adjoint convolution and the program 470.1bm from SPEC CPU2006 - implementing the Lattice Boltzman Method - on the state-of-the-art 4, 2-way SMT cores Intel Sandy Bridge architecture. Specifically, our technique attains nearly optimal speedup for the adjoint convolution and up to 65% performance improvement for 470.1bm.

Acknowledgments. This work was partially supported by the NSF grant number CCF-0811882 and the NSF Variability Expedition Grant number CCF-1029783.

References

1. Henning, J.L.: Spec cpu2000: Measuring cpu performance in the new millennium. IEEE Computer 33(7), 28–35 (2000)
2. Henning, J.L.: SPEC CPU2006 benchmark descriptions. SIGARCH Computer Architecture News 34(4), 1–17 (2006)
3. Lundstrom, S.F., Barnes, G.H.: A controllable MIMD architecture. In: Advanced Computer Architecture, IEEE Computer Society Press, Los Alamitos (1986)

4. Polychronopoulos, C.D., Kuck, D.J.: Guided self-scheduling: A practical scheduling scheme for parallel supercomputers. IEEE Trans. Comput. 36(12), 1425–1439 (1987)
5. Hummel, S., Schonberg, E., Flynn, L.E.: Factoring: a method for scheduling parallel loops. Commun. ACM 35(8), 90–101 (1992)
6. Lucco, S.: A dynamic scheduling technique for irregular parallel programs, pp. 200–211 (1992)
7. Tzen, T.H., Ni, L.M.: Trapezoid self-scheduling: A practical scheduling scheme for parallel compilers. IEEE Trans. Parallel Distrib. Syst. 4(1), 87–98 (1993)
8. Yue, K.K., Lilja, D.J.: Parameter estimation for a generalized parallel loop scheduling algorithm. In: HICSS, p. 187 (1995)
9. Hancock, D.J., Ford, R.W., Freeman, T.L., Bull, J.M.: An investigation of feedback guided dynamic scheduling of nested loops. In: Proceedings of the International Workshop on Parallel Processing (2000)
10. Kejariwal, A., Nicolau, A., Banerjee, U., Veidenbaum, A.V., Polychronopoulos, C.D.: Cache-aware partitioning of multi-dimensional iteration spaces. In: Proceedings of SYSTOR (2009)
11. Williams, S., Waterman, A., Patterson, D.: Roofline: an insightful visual performance model for multicore architectures. Commun. ACM 52(4) (2009)
12. Openmp, http://www.openmp.org
13. Gnu gcc v4.6, http://gcc.gnu.org/gcc-4.6/
14. Intel compilers, http://software.intel.com/en-us/articles/intel-compilers/
15. Aslot, V., Domeika, M., Eigenmann, R., Gaertner, G., Jones, W.B., Parady, B.: SPEComp: A New Benchmark Suite for Measuring Parallel Computer Performance. In: Eigenmann, R., Voss, M.J. (eds.) WOMPAT 2001. LNCS, vol. 2104, pp. 1–10. Springer, Heidelberg (2001)
16. Zhang, Y., Voss, M.: Runtime empirical selection of loop schedulers on hyperthreaded smps. In: 19th International Parallel and Distributed Processing Symposium (2005)
17. Bull, J.M., O'Neill, D.: A microbenchmark suite for openmp 2.0. SIGARCH Comput. Archit. News 29, 41–48 (2001)
18. Novillo, D.: Openmp and automatic parallelization in gcc. In: GCC Developers Summit (2006)
19. Mucci, P.J., Browne, S., Deane, C., Ho, G.: Papi: A portable interface to hardware performance counters. In: Proceedings of the Department of Defense HPCMP Users Group Conference, pp. 7–10 (1999)
20. Kernighan, B.W.: The C Programming Language, 2nd edn. Prentice Hall Professional Technical Reference (1988)
21. Pohl, T., Kowarschik, M., Wilke, J., Iglberger, K., Rüde, U.: Optimization and profiling of the cache performance of parallel lattice boltzmann codes. Parallel Processing Letters 13(4) (2003)
22. Flatt, H.P., Kennedy, K.: Performance of parallel processors. Parallel Computing 12(1), 1–20 (1989)
23. Lamport, L.: The Hyperplane Method for an Array Computer. In: Tse-Yun, F. (ed.) Parallel Processing. LNCS, vol. 24, pp. 113–131. Springer, Heidelberg (1975)
24. Banerjee, U.: Loop transformations for restructuring compilers - the foundations. Kluwer (1993)
25. Kruskal, C.P., Weiss, A.: Allocating independent subtasks on parallel processors. IEEE Trans. Softw. Eng. 11(10) (1985)
26. Aycock, J.: A brief history of just-in-time. ACM Comput. Surv. 35(2), 97–113 (2003)
27. Rauchwerger, L., Amato, N.M., Padua, D.A.: A scalable method for run-time loop parallelization. International Journal of Parallel Programming 23(6) (1995)

AlphaZ: A System for Design Space Exploration in the Polyhedral Model[*]

Tomofumi Yuki[1], Gautam Gupta[2], DaeGon Kim[2],
Tanveer Pathan[2], and Sanjay Rajopadhye[1]

[1] Colorado State University
[2] CORESPEQ Inc.

Abstract. The polyhedral model is now a well established and effective formalism for program optimization and parallelization. However, finding optimal transformations is a long-standing open problem. It is therefore important to develop tools that, rather than following predefined optimization criteria, allow practitioners to explore different choices through script-driven or user-guided transformations. More than practitioners, such flexibility is even more important for compiler researchers and auto-tuner developers. In addition, tools must also raise the level of abstraction by representing and manipulating reductions and scans explicitly. And third, the tools must also be able to explore transformation choices that consider memory (re)-allocation.

AlphaZ is a system that allows exploration of optimizing transformations in the polyhedral model that meets these goals. We illustrate its power through two examples of optimizations that existing parallelization tools cannot perform, but can be systematically applied using our system. One is time-tiling of a code from PolyBench that resembles the Alternating Direction Implicit (ADI) method, and the other is a transformation that brings down the algorithmic complexity of a kernel in UNAfold, a sequence alignment software, from $O(N^4)$ to $O(N^3)$.

1 Introduction

The recent emergence of many-core architectures has given a fillip to automatic parallelization, especially through "auto-tuning" and iterative compilation, of compute- and data-intensive kernels. The *polyhedral model* is a formalism for automatic parallelization of an important class of programs. This class includes *affine control loops* which are the important target for aggressive program optimizations and transformations. Many optimizations, including loop fusion, fission, tiling, and skewing, can be expressed as transformation of polyhedral specifications. Vasillache et al. [21, 28] make a strong case that a polyhedral representation of programs is especially needed to avoid the blowup of the intermediate program representation (IR) when many transformations are repeatedly applied, as is becoming increasingly common.

[*] This work was funded in part by the National Science Foundation, Award Number: 0917319.

H. Kasahara and K. Kimura (Eds.): LCPC 2012, LNCS 7760, pp. 17–31, 2013.
© Springer-Verlag Berlin Heidelberg 2013

A number of polyhedral tools and components for generating efficient code are now available [2, 3, 7, 9–11, 17, 22]. Typically, they are source-to-source, and first extract a section of code amenable to polyhedral analysis, then perform a sequence of analyses and transformations, and finally generate output.

Many of these tools are designed to be fully automatic. Although this is a very powerful feature, and is the ultimate goal of the automatic parallelization community, it is still a long way away. Most existing tools give little control to the user, making it difficult to reflect application/domain specific knowledge and/or to keep up with the evolving architectures and optimization criteria. Some tools (e.g., CHiLL [3]) allow users to specify a set of transformations to apply, but the design space is not fully exposed.

In particular, few of these systems allow for explicit modification of the memory (data-structures) of the original program. Rather, most approaches assume that the allocation of values to memory is an inviolate constraint that parallelizers and program transformation systems must always respect. There is a body of work towards finding the "optimal" memory allocation [4, 23, 25, 26]. However, there is no single notion of optimality, and existing approaches focus on finding memory allocation given a schedule or finding a memory allocation that is legal for a class of schedules. Therefore, it is critical to elevate data remapping to first-class status in compilation/transformation frameworks.

To motivate this, consider a widely accepted concept, *reordering*, namely changing the temporal order of computations. It may be achieved through tiling, skewing, fusion, or a plethora of traditional compiler transformations. It may be used for parallelism, granularity adaptation, or locality enhancement. Regardless of the manner and motivation, it is a fundamental tool in the arsenal of the compiler writer as well as the performance tuner.

An analogous concept is *"data remapping,"* namely changing the memory locations where (intermediate as well as final) results of computations are stored. Cases where data remapping is beneficial have been noted, e.g., in array privatization [16] and the manipulation of buffers and "stride arrays" when sophisticated transformations like time-skewing and loop tiling are applied [30]. However, most systems implement it in an ad hoc manner, as isolated instances of transformations, with little effort to combine and unify this aspect of the compilation process into loop parallelization/transformation frameworks.

In this paper, we present an open source polyhedral program transformation system, called AlphaZ, that provides a framework for prototyping analyses and transformations. We illustrate possible uses of our system through two examples that benefit from explicit representation of reductions and memory re-mapping.

2   Background

In this section we provide the necessary background of the polyhedral model, and summarize related work that use it for compiler optimization.

2.1   The Polyhedral Model

The strength of the polyhedral model as a framework for program analysis and transformation are its mathematical foundations for two aspects that should be (but are often not) viewed separately: program *representation/transformation* and *analysis*. Feautrier [5] showed that a class of loop nests called Affine Control Loops (or Static Control Parts) can be represented in the polyhedral model. This allows compilers to extract regions of the program that are amenable to analyses and transformations in the polyhedral model, and to optimize these regions. Such code sections are often found in kernels of scientific programs, such as dense linear algebra, stencil computations, or dynamic programming.

In the model, each instance of each statement in a program is represented as an *iteration point*, in a space called *iteration domain* of the statement. Each such point is hence, an *operation*. The iteration domain is described by a set of linear inequalities forming a convex polyhedron using the following notation, where z is iteration point, A is a constant matrix, and b is a constant vector.

$$D = \{z \mid Az + b \geq 0, \, z \in Z^n\}$$

Dependences are affine functions, expressed as[1] $(z \to z')$, where z' consists of affine expressions of z. *What* a program computes is completely specified by the set of operations and the (flow) dependences between them. As noted by Feautrier, program memory and data-structures need not figure in this representation.

2.2   Memory-Based Dependences

The results of array dataflow analysis are based on the values computed by instances of statements, and therefore do not need any notion of memory. Therefore, program transformation using dataflow analysis results usually requires re-considering memory allocation of the original program. Most existing tools have made the decision to preserve the original memory allocation, and include memory-based dependences as additional dependences to be satisfied.

2.3   Polyhedral Equational Model

The AlphaZ system adopts an *equational* view, where programs are described as mathematical equations using the Alpha language [15]. After array dataflow analysis of an imperative program, the polyhedral representation of the flow dependences can be directly translated to an Alpha program. Furthermore, Alpha has reductions as first-class expressions [12] providing a richer representation.

We believe that application programmers (i.e., non computer scientists), can benefit from being able to program with equations, where performance considerations like schedule or memory remain unspecified. This enables a separation

---

[1] In the literature of the polyhedral model, the word dependence is sometimes used to express flow of data, but here the arrow is from the consumer to the producer.

of what is to be computed, from the mechanical, implementation details of *how* (i.e., in which order, by which processor, thread and/or vector unit, and where the result is to be stored).

To illustrate this, consider a Jacobi-style stencil computation, that iteratively updates a 1-D data grid over time, using values from the previous time step. A typical C implementation would use two arrays to store the data grid, and update them alternately at each time step. This can be implemented using modulo operations, pointer swaps, or by explicitly copying values. Since the former two are difficult to describe as affine control loops, the Jacobi kernel in PolyBench/C 3.2 [20] uses the latter method, and the code (jacobi_1d_imper) looks as follows:

```
for (t = 0; t < T; t++)
    for (i = 1; i < N-1; i++)
        A[i] = foo(B[i-1] + B[i] + B[i+1]);
    for (i = 1; i < N-1; i++)
        B[i] = A[i];
```

When written equationally, the same *computation* would be specified as:

$$A(t,i) = \begin{cases} t = 0: & B_{\texttt{init}}(i); \\ t > 0 \leq i < N-1: & \texttt{foo}(A(t-1,i-1), A(t-1,i), A(t-1,i+1)); \\ t > 0 = i: & A(t-1,i); \\ t > 0 \wedge i = N-1: & A(t-1,i); \end{cases}$$

where A is defined over $\{t,i | 0 \leq t < T \wedge 0 \leq i < N\}$, and B_{init} provides the initial values of the data grid. Note how the loop program is already influenced by the decision to use two arrays, an implementation decision, not germane to the computation.

2.4   Related Work

The polyhedral model has a long history, and there are many existing tools that utilize its power. Moreover, it is now used internally in the IBM XL compiler family. We now contrast AlphaZ with such tools. The focus of our framework is to provide an environment to try many different ways of transforming a program. Since many automatic parallelizers are far from perfect, manual control of transformations can sometimes guide automatic parallelizers as we show later.

PLuTo is a fully automatic polyhedral source-to-source program optimizer tool that takes C loop nests and generates tiled and parallelized code [2]. It uses the polyhedral model to explicitly model tiling and to extract coarse grained parallelism and locality. Since it is automatic, it follows a specific strategy in choosing transformations.

Graphite is an optimization framework for high-level optimizations that are being developed as part of GCC now integrated to its trunk [19]. Its emphasis is to extract polyhedral regions from programs that GCC encounters, significantly more complex task than what research tools address, and to perform loop optimizations that are known to be beneficial.

AlphaZ is not intend to be full fledged compiler. Instead, we focus on intermediate representations that production compilers may eventually be able to extract. Although codes produced from our system can be integrated into a larger application, we do not insist that the process has to be fully automatic, thus expanding the scope of transformations.

PIPS is a framework for source-to-source polyhedral optimization using interprocedural analysis [8]. Its modular design supports prototyping of new ideas by *developers*. However, the end-goal is an automatic parallelizer, and little control over choices of transformations are exposed to the user.

Polyhedral Compiler Collections (PoCC) is another framework for source-to-source transformations, designed to combine multiple tools that utilize the polyhedral model [22]. POCC also seeks to provide a framework for developing tools like Pluto, and other automatic parallelizers. However, their focus is oriented towards automatic optimization, and they do not explore memory (re)-allocation.

MMAlpha is another system with similar goals to AlphaZ [9]. It is also based on the Alpha language. The significant differences between the two are that MMAlpha emphasizes hardware synthesis. It does not treat reductions as first class , and does no tiling. MMAlpha does provide memory reuse in principle, but in its context, simple projections that directly follow processor allocations are all that it needs to explore.

RStream from Reservoir Labs performs automatic optimization of C programs [17]. It uses the polyhedral model to translate C programs into efficient code targeting multi-cores and accelerators. Vasillache et al. [27] recently gave an algorithm to perform a limited form of memory (re)-allocation (the new mapping must *extend* the one in the original program).

Omega Project has led to development of a collection of tools [10, 24] that cover a larger subset of the design space than most other tools. The Omega calculator partially handles *uninterpreted function symbols*, which no other tools support. Their code generator can also re-allocate memory [24]. However, reductions are not handled by Omega tools.

CHiLL is a high-level transformation and parallelization framework using the polyhedral model [3]. It also allows users to specify transformation sequences through scripts. However, it does not expose memory allocation.

POET is a script-driven transformation engine for source-to-source transformations [31]. One of its goals is to expose parameterized transformations via scripts. Although this is similar to AlphaZ, POET relies on external analysis to verify the transformations in advance.

Finally, we note that none of these tools do anything with reductions.

3   The AlphaZ System

In this section we present an overview of AlphaZ, focusing, due to space limitations, on only the specific features needed for the examples in later sections (see our technical report [32] for more details).

AlphaZ is designed to manipulate Alpha equations, either written directly or extracted from an affine control loop. It does this through a sequence of commands, written as a separate script. The program is manipulated through a sequence of transformations, as specified in the script. Typically, the final command in the script is a call to generate code (OpenMP parallel C, with support for parameterized tiling [7, 11]). The pen-ultimate set of commands specify, to the code generator, the (i) schedule, (ii) memory allocation, and (iii) additional (i.e., tiling related) mapping specifications.

The key design difference from many existing tools is that AlphaZ gives the user full control of the transformations to apply. Our ultimate goal is to develop techniques for automatic parallelizers, and the system can be used as an engine to try new strategies. This allows for trying out new program optimizations that may not be performed by existing tools with high degree of automation. The key benefits for this are:

- Users can *systematically* apply sequences of transformations without rewriting the program by hand.
- Compiler writers can *prototype* new transformations/code generators. New compiler optimizations may eventually be re-implemented for performance/robustness, but prototyping requires much less effort.

In the following, we use two examples to illustrate benefits of the ability to reconsider memory allocation, and to manipulate reductions. Section 4 illustrates the importance of memory re-mapping, with a benchmark from PolyBench/C 3.2 [20], and Section 5, presents an application of a very powerful transformation on reductions, called Simplifying Reductions. We show that the algorithmic complexity of an implementation of RNA secondary structure prediction alignment algorithm from UNAfold package [14] can be reduced from $O(N^4)$ to $O(N^3)$ through a systematic application of AlphaZ transformations.

4   Time-Tiling of ADI-like Computation

The Alternating Direction Implicit method is used to solve partial differential equations (PDEs). One of the stencil kernels in PolyBench/C 3.2 [20], adi/adi.c resembles ADI computation.[2]

ADI with 2D discretization solves two sets of tridiagonal matrices in each time step. The idea behind ADI method is to split the finite difference system of

---

[2] There is an error in the implementation, and time-tiling would not be legal for a correct implementation of ADI. The program in the benchmark nevertheless illustrates our point that existing tools are incapable of extract the best performance, largely because of lack of memory remapping.

equations of a 2D PDE into two sets: one for the x-direction and another for y. These are then solved separately, one after the other, hence the name *alternating direction implicit*.

Shown below is a code fragment from PolyBench, corresponding to the solution for one direction in ADI. When this code is given to PLuTo [2] for tiling and parallelization, PLuTo fails to find that all dimensions can be tiled, and instead, tiles the inner two loops individually. The key reason is as follows: the value written by S0 is later used in S3, since computing S3 at iteration [t,i1,i2] (written S3[t,i1,i2]) depends on the result of S0[t,i1,i2] and S0[t,i1,i2-1]. Since the dependence vector is in the negative orthant, this *value-based dependence* does not hinder tiling in any dimension.

```
for (t = 0; t < tsteps; t++) {
    for (i1 = 0; i1 < n; i1++)
    for (i2 = 1; i2 < n; i2++) {
S0:     X[i1][i2] = X[i1][i2] - X[i1][i2-1] * A[i1][i2]
                    / B[i1][i2-1];
S1:     B[i1][i2] = B[i1][i2] - A[i1][i2] * A[i1][i2]
                    / B[i1][i2-1];
    }

S2 ... // 1D loop updating X[*,n-1] (details irrelevant here)

    for (i1 = 0; i1 < n; i1++)
    for (i2 = n-1; i2 >= 1; i2--)
S3:     X[i1][i2] = (X[i1][i2] - X[i1][i2-1]
                 * A[i1][i2-1]) / B[i1][i2-1];

    ... //second pass for i1 direction

}
```

However, the original C code reuses the array X to store the result of S0 as well as S3. This creates a memory-based dependence $S3[t, i1, i2] \rightarrow S3[t, i1, i2 + 1]$ because S3[t,i1,i2] overwrites X[i1,i2] used by S3[t,i1,i2+1]. Hence, S3 must iterate in a reverse order to reuse array X as in the original code, whereas allocating another copy of X allows all three dimensions to be tiled.

4.1   Additional Complications

The memory-based dependences are the critical reason why the PLuTo scheduler (actually, we use a variation implemented in Integer Set Library by Verdoolaege [29]) cannot find all three dimensions to be tilable in the above code. Moreover, two additional transformations are necessary to enable to scheduler to identify this. These transformations can be viewed as partially scheduling the polyhedral representation before invoking the scheduler. AlphaZ provides a command, called Change of Basis (CoB), to apply affine transforms to statements of polyhedral domains.[3]

One of them *embeds* S2 which nominally has a 2D domain (and the corresponding statement in the second pass) into 3D space, *aligning* it to be adjacent to a boundary of the domain of S1. The new domain of S2 becomes (note the last equality) $\{t, i1, i2 \mid 0 \leq t < \mathtt{tsteps} \wedge 0 \leq i1 < N \wedge i2 == n - 1\}$.

The other complication is that because of the reverse traversal of the i2 loop of S3, dependences obtained by dataflow analysis [5] are affine, not uniform: $S3[t, i1, i2] \rightarrow S2[t, i1, n - i2 - 1]$. If a CoB $(t, i1, i2 \rightarrow t, i1, n - i2 - 1)$ is applied to the domain of S3 we get a uniform dependence. After these three transformations (removing memory-based dependences, and the two CoBs) the PLuTo scheduler discovers that all loops are fully permutable.

We are not sure of the precise reason why PLuTo scheduling is not able to identify all dimensions are tilable without these transformations. Parts of PLuTo scheduling is driven by heuristics, and our conjecture is that these cases are not well handled. We expect these difficulties can be resolved, and that it is not an inherent limitation of PLuTo. However, a fully automated tool, prevents a smart user from so guiding the scheduler. We believe that guiding automated analyses can significantly help refining automated components of tools.

4.2   Performance of Time Tiled Code

Since PLuTo cannot tile the outer time loop, or fuse many of the loops due to the issues described above, PLuTo parallelized code contains 4 different parallel loops within a time step. On the other hand, AlphaZ generated code with time-tiling consists of a single parallel loop, executing wave-fronts of tiles in parallel. Because of this we expect the new code to perform significantly better.

We measured the performance of the transformed code on a workstation, and also on a node in Cray XT6m. The workstation uses two 4 core Xeon5450 processors (8 cores total), 16GB of memory, and running 64-bit Linux. A node in the Cray XT6m has two 12 core Opteron processors, and 32GB of memory. We used GCC/4.6.3 with -O3 -fopenmp options on the Xeon workstation, and CrayCC/5.04 with -O3 option on the Cray. PLuTo was used with options --tile --parallel --noprevector, since prevector targets ICC.

AlphaZ was supplied with the original C code along with a script file specifying pre-scheduling transformations described above, and then used the PLuTo scheduler to complete the scheduling. Memory allocation was specified in the script as well, and additional copies of X were allocated to avoid the memory-based dependences discussed above.

For all generated programs, only a limited set of tile sizes were tried (8, 16, 32, 64 in all dimensions), and we report the best performance out of these. The

---

[3] This is similar to the preprocessing of code generation from unions of polyhedra [1], where affine transforms are applied such that the desired schedule is followed by lexicographic scan of unions of polyhedra. Since the program representation in AlphaZ is equational, any bijective affine transformation is a legal CoB.

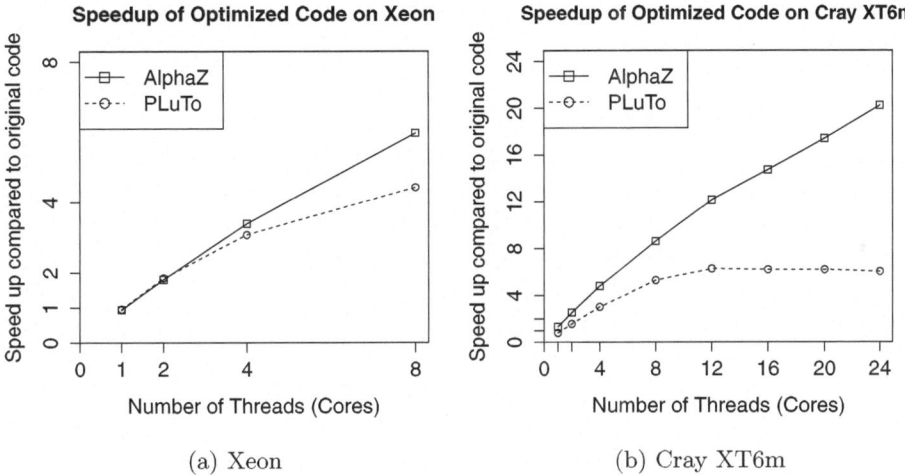

Fig. 1. Speedup of `adi.c` parallelized with PLuTo and `AlphaZ`, with respect to the execution time of the unmodified `adi.c` from `PolyBench/C 3.2`. Observe that coarser grained parallelism with time-tiling leads to significantly better scalability with higher core count on the Cray.

problem size was selected to have cubic iteration space that runs for roughly 60 seconds with the original benchmark on Xeon environment (`tsteps = n = 1200`).

The results are summarized in Figure 1, confirming that the time-tiled version performs much better. On the Cray, we can observe diminishing returns of adding more cores with PLuTo parallelized codes, since only the inner two loops are parallelized. `AlphaZ` generated code does require more memory (this can actually, be further reduced), but at the same time, time-tiling exposes temporal reuse of the memory hierarchies.

5   Reducing Complexity of RNA Folding

In this section, we outline steps to reduce the complexity of an application for RNA folding. Complete details, including the source `Alpha` program as well as the script, can be found in related Master's thesis and technical report [18, 33]. RNA secondary structure prediction, or RNA folding, is a widely used algorithm in bio-informatics. The original algorithm has $O(N^4)$ complexity, but an $O(N^3)$ algorithm has been proposed by Lyngso et. al [13]. However, no implementation of the $O(N^3)$ algorithm is publicly available.[4] This example illustrates one of the most powerful transformations in `AlphaZ` that is enabled through explicit

---

[4] Discussion with the original authors elicited the response that (i) the algorithm was "too complicated to implement" except in an early prototype, and (ii) limiting one of the parameters to 30 was "good enough" in practice.

representation of reductions. Specifically, we show how the equations that describe the algorithm can be systematically transformed to derive the $O(N^3)$ algorithm.

5.1   Reductions in AlphaZ

Reductions, associative and commutative operators applied to collections of values, are first class `Alpha` expressions [12]. It is well known that reductions are important patterns and have important performance implications. Moreover, reductions raise the level of abstraction over chains of dependences.

Alpha reductions are written as $\mathtt{reduce}(op, f_p, E)$, where op is the reduction operator, f_p is a projection function, and E is the expression being reduced. The projection function f_p is an affine function that maps points in Z^n to Z^m, where m is usually smaller than n. When multiple points in Z^n is mapped to the same point in Z^m, the values of E at these points are combined using the reduction operator. For example, commonly used mathematical notations such as $X_i = \sum_{j=0}^{n} A_{i,j}$ is expressed as $X(i) = \mathtt{reduce}(+, (i, j \to i), A(i, j))$. This is more general than mathematical notations, allowing us to easily express reductions with non-canonic projections, such as $(i, j \to i + j)$.

5.2   Simplifying Reductions

Simplifying Reductions [6] is the key transformation for reducing complexity of programs. We first explain the key idea behind this transformation with a simple (almost trivial) example. Consider an `Alpha` program computing a single variable, X_i, over a domain $\{i \mid 0 \le i < N\}$ using the following equation

$$X[i] = \mathtt{reduce}(+, \{j < i\} : A[j])$$

where each element is the sum of subsets of values $A_j, 0 \le j < i < N$. Viewed naively, this would specify that each element of X is an (independent) reduction, and this would take $O(N^2)$ time to compute. Of course this is actually a prefix (scan) computation, and can be written as:

$$X_i = \begin{cases} i = 0 : A_i \\ i > 0 : A_i + X_{i-1} \end{cases}$$

Automatically detecting scans is the core of the reduction simplification algorithm [6]. The key idea is based on the observation that the expression inside the reduction (i.e., the reduction body) exhibits reuse: for the example above, at all points in a 2D space the value of the expression is $X[j]$ so there is reuse along the i direction. Reuse in the body of a reduction and its interaction with the domain boundaries leads to a scan. All the required transformations are implemented as `AlphaZ` commands. Some of the analyses performed are also implemented, but applying simplifying reductions to RNA folding requires additional human analysis, and thus human guided transformation.

5.3   RNA Folding in UNAfold

UNAfold computes the RNA secondary structure through a dynamic programming algorithm, that uses a prediction model based on thermodynamics [14] and finds a structure with minimal free energy. For an RNA sequence of length N, the algorithm computes, for each subsequence from i to j, three tables (arrays) of free energy such that $1 \leq i \leq j \leq N$. The tables $Q(i,j)$, $Q'(i,j)$, and $QM(i,j)$ represent the free energy for three different substructures that may be formed. The following equation is the part of the original formulation corresponding to the dominant term that makes the algorithm $O(N^4)$.

$$
Q'(i,j) = \min \left\{
\begin{array}{l}
\cdots \\
\min_{i<i'<j'<j} \left\{
\begin{array}{l}
E_{BI}(i,j,i',j') \\
Q'(i',j')
\end{array}
\right. \\
\cdots
\end{array}
\right.
\tag{1}
$$

Notice that the term uses four free variables i,j,i' and j', and since the constraints on these indices constitute the domain $\{i,j,i',j'|1 \leq i < i' < j' < j \leq N\}$, it is easy to see the $O(N^4)$ complexity. The term corresponds to a substructure called *internal loops*.

5.4   Simplification

We focus on the dominating term in calculating the energy to illustrate the simplification. The term rewritten as a separate equation in `Alpha` is as follows

$$
Q'(i,j) = \texttt{reduce}(\min, (i,j,i',j' \rightarrow i,j), E_{BI}(i,j,i',j') + Q'(i',j'));
$$

where, the function E_{BI} is defined as follows:

$$
E_{BI}(i,j,i',j') = Asym(i'-i-j+j') + S_P(i'-i+j-j'-2) + E_S(i,j) + E_S(i',j')
$$

The body of the reduction does not exhibit any reuse, so we need to first inline the energy function E_{BI}. Doing this, and distributing out $E_S(i,j)$ gives the following:

$$
Q'(i,j) = E_S(i,j) + \texttt{reduce} \left(
\min, (i,j,i',j' \rightarrow i,j),
\begin{cases}
Asym(i'-i-j+j') & + \\
S_P(i'-i+j-j'-2) & + \\
E_S(i',j') + Q'(i',j')
\end{cases}
\right)
\tag{2}
$$

The reduction still cannot be simplified, and the simplification algorithm [6] algorithm attempts to decompose the reduction from into two reductions (like expressing a double summation as a sum of a sum). The algorithm uses a dynamic programming algorithm to search through possible decompositions. One of the decompositions that lead to complexity reduction is the following:

$$Q'(i,j) = E_S(i,j) + \mathtt{reduce}\,(\min, (i,j,d \to i,j), Q''(i,j,d))$$

$$Q''(i,j,d) = \mathtt{reduce}\left(\min, (i,j,i',j' \to i,j,j'-i'), \begin{cases} Asym(i'-i-j+j') & + \\ S_P(i'-i+j-j'-2) & + \\ E_S(i',j') & + \\ Q'(i',j') & \end{cases}\right)$$

After the decomposition, the expression $S_P(i'-i+j-j')$ can be distributed out from the inner reduction. This can be found through analysis using null spaces of projection and access functions, which is also part of the simplifying reduction algorithm. In short, the analysis finds that null space of the access $S_p(i'-i+j-j'-2)$ contains the null space of the projection function $(i,j,i',j' \to i,j,j'-i')$. Thus, S_p term can be factored out from the reduction.

Then the remaining expressions evaluate to the same value for all points $[i',j',x]; x = j - i$. Taking advantage of this reuse and the property of the $\langle \min, + \rangle$ semi-ring allows the reduction to be simplified.

5.5   Need for Human Guidance

The above steps leading to reduction simplification can be mostly automated. In fact, once we have Equation 2, all the analyses required to apply the sequence of transformations are available. However, extracting Equation 2 from Equation 1 requires separating out boundary cases and other branches. In addition, E_{BI} must be inlined for the algorithm to detect reuse in the reduction.

Although our eventual goal would be fully automatic these steps, the current implementation of AlphaZ provides a powerful set of transformations that enable the user to systematically derive the lower complexity program. For RNA folding, the presence of reuse in the reduction was known [13], and such domain specific knowledge can be utilized by our system that gives the users flexible control over different transformations when needed. The specific semantics preserving transformations that we used are:

- SimplifyingReduction This is the key transformation that replaces a reduction with reuse by a scan.
- Inline (Inline EBI)
- FactorOutFromReduction Use distributivity to factor out terms from within reductions, where possible.
- ReductionDecomposition Decomposition of multidimensional reductions into a reduction of (sub) reductions.

In addition, some pre-processing transformations were also used.

5.6   Validation

We have applied the above transformation using AlphaZ to the UNAfold 3.8 [14]. The function fillMatrices_1 in hybrid-ss-min.c was written in Alpha, and

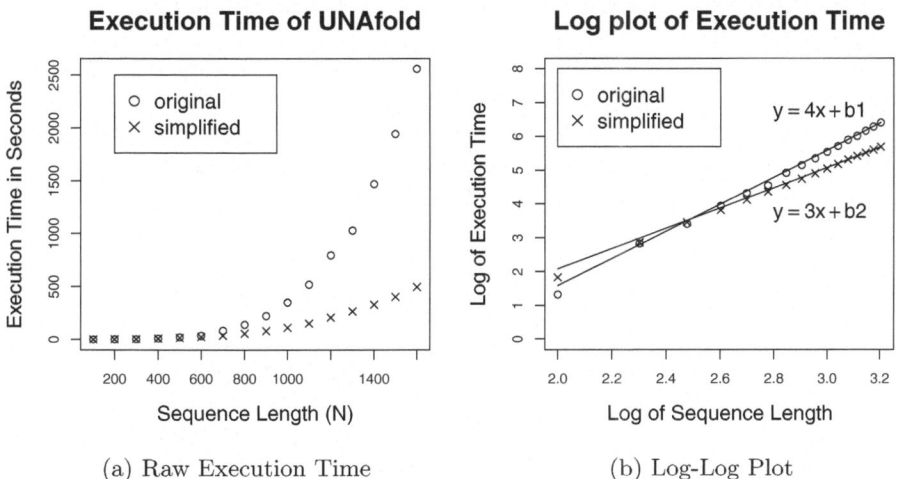

(a) Raw Execution Time   (b) Log-Log Plot

Fig. 2. Execution Time of UNAfold after simplifying reduction compared with the original implementation. The two lines shown are with slopes 4 and 3.

the simplifying transformation was applied. The sequential code generator in AlphaZ code was used to generate the simplified version of fillMatrices_1 and replaced with the original function. Both the original and the simplified versions were compiled with GCC/4.5.1, with -O3 option and the execution times were measured on a machine with Core2Duo 1.86GHz and 6GB of memory.

Figure 2 shows the measured performance (raw and log-log). It clearly shows the reduction in complexity, and, as expected, the speedups with transformed code becomes greater and greater as the sequence length grows.

6   Conclusions and Future Work

We have presented a system for exploring analyses and transformations in the polyhedral model. The two key features in our system are (i) the ability to re-consider memory allocations, and (ii) explicit representation of reductions.

Polyhedral representations of programs are expressed as systems of equations; which can either be extracted from loop nests, or programmed directly in an equational language. These polyhedral programs are manipulated using script driven transformations, to reflect human analyses or domain specific knowledge to help guide optimizing translations. Then executable code is generated by specifying schedule, memory allocation, and other implementation details.

AlphaZ has a number of transformations and code generators, and others are actively being developed. In addition to what previous tools have focused on, we believe that exploring memory allocations is very important. We expect it to become even more important as we target distributed memory machines.

While many tools focus on fully automated program transformations, a tool like AlphaZ that expose as much control to the user is helpful in developing and prototyping new ideas.

Although we have not presented details of our code generators, our code generators are highly modularized and extensible, enabling exploration of code generators as well. Our ongoing efforts are towards extending the code generators to other platforms such as CUDA, OpenCL, etc., and in implementing high level optimizations involving reductions, and many more.

References

1. Bastoul, C.: Code generation in the polyhedral model is easier than you think. In: Proceedings of the 13th IEEE International Conference on Parallel Architecture and Compilation Techniques, PACT 2004, Washington, DC, USA, pp. 7–16 (2004)
2. Bondhugula, U., Hartono, A., Ramanujam, J., Sadayappan, P.: A practical automatic polyhedral parallelizer and locality optimizer. In: Proceedings of the 29th ACM SIGPLAN Conference on Programming Language Design and Implementation, PLDI 2008, pp. 101–113. ACM, New York (2008)
3. Chen, C., Chame, J., Hall, M.: Chill: A framework for composing high-level loop transformations. U. of Southern California, Tech. Rep., pp. 08–897 (2008)
4. Darte, A., Schreiber, R., Villard, G.: Lattice-based memory allocation. IEEE Transactions on Computers 54(10), 1242–1257 (2005)
5. Feautrier, P.: Dataflow analysis of array and scalar references. International Journal of Parallel Programming 20(1), 23–53 (1991)
6. Gautam, G., Rajopadhye, S.: Simplifying reductions. In: POPL 2006: Conference Record of the 33rd ACM SIGPLAN-SIGACT Symposium on Principles of Programming Languages, pp. 30–41. ACM, New York (2006)
7. Hartono, A., Baskaran, M.M., Bastoul, C., Cohen, A., Krishnamoorthy, S., Norris, B., Ramanujam, J., Sadayappan, P.: Parametric multi-level tiling of imperfectly nested loops. In: Proceedings of the 23rd International Conference on Supercomputing, pp. 147–157. ACM, New York (2009)
8. Irigoin, F., Jouvelot, P., Triolet, R.: Semantical interprocedural parallelization: An overview of the pips project. In: Proceedings of the 5th International Conference on Supercomputing, pp. 244–251. ACM (1991)
9. Irisa, C.: The MMAlpha environment
10. Kelly, W., Pugh, W., Rosser, E.: Code generation for multiple mappings. In: Proceedings of the Fifth Symposium on the Frontiers of Massively Parallel Computation, pp. 332–341. IEEE (1995)
11. Kim, D., Rajopadhye, S.: Efficient Tiled Loop Generation: D-Tiling. In: Gao, G.R., Pollock, L.L., Cavazos, J., Li, X. (eds.) LCPC 2009. LNCS, vol. 5898, pp. 293–307. Springer, Heidelberg (2010)
12. Le Verge, H.: Reduction Operators in Alpha. In: Etiemble, D., Syre, J.-C. (eds.) PARLE 1992. LNCS, vol. 605, pp. 397–411. Springer, Heidelberg (1992), see also, Le Verge Thesis (in French)
13. Lyngs, R., Zuker, M., Pedersen, C., et al.: Fast evaluation of internal loops in rna secondary structure prediction. Bioinformatics 15(6), 440–445 (1999)
14. Markham, N., Zuker, M.: Software for nucleic acid folding and hybridization. Methods Mol. Biol. 453, 3–31 (2008)

15. Mauras, C.: ALPHA: un langage équationnel pour la conception et la programma-
    tion d'architectures parallèles synchrones. Ph.D. thesis, L'Université de Rennes I,
    IRISA, Campus de Beaulieu, Rennes, France (December 1989)
16. Maydan, D., Amarasinghe, S., Lam, M.: Array-data flow analysis and its use in
    array privatization. In: Proceedings of the 20th ACM SIGPLAN-SIGACT Sympo-
    sium on Principles of Programming Languages, pp. 2–15. ACM (1993)
17. Meister, B., Leung, A., Vasilache, N., Wohlford, D., Bastoul, C., Lethin, R.: Pro-
    ductivity via automatic code generation for PGAS platforms with the R-Stream
    compiler. In: Workshop on Asynchrony in the PGAS Programming Model (2009)
18. Pathan, T.: RNA Secondary Structure Prediction using AlphaZ. Master's thesis,
    Colorado State University, Computer Science Department (August 2010)
19. Pop, S., Cohen, A., Bastoul, C., Girbal, S., Silber, G., Vasilache, N.: Graphite:
    Loop optimizations based on the polyhedral model for gcc (2006)
20. Pouchet, L.N.: PolyBench, http://www.cs.ucla.edu/ pouchet/software/
    polybench/
21. Pouchet, L.N., Bastoul, C., Cohen, A., Vasilache, N.: Iterative optimization in the
    polyhedral model: Part I, one-dimensional time. In: IEEE/ACM Fifth International
    Symposium on Code Generation and Optimization (CGO 2007), pp. 144–156. IEEE
    Computer Society Press, San Jose (2007)
22. Pouchet, L.N., Bondhugula, U., Bastoul, C., Cohen, A., Ramanujam, J., Sadayap-
    pan, P.: Hybrid iterative and model-driven optimization in the polyhedral model.
    Tech. Rep. 6962, INRIA Research Report (June 2009)
23. Quilleré, F., Rajopadhye, S.: Optimizing memory usage in the polyhedral model.
    ACM Trans. Program. Lang. Syst. 22(5), 773–815 (2000)
24. Shen, T., Wonnacott, D.: Code generation for memory mappings. In: Proceedings of
    the 1998 Mid-Atlantic Student Workshop on Programming Languages and Systems
    (1998)
25. Strout, M., Carter, L., Ferrante, J., Simon, B.: Schedule-independent storage map-
    ping for loops. ACM SIGOPS Operating Systems Review 32(5), 24–33 (1998)
26. Thies, W., Vivien, F., Sheldon, J., Amarasinghe, S.: A unified framework for sched-
    ule and storage optimization. ACM SIGPLAN Notices 36(5), 232–242 (2001)
27. Vasilache, N., Meister, B., Hartono, A., Baskaran, M., Wohlford, D., Lethin, R.:
    Trading off memory for parallelism quality. In: International Workshop on Polyhe-
    dral Compilation Techniques, IMPACT (2012)
28. Vasilache, N.: Scalable Program Optimization Technique. The Polyhedral Model.
    Ph.D. thesis, University of Paris-Sud 11 (2007)
29. Verdoolaege, S.: *isl*: An Integer Set Library for the Polyhedral Model. In: Fukuda,
    K., van der Hoeven, J., Joswig, M., Takayama, N. (eds.) ICMS 2010. LNCS,
    vol. 6327, pp. 299–302. Springer, Heidelberg (2010)
30. Wonnacott, D.: Achieving scalable locality with time skewing. International Jour-
    nal of Parallel Programming 30(3), 181–221 (2002)
31. Yi, Q.: Poet: a scripting language for applying parameterized source-to-source pro-
    gram transformations. Software: Practice and Experience (2011)
32. Yuki, T., Basupalli, V., Gupta, G., Iooss, G., Kim, D., Pathan, T., Srinivasa, P.,
    Zou, Y., Rajopadhye, S.: Alphaz: A system for analysis, transformation, and code
    generation in the polyhedral equational model. Tech. rep., CS-12-101, Colorado
    State University (2012)
33. Yuki, T., Gupta, G., Pathan, T., Rajopadhye, S.: Systematic implementation of
    fast-i-loop in UNAfold using AlphaZ. Tech. rep., CS-12-102, Colorado State Uni-
    versity (2012)

Compiler Optimizations: Machine Learning versus O3

Yuriy Kashnikov[1,3], Jean Christophe Beyler[2,3], and William Jalby[1,3]

[1] Université de Versailles Saint-Quentin-en-Yvelines
[2] Intel France
[3] Exascale Computing Research Center
{yuriy.kashnikov,william.jalby}@exascale-computing.eu,
jean.christophe.beyler@intel.com

Abstract. Software engineers are highly dependent on compiler technology to create efficient programs. Optimal execution time is currently the most important criteria in the HPC field; to achieve this the user applies the common compiler option -O3. The following paper extensively tests the other performance options available and concludes that, although old compiler versions could benefit from compiler flag combinations, modern compilers perform admirably at the commonly used -O3 level.

The paper presents the Universal Learning Machine (ULM) framework, which combines different tools together to predict the best flags from data gathered offline. The ULM framework evaluates three hundred kernels extracted from 144 benchmark applications. It automatically processes more than ten thousand compiler flag combinations for each kernel. In order to perform a complete study, the experimental setup includes three modern mainstream compilers and four different architectures. For 62% of kernels, the optimal flag is the generic optimization level -O3.

For the remaining 38% of kernels, an extension to the ULM framework allows a user to instantly obtain the optimal flag combination, using a static prediction method. The prediction method examines four known machine learning algorithms, Nearest Neighbor, Stochastic Gradient Descent, and Support Vector Machines (SVM). ULM used SVM for the best results of a 92% accuracy rate for the considered kernels.

Keywords: compilers, optimization, machine, learning, performance, modeling, high, performance, computing.

1   Introduction and Motivation

During the last decade, hardware and compilers have changed dramatically, which is why it is necessary to revise the existing optimization methods [1–5] and propose new ones. Unlike previous studies, this study shows for 62% of cases, the code achieves the best performance with -O3 and no further tweaking of compiler flags helps. The precise evaluation methodology and accurate flag selection procedure presents reproducible results.

Compiler optimization efficiency depends not only the code, but also on the architecture, workload, and other parameters. Unpredictable dependencies between

H. Kasahara and K. Kimura (Eds.): LCPC 2012, LNCS 7760, pp. 32–45, 2013.

optimizations only complicate the problem. In an attempt to find a solution, compiler developers couple useful optimizations in groups, also called levels. Default optimization levels like -O3 and -fast are the most common combination of flags among users. Generally efficient, -O3 can be a potential cause of sub-optimal performance, thus careful evaluation is vital to achieving maximum performance.

The compiler research community proposed a practical approach. For example, Bodin et al. [6] describe the flag selection as an optimization problem in the transformation space. They introduced an iterative compilation technique and demonstrated a way to find an optimal combination after exploring less than 1% of the transformation space. Unfortunately, transformation space for modern compilers is large and keeps growing. Therefore, it is infeasible to exhaustively explore even 1% of the whole transformation space; because for example, the GNU compiler has more than 208 independent options and the size of the exploration space is 2^{208}, i.e. 1% is close to 2^{201}. Moreover, in the last five years, the total number of GNU compiler options grew from sixty to more than two hundred! To speedup the search, researchers apply modern machine learning techniques. Machine learning for selecting compiler flags is a mainstream concept [2–5, 7]. Using pre-trained model machine learning based solution allows the user to infer optimal flags on-demand.

The major contributions of the paper are:

- a diverse set of 144 industrial applications with 326 kernels; evaluated with three optimizing compiler on four mainstream architectures
- an application model for comparison with fifty-six static and twenty-three dynamic features
- frequently, performance with -O3 is optimal or near optimal
- for the exceptional applications the created framework predicts optimal flags with 92% accuracy

The initial step to characterizing applications is to consider static and dynamic features. Section 2 presents the chosen features to characterize applications. Once the initial study was performed, Section 3 describes the framework and its contributions. Evaluating three compilers on four architectures led to the conclusion that a classification phase is necessary. Section 4 explains how different application classes divide the considered 326 kernels. For about 38% of the kernels, -O3 does not provide the best performance. Therefore, Section 5 describes a machine learning based method to predict the optimal flag, which results in 92% of correct compiler flag selection. Finally, Sections 6 and 7 present related works on machine learning techniques applied to the compilation field and conclude the paper.

2 Application Characterization and Analysis

The Universal Learning Machine (ULM) framework is a fully automated tool to extract and analyze applications. As a result ULM derives optimal combination of flags from the analyzed data using machine learning. While the next section presents a complete evaluation of ULM, this section introduces its application characterization and analysis.

To predict optimal compiler flags, the ULM framework uses a combination of program internal properties and behavioral characteristics, which compose a feature space. The training sample of vectors in the feature space construct a prediction model. A model's efficiency is its prediction accuracy rate. The accuracy rate directly depends on the chosen feature space and prediction method.

Feature space vectors consist of internal properties and behavioral characteristics, which construct an application vector feature space. Each vector consists of floating-point numbers, logical, or categorical values. Finding a representative set of features is a well-known problem in the machine learning field[8].

It is important to keep the feature space as small as possible to improve classification accuracy and reduce a model's training time. There are two main approaches to characterize an application. First, the ULM framework extracts static features from the source or the compiler's intermediate, or low level program representation. Features reflect inner properties of an application and are independent from the hardware, workload, and other execution conditions. Static features do not require any execution. Contrary to static features, dynamic features are a result of measurement. Dynamic features are highly dependent on execution conditions. In terms of a training time dynamic features are more costly to extract than static features, but at the same time dynamic features can dramatically improve the prediction accuracy.

2.1   Static Features

The classic approach to static feature selection is based on the general knowledge of compiler construction and program optimizations fields. The presented work reuses static features from the MILEPOST GCC project [5, 9, 10]. MILEPOST GCC extracts fifty-six static features from an application's intermediate representation reused in the work [5, 10]. The grouped representation is illustrated in Table 1. Groups represent characteristics of basic blocks, edges between them, variables dependencies through phi-nodes, number of variables, their types, and etc. Finally, all groups are combined in a fifty-six feature vector and further used in the machine learning algorithms to predict flags for optimal performance.

In the work by Namolaru et al. [10], the authors used deductive methods, and Datalog-like language, to infer characteristics dependent on optimizations.

Table 1. The static semantic feature groups

Group	Description
Plain Basic Blocks	number and type of basic blocks
Edges	number and type of edges
Number of Instructions	normalization metric to render the comparison between different programs [5, 10]
Phi-Nodes	different types of dependencies in the code
Constants	number and type of constants
Variables	number, type, and scope of variables
Branches	number and type of branches in the method

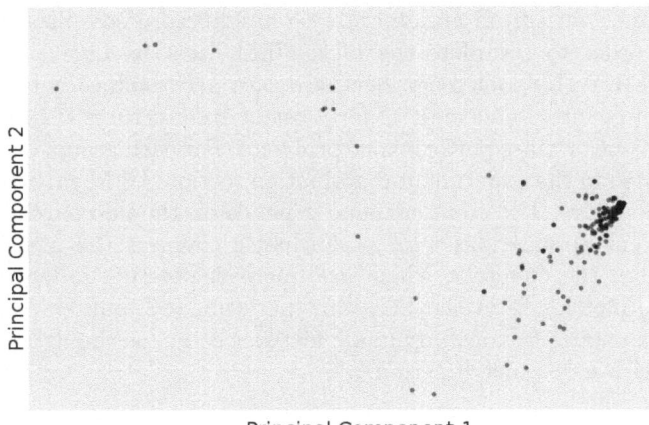

Fig. 1. Principal component analysis applied to static features illustrates program clusters

Even though the original study presents work for a custom embedded system, it was further evaluated on a general purpose desktop and server systems [5], which proved to be useful to represent different applications. In order to compare different applications, the extracted features should be normalized, as large codes tend to have large absolute values, but might be relatively similar to smaller codes. Similar to works by Fursin et al. [5, 10], the normalization metric is the number of instructions.

The scatter plot of the first two principal components for static features space is illustrated in Figure 1. The Principal Component Analysis (PCA) is a technique of orthogonal transformations to convert observations from the original feature space into a set of uncorrelated and independent variables, called principal components [8]. There are two large clusters and a few single outliers visible in Figure 1. Even though the codelets come from a diverse domain set, from the static features point of view the majority of kernels are sensitive to compiler transformations. Further, experimental evaluation confirms this sensitivity hypothesis in Section 3.

2.2   Dynamic Features

Static features are not enough to capture dynamic behavior. For example, a dramatic changes in modern memory systems hide some performance problems. Workload, execution environment, and hardware architecture precisely characterize the application's behavior. Without dynamic features it would be impossible to detect such changes and correct the model accordingly. The overall optimal flags prediction accuracy improves with dynamic features. To capture dynamic behavior the ULM framework uses hardware performance counters as dynamic features. The use of hardware performance counters for application performance analysis and tuning became mainstream almost a decade ago [11].

Counter names vary from architecture to architecture complicating counter gathering. In order to complete the task, ULM uses the Like I Knew What I am Doing (LIKWID) tool to gather hardware performance counters, which ships groups of counters and metrics for a set of architectures [12]. Each group corresponds to one or more performance problems. For each group, on all four architectures, listed in the experimental evaluation section, ULM gathers hardware performance counters. The counter name depends on the microarchitecture. To compare different applications with performance counters the framework uses the metrics from the counters, which are microarchitecture independent. The system derives metrics from the hardware performance counters listed in Table 2. Similar to static features, dynamic features compose the dynamic feature vector space with a distance function.

Table 2. The list of dynamic feature groups

Group	Description
Cycle Count Group	count core cycles
Branch Prediction	the branch miss prediction
Data Cache Performance	data cache miss and cache utilization ratios for L1, L2, and L3
Vectorization Group	number of single and double precision floating-point operations per second

ULM uses both static and dynamic features to classify applications. Using such classification and training results, ULM instantly predicts optimal flags. The next section describes the created framework and the classification procedure.

3   The ULM Framework

ULM automatically predicts the optimal combination of flags for any given application, using offline trained models and requiring no execution. It only uses compiler flags to optimize applications. To predict optimal compiler flags for a given application, the framework first needs to recognize the application's class. Each application has its optimal combination as a class label. For any new application, ULM predicts optimal flags by searching for a similar classified application and reuses the class label, e.g. an optimal combination of flags.

ULM uses three optimization strategies to select compiler flags for evaluation. The first strategy is the compiler's approach - the ULM framework selects default compiler optimization levels -O0, -O1, -O2, -O3, and -fast to optimize hot functions. The second strategy is the performance engineer approach - a collection of performance engineer recipes for optimization based on the kernel knowledge, optimization manuals [13, 14], and personal experience. ULM selects flags for loop unrolling optimization and further vectorization with -O3 to optimize kernels. The third strategy is the auto-tuning researcher's approach.

ULM randomly selects different compiler flags and, through trial and error, determines the best combination. After selecting ten thousand different randomly generated combinations of flags, ULM prunes each to the minimum, while maintaining the performance. All three methods result in more than ten thousand different flags, which ULM applies to applications and selects the one with the highest performance.

The evaluation methodology the ULM framework uses to compute application execution time is a reproducible process. Reproducibility is important for reusing the experimental results and applying them to real world codes. Execution time value implicitly drives ULM's decisions on the flag combination to apply. Prediction quality depends not only on the feature space and classification method, but also on the training set. The quality improves, when the training set covers the most possible cases. Thus, it is important to construct a model from a large and diverse set of kernels.

3.1 Applications and Codelets

The ULM framework uses a large training set of kernels for training and validation. Each kernel together with its data set form a codelet. A codelet is a pure function with data. Here, a pure function is a function with a single entry, single exit, and without side effects. The difference between the execution time of a codelet and the original application could be of one order of magnitude.

ULM uses the Automatic Speculative Thread EXtractor (ASTEX) [15] tool to extract codelets from applications. ASTEX extracts codelets by capturing hot paths with static analysis and profiling the application. Then, ASTEX saves the memory state and provides wrapper functions to load the memory back on demand. From the considered 144 applications, the ASTEX tool extracted 326 codelets, approximately two codelets per application. The full list of applications used and the number of kernels extracted from the application is presented in Table 3. The considered applications represent a diverse domain set from bit manipulation to complex graph problems.

Using the ASTEX tool, the ULM framework focuses on codelet optimization without paying the price for full application execution. The execution time is a result of the following factors: the compiler, runtime environment, architecture, and workload. In order to present a complete view, ULM performs iterative compilation for four different architectures and three optimizing compilers.

3.2 Experimental Setup

Modern compilers rapidly evolve, adapting to new architectures. In order to present the most up to date results, ULM evaluates recent versions of the main industrial and open source compilers, such as Intel Parallel Studio version 12.1, GNU Compiler Collection version 4.6.1, and LLVM version 2.9. The Intel Parallel Studio version 12.1 is an industrial optimizing compiler set for C, C++, and FORTRAN programming languages. For Intel Parallel Studio, eighty-six different options are available for tuning. The GNU Compiler Collection version 4.6.1

Table 3. The list of evaluated applications and the associated number of extracted codelets

MiBench		NAS		UTDSP	
Math and bit manipulation	5	Conjugate gradient (CG)	1	Multimedia	8
Multimedia	6	Embarrassingly parallel (EP)	1	Video codecs	3
Graphs and trees	2	FFT (FT)	1	Graph	6
Text manipulation	4	Lower-up Gauss-Seidel (LU)	1	Compression	6
Cryptography	6	Scalar pentadiagonal (SP)	1	FFT	5
Telecommunication	4	Block triagonal (BT)	1	Lattice filter	8
				LMS FIR filter	9

SPEC 2000		SPEC 2006		SNU-RT	
177.mesa	1	445.gobmk_engine	1	Video codec	3
179.art	1	462.libquantum	1	Graph	6
188.ammp	1	458.sjeng	1		
		464.h264ref	1		
		401.bzip	1		
		429.mcf	1		
		433.milc	1		

Powerstone		Miscellaneous	
Bit manipulation	2	libquantum 0.2.4 and 0.9.1	2
Graphics	2		
Encoding/decoding	1		
Control	1		
Integer arithmetic	1		
Encryption	1		
Pattern recognition	1		

is a standard open source set of compilers for a broad range of programming languages like C, C++, and FORTRAN, which has more than two hundred different options available for the compiler suite. Among the possibilities are eighty parameters with logical or integer values. LLVM version 2.9 is an alternative open source compiler famous for its clean and prototyping-friendly source code. Version 2.9 provides about one hundred different compiler options. For each compiler, ULM randomly generates ten thousand unique combinations.

The ULM framework removes flags, which do not contribute any observable performance gain, from all selected combinations of flags. Different flag combinations may still result in the same binaries. After pruning, ULM compiles the application with a flag combination and executes the generated binary, if

Table 4. The test machines configurations

Processor	Frequency	L1	L2	L3
Atom	1.66 GHz	32Kb	512Kb	-
Core 2 Duo	2.40 GHz	64Kb	3Mb	-
Nehalem	1.86 GHz	64Kb	256Kb	12Mb
Sandy Bridge	3.30 GHz	64Kb	256Kb	8Mb

a check-sum for the binary is not found in the already tested binaries. The list of experimental architectures is presented in Table 4. Nehalem and Sandy Bridge are current architectures. The Core2 is an old architecture, thus the optimization heuristics are well-tuned for producing optimal code. Finally, Atom is a low-power in-order architecture and is closer to embedded systems than the other three architectures. The test machines run the Debian GNU/Linux operating system for x86 64-bit architecture, with a 2.6.38.8 kernel version. Indeed, the presented evaluation setup covers the vast majority of architectures commonly used at the moment.

3.3   Measurement Methodology

The measurement methodology is an accurate procedure, with precise metrics and parameters. The main performance metric is the number of processor cycles. The measurement process organization is presented in Figure 2. First, the ULM framework's execution harness implements the measurement methodology from Figure 2. The harness calls the codelet a fixed amount of times to smooth side effects, such as operating system's context switches. The result is the execution time metrics, the total execution time divided by the number of repetitions. A repetition of a repetition is a metarepetition. The metarepetition result is an execution time series. Furthermore, for each series the execution harness computes statistical metrics: average, median, min, max, and variance. Finally, ULM repeats the whole process thirty times to gather statistically rigorous

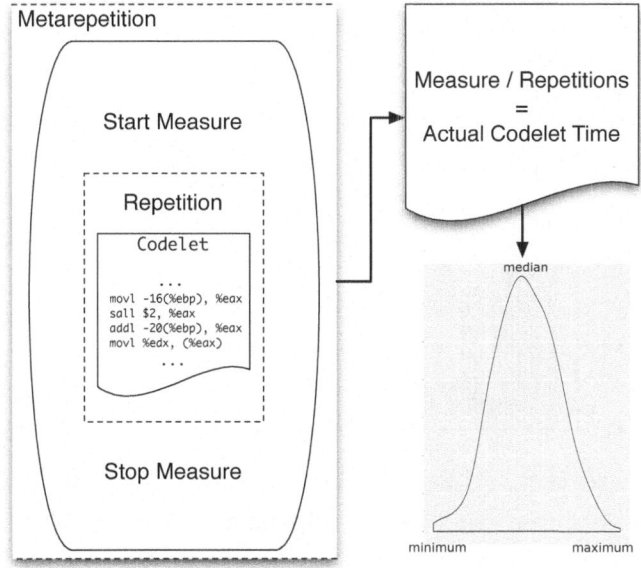

Fig. 2. Measurement process diagram

execution data. ULM repeats the whole process thirty times to gather statistically rigorous execution data.

One of the biggest problems in performance optimization is reproducibility. To reuse the performance optimization knowledge for an application, it is important for results to be reproducible. The experimental setup configuration keeps the variance of execution time at less than 0.3%. The low variance allows ULM to apply tuning data obtained for one application to optimize another with a high confidence in achieved result.

3.4   Results and Analysis

According to the experimental data, 62% of codelets compiled with Intel Parallel Studio, 65% of codelets compiled with gcc, and 100% of codelets compiled with LLVM, the -O3 optimization level is the optimal flag combination. For the rest of the codes, the ULM framework is able to achieve a significant performance gain from 1.15 to 2.2 times. According to Figure 3, most codelets achieve no more than 20% speedup. Additionally, for a majority of the codelets it is not possible to improve the performance compared to -O3 only by tweaking compiler flags. Using the pre-trained data, ULM is able to instantly predict the optimal flags.

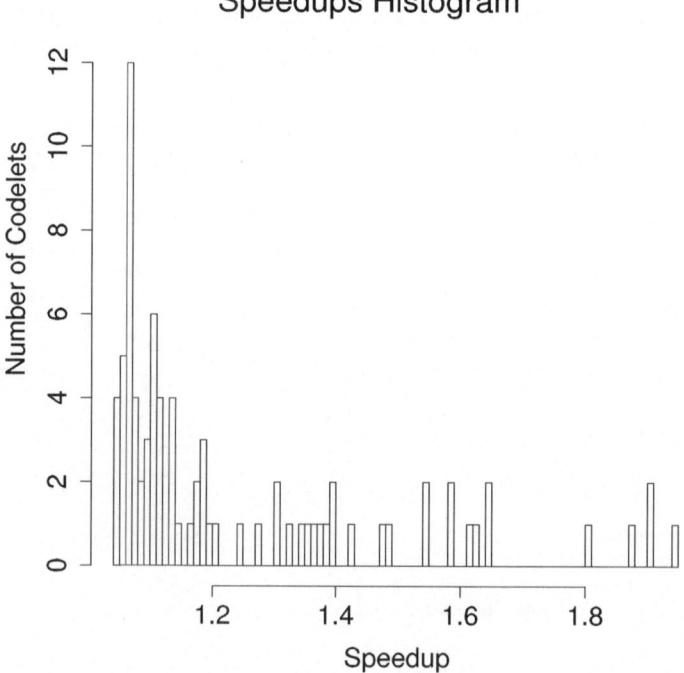

Fig. 3. Speedup over -O3

4   Predicting Optimal Flags

At the classification phase, ULM predicts a class for a given application. The class is optimal flag combination for a given application. The prediction might result with several classes for a given application. If so, the ULM framework selects the class with the smallest combination of flags within 5% of the best speedup. The majority of applications belong to the -O3 class. For these applications -O3 is the optimal flag and no prediction is needed. However, for other applications, it is possible to achieve a substantial performance gain by tweaking compiler flags. For such applications ULM predicts optimal compiler flags based on the trained classes and application characteristics.

The prediction quality depends on the feature space and the classification method. The ULM framework measures the efficiency of each classification method and selects the most efficient one. Classification methods efficiency, or the accuracy ratio, is the number of correctly predicted cases to the total number of cases. Next, ULM calculates the accuracy level using the standard leave-one-out validation method [8]. Finally, ULM automatically recommends user the most accurate prediction method.

Most previous works concentrate on one prediction method. Unlike these [1–5] previous works, The ULM framework compares popular classification methods from the previous studies: support vector machines, nearest neighbor, and stochastic gradient descent [8]. Each classification method is evaluated with leave-one-out method.

The leave-one-out method is one of the most precise methods to validate a classification algorithm and calculate its accuracy rate. The principle of leave-one-out validation procedure selects one observation and builds a model for all other observations except the selected one, then computes the error. The procedure continues for each available observation. The result of such a procedure is an accumulated error. However, the leave-one-out validation method is slow and requires a large amount of time and computational resources. The total validation time is proportional to the number of observations and depends on the time spent building a model.

First, for each architecture, application, and compiler, the framework compiles an application with all the selected flags: default optimization levels, flags with unrolling, and ten thousand randomly generated flags. Then, ULM executes the application, computes the execution time according to the measurement methodology, selects beneficial combinations, and uses them as class labels. Finally, ULM groups applications by class. The accuracy rates for Intel icc compiler

Table 5. Average Classification for Intel icc compiler

Classification Method	Sandy Bridge Nehalem	Atom Core 2
Nearest Neighbor	53%	50%
SGD	60%	55%
SVM	92%	90%

are presented in Table 5. Gcc compiler had almost identical values as the ones showed in Table 5. The results for LLVM compiler do not appear in Table 5 as the prediction is always correct for any method. In fact, for the LLVM compiler -O3 is the optimal combination for 100% of kernels. Using dynamic features the average prediction accuracy is higher than using static features. ULM achieves the highest accuracy level using multi-class support vector machines with Gaussian Radial Bases Function [8].

5   Related Work

Currently, iterative compilation techniques are almost the standard approach to select the best flags. The researchers proposed different methods to reduce flag combination search time: genetic algorithms [4, 16], iterative algorithms like Combined Elimination [17], and even manually constructed models [18, 19]. The main drawback of iterative compilation is its long time to derive optimal flags. In order to reduce the search time, researchers construct models offline. Similar to genetic algorithms, decision based schemes [2, 20, 21] analyze the micro-architecture independent characteristics and infer beneficial optimizations from these characteristics. Finally, manually constructed models [18, 19] use a human expert's knowledge to select the best flags. Existing solutions rarely reuse models constructed for one application to optimize another application. Building a model for each new application makes the whole process too costly to be practically applied. Using pre-trained models, the ULM framework can instantly propose the best options, by simply looking for an application similar to the given one.

Fursin et al. [5] used pre-trained models to predict flags for a new application implemented in the MILEPOST GCC project. Contrary to MILEPOST GCC, the created ULM framework is not limited to static features and selects the best machine learning algorithm, thus achieving higher prediction accuracy.

Some previous work uses static features [9] and performance counters [1] to build a model and predict optimization combinations. According to the results by Cavazos et al. [1] an approach with performance counters outperforms a method based on static features. Cavazos et al. [1] use multiplexing to gather more counters with less executions. The multiplexing is a useful technique, but imprecise, thus degrading prediction accuracy. The ULM framework does not use multiplexing, but precise counter values. Gathering precise counter values requires more executions, but using codelets instead of the whole applications dramatically reduces the overhead. The focus on hot functions allows the framework to gather all the hardware performance counters with low overhead and high precision.

Recently, there are two machine learning compilers available: MILEPOST GCC, an open source compiler[5] and IBM Testarossa, a proprietary JIT compiler [7]. The MILEPOST GCC authors evaluated their compiler on the multi-objective optimization of MiBench benchmarks and industrial database Berkeley DB. The MILEPOST's results opened opportunities for machine learning in compilers and performance optimization.

The presented study reuses features from MILEPOST GCC [5, 10] to build a model, but also improves the feature space with performance counters. Similar to IBM Testarossa [7] the ULM framework uses SVM to select the best flags. The framework presented in this paper is not limited to SVM, but evaluates several machine learning algorithms to select the best one. Contrary to previous studies, the presented evaluation process focuses on kernels, rather than whole applications, which allows ULM to examine large experimental data for more architectures, compilers, and compiler options. Thus providing practical results for a user.

6   Conclusions

This work demonstrates the quality of the code produced by the modern optimizing compilers. Indeed, for 62% of considered kernels, four different architectures, and all three compilers -O3 is enough. However, for the other 38% of applications the default compiler heuristics are not even near optimal and it is possible to produce a better code with a combination of flags, found with iterative compilation.

For any given application the proposed ULM framework instantly predicts the optimal combination of flags from a pre-trained model In this study, ULM evaluated a large set of more than three hundred codelets extracted from 144 benchmark applications. Finally, using Support Vector Machines ULM achieved found the best optimization flag for 92% of kernels with a low overhead. The ULM framework thus provides the user with an easy to use tool to determine the best compiler flags before compiling. Doing so augments the usability of the tool since the user is no longer required to go through the long and complex procedures of iterative compilation once the initial classification is performed.

Future work consists in considering different architectures to augment ULM's coverage and augment the codelet test set to improve application coverage. Though the initial 300+ codelets provide a solid coverage due to the chosen applications' diversity, there is still room to add new applications to the test suite. There is also a direction that pushes ULM directly into the compiler by defining a new optimization flag. The new flag will automatically determine the best compiler flag using ULM's methodology. Finally, ULM will shift from a prototype project to a user open-source project in the near future.

Acknowledgments. This paper is a result of work performed in Exascale Computing Research Lab with support provided by CEA, Genci, Intel, and UVSQ. Any opinions, findings, conclusions, or recommendations expressed in this material are those of the author(s) and do not necessarily reflect the views of the CEA, Genci, Intel or UVSQ. The authors thank Grigori Fursin, Eric Petit, Pablo Oliveira and anonymous reviewers for their valuable feedback on this work.

References

1. Cavazos, J., Fursin, G., Agakov, F., Bonilla, E., O'Boyle, M.F.P., Temam, O.: Rapidly selecting good compiler optimizations using performance counters. In: Proceedings of the International Symposium on Code Generation and Optimization, CGO 2007, pp. 185–197. IEEE Computer Society, Washington, DC (2007)
2. Agakov, F., Bonilla, E., Cavazos, J., Franke, B., Fursin, G., O'Boyle, M.F.P., Thomson, J., Toussaint, M., Williams, C.K.I.: Using machine learning to focus iterative optimization. In: Proceedings of the International Symposium on Code Generation and Optimization, CGO 2006, pp. 295–305. IEEE Computer Society, Washington, DC (2006)
3. Pan, Z., Eigenmann, R.: Fast and effective orchestration of compiler optimizations for automatic performance tuning. In: Proceedings of the International Symposium on Code Generation and Optimization, CGO 2006, pp. 319–332. IEEE Computer Society, Washington, DC (2006)
4. Hoste, K., Eeckhout, L.: Cole: compiler optimization level exploration. In: Proceedings of the 6th Annual IEEE/ACM International Symposium on Code Generation and Optimization, CGO 2008, pp. 165–174. ACM, New York (2008)
5. Fursin, G., Kashnikov, Y., Wahid, A., Chamski, M.Z., Temam, O., Namolaru, M., Yom-tov, E., Mendelson, B., Zaks, A., Courtois, E., Bodin, F., Barnard, P., Ashton, E., Bonilla, E., Thomson, J., Williams, C.K.I.: Milepost GCC: machine learning enabled self-tuning compiler (2011)
6. Bodin, F., Kisuki, T., Knijnenburg, P., O'Boyle, M., Rohou, E.: Iterative compilation in a non-linear optimisation space (1998)
7. Sanchez, R.N., Amaral, J.N., Szafron, D., Pirvu, M., Stoodley, M.: Using support vector machines to learn how to compile a method. In: Proceedings of the 2010 22nd International Symposium on Computer Architecture and High Performance Computing, SBAC-PAD 2010, pp. 223–230. IEEE Computer Society, Washington, DC (2010)
8. Bishop, C.M.: Pattern recognition and machine learning, 1st edn., corr. 2nd printing edn. Springer (October 2006)
9. Dubach, C., Cavazos, J., Franke, B., Fursin, G., O'Boyle, M.F., Temam, O.: Fast compiler optimisation evaluation using code-feature based performance prediction. In: Proceedings of the 4th International Conference on Computing Frontiers, CF 2007, pp. 131–142. ACM, New York (2007)
10. Namolaru, M., Cohen, A., Fursin, G., Zaks, A., Freund, A.: Practical aggregation of semantical program properties for machine learning based optimization. In: Proceedings of the 2010 International Conference on Compilers, Architectures and Synthesis for Embedded Systems, CASES 2010, pp. 197–206. ACM, New York (2010)
11. Azimi, R., Stumm, M., Wisniewski, R.W.: Online performance analysis by statistical sampling of microprocessor performance counters. In: Proceedings of the 19th Annual International Conference on Supercomputing, ICS 2005, pp. 101–110. ACM, New York (2005)
12. Treibig, J., Hager, G., Wellein, G.: LIKWID: Lightweight Performance Tools. CoRR abs/1104.4874 (2011)
13. Intel Corp.: Intel 64 and IA-32 Architectures Optimization Reference Manual (2011)
14. Intel Corp.: Intel 64 and IA-32 Architectures Software Developer's Manual (2011)

15. Petit, E., Papaure, G., Dru, F., Bodin, F.: ASTEX: a Hot path Based Thread Extractor for Distributed Memory System on a Chip. In: 1st HiPEAC Industrial Workshop, Grenoble, France (2006)
16. Cooper, K.D., Schielke, P.J., Subramanian, D.: Optimizing for reduced code space using genetic algorithms. SIGPLAN Not. 34, 1–9 (1999)
17. Triantafyllis, S., Vachharajani, M., Vachharajani, N., August, D.I.: Compiler optimization-space exploration. In: Proceedings of the International Symposium on Code Generation and Optimization: Feedback-Directed and Runtime Optimization, CGO 2003, pp. 204–215. IEEE Computer Society, Washington, DC (2003)
18. Parello, D., Temam, O., Cohen, A., Verdun, J.M.: Towards a systematic, pragmatic and architecture-aware program optimization process for complex processors. In: Proceedings of the 2004 ACM/IEEE Conference on Supercomputing, p. 15. IEEE Computer Society, Washington, DC (2004)
19. Zhao, M., Childers, B.R., Soffa, M.L.: A model-based framework: An approach for profit-driven optimization. In: Proceedings of the International Symposium on Code Generation and Optimization, CGO 2005, pp. 317–327. IEEE Computer Society, Washington, DC (2005)
20. Vuduc, R., Demmel, J.W., Bilmes, J.A.: Statistical models for empirical search-based performance tuning. Int. J. High Perform. Comput. Appl. 18, 65–94 (2004)
21. Stephenson, M., Amarasinghe, S.: Predicting unroll factors using supervised classification. In: Proceedings of the International Symposium on Code Generation and Optimization, CGO 2005, pp. 123–134. IEEE Computer Society, Washington, DC (2005)

The STAPL Parallel Graph Library*

Harshvardhan, Adam Fidel, Nancy M. Amato, and Lawrence Rauchwerger

Parasol Lab, Dept. of Computer Science and Engineering, Texas A&M University
{ananvay,fidel,amato,rwerger}@cse.tamu.edu

Abstract. This paper describes the STAPL Parallel Graph Library, a high-level framework that abstracts the user from data-distribution and parallelism details and allows them to concentrate on parallel graph algorithm development. It includes a customizable distributed graph container and a collection of commonly used parallel graph algorithms. The library introduces pGraph pViews that separate algorithm design from the container implementation. It supports three graph processing algorithmic paradigms, level-synchronous, asynchronous and coarse-grained, and provides common graph algorithms based on them. Experimental results demonstrate improved scalability in performance and data size over existing graph libraries on more than 16,000 cores and on internet-scale graphs containing over 16 billion vertices and 250 billion edges.

1 Introduction

Processing large graphs is essential in many domains, from social network and web-scale graphs to scientific meshes and nuclear reactor-design [2]. As the graphs span billions of vertices and edges, they may not fit in the memory of a single-processor system. Using a distributed data-structure allows massive graphs to be processed quickly and concurrently.

There have been many attempts over the past decade [7,3,8] to allow programmers to easily express their graph computations in parallel. Despite this, graph algorithms remain notoriously hard to scalably parallelize, and existing graph libraries are restrictive in allowing users to express algorithms and require them to manage many details regarding data-distribution and communication.

This paper describes the STAPL Parallel Graph Library (SGL), a generic parallel graph library that provides a high-level framework that allows the user to concentrate on parallel graph algorithm development and relieves them from the details of the underlying distributed environment. It consists of the STAPL

* This research supported in part by NSF awards CRI-0551685, CCF-0833199, CCF-0830753, IIS-096053, IIS-0917266, NSF/DNDO award 2008-DN-077-ARI018-02, by DOE NNSA under the Predictive Science Academic Alliances Program grant DE-FC52-08NA28616, by THECB NHARP award 000512-0097-2009, by Chevron, IBM, Intel, Oracle/Sun and by Award KUS-C1-016-04 made by King Abdullah University of Science and Technology (KAUST). This research used resources of the National Energy Research Scientific Computing Center, which is supported by the Office of Science of the U.S. Department of Energy under Contract No. DE-AC02-05CH11231.

H. Kasahara and K. Kimura (Eds.): LCPC 2012, LNCS 7760, pp. 46–60, 2013.

pGraph pContainer, pGraph pViews that allow for the separation of the algorithm design from the container implementation, and a collection of parallel graph algorithms. In addition, the library supports level-synchronous, asynchronous and coarse-grained algorithmic paradigms, which are designed to support graph processing applications and algorithms. Further, it automates load balancing and simplifies some locality-related optimizations.

The STAPL Parallel Graph Library makes several contributions:

Programmability. One of the main goals of SGL is to provide a similar interface and level of abstraction as sequential graph libraries by allowing seamless access to local and remote elements through virtualization using Shared-Object Views, while providing good performance.

Abstraction. The pGraph pView – a high-level graph abstraction – allows programmers to completely decouple the design of the graph algorithm from the implementation of the graph container. Users are left free to express the graph as is most natural to the problem, while the underlying data-structure and implementation can be chosen to offer maximum performance.

Multiple Algorithmic Paradigms. We provide three paradigms for expressing graph algorithms, including two fine-grained (level-sync and async) and one coarse-grained paradigm. These enable natural expression of algorithms while extracting the best performance from different input graphs.

Scalable Performance. We demonstrate improved scalability in performance and data size over tens of thousands of cores compared with existing graph libraries on standard benchmarks. Moreover, we provide light-weight support for load balancing through asynchronous data migration, and demonstrate improved performance and scalability in a real-world production application by mitigating load-imbalance through automatic redistribution of vertices.

2   STAPL Overview

The pGraph pContainer is built using the pContainer framework (PCF) provided by the Standard Template Adaptive Parallel Library (STAPL). STAPL [4,5,13] is a framework for parallel C++ code development. STAPL's core is a library of C++ components implementing parallel algorithms (pAlgorithms) and distributed data structures (pContainers) that have interfaces similar to the C++ standard library (STL) [10]. Analogous to STL algorithms that use *iterators*, pAlgorithms are written in terms of pViews [4] so that the same algorithm can operate on multiple pContainers. pViews facilitate parallel processing by supporting independent random access to ranges (partitions) of a container's elements. The PARAGRAPH represents computations as parallel task graphs.

STAPL abstracts the physical parallel elements to the notion of *locations* – units of a parallel machine capable of performing computations that have a contiguous memory address space. Asynchronous communication is allowed through remote method invocations (RMIs) on shared objects. The STAPL runtime system is portable to different platforms and architectures without modifying other STAPL components.

```
//create pgraph with 10 vertices :
p_graph<Directed, Multiedges> pg(10);
size_t  V = pg.num_vertices();
pg.add_vertex(11);

  parallel_for_each  (i = 0..E)
    pg.add_edge(rand() % V, rand() % V);

// get the out−degree of vertex 3
size_t  deg_3 = pg[3].edges(). size ();
// delete a specific  edge between two vertices
bool success = pg.delete_edge (3,2);
```

```
// directed  graph,  multiple allowed edges b/w
// same source & target
p_graph<Directed, Multiedges>

// graph with custom vertex and edge properties
p_graph<Directed, Multiedges,  vertex_prop , edge_prop>

// vertices  block−partitioned,
// with custom  traits  for graph
p_graph<Directed, Multiedges,  int , bool,
        blocked_partition ,  my_traits >
```

Fig. 1. Typical interaction with the pGraph pContainer through methods

Fig. 2. Example traits of the pGraph

3   The pGraph Container and Implementation

Graphs can be *directed* or *undirected*, with *weighted* or *unweighted* edges, and may or may not allow multiple edges between the same source and target (*multigraph*) or self-loops. Applications may associate information (properties/weights) with vertices and edges.

API. The pGraph pContainer exports a uniform interface for accessing and manipulating all types of graphs. Every vertex and edge in the graph is uniquely identified by a vertex (or edge) descriptor that is used for accessing and referencing the element, and for adding or deleting elements.

The pGraph API makes it simple to create graphs and perform common graph operations (Fig. 1), such as adding, deleting or accessing vertices and edges, applying functors on graph elements, etc. Issues of concurrency and consistency are handled by the pGraph. Importantly, users do not have to reason or know about the locality of the graph elements – they refer to vertices and edges using descriptors and the pGraph handles the details of locality and forwarding requests to the required location. This is not the case with many other graph libraries, e.g., in PBGL, the user can only get the out-degree of a vertex from a local process, whereas in our model this information is available from all locations.

Users can customize a pGraph by selecting properties and traits (e.g., directedness, graph representation, storage). SGL provides common options and implementations for storages, etc., but users may provide their own, or implement bridges to adapt their data structures to our algorithms. These choices may affect the performance. For example, a pGraph using vector storage may be faster than one using map storage if the graph is static (i.e., the number of vertices is known *a priori*). It is straightforward to customize a pGraph (Fig. 2). Further customizations are possible through trait-classes.

Implementation. The pGraph is built using the STAPL pContainer framework (PCF), which provides base classes that handle issues dealing with data distribution and parallelism and allows the design of the pGraph pContainer to focus on graph-specific concerns. The pGraph pContainer consists of a set of base containers (bContainers) and the infrastructure to make them work together in parallel. For the pGraph, a bContainer is a base graph data structure that exports the pGraph's interface. The bContainer has three layers: the representation of the graph, the graph storage, and the underlying storage. The graph storage is tied to the representation, exporting an interface that allows the representation to work with the underlying storage. It provides the policies for the type of underlying storage used by the graph (e.g., vector, hash map, map) for vertices and edges. It also specifies the type for a vertex and type for an edge, along with how properties are stored on these. The underlying storage may be a sequential container unaware of parallelism that is used by the graph to store vertices and edges, or possibly another pContainer.

The PCF provides a shared-object view [14] that allows users to address any element globally. pGraph users interact with the container by method invocation, which the framework forwards to the location where the needed graph elements reside. Fig. 3 shows the internal base-class implementation for apply_async, which provides an example of address resolution for graph elements using asynchronous communication. The apply_async method is provided by the PCF for applying a higher-order function object on an element of the container. This may be used to implement methods such as add_edge and set_vertex_property for the pGraph. Internally, this forwarding is supported by a distributed directory service – which is contained within the pGraph – that provides a two-level lookup of the requested vertex's location. This is described in the next section.

Shared-Object View Provided by Distributed Directory. The pGraph is a dynamic container, where vertices may be added and removed, and so vertex IDs need not be contiguous or even ordered. The pGraph uses a distributed directory to provide a shared-object view to users and abstract them from dealing with the details of distribution. While a distributed directory can increase access costs, other solutions such as centralized models (e.g., the master-slave model employed by Pregel [8]) which store the entire directory information in a single location, or replicated directory on all locations, may not scale to large systems.

In this two-level distributed directory scheme, every vertex has a *home location* associated with it, which may not be the location of the vertex, but is rather the location that stores information about the vertex's locality. It is calculated using simple closed-form solution (a hash of the vertex's descriptor), so any requesting location knows quickly and precisely where to send the request.

In this mechanism, the pGraph first checks if the graph vertex is local, and if so, then services the request immediately. If the vertex is not found locally, the local directory computes the *home location* of that vertex and forwards the request there. The *home location* is responsible for knowing the exact location of the vertex. In some cases, the *home location* may own the vertex itself, at which point, the requested action is performed on the vertex. However, in the case that it does not, the request is forwarded to the location that owns the vertex, where the request is serviced. As shown by Tanase et. al. [14], address resolution using asynchronous forwarding provides improved performance over a directory that determines the element's location using synchronous communication.

// *asynchronous migration and redistribution :*
g.migrate(vertex , location)
g. redistribute (cost_map, action_function =no_op)

```
void _base :: apply_async( vertex_descriptor  s,
                           Functor f)
if  base_container . contains(s)
  base_container . apply(s,  f)
else
  home = home_location(s) // hash−based lookup
  if  my_location == home
    owner = directory . lookup(s)
    async_rmi (owner, apply_async(s, f))
  else
    async_rmi (home, apply_async(s, f))
```

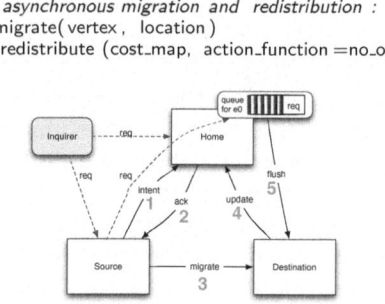

Fig. 3. Internal base-class implementation of `apply_async` method illustrating address resolution

Fig. 4. Asynchronous migration protocol for `pGraph`

Vertex Migration. The SGL provides the novel ability to migrate vertices asynchronously between locations during the execution of the program. An important property of the migration protocol is that it ensures that SGL algorithms can be oblivious to the data distribution and also to any migration occurring during the execution of an algorithm.

The protocol for migration of graph elements implemented by the pGraph is inspired by directory-based cache coherence techniques [6] and is described in Fig. 4. When processing an element-migration request from a source location to a destination location, the source first informs the home location of its intent to migrate (1). The home location, upon receiving this request, marks the element as in the process of migration and creates a queue for all requests addressed to that element. It then sends an acknowledgement (2) to the source location allowing the source to then proceed to migrate the element data to the destination (3). When the destination receives the element's data, it stores it and informs the home location (4) to update its metadata to record that the destination is now the owner of that element. Finally, the home location updates its metadata and forwards all pending requests for that element to the destination location (5). If at any point during migration a location requests access to the element that is currently being migrated, the requests are forwarded to the home location for that element, where they are buffered in the queue. The queue is flushed at the end of migration and requests are forwarded to the new location of the element.

Redistribution. As users of SGL generally may be unaware of localilty, SGL provides a convenient way to rebalance a pGraph.

Redistribution of a pGraph requires some process for determining the new distribution. This can be user provided or it can be computed based on some cost function. For many graph-based scientific applications, a cost function (cost map) can be determined representing the expected computational costs associated with vertices and edges. In SGL, such cost maps can be user provided, or if no additional information is available, uniform costs can be assumed for all elements. Given a cost map, a new partition that attempts to address the

```
p_graph<Directed, Multiedges> pg(N);
graph_view view(pg);

strongly_connected_components(view);
connected_components(undirected_view(pg));
page_rank( implicit_view (N, binary_tree_func ()));
```

```
struct  binary_tree_func
  size_t  size ( size_t  parent)  { return 2; }

  size_t  operator()( size_t  parent,  size_t  idx)
    if ( idx == 0)
      return 2*parent+1;
    else   return 2*parent+2;
```

Fig. 5. A few examples of creating and using pGraph pViews, with binary-tree functor

imbalance can be computed by an SGL graph partitioning algorithm. Given a desired partition, each location computes the vertices that need to be migrated to itself from other locations and invokes a migrate call on those vertices. Internally, the asynchronous directory forwards the migration request to the correct location where the element is located and initiates the migration of that vertex. Fig. 4 illustrates how redistribution is invoked, and the protocol used in SGL. SGL allows application programmers to optionally provide callback functions that are invoked along with each migration call on the corresponding element to allow any action that needs to be performed during the process of migrating a single element, such as updating auxiliary data structures.

4   pGraph pViews

pGraph algorithms are written in terms of pViews that export the full interface of the pGraph and allow iteration over vertices and edges. While arbitrary partitions can be specified, the default partition of a pGraph pView matches the physical partition of the graph on the system. This is the pView that can offer the best performance and it should be used unless it is not suitable for the algorithm. The pGraph supports the standard pViews provided by STAPL, as well as some graph-specific pViews that are described in this section.

Useful pGraph pViews. The pGraph provides many useful views that can be used to logically view and manipulate the structure of a graph. For example, by applying an undirected pGraph pView to a directed graph, one can use an algorithm that was designed for undirected graphs on a directed graph without explicitly modifying the graph. Fig. 5 shows the creation of an undirected view over a directed pGraph which is then used as input for a parallel connected components algorithm. This is a particular need for a motion planning application which constructs a digraph and uses this connectivity information to view the results and as a stopping condition [16]. We also evaluate the performance of a parallel connected components algorithm using this pView in Sec. 6.

As another example, some strongly connected components algorithms [9] need access to the predecessors of a vertex in a digraph. For this, a predecessor pView can be used to provide the predecessor information without modifying the underlying graph. Or, in some cases, one may wish to work with the complement of a graph which has the edges of the graph complemented. In this case, instead of constructing another graph, one could simply apply a complement view.

Implicit pGraph pViews. A pView is a partitioned collection of element descriptors. While these collections are often explicit, with memory associated with each element, STAPL provides for the creation of pViews that do not have an underlying collection of elements, but instead evaluate expressions to provide vertices and edges lazily. These views may be used when the graph structure can be described by a series of formulae, with the benefit of having virtually no storage overhead, e.g., users can specify the formula using a functor that, given the descriptor of a vertex, returns the descriptor of its neighboring vertices. This is most useful in scientific applications that work on regular meshes, where the structure may be expressed by formulae. This allows the application to avoid storing the vertices and edges of the graph, freeing up memory for larger problems, or allowing the program to run on memory-constrained systems.

In Fig. 5, the PageRank algorithm is invoked on an implicit binary tree pView by specifying the view size and the function object (binary_tree_func) that describes the parent-child relationship for a complete binary tree (Fig. 5). This pView can be passed as input to any generic pGraph algorithm, the execution of the algorithm lazily creates graph elements on which to operate. Similarly, an n-dimensional hypercube, a mesh, a torus and other classes of regular graphs can be generated by using the appropriate algrebraic expressions.

5   Parallel Graph Algorithms

The SGL provides three paradigms to help users design parallel graph algorithms: the level-synchronous paradigm, the asynchronous paradigm and the coarse-grained paradigm. Using these paradigms, the SGL provides standard fundamental graph algorithms, including breadth-first search, connected components, single-source shortest path, and topological sort, and also more specialized algorithms such as page rank and particle-swarm optimization.

These paradigms are built on top of algorithmic primitives provided by STAPL (e.g., map_func, map_reduce) that execute higher-order functions (workfunction) on elements of a view. To express a new parallel graph algorithm, users choose a suitable paradigm and provide a workfunction that describes the computation, either in a fine-grained manner for the level-sync and async paradigms, or in a coarse-grained manner for the coarse-grained paradigm. Fig. 6 is an example of a workfunction for SGL's parallel breadth-first search (BFS).

The workfunction is generic and oblivious to the paradigm (either level-sync or async). The differences between level-sync and async versions are taken care of by the paradigm itself. For example, the generic BFS workfunction (bfs_wf) will use the visitor (visit_wf) (Fig. 6), and may be used in both, the level-sync or async paradigms. For fine-grained algorithms (workfunctions that operate on individual vertices), the pViews provide optimizations that are transparent to the user to better exploit data locality. Coarse-grained workfunctions receive a partition of the graph on which to work.

```
void BFS (graph_view graph, vertex source)
  source. color = GREY;
  Paradigm(graph_view, bfs_wf (),  bfs_visitor ());

bool  bfs_visitor (Vertex v,  int  level )
  if (v. level > level )
    v. level = level ;
    v. color = GREY;
    return true;
  return false ;
```

```
bool bfs_wf(Vertex v)
  if (v. color == GREY)
    for (u : v.neighbors())
      spawn(Visit( bfs_visitor (_1, v. level +1)), u)
    v. color = BLACK;
    return true;
  return false ;
```

Fig. 6. Pseudocode for generic BFS and workfunctions (**bfs_wf** and **bfs_visitor**)

Level-Synchronous Algorithms. The Level-synchronous paradigm iteratively executes tasks on the active vertices of the graph in a BSP fashion [20], with a global synchronization between each level. Iterative application of the map/reduce pattern is one way to express the level-sync paradigm.

The algorithm's communication happens asynchronously during and after a level, but is guaranteed to have completed before the next level. In this paradigm, each level is a phase that works on some set of active vertices, which may change through the levels. Level-synchronous algorithms tend to perform best when the number of levels is small since each level requires a costly global synchronization.

Examples of level-sync algorithms are PageRank [11] and level-sync BFS [18]. To create a level-sync BFS, a user would plug-in the generic BFS workfunction (Fig. 6) into the level-sync paradigm. The workfunction should return true if it was active for a vertex, and false otherwise. This is used to decide the termination condition, which occurs when all vertices are inactive (all vertices return false).

Asynchronous Algorithms. The async paradigm, on the other hand, has no internal synchronizations, and therefore, may perform better on graphs with high diameter. However, asynchronous algorithms may perform redundant work, as there are no guarantees for the execution order. For example, an async BFS may re-visit a vertex multiple times as shorter paths are discovered [12].

The algorithm typically starts with a few fine-grained *source tasks* over an initial set of vertices. These may spawn additional tasks on their neighboring vertices that are asynchronously forwarded to the location where the neighbor target vertex is currently located (using task forwarding). The algorithm execution ends when there are no more tasks currently executing or in-flight, as detected by a termination-detection algorithm. Termination detection is supported by internal mechanisms that track the number of tasks executing and in waiting and that performs a reduction across locations.

Since most libraries for graph processing provide one of the two paradigms, users either have to use different libraries for different input graphs, or potentially settle for lower performance depending on their input graphs. SGL provides both paradigms, such that the user workfunction is oblivious to the paradigm selected, so it is easy to switch paradigms to obtain the best performance in different cases.

Coarse-Grained Algorithms. The coarse-grained paradigm is useful to express graph computations in which a pGraph may be partitioned into subgraphs,

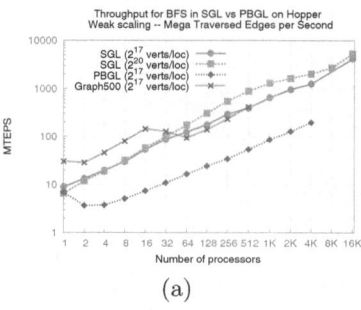
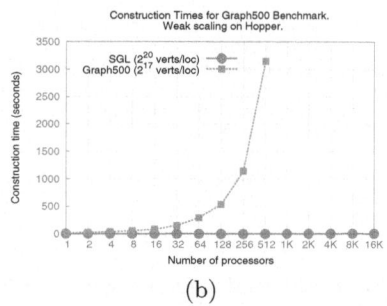

(a)   (b)

Fig. 7. Comparison of MTEPS (a) and construction times (b) for `pGraph`, PBGL and Graph 500 ref. implementation. Note log-scale y-axis for (a)

each of which is processed separately. An example of this type of computation is the coarse-grained connected components algorithm [21]. The first level of the algorithm computes the connected-components of the local subgraph, ignoring remote edges. In the second level, the local connected components are merged by applying a level-synchronous connected components to the graph. Then, the CC vertices are relabeled with the CC-identifier of their connected component. This allows the algorithm to reduce communication by coarsening local computation.

As an example, the Motion-Planning applications [17] follow this paradigm, where they build the graph locally in coarse-grained partitions, and then merge the graphs to get the final result.

6   Results

We evaluate SGL using multiple input graphs and over multiple platforms and show that our library performs better, both in terms of scalability and memory used, than other available graph libraries, Parallel Boost Graph Library (PBGL) (v0.7.0), Multi-Threaded Graph Library (MTGL) (v1.1.1), and the Graph500 MPI Reference Implementation (benchmark) (v1.2). (see Sec. 7).

We show scalability of SGL algorithms over a representative subset of input graphs, including the Graph500 Benchmark-generated input (that simulates internet-scale webgraphs and social-networks) and torus graphs (that simulate scientific meshes). Our experimental studies are conducted on two massively parallel systems: a 153,216 core Cray XE6 (HOPPER) and a 832 core Power5 cluster (P5-CLUSTER). For testing MTGL, we run strong-scaling on an 8-core node of a 2,400 core Opteron cluster (OPTERON). We also run a strong-scaling experiment on a real-world production application using SGL on OPTERON.

Graph 500 Benchmark. We implemented the Graph 500 benchmark [1] for SGL, using the level-sync BFS. We show the results and scalability on HOPPER.

In our experiments, while PBGL and benchmark could only accomodate 2^{17} vertices per core at scale, SGL was able to fit a maximum of 2^{20} vertices per core due to less memory needed for storing outstanding communication requests. We

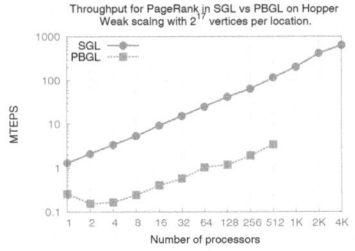
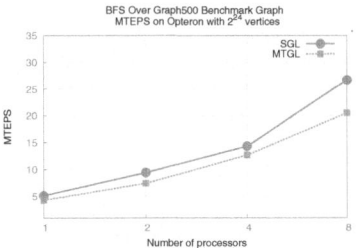

Fig. 8. Level-Sync PageRank on Hopper: SGL and PBGL

Fig. 9. Strong scaling for the Graph 500 benchmark: MTGL vs pGraph

show a weak-scaling plot comparing the scalability of the Graph500 benchmark, PBGL, and SGL for 2^{17} and SGL for 2^{20} vertices per location in Fig. 7(a). The y-axis reports the throughput in Mega Traversed Edges Per Second (MTEPS). Both the benchmark and PBGL suffered from memory bottlenecks. While the Graph500 reference implementation was able to construct the graph, it crashed during the execution of the algorithm on 1,024 cores and PBGL was unable to run the algorithm beyond 4,096 cores. On a single core, PBGL performed similar to SGL, whereas the Graph500 benchmark implementation was 5x faster due to the use of Compressed Sparse-Row (CSR) representation of the graph, while PBGL and SGL used the adjacency-list representation. While CSR is faster for executing the algorithm, it takes a considerable amount of time to build the graph (Fig. 7(b)) as edges need to be globally shuffled to maintain contiguous access through the edgelist. The high overhead of generating the CSR prompted us to use the adjacency-list representation (which is also timed by the Graph500 benchmark specification). We also observed that SGL scaled better than both the benchmark and PBGL. This is more evident for larger inputs, as more local work better hides the communication overhead.

The poor scalability of PBGL and the reference implementation may be explained in part due to insufficient aggregation of messages and the use of ghost nodes for PBGL. The benchmark generates a large number of small messages while executing the algorithm, which overloads the MPI buffers of the machine. The STAPL runtime-system aggregates messages by combining messages being sent to the same location, as well as buffering them and then sends fewer messages, of bigger size through MPI. This helps achieve better performance – as is more evident when going off-node (24 cores) – due to sending messages in bulk, as well as prevents the communication sub-system from running out of memory. This is also why SGL can run on larger graphs than PBGL and benchmark.

We also compare SGL's level-sync BFS with MTGL's BFS implementation using Qthreads in Fig. 9. We can see that MTGL and SGL exhibit similar behavior on a shared-memory node in terms of strong scaling.

Parallel Graph Algorithms. In this section, we analyze the performance of several parallel graph algorithms for various input types.

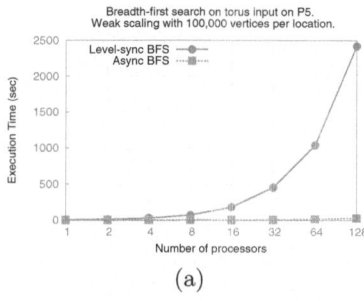
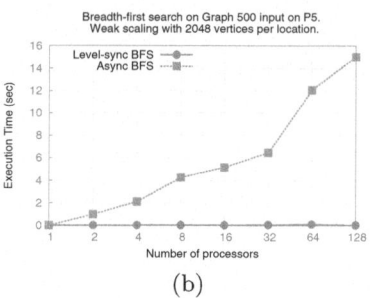

(a)   (b)

Fig. 10. Scalability (time) for both async and level-sync BFS over (a) torus and (b) the Graph 500 Benchmark graph

Level-Synchronous vs Asynchronous Paradigms. Fig. 10 compares SGL's async and level-sync BFS variants on a torus and a Graph500 Benchmark graph. The async BFS spawns new computation (tasks) asynchronously as it reaches a remote edge, whereas the level-sync algorithm (used in the Graph500 benchmark) is a BSP-style [20] computation with asynchronous communication-phases. In both cases, communication is proportional to the number of remote edges.

The torus graph represents the worst-case scenario for parallel BFS scalability – the algorithm is serialized due to the topology of the torus, and its mapping on the machine (blocked distribution, sliced vertically). In this worst-case scenario (Fig. 10 (a)), the async BFS performs much better than the level-sync BFS, due to the absence of synchronization-points. This trend continues at scale, (upto 4,096 cores shown in Fig. 11). However, for the Graph500 input graph, where there are vertices with massive out-degree, the async BFS performs much worse due to the large number of asynchronous tasks created that may need to be re-created if the vertex is revisited in the traversal (with a smaller distance-from-source, for example, as the ordering of tasks is not guaranteed). The level-sync BFS performs well in this case due to the input graph's low diameter, which implies fewer synchronization points (one fence per level of BFS, i.e., the number of global synchronizations is directly proportional to the diameter of the graph).

These experiments suggest that the async paradigm is better suited for large-diameter graphs, while graphs with smaller diameters and high out-degrees are better suited to the level-sync paradigm.

Coarse Grained Paradigm. To compare the fine-grained and `coarse-grained` paradigms, we ran three versions of the connected components algorithm on a torus graph: a naive fine-grained, level-sync algorithm, a fine-grained connected components algorithm on an undirected view of a directed input graph (Sec. 4), and the coarse-grained connected components algorithm.

Fig. 12 shows weak scaling results for these algorithms. The coarse-grained algorithm provides better performance and scalability since it reduces the communication and the graph size significantly for the subsequent phases by coarsening local connected-components. Up to four-cores, the level-sync paradigms are faster due to communication-overhead being negligible and the overhead of

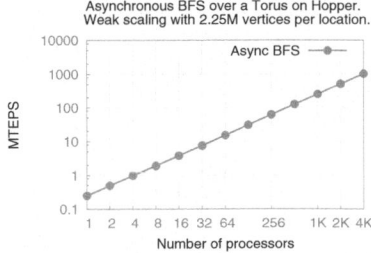

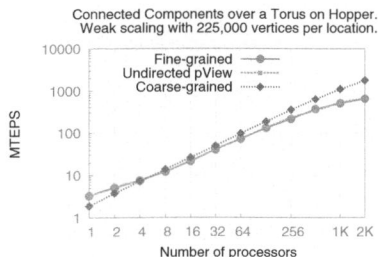

Fig. 11. Asynchronous BFS over a torus pGraph on Hopper

Fig. 12. Weak scaling for connected components over a torus pGraph

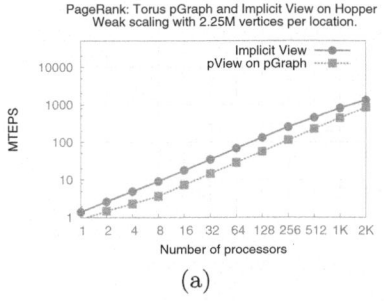

(a)

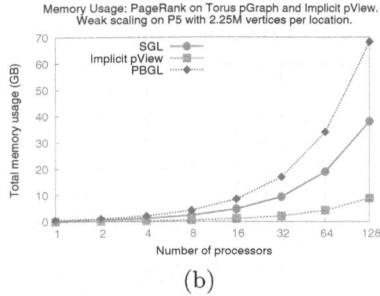

(b)

Fig. 13. Evaluation of PageRank execution time (a) and memory usage (b) using pGraph vs. Implicit View on a Torus graph

coarsening. However, at scale (>256 cores), the communication overhead starts becoming more significant. In this scenario, doing extra local work to reduce communication benefits the performance of the algorithm at high core-counts. The performance for the level-sync paradigms degrades beyond 1,024 cores, while the coarse-grained variant scales better. There is also no significant overhead of the undirected-view over a digraph vs. using the undirected graph as input.

PageRank. We ran SGL PageRank on the input graph generated by the Graph 500 benchmark. Fig. 8 shows weak-scaling results for PageRank on the Graph500 input for pGraph compared to PBGL's implementation. SGL scales better than PBGL on HOPPER up to 512 cores, after which PBGL crashes while executing the algorithm, while SGL PageRank continues to scale to the tested 4,096 cores.

Implicit Views. We evaluate the performance and impact of Implicit Views in (Fig. 13), which are based on evaluation of expressions and use negligible storage (Sec. 4). We run the PageRank algorithm on a torus graph (weak-scaling), and compare it with a view over a pGraph in terms of the throughput (Fig. 13(a)). The Implicit View outperforms the pGraph, as the edges are generated with simple formulae and do not have the overhead of accessing and traversing the underlying container storage. In addition, the pGraph exhibits a slight increase in execution time going from 8 to 16 cores. This can be attributed to the saturation

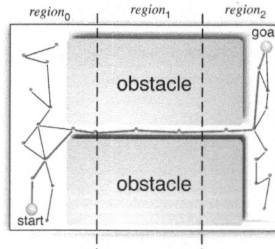
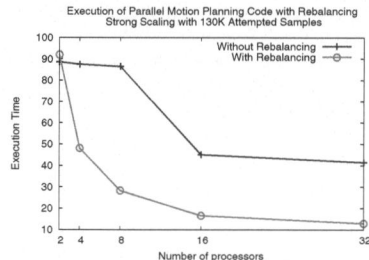

Fig. 14. Strong scaling for a parallel motion planning application on a poorly balanced environment with and without rebalancing techniques

of the memory bus on a node for this particular architecture. The performance of the Implicit View is not affected by this phenomenon, as it does not need to go to memory but evaluates formulae to generate temporary vertices and edges instead. We can also observe that the amount of memory consumed (Fig. 13(b)) by Implicit Views is much less, as there is no memory used for storing the vertices and edges of the graph. The only storage needed is for storing properties that are written to by PageRank. Also shown is memory consumed by PBGL.

Redistribution: Application and Performance. Motion planning is the problem of finding a path for a movable object through an environment from a start to a goal configuration. Sampling-based motion planning is a probabilistic method consisting of two phases: generation and connection of samples representing valid (e.g., collision-free) points in configuration space (C-space) of the object, and querying of the roadmap for valid paths.

Jacobs et. al [17] introduced a scalable parallel application for sampling-based motion planning that subdivides the C-space into regions and constructs independent roadmaps for each region. The regions are then connected to form a single roadmap. This algorithm was implemented using SGL where both the regions and roadmap are pGraphs. In complex environments, regions could have varying numbers of obstacles, creating regions with fewer nodes, and leading to an imbalance in computation during the connection phase. Instrumenting this real-world production application to invoke pGraph redistribution support on the region graph helps the application scale, as well as run faster on unbalanced inputs (Fig. 14) with minimal input from the application, as the application needs only provide the costs it associates with each vertex.

7   Related Work

While much effort has been put into making array-based data structures suitable for parallel programming, graphs have not received as much attention. This section reviews some of the more relevant projects in this area.

Graph500 [1] provides a reference implementation for its benchmark, but is not intended to be a generic library. It provides a baseline for our performance comparisons as it is how users naturally express parallel BFS in MPI.

The Parallel Boost Graph Library (PBGL) [7] is a stand-alone graph library that is closest to the goals of SGL. An important difference from SGL is that since PBGL does not have a shared-object view, it exposes users to explicit knowledge of parallelism and data distribution details through the use of process groups. PBGL's interface requires the user to know explicitly the location of a vertex before any operations may be performed on it. In particular, many methods in PBGL require the vertex/edge they are operating on to be local to the process, and therefore, there is no locality-agnostic way to access remote vertices and edges. This added complexity affects the programmer's ability to create scalable graph algorithms. Another difference is that PBGL only provides the ability to express level-sync algorithms. Further, PBGL is based on MPI, whereas SGL can use different communication libraries through the portable STAPL runtime system.

The Multi-Threaded Graph Library (MTGL) [3] is designed to work on Cray XMP massively multithreaded machines, and utilize their unique architectural features. It can be ported to other platforms using the QThreads library, which requires the programmer to know the QThreads API, as well as details of multi-threaded programming. However, MTGL is limited to shared-memory systems.

Google's Pregel [8] is a library for processing graphs in parallel that emphasizes vertex-centric computation and algorithm design that only supports Bulk Synchronous Processing (BSP) style [20] algorithms. It is restrictive in allowing users to read remote vertices, as it does not provide a shared-memory view. Further, the representation of the graph and its storage cannot be customized to suit the needs of the application. Pregel is also a stand-alone framework that does not provide other containers. Finally, Pregel employs a master-slave model which may limit scalability. Neither Pregel, nor MTGL, nor PBGL provide asynchronous or coarse-grained paradigms.

Green-Marl is a domain-specific language for graph analysis and provides an implementation for shared-memory systems [19]. It allows users to write algorithms naturally, while the compiler generates parallel code for different targets.

8 Conclusion

This work describes the STAPL Parallel Graph Library, a generic, extensible and scalable parallel graph library built on the STAPL infrastructure. It provides a highly customizable parallel graph container, support for various algorithmic paradigms to express parallel graph algorithms, and useful abstractions in the form of pGraph pViews. We presented the general design for the pGraph, along with various features to improve the performance of graph applications. We compared against relevant graph benchmarks and libraries, and showed that SGL algorithms scale beyond tens of thousands of cores and are comparable to a real-world tuned benchmark code implementation. Further, algorithms were able to scale to more cores and run on larger graphs than comparable graph libraries without sacrificing expressivity.

Acknowledgements. The authors would like to thank Sam Jacobs and Nicolas Castet for their help with implementing, instrumenting and running the Motion Planning application.

References

1. The graph 500 list, http://www.graph500.org
2. Adams, M., Larsen, E.: Fast iterative methods for discrete-ordinates particle transport calculations. Progress in Nuclear Energy 40(1), 3–159 (2002)
3. Berry, J.W., et al.: Software and algorithms for graph queries on multithreaded architectures. In: Par. and Dist. Proc. Symp., Int., p. 495 (2007)
4. Buss, A., Fidel, A., Harshvardhan, Smith, T., Tanase, G., Thomas, N., Xu, X., Bianco, M., Amato, N.M., Rauchwerger, L.: The STAPL pView. In: Cooper, K., Mellor-Crummey, J., Sarkar, V. (eds.) LCPC 2010. LNCS, vol. 6548, pp. 261–275. Springer, Heidelberg (2011)
5. Buss, A., et al.: STAPL: Standard template adaptive parallel library. In: Proc. Annual Haifa Exp. Sys. Conf, pp. 1–10. ACM, New York (2010)
6. Culler, D., et al.: Par. Comp. Architecture: A Hardware/Software Approach. The Morgan Kaufmann Series in Comp. Arch. and Design (1998)
7. Gregor, D., Lumsdaine, A.: The parallel BGL: A generic library for distributed graph computations. Par. Object-Oriented Scientific Computing (July 2005)
8. Malewicz, G., et al.: Pregel: a system for large-scale graph processing. In: Proc. Int. Conf. on Management of Data, pp. 135–146. ACM, New York (2010)
9. McLendon III, W., et al.: Finding strongly connected components in distributed graphs. J. Par. Dist. Comp. 65(8), 901–910 (2005)
10. Musser, D., et al.: STL Tutorial and Ref. Guide, 2nd edn. Addison-Wesley (2001)
11. Page, L., et al.: The pagerank citation ranking: Bringing order to the web (1998)
12. Pearce, R., et al.: Multithreaded asynchronous graph traversal for in-memory and semi-external memory. In: Proc. of the ACM/IEEE Int. Conf. for High Performance Computing, Networking, Storage and Analysis, Washington, DC, USA, pp. 1–11 (2010)
13. Saunders, S., Rauchwerger, L.: ARMI: an adaptive, platform independent communication library. In: Proc. ACM SIGPLAN Symp. Prin. Prac. Par. Prog, pp. 230–241. ACM, San Diego (2003)
14. Tanase, G., et al.: The STAPL Parallel Container Framework. In: Proc. ACM SIGPLAN Symp. Prin. Prac. Par. Prog., San Antonio, TX, USA, pp. 235–246 (2011)
15. Thomas, N., et al.: A framework for adaptive algorithm selection in STAPL. In: Proc. ACM SIGPLAN Symp. Prin. Prac. Par. Prog, Chicago, IL, USA, pp. 277–288 (2005)
16. Thomas, S., et al.: Parallel protein folding with STAPL. Concurrency and Computation: Practice and Experience 17(14), 1643–1656 (2005)
17. Jacobs, S.A., et al.: A scalable method for parallelizing sampling-based motion planning algorithms. Proc. IEEE Int. Conf. Robot. Autom. (2012)
18. Quinn, M.J., et al.: Parallel graph algorithms. ACM Comp. Surv., 319–348 (1984)
19. Hong, S., et al.: Green-marl: a dsl for easy and efficient graph analysis. In: Proc. Int. Conf. Arch. Sup. Prog. Lang. Operat. Sys., pp. 349–362. ACM, New York (2012)
20. Valiant, L.: Bridging model for parallel computation. Comm. ACM, 103–111 (1990)
21. Dehne, F., et al.: Efficient Parallel Graph Algorithms for Coarse-Grained Multicomputers and BSP. Algorithmica, 183–200 (2002)

Set and Relation Manipulation
for the Sparse Polyhedral Framework

Michelle Mills Strout, Geri Georg, and Catherine Olschanowsky

Colorado State University
{mstrout,georg,cathie}@cs.colostate.edu

Abstract. The Sparse Polyhedral Framework (SPF) extends the Polyhedral Model by using the uninterpreted function call abstraction for the compile-time specification of run-time reordering transformations such as loop and data reordering and sparse tiling approaches that schedule irregular sets of iteration across loops. The Polyhedral Model represents sets of iteration points in imperfectly nested loops with unions of polyhedral and represents loop transformations with affine functions applied to such polyhedra sets. Existing tools such as ISL, Cloog, and Omega manipulate polyhedral sets and affine functions, however the ability to represent the sets and functions where some of the constraints include uninterpreted function calls such as those needed in the SPF is non-existant or severely restricted. This paper presents algorithms for manipulating sets and relations with uninterpreted function symbols to enable the Sparse Polyhedral Framework. The algorithms have been implemented in an open source, C++ library called IEGenLib (The Inspector/Executor Generator Library).

1 Introduction

Particle simulations, irregular mesh based applications, and sparse matrix computations are difficult to parallelize and optimize with a compiler due to indirect memory accesses such as x[k-1][col[p]] Saltz et al. [1, 2] pioneered inspector/executor strategies for creating parallel communication schedules for such computations at run time. An *inspector/executor* strategy involves generating inspector and executor code at compile time. At runtime an *inspector* traverses index arrays to determine how loop iterations are accessing data, create communication and/or computation schedules, and/or reorder data. An *executor* is the transformed version of the original code. The executor re-uses the schedules and/or reordered data created by the inspector multiple times.

In the late 90s and early 2000s, researchers developed additional inspector/executor strategies to detect fully parallel loops at runtime [3], expose wavefront parallelism [4], improve data locality [5–9], improve the locality in irregular producer/consumer parallelism [10, 11], and schedule sparse tiles across loops so as to expose a level of course-grain parallelism with improved temporal locality [12–14]. The Sparse Polyhedral Framework (SPF) research [15, 16, 13] seeks to provide a compilation framework for automating the application of inspector /executor strategies and their many possible compositions.

H. Kasahara and K. Kimura (Eds.): LCPC 2012, LNCS 7760, pp. 61–75, 2013.
© Springer-Verlag Berlin Heidelberg 2013

```
for (k=1; k<=m; k++) {
   for (p=0; p<nz; p++) {
      x[k][row[p]]  += a[p]*x[k-1][col[p]];
} }
```

Fig. 1. Matrix powers kernel where the matrix is stored in coordinate storage (COO). The Matrix Powers kernel computes a set of vectors $\{A^0x, A^1x, ..., A^mx\}$. This loop is performing k sparse matrix vector products.

```
for (t=0; t<Nt; t++) {
   for (k=1; k<=m; k++) {
      for (i=0; i<N; i++) {
         for (p=0; p<nz; p++) {
            if (sigma[row[p]]==i && tile(k,i)==t))
               x[k][sigma[row[p]]]
                  += a[p]*x[k-1][sigma[col[p]]];
} } } }
```

Fig. 2. The transformed matrix powers kernel after the second dimension of x has been reordered and a full sparse tiling has been performed. Note that further optimizations are done to remove the conditional from the inner loop and remove double indirections, but such optimizations are not within the scope of this paper.

Transformation frameworks such as the polyhedral framework [17–22] enable the specification and exploration of a space of possible *compile-time* reordering transformations for static control parts [23]. *Static control parts (SCoP)* require that the loop bounds and array accesses in the loops being transformed be affine functions of the loop iterators and variables that do not change in the loops.

A portion of the matrix powers, A^mx, kernel in Figure 1 falls within the polyhedral model, specifically the iteration space that contains all integer tuples $[k, p]$ within the specified loop bounds. However, the indirect memory accesses x[k-1][col[p]] and x[k][row[p]] do not fall directly within the polyhedral model. In previous work, the polyhedral model has been extended to handle indirect memory references by using uninterpreted function calls to represent such memory accesses and using this information to make data dependence analysis more precise [24], approximate data dependences in spite of indirect memory references [25, 26], and handle while loops [22].

A problem arose when the Sparse Polyhedral Framework [15, 16] extended the polyhedral framework further by using uninterpreted function calls to represent run-time reordering transformations. We are aware of only one loop transformation tool that attempts to deal with uninterpreted function calls: omega [27] and a newer version of omega called omega+ [28, 29]. Omega uses uninterpreted function calls to aid in the precision of data dependence analysis.

However, Omega does not use uninterpreted function calls to represent run-time reordering transformations and, therefore, manipulations of the intermediate representations for the computation and for the transformations are not precise enough. For example, the conversion of the memory access x[k][row[p]] in Figure 1 to x[k][sigma[row[p]]] in Figure 2 is not possible with omega.

Transforming code with the SPF requires composing relations, inverting relations, and applying relations to sets when both the relation(s) and the set can have uninterpreted function call constraints as well as affine constraints. In this paper, we make the following contributions:

- Practical algorithms for performing compositions and applying relations to sets based on the relations typically used in the SPF.
- An open source library that makes the algorithm implementation available for general use.

Section 2 reviews the Sparse Polyhedral Framework terminology revolving around sets and relations and the compose and apply operations. Section 3 presents the compose and apply algorithms. Section 4 presents the IEGenLib software package available at http://www.cs.colostate.edu/hpc/PIES that implements the presented algorithms. In Section 5 we conclude.

2   The Sparse Polyhedral Framework (SPF)

Within a polyhedral transformation framework such as Omega [20], Pluto [30], Orio [31], Chill [32, 29], AlphaZ [33], or POET [34], the intermediate representation includes an iteration space set to represent all of the iterations in the loop, a function that maps each iteration in the loop to an array index for each array access, data dependence relations between iterations in the loop, and some representation of the statements themselves.

We originally introduced the sparse polyhedral framework in [15] where it was described as a compile-time framework for composing run-time reordering transformations. In this section, we provide a basic introduction to the SPF: how to represent computations in the SPF, how to transform these computations, and describe the problem of projecting out existential variables that arises in this context.

2.1   Sets and Relations in SPF

Sets and relations are the fundamental building blocks for the SPF. Data and iteration spaces are represented with sets, and access functions, data dependences, and transformations are represented with relations. Sets are specified as $s = \{[x_1, \ldots, x_d] : c_1 \wedge \ldots \wedge c_p\}$, where each x_i is an integer tuple variable/iterator and each c_j is a constraint. The *arity* of the set is the dimensionality of the tuples, which for the above is d.

The constraints in a set are equalities and inequalities. Each equality and inequality is a summation expression containing terms with constant coefficients, where the terms can be tuple variables x_i, symbolic constants, or uninterpreted function calls. A symbolic constant represents a constant value that does not change during the computation, but may not be known until runtime. An uninterpreted function call $f(p_1, p_2, ..., p_3)$ is a function, therefore, $p = q$ implies that $f(p) = f(q)$, however the actual output values are not known until compile time. We also allow the actual parameters p_v passed to any uninterpreted function symbol to be affine expressions of the tuple variables, symbolic constants, free variables, or uninterpreted function symbols, whereas in omega [24] uninterpreted function calls are not allowed as parameters to other uninterpreted function calls. We represent the iteration space I in Figure 1 as a set with only affine constraints, $I = \{[k, p] \mid 1 \le k < N_k \wedge 0 \le p < nz\}$.

A relation represents a set of integer tuple pairs, where the first tuple in the pair is called the input tuple (often the relation is a function) and the second tuple in the pair is called the output tuple. Relations are specified as $r = \{[x_1, \ldots, x_m] \to [y_1, \ldots, y_n] : c_1 \wedge \ldots \wedge c_p\}$, where each x_i is an input tuple variable in $\mathbb{Z}$, each y_j is an output tuple variable in $\mathbb{Z}$, and each c_v is a constraint. The constraints of a relation follow the same restrictions as set constraints and additionally the relation needs to include equalities that make the relation a function or the inverse of a function (see Section 3 for more details).

It is possible to represent the array access functions in Figure 1 (A1: x[k-1][col[p]] and A2: x[k][row[p]]) as follows:

$$A1_{I \to X} = \{[k, p] \to [v, w] \mid v = k - 1 \wedge w = col(p)\}$$
$$A2_{I \to X} = \{[k, p] \to [v, w] \mid v = k \wedge w = row(p)\}.$$

As a notational convenience we subscript the names of abstract relations to indicate which sets are the domain and range of the relation. For example, the array access function $A1_{I \to X}$ has the iteration space set I as its domain and data space set X as its range.

2.2   Transforming Iteration and Data Spaces

The SPF uses relations to represent transformation functions for iteration and data spaces. Given sets that express iteration and data spaces, relations that specify how an iteration space accesses data spaces (access functions), and relations that represent dependences between iteration points (data dependence relations), we can express how data and/or iteration reordering transformations affect these entities by performing certain set and relation operations.

For the matrix powers kernel computation $A^k x$ in Figure 1, assume we plan to reorder the rows and columns of the sparse matrix by reordering the rows of the x array to improve the data locality [35]. This *run-time data reordering transformation* can be specified as follows:

$$R_{X \to X'} = \{[k, i] \to [k, i'] \mid i' = \sigma(i)\},$$

where $\sigma()$ is an uninterpreted function that represents the permutation for the data that will be created by a heuristic in the inspector at runtime.

The data reordering transformation affects the data space for the array x, therefore, any access functions that target the data space X need to be modified. We use relation composition to compute the new access function:

$$A1_{I \to X'} = R_{X \to X'} \circ A1_{I \to X} = \{[k,p] \to [v,w] \mid v = k - 1 \wedge w = \sigma(col(p))\}.$$

An *iteration-reordering* transformation is expressed as a mapping between the original iteration space and the transformed iteration space. The new execution order is given by the lexicographic order of the iterations in I'. In the example, we transform Figure 1 to Figure 2 using full-sparse tiling, a run-time reordering transformation [13] (also equivalent to the "implicit sequential algorithm" in [14]) that provides task graph asynchronous parallelism [36]. The tile() function aggregates iteration points into atomically executable groups of computation.

$$T_{I \to I'} = \{[k,p] \to [t,k,i,p] \mid t = tile(k,i) \wedge i = \sigma(row(p))$$
$$\wedge 1 \le t < N_t \wedge 0 \le i < N_r\}.$$

This requires modifying the access functions $A1_{I' \to X'} = A1_{I \to X'} \circ T_{I' \to I}$ $= A1_{I \to X'} \circ T_{I \to I'}^{-1}$ and $A2_{I' \to X'} = A2_{I \to X'} \circ T_{I' \to I} = A2_{I \to X'} \circ T_{I \to I'}^{-1}$, and transforming the iteration space $I' = T_{I \to I'}(I)$. Given the transformed access functions, scheduling functions, and dependences, we can specify further run-time reordering transformations (RTRTs).

2.3   Necessary Set and Relation Operations

Modifying the iteration space and access functions to reflect the impact of run-time reordering transformations requires the following set of operations:

- relation inverse $r = r_1^{-1} = (\boldsymbol{x} \to \boldsymbol{y} \in r) \Longleftrightarrow (\boldsymbol{y} \to \boldsymbol{x} \in r_1)$,
- relation composition
  $r = r_2 \circ r_1 = (\boldsymbol{x} \to \boldsymbol{y} \in r) \Longleftrightarrow (\exists \boldsymbol{z} \mid \boldsymbol{x} \to \boldsymbol{z} \in r_1 \wedge \boldsymbol{z} \to \boldsymbol{y} \in r_2)$,
- and applying a relation to a set
  $s = r_1(s_1) = (\boldsymbol{x} \in s) \Longleftrightarrow (\exists \boldsymbol{z} \mid \boldsymbol{z} \in s_1 \wedge \boldsymbol{z} \to \boldsymbol{x} \in r_1)$.

2.4   The Problem: Implementing Compose and Apply Is Difficult

The inverse operation can easily be implemented by swapping the input and output tuple variables in a relation. However, implementing relation composition and applying a relation to a set is difficult due to the existential variables (i.e. the vector $\boldsymbol{z}$ in Section 2.3) introduced while computing both. These existential variables need to be projected out of the resulting set or relation so that the remaining constraints only involve tuple variables, symbolic constants, and uninterpreted function calls.

When all of the constraints are affine, then each conjunct is a polyhedron. It is possible to use integer versions of Fourier Motzkin [27, 37] to project out any existential variables. The Omega library and calculator [27] enable the expression of constraints with uninterpreted function calls, but it has two key limitations in terms of manipulating uninterpreted function calls. One limitation is that the arguments to an uninterpreted function have to be a prefix of the input or output tuples. Therefore, the following input and output occurs (the example uses omega+, which was built on omega and has similar behavior with respect to uninterpreted function calls):

```
Omega+ and CodeGen+ v2.2.3 (built on 08/15/2012)
Copyright (C) 1994-2000 the Omega Project Team
Copyright (C) 2005-2011 Chun Chen
>>> symbolic col(1);
>>> A1_I_to_X := { [k,p] -> [k,w] : w=col(p) };
arguments to function must be prefix of input or output tuple ...
```

Even when working around this constraint by using a prefix of the input or output tuple as input to the uninterpreted function call, when a compose or apply operation results in an existential variable that is the parameter to an uninterpreted function call, the UNKNOWN term is included within the conjunct thus making the resulting set or relation lose its precision.

```
>>> symbolic col(2),row(2);
>>> A1_I_to_X := { [k,p] -> [k,w] : w=col(k,p) };
>>> symbolic sigma(2);
>>> R_X_to_X' := {[k,i] -> [k,i'] : i'=sigma(k,i)};
>>> R_X_to_X' compose A1_I_to_X;
{[k,p] -> [k,i] : UNKNOWN}
```

Since in the SPF we are representing computation with iteration spaces and access functions, this level of precision loss is problematic.

Previously, we developed heuristics for eliminating existential variables involved in uninterpreted function call constraints [16]. The heuristics involved solving for existential variables and then substituting the resulting expression in an attempt to remove such existential variables from the constraints. The approach we present in Section 3 is much simpler to explain and prove correct, but is more restrictive in the kinds of relations handled.

3   Algorithms for Implementing Compose and Apply

In the Sparse Polyhedral Framework (SPF), relations and sets have certain characteristics because of what they represent and how the relations are used. A relation can represent (1) a function mapping an iteration point to a memory location integer tuple (access function), (2) the mapping of an iteration point for a statement to a shared iteration space that represent space and lexicographical time (scheduling/scattering function [38]), or (3) a transformation function mapping each iteration (or data point) to a new shared iteration space (or data layout). For (1), (2), and (3), the output tuple is a function of the input tuple.

Based on the above uses of relations in SPF, a relation in SPF is either a function $\{x \rightarrow y \mid y = F(x) \wedge C\}$ or the inverse of a function $\{x \rightarrow y \mid x = G(y) \wedge C\}$ such that x is the input tuple, y is the output tuple, F and G are affine or uninterpreted functions, and C is a set of constraints involving equalities, inequalities, linear arithmetic, and uninterpreted function calls. We can use this information to develop algorithms for relation composition and applying a relation to a set.

This section shows that there are closed form solutions for composing relations and applying a relation to a set that do not involve existential variables when the relations satisfy certain assumptions. The algorithms can be implemented directly by using the closed form solution provided in each theorem and implementing a routine that solves for one set of tuple variables with respect to another set and provides substitution for a set of tuple variables.

3.1   Relation Composition Theorems

Our algorithms for implementing relation composition requires that either both relations must be functions or both relations must be the inverse of a function. By making this assumption, the relation resulting from a composition will be either a function and/or the inverse of a function.

Theorem 1 (Case 1: Both Relations are Functions). *Let x, y, v, and z be integer tuples where $|y| = |v|$, $F1()$ and $F2()$ be either affine or uninterpreted functions, and $C1$ and $C2$ be sets of constraints involving equalities, inequalities, linear arithmetic, and uninterpreted function calls in*

$$\{v \rightarrow z \mid z = F1(v) \wedge C1\} \circ \{x \rightarrow y \mid y = F2(x) \wedge C2\}.$$

The result of the composition is $\{x \rightarrow z \mid \exists y, v \mid y = v \wedge z = F1(v) \wedge C1 \wedge y = F2(x) \wedge C2\}$, which is equivalent to

$$\{x \rightarrow z \mid z = F1(F2(x)) \wedge C1[v/F2(x)] \wedge C2[y/F2(x)]\}$$

where $C1[v/F2(x)]$ indicates that v should be replaced with $F2(x)$ in the set of constraints $C1$.

Proof
Starting from $\{x \rightarrow z \mid \exists y, v \mid y = v \wedge z = F1(v) \wedge C1 \wedge y = F2(x) \wedge C2\}$, we first substitute y with v to obtain $\{x \rightarrow z \mid \exists v \text{ s.t. } \wedge z = F1(v) \wedge C1 \wedge v = F2(x) \wedge C2[y/v]\}$. Then we substitute v with $F2(x)$ to obtain the forward equivalence $\{x \rightarrow z \mid z = F1(F2(x)) \wedge C1[v/F2(x)] \wedge C2[y/F2(x)]\}$. The backward direction of the equivalence requires performing the reverse substitutions in the reverse order where instead of removing existential variables we are introducing them. ∎

From the running example, both the access relation $A1_{I \rightarrow X'}$ and the transformation $T_{I \rightarrow I'}$ are functions. Therefore, to compute the effect of the transformation on A1 ($A1_{I' \rightarrow X'} = A1_{I \rightarrow X'} \circ T_{I' \rightarrow I}$), we can use Theorem 1. For $A1_{I \rightarrow X'}$, the output tuple variables are a function of the input tuple variables: $[v, w] = F1([k, p]) = [k - 1, \sigma(col(p))]$. For $T_{I' \to I}$, we have the following function: $[k, p] = F2([t, k, i, p]) = [k, p]$. Therefore the result of the composition is

$$A1_{I' \to X'} = \{[t, k, i, p] \to [v, w] \mid v = k - 1 \wedge w = \sigma(col(p))\}.$$

Theorem 2 (Case 2: The Inverses of both Relations are Functions).
Let x, y, v, and z be integer tuples where $|y| = |v|$, $G1()$ and $G2()$ be either affine or uninterpreted functions, and $C1$ and $C2$ be sets of constraints involving equalities, inequalities, linear arithmetic, and uninterpreted functions in

$$\{v \to z \mid v = G1(z) \wedge C1\} \circ \{x \to y \mid x = G2(y) \wedge C2\}.$$

The result of the Case 2 composition is $\{x \to z \mid \exists y, v \text{ s.t. } y = v \wedge v = G1(z) \wedge C1 \wedge x = G2(y) \wedge C2\}$, which is equivalent to

$$\{x \to z \mid x = G2(G1(z)) \wedge C1[v/G1(z)] \wedge C2[y/G1(z)]\}.$$

Proof. As with Theorem 1, we can perform substitutions to show the equivalence. For Theorem 2, we substitute y with v and then substitute v with $G1(z)$. ∎

3.2 Relation Application to Set Theorem

For applying a relation to a set, the relation must be the inverse of a function. This is necessary because the existential variables resulting from the application are replaced by functions of the output tuple variables. The below theorem shows why this is the case.

Theorem 3 (Relation to Set Application). *Let x, y, and z be integer tuples where $|x| = |z|$, $G()$ be either an affine or uninterpreted function, and C and D be sets of constraints involving equalities, inequalities, linear arithmetic, and uninterpreted function calls in*

$$\{x \to y \mid x = G(y) \wedge C\}(\{z \mid D\}).$$

The result of applying the relation to the set is $\{y \mid \exists x, z \mid z = x \wedge x = G(y) \wedge C \wedge D\}$, which is equivalent to

$$\{y \mid C[x/G(y)] \wedge D[z/G(y)]\}.$$

Proof. As with Theorem 1, we can perform substitutions to show the equivalence. For Theorem 3, we substitute z with x and then substitute x with $G(y)$. ∎

4   The Inspector/Executor Generator Library

The Inspector/Executor Generator Library (IEGenLib) enables the programmatic manipulation of sets and relations with constraints involving affine expressions where terms can be uninterpreted function calls for the use in specifying run-time reordering transformations. This section provides an overview of typical IEGenLib usage and functionality. Release 1 of the IEGenLib along with a user manual and API documentation can be found at
http://www.cs.colostate.edu/hpc/PIES.

The IEGenLib is similar to the Omega library [27] in that IEGenLib provides a C++ API for manipulating sets and relations with inequality and equality constraints. The main differences are that IEGenLib enables uninterpreted function calls to have any affine expressions as arguments including those with uninterpreted function calls, and IEGenLib maintains more detail when performing relation to set application and relation composition when the constraints involved include uninterpreted function calls.

IEGenLib Release 1 has fewer features than the current Omega library and new versions of that library such as Omega+ [28]. For example, the IEGenLib calculator **iegenlib_calc** does not generate code at this time. Additionally the IEGenLib calculator and library provide a subet of set and relation operations. IEGenLib does provide the following operations: composition of two relations, applying a relation to a set, union, and relation inverse.

4.1   Typical Usage of IEGenLib

The IEGenLib ships with three convenient interfaces: the IEGenLib API available through a C++ library, the IEGenLib calculator (a sample program using

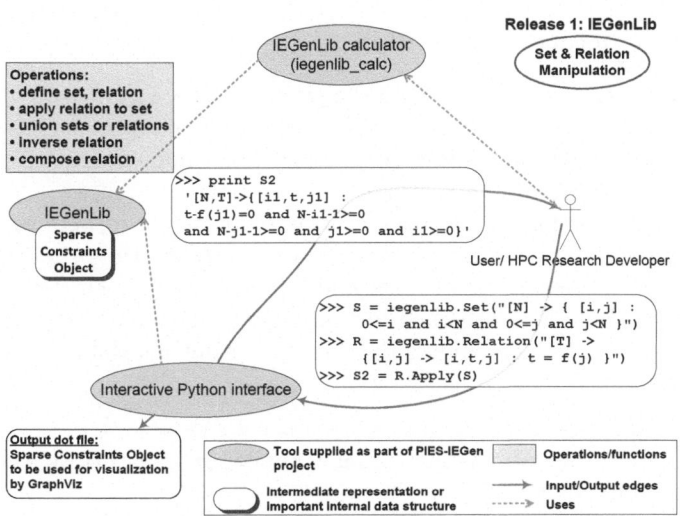

Fig. 3. Shows how the iegenlib is typically used

Table 1. Set and Relation Operations

Operation	Notation	Semantics
		Syntax using Python Bindings
constant Apply	$s = r_1(s_1)$	$(x \in s) \iff (\exists y \text{ s.t. } y \in s_1 \land y \to x \in r_1)$
		`Iprime = T_I_to_Iprime.Apply( I )`
Union	$s = s_1 \cup s_2$	$(x \in s) \iff (x \in s_1 \lor x \in s_2)$
	$r = r_1 \cup r_2$	$(x \to y \in r) \iff (x \to y \in r_1 \lor x \to y \in r_2)$
Inverse	$r = r_1^{-1}$	$(x \to y \in r) \iff (y \to x \in r_1)$
		`T_I_to_I = T_I_to_Iprime.Inverse()`
Compose	$r = r_2 \circ r_1$	$(x \to y \in r) \iff (\exists z \text{ s.t. } x \to z \in r_1 \land z \to y \in r_2)$
		`A1_I_to_Xprime = R_X_to_Xprime.Compose(A1_I_to_X)`

the library that enables interactive experimentation), and the interactive Python interface (i.e. python bindings). Section 4.2 provides an overview of the IEGenLib API and underlying class structure. The IEGenLib calculator and Python interface are each supplied to allow users quick access to the IEGenLib capabilities.

The IEGenLib calculator (iegenlib_calc) is a C++ program written using the IEGenLib. It is both useful as a standalone tool and the source code is provided as an example of how to use the library API.

The interactive Python interface is automatically created using SWIG. After the application of SWIG it is possible to access the C++ library directly from Python scripts and the interactive Python interface. All of the examples in the following section are written using the Python syntax. Figure 3 shows the usage relationship between the three interfaces and gives a brief example of using the Python interface.

4.2   Class Structure of IEGenLib

This section gives an overview of both the programmatic interface exposed by the IEGenLib and the class structure that supports the given interface. The interface is designed to be easily accessible and at the same time enable advanced users direct access to the internal structures.

The primary function of the IEGenLib is to provide a programmatic interface for the manipulation of sets and relations, therefore, the primary high-level objects are exposed as two classes, Set and Relation (each in the iegenlib namespace). Sets and Relations are each instantiated using a constructor that takes a string as a parameter. As an example, instantiating the Relations used in the example in Section 1 is done as follows.

$A1_{I \to X} = \{[k,p] \to [v,w] \mid v = k - 1 \land w = col(p)\}$
```
# Python code to represent access function for x[k-1][col[p]]
import iegenlib
A1_I_to_X = Relation("{[k,p] → [v,w] : v=k-1 && w=col(p)}")
```

$A2_{I \to X} = \{[k, p] \to [v, w] \mid v = k \wedge w = row(p)\}$
# Python code to represent access function for x[k][row[p]]
A2_I_to_X = Relation("{[k,p] → [v,w] : v=k && w=row(p) }")

$T_{I \to I'} = \{[k, p] \to [t, k, i, p] \mid t = tile(k, i) \wedge i = sigma(row(p))$
$\wedge 0 \leq t < N_t \wedge 0 \leq i < N_r\}$
# Python code to represent sparse tiling transformation
T_I_to_Iprime = Relation("{[k,p] → [t,k,i,p] : t=tile(k,i)
&& i=sigma(row(p)) && 0 ≤ t && t < N_t && 0 ≤ i && i < N_r }")

Table 1 lists the high-level operations available for the Set and Relation classes: apply, union, inverse, and compose. The table shows the syntax used to use these functions through the Python bindings. The examples in the table use the objects that result from the above construction examples.

An internal class structure supports the Set and Relation class operations. The class structure is centralized around Expressions. Expressions (class name Exp) consist of at least one Term. A Term can fall into one of four categories. First, a Term may be an integer constant, in that case it is implemented using the Term class directly. In the other three cases a Term may be coefficient multiplied by a variable (VarTerm), a coefficient multiplied by a tuple variable (TupleVarTerm),

```
Relation R_X_to_Xprime (2 ,2);
Conjunction *c = new Conjunction (2+2);
c->setTupleElem (0 ,"k");
c->setTupleElem (1 ,"i");
c->setTupleElem (2 ,"k");
c->setTupleElem (3 ,"i'");

// Create the expression
Exp* exp = new Exp ();
exp->addTerm (new VarTerm ("i'"));
std::list<Exp*> *args = new std::list<Exp*>;
Exp *arg0 = new Exp ();
arg0->addTerm (new VarTerm ("i"));
args->push_back (arg0);
exp->addTerm (new UFCallTerm (-1, "sigma", args ));

// add the equality to the conjunction
c->addEquality (exp);

// add the conjunction to the relation
R_X_to_Xprime.addConjunction (c);
```

Fig. 4. Building the Relation in Figure 5 manually

```
Relation R_X_to_Xprime =
        Relation("{[k,i] -> [k,i'] : i' = sigma(i) }")
```

Fig. 5. Building the Relation in Figure 4 using the parser

or a coefficient multiplied by an uninterpreted function call (UFCallTerm). A UFCallTerm contains a list of parameters that are instances of the Exp class.

While it is possible to utilize the IEGenLib to create Sets and Relations using the class structure directly a parser is included in the library that allows for much more simple construction. A built-in parser enables constructors in the Set and Relation classes that accept a string. The string can use the Omega or ISL syntax. The parser does all of the internal work to build the appropriate underlying structure that represents the Set or Relation desired. Figures 4 and 5 demonstrate the significant reduction in user code size that results from using this feature.

Another helpful capability of the IEGenLIb is that each class implements a function that writes a representation of that object to dot. Dot is a syntax for creating "hierarchical" or layered drawings of directed graphs. Tools such as

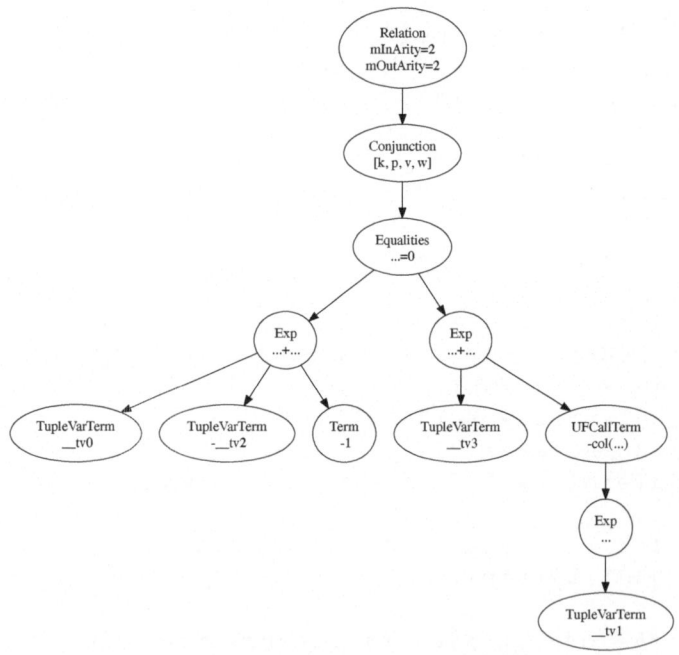

Fig. 6. The dot visualization for the relation $A1_{I \to X}$

Graphviz create images using the dot files as input. The visual representations of sets and relations is a quick way to understand the underlying structure for a specific Set or Relation. Figure 6 shows an example taken from the introduction.

5   Conclusions

This work is another step in automating the process of generating inspector/executor code. We present algorithms for composing relations and applying relations to sets, when the relation(s) and set involved in those operations include affine constraints and constraints involving uninterpreted function calls. The IEGenLib software package implements the presented algorithms. This paper also shows how a user of IEGenLib can specify and perform relation composition and the application of a relation to a set.

Acknowledgements. We would like to thank previous participants of the IEGenLib project for their implementation work including Brendan Sheridan, Mark Heim, Mohammed Al-Refai, Nicholas Wes Jeannette, and Ian Craig. We would especially like to thank Alan LaMielle who developed an earlier prototype of IEGenLib and Joseph Strout who made significant programming contributions to the current version. This project is supported by a Department of Energy Early Career Grant DE-SC0003956, by a National Science Foundation CAREER grant CCF 0746693, and by the Department of Energy CACHE Institute grant DE-SC04030.

References

1. Mirchandaney, R., Saltz, J.H., Smith, R.M., Nico, D.M., Crowley, K.: Principles of runtime support for parallel processors. In: ICS 1988: Proceedings of the 2nd International Conference on Supercomputing, pp. 140–152. ACM, New York (1988)
2. Saltz, J., Chang, C., Edjlali, G., Hwang, Y.S., Moon, B., Ponnusamy, R., Sharma, S., Sussman, A., Uysal, M., Agrawal, G., Das, R., Havlak, P.: Programming irregular applications: Runtime support, compilation and tools. Advances in Computers 45, 105–153 (1997)
3. Rauchwerger, L.: Run-time parallelization: Its time has come. Parallel Computing 24, 527–556 (1998)
4. Rauchwerger, L., Amato, N.M., Padua, D.A.: A scalable method for run-time loop parallelization. International Journal of Parallel Programming 23, 537–576 (1995)
5. Ding, C., Kennedy, K.: Improving cache performance in dynamic applications through data and computation reorganization at run time. In: Proceedings of the ACM SIGPLAN Conference on Programming Language Design and Implementation, pp. 229–241. ACM, New York (1999)
6. Mitchell, N., Carter, L., Ferrante, J.: Localizing non-affine array references. In: Proceedings of the International Conference on Parallel Architectures and Compilation Techniques (PACT), pp. 192–202. IEEE Computer Society, Los Alamitos (1999)

7. Im, E.J.: Optimizing the Performance of Sparse Matrix-Vector Multiply. Ph.d. thesis, University of California, Berkeley (2000)
8. Mellor-Crummey, J., Whalley, D., Kennedy, K.: Improving memory hierarchy performance for irregular applications using data and computation reorderings. International Journal of Parallel Programming 29, 217–247 (2001)
9. Pingali, V.K., McKee, S.A., Hsieh, W.C., Carter, J.B.: Restructuring computations for temporal data cache locality. International Journal of Parallel Programming 31, 305–338 (2003)
10. Basumallik, A., Eigenmann, R.: Optimizing irregular shared-memory applications for distributed-memory systems. In: Proceedings of the Eleventh ACM SIGPLAN Symposium on Principles and Practice of Parallel Programming, pp. 119–128. ACM Press, New York (2006)
11. Ravishankar, M., Eisenlohr, J., Pouchet, L.N., Ramanujam, J., Rountev, A., Sadayappan, P.: Code generation for parallel execution of a class of irregular loops on distributed memory systems. In: The International Conference for High Performance Computing, Networking, Storage, and Analysis, SC (2012)
12. Douglas, C.C., Hu, J., Kowarschik, M., Rüde, U., Weiß., C.: Cache Optimization for Structured and Unstructured Grid Multigrid. Electronic Transaction on Numerical Analysis, 21–40 (2000)
13. Strout, M.M., Carter, L., Ferrante, J., Kreaseck, B.: Sparse tiling for stationary iterative methods. International Journal of High Performance Computing Applications 18, 95–114 (2004)
14. Mohiyuddin, M., Hoemmen, M., Demmel, J., Yelick, K.: Minimizing communication in sparse matrix solvers. In: Supercomputing, ACM, New York (2009)
15. Strout, M.M., Carter, L., Ferrante, J.: Compile-time composition of run-time data and iteration reorderings. In: Proceedings of the ACM SIGPLAN Conference on Programming Language Design and Implementation (PLDI), ACM, New York (2003)
16. LaMielle, A., Strout, M.M.: Enabling code generation within the sparse polyhedral framework. Technical report, Technical Report CS-10-102 Colorado State University (2010)
17. Wolf, M.E., Lam, M.S.: Loop transformation theory and an algorithm to maximize parallelism. IEEE Transactions on Parallel and Distributed Systems 2, 452–471 (1991)
18. Feautrier, P.: Some efficient solutions to the affine scheduling problem. part II. multidimensional time. International Journal of Parallel Programming 21, 389–420 (1992)
19. Sarkar, V., Thekkath, R.: A general framework for iteration-reordering loop transformations. In: Fraser, C.W. (ed.) Proceedings of the ACM SIGPLAN Conference on Programming Language Design and Implementation (PLDI), pp. 175–187. ACM, New York (1992)
20. Kelly, W., Pugh, W.: A unifying framework for iteration reordering transformations. Technical Report CS-TR-3430, University of Maryland, College Park (1995)
21. Cohen, A., Donadio, S., Garzaran, M.J., Herrmann, C., Kiselyov, O., Padua, D.: In search of a program generator to implement generic transformations for high-performance computing. Sci. Comput. Program. 62, 25–46 (2006)
22. Benabderrahmane, M.-W., Pouchet, L.-N., Cohen, A., Bastoul, C.: The Polyhedral Model Is More Widely Applicable Than You Think. In: Gupta, R. (ed.) CC 2010. LNCS, vol. 6011, pp. 283–303. Springer, Heidelberg (2010)
23. Xue, J.: Transformations of nested loops with non-convex iteration spaces. Parallel Computing 22, 339–368 (1996)

24. Pugh, B., Wonnacott, D.: Nonlinear array dependence analysis. Technical Report CS-TR-3372, Dept. of Computer Science, Univ. of Maryland (1994)
25. Lin, Y., Padua, D.: Compiler analysis of irregular memory accesses. SIGPLAN Notices 35, 157–168 (2000)
26. Barthou, D., Collard, J.F., Feautrier, P.: Fuzzy array dataflow analysis. Journal of Parallel and Distributed Computing 40, 210–226 (1997)
27. Kelly, W., Maslov, V., Pugh, W., Rosser, E., Shpeisman, T., Wonnacott, D.: The omega calculator and library, version 1.1.0 (1996)
28. Chen, C., Hall, M., Venkat, A.: Omega+ (2012),
    http://ctop.cs.utah.edu/ctop/?page_id=21
29. Chen, C.: Polyhedra scanning revisited. In: Proceedings of the 33rd ACM SIG-PLAN Conference on Programming Language Design and Implementation, PLDI 2012, pp. 499–508. ACM, New York (2012)
30. Bondhugula, U., Hartono, A., Ramanujam, J., Sadayappan, P.: A practical automatic polyhedral program optimization system. In: Proceedings of the ACM SIG-PLAN Conference on Programming Language Design and Implementation (PLDI), ACM, New York (2008)
31. Hartono, A., Norris, B., Ponnuswamy, S.: Annotation-based empirical performance tuning using Orio. In: 23rd IEEE International Parallel & Distributed Processing Symposium (IPDPS), Rome, Italy (2009)
32. Hall, M., Chame, J., Chen, C., Shin, J., Rudy, G., Khan, M.M.: Loop Transformation Recipes for Code Generation and Auto-Tuning. In: Gao, G.R., Pollock, L.L., Cavazos, J., Li, X. (eds.) LCPC 2009. LNCS, vol. 5898, pp. 50–64. Springer, Heidelberg (2010)
33. Yuki, T., Basupalli, V., Gupta, G., Iooss, G., Kim, D., Pathan, T., Srinivasa, P., Zou, Y., Rajopadhye, S.: Alphaz: A system for analysis, transformation, and code generation in the polyhedral equational model. Technical report, Colorado State University CS-12-101 (2012)
34. Yi, Q., Seymour, K., You, H., Vuduc, R., Quinlan, D.: Poet: Parameterized optimizations for empirical tuning. In: Proceedings of the Parallel and Distributed Processing Symposium (2007)
35. Wood, S., Strout, M.M., Wonnacott, D.G., Eaton, E.: Smores: Sparse matrix omens of reordering success. Winning Poster at the PLDI Student Research Competition (2011)
36. Strout, M.M., Carter, L., Ferrante, J., Freeman, J., Kreaseck, B.: Combining Performance Aspects of Irregular Gauss-Seidel Via Sparse Tiling. In: Pugh, B., Tseng, C.-W. (eds.) LCPC 2002. LNCS, vol. 2481, pp. 90–110. Springer, Heidelberg (2005)
37. Verdoolaege, S.: An integer set library for program analysis. In: Advances in the Theory of Integer Linear Optimization and its Extensions, AMS 2009 Spring Western Section Meeting, San Francisco, California (2009)
38. Bastoul, C.: Code generation in the polyhedral model is easier than you think. In: Proceedings of the 13th Interntional Conference on Parallel Architecture and Compilation Techniques, PACT (2004)

Parallel Clustered Low-Rank Approximation of Graphs and Its Application to Link Prediction

Xin Sui[1], Tsung-Hsien Lee[2], Joyce Jiyoung Whang[1], Berkant Savas[3,*],
Saral Jain[1], Keshav Pingali[1], and Inderjit Dhillon[1]

[1] Department of Computer Science, The University of Texas at Austin
[2] Department of Electrical and Computer Engineering,
The University of Texas at Austin
[3] Department of Mathematics, Linköping University

Abstract. Social network analysis has become a major research area
that has impact in diverse applications ranging from search engines to
product recommendation systems. A major problem in implementing social network analysis algorithms is the sheer size of many social networks,
for example, the Facebook graph has more than 900 million vertices and
even small networks may have tens of millions of vertices. One solution to dealing with these large graphs is dimensionality reduction using
spectral or SVD analysis of the adjacency matrix of the network, but
these global techniques do not necessarily take into account local structures or clusters of the network that are critical in network analysis. A
more promising approach is *clustered* low-rank approximation: instead
of computing a global low-rank approximation, the adjacency matrix is
first clustered, and then a low-rank approximation of each cluster (*i.e.*,
diagonal block) is computed. The resulting algorithm is challenging to
parallelize not only because of the large size of the data sets in social
network analysis, but also because it requires computing with very diverse data structures ranging from extremely sparse matrices to dense
matrices. In this paper, we describe the first parallel implementation of
a clustered low-rank approximation algorithm for large social network
graphs, and use it to perform link prediction in parallel. Experimental
results show that this implementation scales well on large distributed-
memory machines; for example, on a Twitter graph with roughly 11
million vertices and 63 million edges, our implementation scales by a
factor of 86 on 128 processes and takes less than 2300 seconds, while
on a much larger Twitter graph with 41 million vertices and 1.2 billion
edges, our implementation scales by a factor of 203 on 256 processes with
a running time about 4800 seconds.

Keywords: Social network analysis, link prediction, parallel computing,
graph computations, clustered low-rank approximation.

* This work was started when Berkant Savas was a postdoctoral researcher in ICES,
University of Texas at Austin.

H. Kasahara and K. Kimura (Eds.): LCPC 2012, LNCS 7760, pp. 76–95, 2013.
© Springer-Verlag Berlin Heidelberg 2013

1 Introduction

Networks are increasingly used to model mechanisms and interactions in a wide range of application areas such as social network analysis, web search, product recommendation, and computational biology. Not surprisingly, the study of large, complex networks has attracted considerable attention from computer scientists, physicists, biologists, and social scientists. Networks are highly dynamic objects; they grow and change quickly over time through the additions of new vertices and edges, signifying the appearance of new interactions in the underlying structure. For example, a specific network analysis problem is link prediction, where the task is to predict the presence or absence of a link between certain pairs of vertices, based on observed links in other parts of the networks [15].

One of the most important issues in addressing such network analysis problems is the sheer size of the data sets; for example, Facebook has over 900 million monthly active users, and even relatively small networks may have millions of vertices and edges. One solution to deal with these large scale networks is dimensionality reduction, which aims to find more compact representations of data without much loss of information. Principal Component Analysis (PCA) and low-rank approximation by truncated Singular Value Decomposition (SVD) are well-known techniques for dimensionality reduction [14,10]. ISOMAP [28] and locally linear embedding [24] are also widely used when we need to retain the non-linear property or manifold structure of the data.

However, these global dimensionality reduction techniques do not necessarily take into account *local structure* such as clusters in the network that are crucial for network analysis. Specifically, global techniques are likely to extract information from only the largest or a few dominant clusters, excluding information about smaller clusters. This is not desirable since different clusters usually have distinct meanings. We need to extract some information from every cluster regardless of its size to preserve important structural information of the original network in a low-dimensional representation. This is the motivation of a recently proposed method called *clustered low-rank approximation* [25], which reflects the clustering structure of the original network in the low-rank representation of the network. It extracts clusters, computes a low-rank approximation of each cluster, and then combines together the cluster approximations to approximate the entire network.

Unfortunately, the only available implementation of the clustered low-rank approximation is a sequential implementation, which precludes its use for processing large scale data sets for two reasons: (1) when the network size is huge, the network usually does not fit into the memory of a single machine, and (2) the running time can be substantial.

In this paper, we describe the first parallel implementation of clustered low-rank approximation, and show its application to link prediction on large scale social networks. It is a challenging problem to develop a parallel algorithm for the clustered low-rank approximation since it requires computing with very diverse data structures ranging from extremely sparse matrices to dense matrices. Experimental results show that our parallel implementation scales well on large distributed-memory machines; for example, on a Twitter graph, a standard data set in the social networks area with roughly 11 million vertices and 63 million edges, our implementation scales by a factor of 86 on 128 processes. The whole procedure, including link prediction, takes less than 2300 seconds on 128 processes. On a much larger Twitter graph with 41 million vertices and 1.2 billion edges, our current algorithm produces encouraging results with a scalability of 203 on 256 processes. In this case, the running time is about 4800 seconds.

The rest of this paper is organized as follows. In Section 2, we present the clustered low-rank approximation algorithm in detail, and introduce the link prediction problem. In Section 3, we describe our parallel algorithm. We present our experimental results in Section 4, and we briefly review some related work in Section 5. Finally, we state our conclusions in Section 6.

2   Preliminaries

In this section, we describe the clustered low-rank approximation method proposed in [25], and introduce the problem of link prediction in social network analysis. Throughout the paper, we use capital letters to represent matrices, lower-case bold letters to represent vectors, and lower-case italics to represent scalars. Note that the terms *graph* and *network* are used interchangeably.

2.1   Clustered Low-Rank Approximation

A graph $G = (\mathcal{V}, \mathcal{E})$ is represented by a set of vertices $\mathcal{V} = \{1, \ldots, m\}$ and a set of edges $\mathcal{E} = \{e_{ij} | i, j \in \mathcal{V}\}$ where e_{ij} denotes an edge weight between vertices i and j. The corresponding adjacency matrix of G is represented by $A = [a_{ij}]$ such that $a_{ij} = e_{ij}$ if there is an edge between vertices i and j, and 0 otherwise. Note that A is an $m \times m$ matrix. For simplicity, we focus our discussion on undirected graphs, which implies that the adjacency matrix of the graph is symmetric.

One of the standard and very useful methods for dimensionality reduction is obtained by spectral or SVD analysis of the adjacency matrix A. For example, if the graph is undirected (A is symmetric), the rank-k spectral approximation of A can be computed by eigendecomposition as follows:

$$A \approx V \Lambda V^T, \tag{1}$$

where $V = [\mathbf{v}_1, \ldots, \mathbf{v}_k]$, $\Lambda = \text{diag}(\lambda_1, \ldots, \lambda_k)$ is a $k \times k$ diagonal matrix, and $\lambda_1, \ldots, \lambda_k$ are the largest eigenvalues (in magnitude) of A, $\mathbf{v}_1, \ldots, \mathbf{v}_k$ are the corresponding eigenvectors of A. One benefit of the spectral approximation is that it gives a globally optimal low-rank approximation of A for a given rank. On the other hand, a drawback with spectral analysis and SVD is that they do not necessarily take into account local structures, such as clusters, of the network that are important for network analysis. These local structures (clusters) of the network are usually discovered by graph clustering which seeks to partition the graph into c disjoint clusters $\mathcal{V}_1, \ldots, \mathcal{V}_c$ such that $\bigcup_{i=1}^{c} \mathcal{V}_i = \mathcal{V}$. Suppose that A is an $m \times m$ adjacency matrix, and that we cluster the graph into c disjoint clusters. We use m_i

to denote the number of vertices in the cluster i. By reordering vertices in order of their cluster affiliations, we can represent the $m \times m$ adjacency matrix A as follows:

$$A = \begin{bmatrix} A_{11} & \cdots & A_{1c} \\ \vdots & \ddots & \vdots \\ A_{c1} & \cdots & A_{cc} \end{bmatrix}, \tag{2}$$

where each diagonal block A_{ii}, for $i = 1, \ldots, c$, is an $m_i \times m_i$ matrix that can be considered as a local adjacency matrix for cluster i. The off-diagonal blocks A_{ij} with $i \neq j$, represent the set of edges between vertices belonging to cluster i and cluster j. Note that A_{ij} is $m_i \times m_j$ matrix. Figure 1 shows the adjacency matrix of an arXiv network in the block form of (2). In the figure, a blue dot represents a non-zero entry of the matrix. Observe that the non-zeros (links) in the adjacency matrix are concentrated in the diagonal blocks A_{ii}, while the off-diagonal blocks are much more sparse.

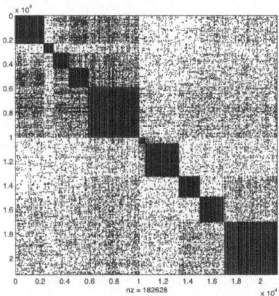

Fig. 1. Clustering structure of an arXiv network. Note that the diagonal blocks are much denser than the off-diagonal blocks.

In the clustered low-rank approximation framework, we first cluster a given network. Then, we independently compute a low-rank approximation of each cluster which corresponds to a diagonal block A_{ii}. With a symmetric matrix A as in (2), we can compute the best rank-k approximation of each A_{ii} as follows:

$$A_{ii} \approx V_i D_{ii} V_i^\mathsf{T}, \quad i = 1, \cdots, c, \tag{3}$$

where D_{ii} is a diagonal matrix with the k largest (in magnitude) eigenvalues of A_{ii}, and V_i is an orthogonal matrix with the corresponding eigenvectors.

Subsequently, the different cluster-wise approximations are combined together to obtain a low-rank approximation of the entire adjacency matrix. That is,

$$A \approx \begin{bmatrix} V_1 & \cdots & 0 \\ \vdots & \ddots & \vdots \\ 0 & \cdots & V_c \end{bmatrix} \begin{bmatrix} D_{11} & \cdots & D_{1c} \\ \vdots & \ddots & \vdots \\ D_{c1} & \cdots & D_{cc} \end{bmatrix} \begin{bmatrix} V_1 & \cdots & 0 \\ \vdots & \ddots & \vdots \\ 0 & \cdots & V_c \end{bmatrix}^\mathsf{T} \equiv \bar{V} \bar{D} \bar{V}^\mathsf{T}, \tag{4}$$

where $D_{ij} = V_i^\mathsf{T} A_{ij} V_j$, for $i, j = 1, \ldots, c$, which makes $\bar{D}$ optimal in the least squares sense.

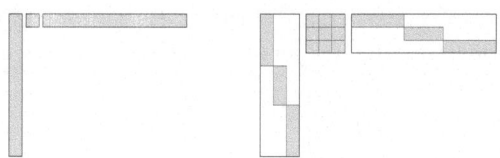

Fig. 2. Left panel shows an illustration of the regular spectral approximation $A \approx V\Lambda V^\mathsf{T}$. Right panel shows an illustration of the clustered low-rank approximation $A \approx \bar{V}\bar{D}\bar{V}^\mathsf{T}$ from (4). In both cases V and $\bar{V}$ are "long-thin" and they both use the same amount of memory as only the diagonal blocks of $\bar{V}$ are stored.

With a rank-k approximation of each cluster A_{ii}, we can observe that the clustered low-rank approximation has rank ck. As a result, compared with a regular rank-k approximation of A, we see that the rank in the clustered low-rank approximation is increased by a factor of c. However, a key observation is that $\bar{V}$ is a block diagonal matrix and uses exactly the same amount of memory as a regular rank-k approximation of A, as only the non-zero V_i blocks are stored while zero blocks of $\bar{V}$ are not stored. A pictorial representation of a regular rank-k approximation and the clustered low-rank approximation is given in Figure 2.

There are a number of benefits of clustered low rank approximation compared to spectral regular low-rank approximation: (1) the clustered low-rank approximation preserves important structural information of a network by extracting a certain amount of information from all of the clusters; (2) it has been shown that the clustered low-rank approximation achieves a lower relative error than the truncated SVD with the same amount of memory [25]; (3) it also has been shown that even a sequential implementation of clustered low rank approximation [25] is faster than state-of-the-art algorithms for low-rank matrix approximation [20]; (4) improved accuracy of clustered low-rank approximation contributes to improved performance of end tasks, e.g., prediction of new links in social networks [26] and group recommendation to community members [29].

2.2   Link Prediction in Social Networks

Link prediction [21] is one of the important tasks in social network analysis. Link prediction is the problem of predicting formation of new links in networks that evolve over time. This problem arises in applications such as friendship recommendation in social networks [26], affiliation recommendation [29], and prediction of author collaborations in scientific publications [23].

In social network analysis, the Katz measure [18] is a widely used proximity measure between the vertices (actors). In an undirected social network A, the Katz measure can be represented as a matrix function $Katz(A)$, where the (i,j)-th element represents the value of a proximity between actor i and actor j, as follows:

$$Katz(A) = \beta A + \beta^2 A^2 + \beta^3 A^3 + ... = \sum_{k=1}^{\infty} \beta^k A^k, \tag{5}$$

where $\beta < 1/\|A\|_2$ is a damping parameter.

Given a network, we sort all the pairs of vertices according to the Katz scores in descending order. By selecting top-k pairs which do not appear in the current network, we predict k links that are likely to be formed in the future. Note that this Katz computation is infeasible when the network size is very large, since it requires $O(m^3)$ time where m is the number of vertices in the network. However, the computation becomes feasible to approximate by leveraging the clustered low-rank approximation. Suppose that A is represented as (4) by using the clustered low-rank approximation. Then, the Katz measure can be approximated by:

$$Katz(A) \approx \hat{K} = \sum_{k=1}^{k_{\max}} \beta^k (\bar{V} \bar{D} \bar{V}^T)^k = \bar{V} (\sum_{k=1}^{k_{\max}} \beta^k \bar{D}^k) \bar{V}^T \equiv \bar{V} \bar{P} \bar{V}^T \tag{6}$$

3   Parallelization Strategy

In this section, we describe the parallelization strategy for each major phase of the clustered low-rank approximation algorithm: (i) graph clustering, (ii) approximation of diagonal blocks (clusters), and (iii) approximation of off-diagonal blocks (inter-cluster edges). We also describe how the parallel low-rank approximation algorithm can be used to solve a parallel link prediction problem on social networks.

On distributed memory machines, a graph is stored across different processes such that each process owns a subset of vertices and their adjacency lists. We use the term *local vertices* to designate the vertices each process owns.

3.1   Parallel Graph Clustering

Recall that for a given graph $G = (\mathcal{V}, \mathcal{E})$, graph clustering (also called graph partitioning) seeks to partition the graph into c disjoint clusters $\mathcal{V}_1, \ldots, \mathcal{V}_c$ such that $\bigcup_{i=1}^{c} \mathcal{V}_i = \mathcal{V}$. We use the term *clusters* and *partitions*, interchangeably.

Parallelization of graph clustering algorithms has long been recognized as a difficult problem. The state-of-the-art parallel library for graph clustering and partitioning is ParMetis [17], which is designed to deal with large scale graphs on distributed memory machines. However, ParMetis was designed for clustering and partitioning graphs that arise in computational science applications, and it does not perform well on social network graphs, which have a very different structure. For example, ParMetis could not cluster one of our data sets which has 40 million vertices and 1 billion edges due to lack of memory. Therefore, as one variation of the algorithm proposed in [30], we developed a custom parallel graph clustering algorithm which (i) scales well for social network graphs, and (ii) produces comparable quality clusters with ParMetis for graphs on which

ParMetis is successful. We name our new parallel graph clustering algorithm PEK[1]. PEK consists of four phases: (1) extraction of a representative subgraph, (2) initial partitioning, (3) partitioning propagation and refinement, and (4) recursive partitioning.

Extraction of a Representative Subgraph. From a given graph, we first select vertices whose degrees are greater than a certain threshold. These vertices induce a representative subgraph of the original graph, which is constructed with these selected vertices and the edges between them. Note that we can typically designate a degree threshold so that a desired number of vertices is included in the subgraph.

This step is easy to parallelize. First of all, each process scans its local vertices to select vertices and then communicates with other processes to decide the location of the selected vertices. According to the location information, a subgraph is created and distributed across different processes.

Initial Partitioning. The extracted subgraph is clustered using ParMetis. The runtime of this initial partitioning step only takes a small fraction of the total runtime if the extracted subgraph is very small compared to the original graph. When a network follows a power-law degree distribution, which is a well-known property of social networks, a very small number of high-degree vertices cover a large portion of the edges in the entire network. So, we usually extract a small number of vertices from the original graph, which are likely to govern the overall structure of the entire network, and then cluster this small network using ParMetis.

Partitioning Propagation and Refinement. At this point, the vertices of the extracted subgraph have been assigned to clusters. These vertices are considered to be the "seeds" for clustering the entire graph. Starting from vertices of the extracted subgraph, we visit the rest of the vertices in the original graph in a breadth-first order. To reduce communication among processes, each process only considers its local vertices when doing a breadth-first traversal. When we visit a vertex, we assign the vertex to some cluster by applying a weighted kernel k-means (WKKM) algorithm. We will explain the WKKM algorithm in detail below. Once we assign all the vertices of the original graph to some clusters, we refine the clustering using the WKKM algorithm repeatedly.

It has been shown that a general weighted kernel k-means objective is mathematically equivalent to a weighted graph clustering objective [13]. Therefore, we can optimize a weighted graph clustering objective by running the WKKM algorithm. At a high level, this algorithm computes the distance between a vertex and the centroid of each of the clusters, and assigns each vertex to its closest cluster.

To describe the WKKM algorithm in detail, we introduce some notation. Recall that for a given graph $G = (\mathcal{V}, \mathcal{E})$, where $\mathcal{V} = \{1, \ldots, m\}$ and $\mathcal{E} = \{e_{ij} | i, j \in \mathcal{V}\}$, the corresponding adjacency matrix of G is represented by $A = [a_{ij}]$ such that $a_{ij} = e_{ij}$, the edge weight between i and j, if there is an edge between

---

[1] The abbreviation PEK represents two key concepts of our Parallel graph clustering algorithm: Extraction of graph, and weighted Kernel k-means.

i and j, and 0 otherwise. Now, let us define $links(\mathcal{V}_p, \mathcal{V}_p)$ to be the sum of the edge weights between vertices in $\mathcal{V}_p$ for $p = 1, ..., c$, i.e., $links(\mathcal{V}_p, \mathcal{V}_p) = \sum_{i \in \mathcal{V}_p, j \in \mathcal{V}_p} a_{ij}$. Similarly, $links(\hat{x}, \mathcal{V}_p)$ denotes the sum of the edge weights between a vertex $\hat{x}$ and the vertices in $\mathcal{V}_p$. Also, we define $degree(\mathcal{V}_p)$ to be the sum of the edge weights of vertices in $\mathcal{V}_p$, i.e., $degree(\mathcal{V}_p) = links(\mathcal{V}_p, \mathcal{V})$. Finally, we use $\hat{x}$ to denote a vertex, and $\hat{w}$ to denote the degree of the corresponding vertex.

There can be many variations of the WKKM algorithm when applying it to a graph clustering problem. In our experiments, we measure the distance between a vertex $\hat{x}$ and a cluster $\mathcal{V}_p$, denoted by $dist(\hat{x}, \mathcal{V}_p)$, using the following expressions (detailed explanation about how this distance measure is derived is stated in [30]):

$$
dist(\hat{x}, \mathcal{V}_p) = \begin{cases} \dfrac{\hat{w} \cdot degree(\mathcal{V}_p)}{(degree(\mathcal{V}_p) - \hat{w})} \left(\dfrac{links(\mathcal{V}_p, \mathcal{V}_p)}{degree(\mathcal{V}_p)^2} - \dfrac{2 links(\hat{x}, \mathcal{V}_p)}{\hat{w} \cdot degree(\mathcal{V}_p)} \right), & \text{if } \hat{x} \in \mathcal{V}_p, \\[3mm] \dfrac{\hat{w} \cdot degree(\mathcal{V}_p)}{(degree(\mathcal{V}_p) + \hat{w})} \left(\dfrac{links(\mathcal{V}_p, \mathcal{V}_p)}{degree(\mathcal{V}_p)^2} - \dfrac{2 links(\hat{x}, \mathcal{V}_p)}{\hat{w} \cdot degree(\mathcal{V}_p)} \right), & \text{if } \hat{x} \notin \mathcal{V}_p. \end{cases} \tag{7}
$$

Once we compute the distance between a vertex and the clusters, we assign the vertex to the closest cluster. If a vertex moves from its current cluster to another cluster, the centroids of the current cluster and the new cluster need to be updated immediately. However, since the cluster centroids are globally shared, the updates will serialize the algorithm. To avoid this serialization, we synchronize the cluster centroids less frequently. In our experiments, we synchronize the centroids of clusters once all of the processes finish considering their local vertices.

In summary, given the current cluster information, each process assigns its local vertices to their closest clusters. After this, the cluster information is updated. This procedure is repeated until the change in the WKKM objective value is sufficiently small or the maximum number of iterations is reached.

Recursive Partitioning. If we observe very large clusters, we can further partition the clusters by recursively applying the above procedures until all the clusters are small enough. To do the recursive partitioning on the large clusters, we need to extract the large clusters from the original graph. Usually, each extracted cluster is not necessarily a single connected component. Therefore, we first find all components in the extracted clusters. If the size of a component is larger than a certain threshold, we recursively partition it using the WKKM procedure. If the size of a component is near the threshold (*i.e.*, a moderate-sized component), we just leave it as a new cluster. Finally, we form new clusters by merging small components. At the end, each cluster contains a reasonably large number of vertices.

This recursive partitioning is required since subsequently each cluster is approximated using eigendecomposition of the corresponding submatrix (described in Section 3.2). If a cluster is too large, the memory consumption increases significantly in the eigendecomposition step. Therefore we partition each cluster until every cluster is small enough to be handled by a single process. In our experiments, we recursively partition the graph until each cluster contains less than 100,000 vertices.

3.2   Approximation of Diagonal Blocks

The clustering step is followed by a reordering of the vertices so vertices in the same cluster are contiguously numbered. The adjacency matrix of the resulting graph G has a block structure as in (2). Each A_{ii} is the local adjacency matrix of cluster i, and off-diagonal blocks A_{ij} contain the edges between cluster i and cluster j. Then each process computes the rank-k eigendecomposition approximation for each of the diagonal matrices A_{ii} it owns according to (3); for example, $A_{11} \approx V_1 D_{11} V_1^\mathsf{T}$.

Since each process can only access a limited amount of memory and computing the eigen-decomposition requires fairly large amount of memory, it is better to compromise the balance of the memory usage and the computation time across processes. Therefore, we assign clusters to processes using a static list scheduling approach. All the clusters are put into an ordered list where the priority of each cluster A_{ii} is determined by (the number of non-zero entries in A_{ii}) $\times k$. Each process is associated with a weight. The clusters are repeatedly extracted from the list and assigned to the process with the current minimum weight. Whenever a cluster is assigned to a process, its weight is increased by an amount equal to the cluster's priority. Since this computation is so small that every process can simultaneously compute the assignment. After the assignment, we redistribute the graph so that the vertices belonging to the same cluster are aggregated into the same process.

The matrices V_i in the low-rank approximation (see Figure 2) will, in general, be dense matrices. They are typically small enough so that they fit on any node of the distributed-memory machine, so we do not distribute individual V_i's across processes, reducing communication further.

3.3   Approximating Off-Diagonal Blocks

The approximations of the off-diagonal blocks A_{ij} is given by $A_{ij} \approx V_i D_{ij} V_j^\mathsf{T}$ where $D_{ij} = V_i^\mathsf{T} A_{ij} V_j$. Given that all V_i are computed in the previous step, what remains is to compute D_{ij} for $i, j = 1, 2, \ldots, c$ and $i \neq j$. Recall that all V_i are dense matrices and off-diagonal blocks A_{ij} are sparse matrices. It follows that matrix products of the type $V_i^\mathsf{T} A_{ij}$ or $A_{ij} V_j$ result in dense matrices. Consequently, computation of each D_{ij} involves two multiplications: one between a dense matrix and a sparse matrix, and the other between two dense matrices.

Since the graph G is undirected, we can exploit the symmetry of its adjacency matrix representation. In this case, we only need to compute D_{ij} or D_{ji}, as the other can be easily obtained with a transpose operation. We define $\mathrm{job}(i, j)$ as computing D_{ij} $(i < j)$, so the total number of jobs is $\frac{c(c-1)}{2}$. From Section 3.2,

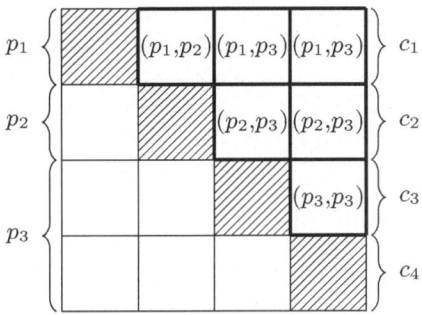

Fig. 3. An example where a pair (p_i, p_j) represents a job shared by processes p_i and p_j in approximation of off-diagonal blocks

it is easy to see that each process contains A_{ij} and V_i for the clusters it owns. In order to compute D_{ij}, we require the matrices V_i, A_{ij}, and V_j. In the easy case, where a process which owns A_{ij} and V_i, also owns the matrix V_j as well, D_{ij} can be computed without any communication. Otherwise, some communication is required between the process owning V_i (and A_{ij}) and the process owning V_j. Therefore, the jobs can be categorized as the ones which can be performed independently and those which need some communication between processes. For the former type, all of V_i, V_j, A_{ij}, and A_{ji} are located in the same process and we call them *private jobs* of the owner process. The latter is a more complicated scenario in which A_{ij} and V_i are co-located in one process while A_{ji} and V_j are co-located in another process. Therefore, either process can execute job(i, j) by fetching the required matrices from the other process. We call these *shared jobs* between the two processes. Since jobs take different amounts of time, a challenging problem that arises here is to evenly divide the shared jobs between every pair of processes, with the aim of minimizing communication and achieving an ideal load balance.

Figure 3 is an example to illustrate this problem. Figure 3 shows a matrix representing the block view of A. Each entry of this matrix represents A_{ij}. In this example, graph A is partitioned into four clusters. Each row of the matrix can be regarded as a cluster including edges that connect to other clusters, denoted as c_i. There are three processes p_1, p_2, and p_3. Process p_1 owns cluster c_1, p_2 owns cluster c_2, and p_3 owns clusters c_3 and c_4. The pair (p_i, p_j) inside each entry in Figure 3 represents that the job (approximation of this entry) can be computed by either process i or process j.

We build a dynamic load balancing framework for performing the jobs. For each pair of processes, we create a *job queue* storing the shared jobs between them. A job queue is a priority queue where jobs are ordered by the amount of work. Each process first works on its private jobs. Once its private jobs are finished, the process starts to ask for jobs from a master process p_{master} dedicated to scheduling jobs. Whenever a process p asks for a new job, p_{master} goes through all job lists that involve p, picks the job queue with the most jobs, extracts the largest job in that job list, and then hands it to the process p. When the process p receives the job, it fetches the corresponding V_j from the process owning V_j using RDMA (Remote Direct Memory Access).

Once this stage is complete, we have computed all necessary factors to approximate A, i.e., $A \approx \hat{A} = \bar{V}\bar{D}\bar{V}^\mathsf{T}$, as in (4). In particular, the approximation of each block A_{ij} in (2) is given by $A_{ij} \approx \hat{A}_{ij} = V_i D_{ij} V_j^\mathsf{T}$, for $i, j = 1, \ldots, c$.

3.4   Parallel Computation of the Katz Measure and Link Prediction

Now, we describe how we compute the Katz measure in parallel, and perform parallel link prediction. Recall (6). The computation of the term $\sum_{k=1}^{k_{\max}} \beta^k \bar{D}^k$ requires a distributed dense matrix multiplication since $\bar{D}$ is a dense matrix. Parallel dense matrix multiplication has been fairly well understood and there are several efficient libraries available. We use the Elemental Matrix class library [2] to perform this step and we set $k_{\max} = 6$ in the experiments. In terms of the block-wise view as in (4), we can rewrite (6) as follows:

$$\hat{K} = \bar{V}\bar{P}\bar{V}^\mathsf{T} \equiv \begin{bmatrix} V_1 & \cdots & 0 \\ \vdots & \ddots & \vdots \\ 0 & \cdots & V_c \end{bmatrix} \begin{bmatrix} P_{11} & \cdots & P_{1c} \\ \vdots & \ddots & \vdots \\ P_{c1} & \cdots & P_{cc} \end{bmatrix} \begin{bmatrix} V_1 & \cdots & 0 \\ \vdots & \ddots & \vdots \\ 0 & \cdots & V_c \end{bmatrix}^\mathsf{T}, \qquad (8)$$

Then, $\hat{K}_{ij}$ is computed as follows: $\hat{K}_{ij} = V_i P_{ij} V_j^\mathsf{T}$, for $i, j = 1, \ldots, c$. We distribute P_{ij} to the same process as A_{ij}. Due to the symmetry of $\bar{P}$, computing $\hat{K}$ is very similar to the approximation of off-diagonal matrices in Section 3.3, so we adopt a similar parallelization stratgy. Since $\hat{K}$ is a $m \times m$ matrix, it is infeasible to compute the whole matrix if m is very large. Therefore, we only compute a subset of $\hat{K}$ and predict links based on the sampled subset. The details of our sampling method is stated in Section 4.

4   Experimental Results

In this section, we present and analyze experimental results on a large-scale parallel platform at the Texas Advanced Computing Center (TACC), Ranger [5]. Ranger has 3,936 nodes, and each node is equipped with a 16-core AMD Opteron 2.2GHz CPU and 32GB memory. Ranger uses InfiniBand networks with 5GB/s point-to-point bandwidth. The MPI library on Ranger is Open MPI 1.3. Our implementation is written in C++. We use ARPACK++ [1] for the eigendecompositions of diagonal blocks, GotoBLAS 1.30 [3] for the dense matrix multiplications involving the off-diagonal blocks, and Elemental Matrix class library [2] for the dense matrix multiplications for the Katz measure.

4.1   Data Sets

We use three different social graphs which are summarized in Table 1. LiveJournal is a free online community with almost 10 million members, and it allows members to select other members as their friends. Twitter is an online social networking website where members *follow* other members they are interested in. In our experiments, we extract the largest connected component from each of the network. Originally, each of these networks were directed networks. So, we transformed them into undirected graphs by adding additional edges. In the experiments, the degree thresholds for PEK are 42 (Soc-LiveJournal), 200 (Twitter-10M) and 2500 (Twitter-40M). The number of vertices of the extracted subgraph is less than 5% of the original graph in all cases.

Table 1. Detailed information of the graph data sets

Data set	#Vertices	#Edges	Description
soc-LiveJournal	3,828,682	39,870,459	LiveJournal on social network [6].
Twitter-10M	11,316,799	63,555,738	Crawled Twitter graph from [7].
Twitter-40M	41,652,230	1,202,513,046	Crawled Twitter graph from [19].

4.2 Parallel Performance Evaluation

We use one process as the scheduling server and the other processes as the workers in the phases of computing the approximation of off-diagonal blocks and link prediction. In other phases, the scheduling process stays idle and does not participate in computation in any phase. The graphs are initially randomly distributed among all the processes other than the scheduling process.

Figure 4 shows the performance of our parallel implementation of the clustered low-rank approximation, on the soc-LiveJournal, Twitter-10M and Twitter-40M graphs. All these social network graphs are too large to be processed in a single node of Ranger. Therefore, we run each graph on the smallest number of nodes on which the program finishes successfully, and then measure the performance as the number of nodes increases. We use only one MPI process on each node to enable us to measure performance without interference from other processes in the same node. From Figure 4, we see that our implementation scales very well on the three different sizes of real social graphs. A speedup of 68 is achieved on 64 processes for soc-LiveJournal, a speedup of 86 is achieved on 128 processes for Twitter-10M and 203 on 256 processes for Twitter-40M. The super-linear speedup is mainly due to the cache effects of matrix multiplication. For soc-LiveJournal and Twitter-10M, performance levels off after 64 nodes, but this is mainly because the problem size is relatively small compared to the number of processes. This is clear from the performance of Twitter-40M: it consistently scales up to 256 processes.

Figure 5 shows how much time is spent on each of the major phases of the algorithm: (i) partitioning, (ii) computing diagonal blocks, (iii) computing the off-diagonal blocks D_{ij}'s, and (iv) link prediction. We divide the link prediction phase into two steps: (a) computing the $\bar{P}$ matrix in (6) which requires dense matrix multiplication, and (b) computing $\hat{K}_{ij} = V_i P_{ij} V_j^{\mathsf{T}}$ in (8). We label (a) as MATRIXPOWER, and label (b) as SCORECOMPUTATION in Figure 5.

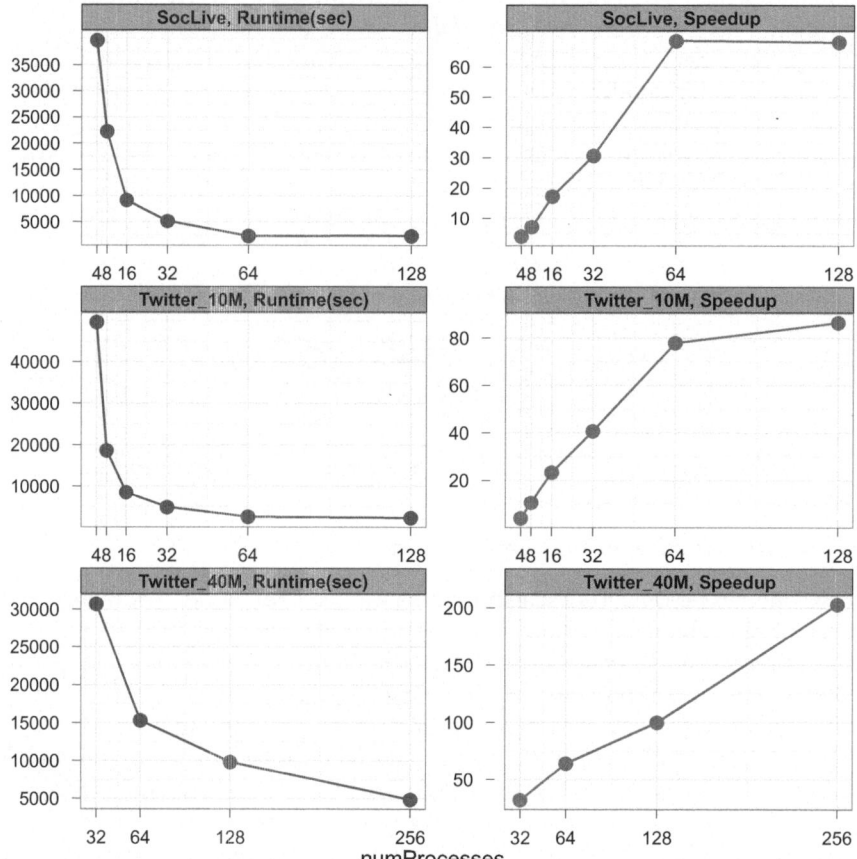

Fig. 4. Runtime and Speedup for soc-LiveJournal, Twitter-10M, and Twitter-40M graphs, where $c = 500$ and $k = 100$ for soc-LiveJournal and Twitter-10M, and $c = 1000$ and $k = 100$ for Twitter-40M

The MATRIXPOWER dominates the running time since this step involves large dense matrix multiplication (square matrix, each dimension is $c \times k$ where c is the number of clusters and k is the number of eigenvalues). To make the runtime of other phases visible in the graph, we show MATRIXPOWER time in a separate figure from other phases.

From Figure 5, we see that most of the phases scale well with increasing numbers of processes, especially with our new parallel graph partitioning algorithm. For soc-LiveJournal and Twitter-10M, the runtime of the diagonal phase does not decrease beyond 32 processes. There are two reasons: first, the clustering algorithm is not deterministic, so running with different number of processes may cluster the graph differently. Cluster sizes will affect the runtime significantly since the complexity of eigendecomposition in the diagonal phase does not increase linearly with cluster size. Second, since the number of eigendecompositions is equal to the number of clusters, the average number of clusters assigned to each process will become smaller when the number of processes becomes large. So, the space available for load balancing among processes to hide unbalanced clustering effects will be less. This problem may be alleviated by dynamic load balancing which we will explore in the future. On the other hand, in the MATRIXPOWER step, the Elemental library [2] we use for parallel dense matrix multiplication does not scale well after 64 processes for small matrix sizes ($50,000 \times 50,000$ for soc-LiveJournal and Twitter-10M), while it can scale consistently to 256 processes for larger sizes ($100,000 \times 100,000$ for Twitter-40M). This phase dominates the total runtime, and it is the main reason why the running time of soc-LiveJounrnal is not improved after 128 nodes.

Load Balancing. Figure 6 shows the load balancing results of three phases: diagonal, off-diagonal and link prediction. The red and green bars denote the maximum and minimum time processes take, respectively. The dynamic load balancing framework is effective in most of the cases for approximating off-diagonal blocks and link prediction. For small number of processes, the diagonal phase is also balanced. When the number of processes increases, the load among processes starts to become unbalanced. As mentioned before, this is mainly due to the very unbalanced partitions.

4.3   Evaluation of Clustering Algorithm

Figure 7 compares our clustering algorithm (PEK) with ParMetis on soc-Live Journal and Twitter-10M, using two measures: (i) the quality of the partition, and (ii) the running time of the algorithm. ParMetis fails to cluster Twitter-40M graph on Ranger because the memory at each node is not enough. To evaluate the quality of clusters, we use two standard measures: the normalized cut measure and the cut-size measure. These measures are defined as:

$$\text{NormCut} = \sum_{k=1}^{c} \frac{links(\mathcal{V}_k, \mathcal{V}\backslash\mathcal{V}_k)}{degree(\mathcal{V}_k)}, \text{Cut-Size} = \sum_{k=1}^{c} links(\mathcal{V}_k, \mathcal{V}\backslash\mathcal{V}_k). \quad (9)$$

where c is the number of clusters, A is the adjacency matrix of a graph $G=(\mathcal{V},\mathcal{E})$, $links(\mathcal{V}_k, \mathcal{V}\backslash\mathcal{V}_k) = \sum_{i\in\mathcal{V}_k, j\in\{\mathcal{V}\backslash\mathcal{V}_k\}} a_{ij}$, and $degree(\mathcal{V}_k) = links(\mathcal{V}_k, \mathcal{V})$ for $k = 1, 2, ..., c$. By definition, the normalized cut is upper-bounded by the number of clusters. Lower normalized cut value indicates better quality of clusters. In Figure 7, we divide the normalized cut by the total number of clusters since PEK probably makes more clusters than the designated number of clusters due to its recursive partitioning phase. We see that PEK performs a little better than ParMetis on both of soc-LiveJournal and Twitter-10M in terms of the normalized cut. We also divide the cut-size by the total number of clusters, and present the results in Figure 7. Note that lower cut-size indicates better quality of clusters. We can see that the cluster quality of PEK and ParMetis are comparable in terms of the cut-size.

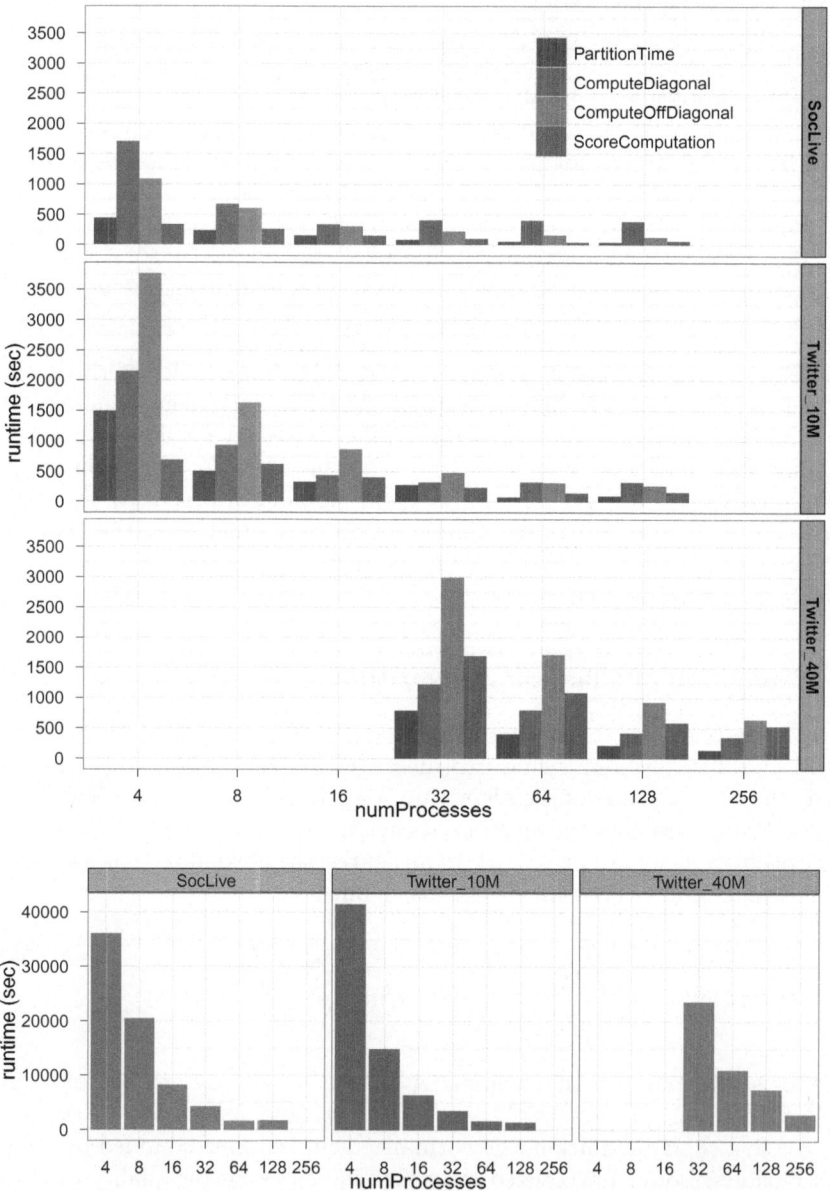

Fig. 5. Time spent in each phase for soc-LiveJournal, Twitter-10M, and Twitter-40M graphs, where $c = 500$ and $k = 100$ for soc-LiveJournal and Twitter-10M, and $c = 1000$ and $k = 100$ for Twitter-40M. The bottom figure shows the time for MATRIXPOWER step. The MATRIXPOWER dominates the running time since this step involves large dense matrix multiplication (square matrix, each dimension is $c \times k$ where c is the number of clusters and k is the number of eigenvalues). To make the runtime of other phases visible in the graph, we show MATRIXPOWER time in a separate figure from other phases.

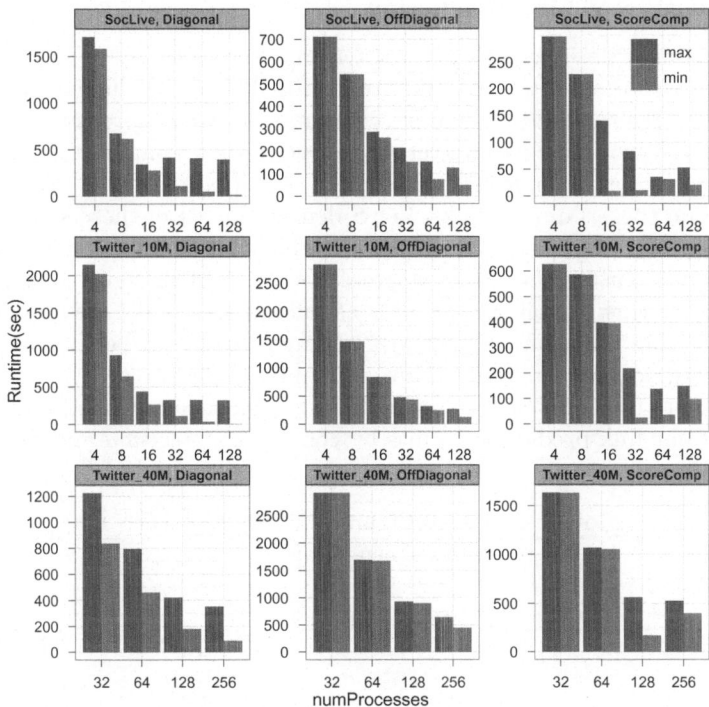

Fig. 6. Load balancing statistics in diagonal, off-diagonal, and link prediction phases for soc-LiveJournal, Twitter-10M, and Twitter-40M graphs, where $c = 500$ and $k = 100$ for soc-LiveJournal and Twitter-10M, and $c = 1000$ and $k = 100$ for Twitter-40M

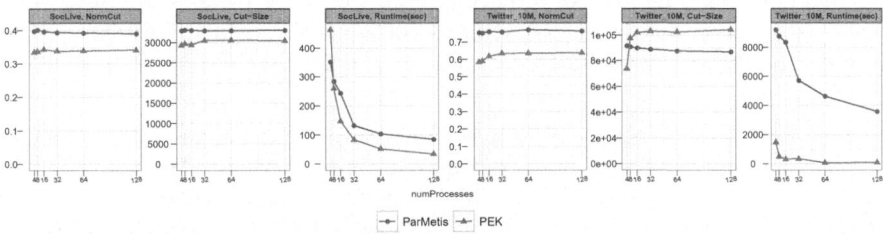

Fig. 7. Comparison between our clustering algorithm (PEK) with ParMetis on soc-LiveJournal and Twitter-10M. The number of clusters is 500. Since our implementation needs one scheduling server for later phases, we leave one process to handle that for both clustering algorithms in the experiments.

We see that PEK is much faster than ParMetis. For soc-LiveJournal, PEK is two times faster than ParMetis on 128 processes. For Twitter-10M, PEK is about seven times faster than ParMetis on 128 processes. Overall, PEK achieves similar quality as ParMetis but can scale better than ParMetis to larger number of processes and larger graphs.

4.4   Evaluation of Link Prediction

We perform our experiments as follows. Given a network $G = (V, E)$, a network $G' = (V, E')$ is obtained by randomly removing 30% of the links of G. We call the removed links *test links*. Then, we compute the Katz scores on the network G'. Since the networks we use are very large, we cannot compute the Katz scores for all the vertex pairs. So, we sample a set of vertex pairs from G', and compute Katz scores on these sampled links. Let S denote the set of these sampled links. We randomly sample a subset of the links which are incident to vertices that are in the same cluster and whose degrees are larger than some threshold. The justification for this sampling method is as follows: new links are more likely to be formed within the same cluster and are more likely to be formed between vertices whose degrees are larger than a certain threshold.

Let R denote the set of top-k scoring links (top-k recommended links). Then, we evaluate our link prediction results by computing *precision* and *recall* which are defined as follows:

$$\text{Precision} = \frac{\text{number of correctly predicted links}}{\text{top-}k\text{ recommendations}} = \frac{|(E - E') \bigcap R|}{|R|}, \qquad (10)$$

$$\text{Recall} = \frac{\text{number of correctly predicted links}}{\text{number of overlapped links between test and sampled links}} = \frac{|(E - E') \bigcap R|}{|(E - E') \bigcap S|}. \qquad (11)$$

By definition, the upper bound of the recall measure is obtained by setting the numerator as $|R|$ (i.e., k). Higher precision and recall indicate better performance. Table 2 shows precision and recall for the soc-LiveJournal and Twitter-10M graphs with different ranks of approximations. We partition each graph into 500 clusters. The only difference among the three rows is the rank of each cluster. For soc-LiveJournal, we achieve 100% precision for predicting the top-10 and top-100 links and 98% precision for predicting the top-1000 links using

Table 2. Link prediction evaluation on soc-LiveJournal and Twitter-10M. We compare the precision and recall with different ranks of approximations. The graph is always partitioned into 500 clusters. Three different rows represent different ranks of each cluster, which results in different rank approximations of the whole graph. UB is the upper bound for the recall. Note the upper bound differs in the experiments since we use a new sample set for each case.

Graph	Top-k	Rank	Precision	Recall(UB)	Graph	Top-k	Rank	Precision	Recall(UB)
SocLive	10	c500r50	100	0.002(0.002)	Twitter-10M	10	c500r50	0	0(0.39)
		c500r100	100	0.002(0.002)			c500r100	100	0.389(0.389)
		c500r200	0	0(0.002)			c500r200	100	0.431(0.431)
	100	c500r50	100	0.024(0.024)		100	c500r50	10	0.431(4.310)
		c500r100	90	0.019(0.021)			c500r100	30	1.167(3.891)
		c500r200	30	0.006(0.021)			c500r200	10	0.431(4.310)
	1000	c500r50	98	0.234(0.239)		1000	c500r50	3	1.293(43.103)
		c500r100	46	0.096(0.209)			c500r100	10	3.891(38.910)
		c500r200	40	0.083(0.208)			c500r200	6	2.586(43.103)

rank 500 × 50 (500 indicates the number of clusters, 50 indicates the rank of each cluster). The recall is also very close to the upper bound. For Twitter-10M graph, precision and recall measures are not as good as for soc-LiveJournal. A contributing factor to this is that the overlap between $E - E'$ and S for the Twitter-10M graph is very small, around 2600 overlapping links with a sample size of 70 millions. (The overlap for soc-LiveJournal is around 500,000.) Even on this setting, we can see that the precision for top-10 is still 100%, and top-100 is 30% for rank 500 × 100. This reflects the effectiveness of clustered low-rank approximation approach.

5   Related Work

The study of parallel graph partitioning, which is a key component of parallel clustered low-rank approximation, has a long history. The most commonly used library is ParMetis [17]. However, ParMetis is not suitable for social networks because ParMetis utilizes a multilevel coarsening approach which is not effective in social networks. This multilevel coarsening is primarily designed for graphs in scientific computing (e.g. finite element meshes) [8,27]. In order to overcome this problem, we develop PEK which is described in Section 3. While PEK is closely related to PGEM which is presented in [30], PEK is a custom clustering algorithm for clustered low-rank approximation framework. PEK includes a recursive partitioning step which allows us to proceed to the next phase of clustering phase. Furthermore, PEK utilizes ParMetis to cluster an extracted graph while PGEM uses weighted kernel k-means.

Cong et al. [12] studied the problem of parallel connected components implemented in UPC for distributed-memory systems. They started from a PRAM-based algorithm and applied several optimizations for sparse graphs. We implemented similar algorithm using MPI in our clustering algorithm. It takes very small fraction of the total clustering time so we do not report it.

Low-rank approximation has been applied to the task of link prediction and has been shown to be successful in practice [22]. Parallel eigendecomposition for dense matrices on multiple machines has been well studied in, e.g., [11,9]. But they are not suitable for large social networks because the adjacency matrices for them are too large to be represented as dense matrices. Recently, [4,16] studied the problem of large scale sparse eigensovler based on Hadoop.

Yoo et al. [31] studied level-synchronized breadth-first search on the Blue-Gene machine. They performed 2D partitions. By optimizing message buffer size and utilizing the processor topology, they achieved scalability of $\sqrt[3]{p}$ with p processors on a very large graph. Their work indicates that exploring processor topology information may be an important aspect for efficiency that we have not explored in this paper.

6   Conclusions

In this paper, we present the first parallel implementation of clustered low-rank approximation. We conduct experiments on distributed-memory machines, and the experimental results show that this parallel implementation is effective in processing large-scale social network graphs with tens of millions of vertices and hundreds of millions of edges. In particular, our parallel implementation scales well according to the number of processes.

Our parallel implementation of clustered low rank approximation provides a critical routine that is a key enabler for efficient analyses of social network graphs. Presently, such analyses are performed in a brute-force manner on the entire graph by using parallel processing in large data-centers; in contrast, low rank approximations of these graphs enable analyses to be performed more efficiently on a smaller graph that distills the essence of the original graph. However, most current low rank approximation techniques compute a global approximation of the graph, and ignore local structure, such as clusters, that must be preserved in the low rank approximation for accurate analysis. Fortunately, the clustered low rank approximation permits the computation of a structure-preserving low rank approximation. Our parallel implementation of this algorithm enables the full power of clustered low rank approximation to be brought to bear on huge social networks for the first time.

Acknowledgments. This research was supported by NSF grants CCF-1117055 and CCF-0916309.

References

1. ARPACK++, http://www.ime.unicamp.br/~chico/arpack++/
2. Elemental, http://elemental.googlecode.com/hg/doc/build/html/core/matrix.html
3. GotoBLAS, http://www.tacc.utexas.edu/tacc-projects/gotoblas2/
4. Mahout, http://lucene.apache.org/mahout/
5. Ranger, http://services.tacc.utexas.edu/index.php/ranger-user-guide
6. SNAP - Stanford Network Analysis Package, http://snap.stanford.edu/snap/
7. Social Computing Data Repository, http://socialcomputing.asu.edu/datasets/Twitter
8. Abou-Rjeili, A., Karypis, G.: Multilevel algorithms for partitioning power-law graphs. In: IPDPS (2006)
9. Alpatov, P., Baker, G., Edwards, C., Gunnels, J., Morrow, G., Overfelt, J., van de Geijn, R., Wu, Y.-J.J.: Plapack: parallel linear algebra package design overview. In: Proceedings of the 1997 ACM/IEEE Conference on Supercomputing, pp. 1–16. ACM (1997)
10. Bishop, C.M.: Neural Networks for Pattern Recognition. Oxford University Press (1995)
11. Blackford, L.S., Choi, J., Cleary, A., D'Azeuedo, E., Demmel, J., Dhillon, I., Hammarling, S., Henry, G., Petitet, A., Stanley, K., Walker, D., Whaley, R.C.: ScaLAPACK user's guide. Society for Industrial and Applied Mathematics, Philadelphia (1997)
12. Cong, G., Almasi, G., Saraswat, V.: Fast pgas connected components algorithms. In: Proceedings of the Third Conference on Partitioned Global Address Space Programing Models, PGAS 2009 (2009)

13. Dhillon, I.S., Guan, Y., Kulis, B.: Weighted graph cuts without eigenvectors: A multilevel approach. IEEE Trans. Pattern Anal. Mach. Intell. 29(11), 1944–1957 (2007)
14. Golub, G.H., Van Loan, C.F.: Matrix Computations, 3rd edn. Johns Hopkins University Press (1996)
15. Huang, Z.: Link prediction based on graph topology: The predictive value of the generalized clustering coefficient. In: Workshop on Link Analysis, KDD (2006)
16. Kang, U., Meeder, B., Faloutsos, C.: Spectral Analysis for Billion-Scale Graphs: Discoveries and Implementation. In: Huang, J.Z., Cao, L., Srivastava, J. (eds.) PAKDD 2011, Part II. LNCS, vol. 6635, pp. 13–25. Springer, Heidelberg (2011)
17. Karypis, G., Kumar, V.: A coarse-grain parallel formulation of multilevel k-way graph partitioning algorithm. In: Proceedings of SIAM International Conference on Parallel Processing for Scientific Computing (1997)
18. Katz, L.: A new status index derived from sociometric analysis. Psychometrika 18, 39–43 (1953)
19. Kwak, H., Lee, C., Park, H., Moon, S.: What is Twitter, a social network or a news media? In: WWW, pp. 591–600. ACM, New York (2010)
20. Lehoucq, R., Sorensen, D., Yang, C.: Arpack Users' Guide: Solution of Large Scale Eigenvalue Problems with Implicitly Restarted Arnoldi Methods. SIAM, Philadelphia (1998)
21. Liben-Nowell, D., Kleinberg, J.: The link-prediction problem for social networks. Journal of the American Society for Information Science and Technology 58(7), 1019–1031 (2007)
22. Liben-Nowell, D., Kleinberg, J.: The link-prediction problem for social networks. J. Am. Soc. Inf. Sci. Technol. 58(7), 1019–1031 (2007)
23. Lu, Z., Savas, B., Tang, W., Dhillon, I.S.: Link prediction using multiple sources of information. In: Proceedings of the IEEE International Conference on Data Mining (ICDM), pp. 923–928 (2010)
24. Roweis, S.T., Saul, L.K.: Nonlinear dimensionality reduction by locally linear embedding. Science 290, 2323–2326 (2000)
25. Savas, B., Dhillon, I.S.: Clustered low rank approximation of graphs in information science applications. In: SIAM Data Mining Conference, pp. 164–175 (2011)
26. Song, H.H., Savas, B., Cho, T.W., Dave, V., Lu, Z., Dhillon, I.S., Zhang, Y., Qiu, L.: Clustered embedding of massive social networks. In: SIGMETRICS (2012)
27. Sui, X., Nguyen, D., Burtscher, M., Pingali, K.: Parallel Graph Partitioning on Multicore Architectures. In: Cooper, K., Mellor-Crummey, J., Sarkar, V. (eds.) LCPC 2010. LNCS, vol. 6548, pp. 246–260. Springer, Heidelberg (2011)
28. Tenenbaum, J.B., de Silva, V., Langford, J.C.: A global geometric framework for nonlinear dimensionality reduction. Science 290(5500), 2319–2323 (2000)
29. Vasuki, V., Natarajan, N., Lu, Z., Savas, B., Dhillon, I.S.: Scalable affiliation recommendation using auxiliary networks. ACM Transactions on Intelligent Systems and Technology 3, 3:1–3:20 (2011)
30. Whang, J., Sui, X., Dhillon, I.: Scalable and memory-efficient clustering of large-scale social networks. In: Proceedings of the IEEE International Conference on Data Mining (2012)
31. Yoo, A., Chow, E., Henderson, K., McLendon, W., Hendrickson, B., Catalyurek, U.: A scalable distributed parallel breadth-first search algorithm on bluegene/l. In: Proceedings of the 2005 ACM/IEEE Conference on Supercomputing, SC 2005, pp. 25–43 (2005)

OmpSs-OpenCL Programming Model
for Heterogeneous Systems

Vinoth Krishnan Elangovan[1,2], Rosa. M. Badia[1,3],
and Eduard Ayguade Parra[1,2]

[1] Barcelona Supercomputing Center
[2] Universitat Politècnica de Catalunya
[3] Artificial Intelligence Research Institute (IIIA),
Spanish National Research Council (CSIC), Spain

Abstract. The advent of heterogeneous computing has forced programmers to use platform specific programming paradigms in order to achieve maximum performance. This approach has a steep learning curve for programmers and also has detrimental influence on productivity and code re-usability. To help with this situation, OpenCL an open-source, parallel computing API for cross platform computations was conceived. OpenCL provides a homogeneous view of the computational resources (CPU and GPU) thereby enabling software portability across different platforms. Although OpenCL resolves software portability issues, the programming paradigm presents low programmability and additionally falls short in performance. In this paper we focus on integrating OpenCL framework with the OmpSs task based programming model using Nanos run time infrastructure to address these shortcomings. This would enable the programmer to skip cumbersome OpenCL constructs including OpenCL plaform creation, compilation, kernel building, kernel argument setting and memory transfers, instead write a sequential program with annotated pragmas. Our proposal mainly focuses on how to exploit the best of the underlying hardware platform with greater ease in programming and to gain significant performance using the data parallelism offered by the OpenCL run time for GPUs and multicore architectures. We have evaluated the platform with important benchmarks and have noticed substantial ease in programming with comparable performance.

1 Introduction

Microprocessor vendors have switched to the many core paradigm to effectively utilize the transistor count afforded by Moore's Law. In accordance with this trend, we are seeing an increase in the number of cores with every successive product generation. It is also predicted that this trend is likely to continue into the future. The software development effort needed to harness the immense computing power, is however growing over the roof and hence presents the developers with a tedious challenge . In addition, with the emergence of heterogeneous computing models, it is imperative that expressive programming models be made available to the programmers to make proper use of the computational resource

H. Kasahara and K. Kimura (Eds.): LCPC 2012, LNCS 7760, pp. 96–111, 2013.
© Springer-Verlag Berlin Heidelberg 2013

available and also ease the task of programming. Although lot of research is being carried out in this direction a clear solution to address this issue is still far from sight. Emerging accelerator architectures address this issue by providing platform specific programming model. Two notable examples of this are GPUs from Nvidia (that use the CUDA programming model) [4] and the CELL processor from IBM (CELL programming API)[5]. Although these models provide the potential to get maximum performance out of the system (after exhaustive programming effort), the portability of applications developed using these models is largely limited. This restricts the application of this programming model to niche domains. Some believe that the trend of using platform specific programming models and development tools is here to continue.

An alternate approach to address the programmability issue involves design of plaform indepèndent paradigms in order to ease off the burden on the developers (by improving portability and code reuse). This approach has received a lot of attention lately. One such initiative currently being undertaken by the Khronos research consortium is OpenCL (Open Computing Language)[1]. OpenCL provides a platform *independent* programming APIs and is targeted towards developers to promote the concept of portability and reusability. OpenCL offers support to both Data and Task parallel execution model. The main drawback of this approach is that programs written using this model are cumbersome when compared to programs written using the platform specific model. This is primarily because the designers have traded-off programming efficiency for portability. In addition to the low programmability the development time involved here is quite overwhelming. In this paper we put forward a proposal to simplify the programming effort to develop applications using the portable programming model. The attempt is to integrate the OpenCL runtime with OmpSs, a Task Based programming model[2] as a back-end execution platform. The pursuit is to offer the programmers a sequential programming flow with annotated pragmas specifying the key attributes for the code which is to be accelerated or the section which is needed to be parallelized for a target architecture. The OmpSs model comprises of Mercurium[2], a source to source compiler and Nanos runtime library[2] for effectively garnering the computing power of the hardware. The source code with pragmas is compiled with mercurium which links with the Nanos runtime hence forming a task-graph based on dependencies available for scheduling. This is scheduled in a appropriate way depending on the target archiecture and uses the OpenCL runtime as a backend for executing the tasks in a data-parallel fashion. The Integration works well with both Data/Task parallel execution model of OpenCL but our focus in the paper would be on data parallel execution as OpenCL task parallel model poorly uses the compute hardware. The key aspect is that GPU hardware is very unfriendly to exploitation of pure task-level parallellism thereby using a single compute unit of the hardware for execution which produces huge performance penalties. Whereas in CPUs, the concept of Device Fission [13] can make way to use task parallel execution model over the entire hardware. To make our integration more robust and competent, device fission or device partitioning of CPUs have also been exercised into the OmpSs-OpenCL programming model. With this we try to offer the programmer a straightfoward way to exploit heterogeneous architecture supporting code portability, reusability and with minimal development time. This work will benefit the programmer to have no knowledge of OpenCL programming constructs and program in conventional way. In this paper we discuss the details of integrating OpenCL with OmpSs programming model and demonstrate how this proposed approach liberates the programmer from laborious development process.

The paper is divided into seven sections. In the Section 2 we give a overview of the OpenCL programming API. Following that in Section 3, we discuss the OmpSs programming model developed at BSC and its key features. In section 4, integration of OpenCL with OmpSs is discussed in detail, giving insight to Nanos-OpenCL execution and memory model. Section 5 demonstrates our evaluation of the plaform with key benchmarks followed by an insight into task parallel OmpSs-OpenCL performance in section 6. Section 7 concludes the paper and discusses possible extensions to this work.

2 OpenCL Overview

OpenCL (Open Computing Language), a Open standard parallel pragramming model introduced by khronos to provide protability and code reusability across heterogeneous plaforms (DSP Processors,CPUs and GPUs)[8]. Its a cross platform programming language with a robust API capable of doing data parallel and task parallel computations across various architectures. It encloses a hierarchy comprising of the platform model, memory model, execution model and programming model[8]. The design essentially is a classical host-client system with a host and others considered as OpenCL devices. The OpenCL devices are further divided into compute units and they are directed by the commands from the Host to do the computations. The computations executed on the compute units is fundamentally the portion of the application(kernel code) which needs to be accelerated.

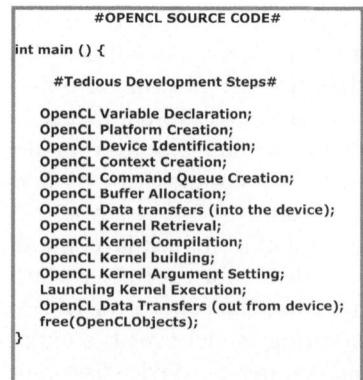
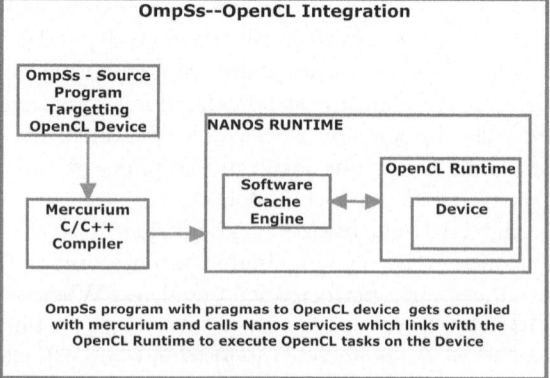

Fig. 1. OpenCL Programing model and OmpSs-OpenCL Integration Perspective

This design involves several complicated steps as shown in figure 1 inorder to execute the kernel in any heterogeneous device. To start with, first the OpenCL platform is created and the device is identified and then corresponding context is created for the device with command queues. All the data transfers have to be accomplished with creation of OpenCL data buffers in the devices. The key aspect of portability here is the kernel code is being compiled and built at runtime [8] to create a executable for the corresponding device (GPU or CPU). Further it is required to set the corresponding kernel arguments for the kernel object created. Then the kernel is enqueued for execution using clEnqueueNDRangeKernel – Data Parallel Launch or clEnqueueTask – Task Parallel launch. This eventually makes the development more tedious and demanding leaving alone the performance optimization. Our contribution largely addresses this issue with OpenCL programming. The integration of OpenCL with OmpSs makes the development process a lot more simpler and subsequently writing a sequential program with added pragmas. OmpSs programming model developed at BSC is a combination of openMP and StarSs which is elaborated in the following section. Due to page constraints, we have provided reference links at appropriate places which covers the details of Language design and in depth explanation for the various concepts of OpenCL.

3   OmpSs-OpenCL Model

OmpSs is an adaptation of OpenMP with extensions based on the StarSs programming model[3]. It was designed to simplify programming for heterogeneous architectures using a unified development framework comprising the Mercurium compiler and the Nanos runtime. The OmpSs model currently encompasses the feature set provided by SMPSs[3], CellSs and GpuSs[7], each of which was developed keeping a specific architecture in mind. Since OpenCL offers cross platform portability and is starting to be recognized by multiple hardware vendors as a viable programming model for the future, we extend and integrate OmpSs with OpenCL to leverage on it. A brief perspective of the integration is shown in figure 1. The OmpSs-OpenCL plaform follows the similar style of representation along with its previous feature sets. The parallel regions of the application are expressed in the form annotated pragmas which are considered to be Tasks by the model. The syntax of specifying the task includes the target device for execution and the neccessary data required for it execution.

```
#pragma omp target device [clauses]
#pragma omp task [clauses]
The list of main clauses is the following:
    input ([list of parameters])
    output ([list of parameters])
    inout ([list of parameters])
```

The clauses to be specified for target device should be OpenCL Device (CPUs, GPUs) and for task is essentially the neccessary data transfers as mentioned above. The clauses input, output and inout primarily express the datatype on which the task performs its computation along with size of data required. In addition their can be as many tasks as possible (eg: iterative task calls (same kernel code)) and as many number of task type (eg: multiple tasks with different kernel code)). A example code of a OmpSs-OpenCL program is mentioned below with 2 kernel calls (vector add (data parallel) and vector sub (task parallel)).

```
#include <stdio.h>
#pragma omp target device (opencl-cpu) copydeps /* Target a
    OpenCL Device (CPU/GPU) */
#pragma omp task input ([size] A) output( [size] B) /* Input/
    Output Parameters for the Task/Kernel  */
void vec_Add(float *A, float *B)

#pragma omp target device (opencl-cpu) copydeps /* Target a
    OpenCL Device (CPU/GPU) */
#pragma omp task input ([size] A) output( [size] B) /* Input/
    Output Parameters for the Task/Kernel  */
void vec_Sub(float *A, float *B, int size)

int main(int argc, char** argv)
{
    int size  = 512;
    double *A;               /**< Array of random numbers */
    double *B;               /**< Array of random numbers */
    A = (double*)malloc(size  * sizeof(double));
    B = (double*)malloc(size  * sizeof(double));
    for(int j = 0; j < size; j++)
      a[j] = rand();     /* Initialize with random values */
    vec_Add (a,b);        /* Calling Vector addition (OpenCL
        Kernel Call)*/
    vec_Sub (a,b,size); /* Calling Vector subtraction (OpenCL
        Kernel call ) */
    #pragma omp taskwait /* Wait for tasks to finish
        Execution */
    return 0;
}
/* OpenCL Data-Parallel Kernel Code*/
__kernel void vec_Add ( __global double * A, __global double
    * B)
{
  int I = get_global_id(0);
    B[I] = A[I] + A[I];
}
/* OpenCL Task-Parallel Kernel Code*/
__kernel void vec_Sub ( __global double * A, __global double
    * B, __const int size)
{
  for (int i = 0; i<size; i++)
    B[i] = A[i] - 4.0;
}
```

The task here is fundamentally the OpenCL kernel, coded according to the OpenCL C99 standard[8] with the appropriate parameters matching with the task data clauses. As we can see above the vector add kernel is written in data parallel style whereas vector sub in task parallel. This is being highlighted here to show that programmer needs basic understanding of the architecture and OpenCL execution model to write data parallel kernels to harness the hardware in the best posssible way. While for task-parallel kernels, the developer needs to have no knowledge of the hardware and is similar to sequential execution(uses single compute unit) with almost no OpenCL constructs hence with understandable performance loses with task parallel model. Moreover the OpenCL kernel can be written in a separate file (for eg .cl file) and can be passed as a command line argument during compilation (multiple .cl files incase of multiple tasks). This annotated sequential program above is compiled by mercurium and generates executable with coresponding calls to the Nanos runtime. Along with this, mercurium makes sure the correctness of the specification and also passing the kernel code to the runtime for compilation. From here the Nanos runtime using the OpenCL data/task execution model tries to bring about the best possible parallel execution of tasks on the device. In the interest of better utilization of hardware for OpenCL task parallelism model we have also integrated the concept of device fission wherein the hardware is divided into multiple sub-devices each capable of running independent OpenCL kernels. The details of the integration with Nanos and mechanisms used for data/task parallelism are explained in the next section.

4   Nanos - OpenCL Model

Nanos is the asynchronous runtime environment used in OmpSs. It is based on a thread-pool execution model where the master thread coordinates and manages multiple slave threads. The executable generated by the compiler includes embedded calls that invoke different runtime services in Nanos for execution. Some of the key services provided by the Nanos runtime include task creation, dependency graph generation, memory transfer management and kernel execution management. Task creation service is responsible for creation and addition of task description to each of new tasks (typical example of descriptions include updating the target device, execution state, copy data information etc.). Following this, dependency graph generation service is responsible for generating the data dependency graph based on the task clauses specified in the application. Once the dependency graph is constructed, data dependencies are tracked and requests are sent to the software cache engine when appropriate to initiate the necessary transfers. Based on the dependency graph flow the task is set to be available for execution and is moved to the ready queue. The slave threads pick up tasks from the ready queue (on the basis of a specified scheduling algorithm) for execution. The slave threads use OpenCL runtime calls to execute the tasks. The integration is diagramatically described in figure 3.

The baseline Nanos runtime environment supports three modes namely Performance, Debug and Instrumentation. Environment variables can be used to choose between any of these modes. Performance mode generally enables application execution in a performance optimal manner. Debug mode is generally used by developers to assist with the identification of issues like memory leaks. Intrumentation mode is used to generate detailed execution traces for further analysis and optimizations. Nanos is linked with instrumentation library paraver[6] inorder to accomplish this. The Nanos-OpenCL model extends support to all the aforementioned modes (with additional support for trace generation to monitor OpenCL runtime activity). In in follwing sub sections we explain how Nanos environment is linked with the OpenCL runtime for doing memory transfers and execution of kernels.

4.1   Execution Model

The master thread as discussed previously is responsible for creating the tasks, generating dependency graph, scheduling tasks for execution and more importantly for creating the OpenCL runtime plaform for Nanos. This happens immediately after the runtime is informed that the tasks are targetted towards an OpenCL device as shown in figure3. Once the platform is created the device is identified and the OpenCL context is created for the corresponding device. The slave thread correspond to a single computing device (eg:1 Nvidia GPU on a board of 4 GPUs) and OpenCL command queues for execution and data transfers are created to the device. In addition to handling execution, the slave threads are responsible for compiling, building and argument setting by calling respective OpenCL calls. The slave thread interact directly with the OpenCL runtime using its constructs. Work flow of slave thread is shown in figure 2. After the slave thread completes execution data is transfered back using OpenCL memory transfer calls initiated by the cache engine and the task state is changed to indicate completion. These data transfers are maintained by the cache engine which keeps detailed track of the inter task depedencies.

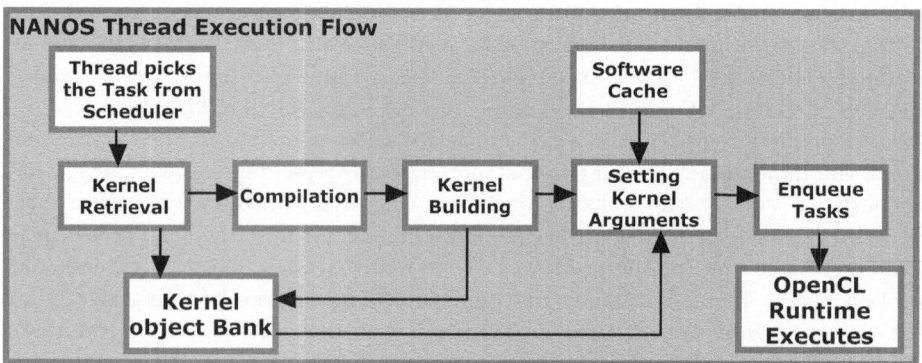

Fig. 2. Nanos Thread Execution Model

4.2   Memory Model

Data dependencies specified using pragmas in the source code help Nanos to maintain a data dependency graph across the tasks. This service in Nanos is managed by the software based cache engine. When a task is created the copy over information is directly sent to the cache engine for each task inorder to maintain the data consistency. Once the task is available in the ready queue, it is ready to be scheduled for execution. The slave thread picks up tasks and send in calls to the cache engine to do the neccessary data transfers prior to slave thread executing its task. The software based cache engine is integrated with the OpenCL runtime and performs allocation of buffers, data transfers using OpenCL runtime calls, for eg clcreatebuffer() to the device memory. The cache engine works with the OpenCL runtime with a separate command queue different from the one being used for launching the kernels by the slave threads, hence making it independent supporting computation-communication overlap. This engine utilizes two different caching strategies: write back and write through. The user can choose any strategy based on the application requirement. Write back policy copies back the data from the device once the application has finished execution so that future tasks can reuse the data hence avoiding unnecessary data transfers whereas write through copies back the data once the task is over. Further the Cache engine also interacts with the slave threads to facililate the OpenCL call of clSetKernelArgs() for each task as shown in figure 3.

4.3   OpenCL Kernel Compilation

The key aspect of OpenCL is the runtime compilation of the kernel and this needs to be carefully handled by the Nanos runtime. With each task that is created it associates a parallel region of the code (kernel code). Since the compiler passes the kernel code to the runtime, each slave thread when picking a task will eventually have the kernel code associated with it. This code is retrived, compiled and build into a kernel object for execution. Incase of compilation failure Nanos throws the corresponding errors in the kernel code (task)to the user asking for debugging. Besides compilation it also tries to vectorize the kernel code for the device architecture (if available with the device package). Once the kernel object is build successfully the slave thread contacts the cache system to set the arguments of the task and eventually enqueue the task for execution. Nanos makes sure that kernel code/task is compiled only once and if repeated or called iteratively, it uses the precompiled kernel hence bypassing compilation. This mechanism is maintained based on the unique kernel name, based on which tasks are built as shown in figure 2. Moreover if multiple slave threads picks the same task(identical kernel code) but with different data addresses (eg: tasks called iteratively with non blocking data) the runtime ensures that only a single thread compiles and the rest locks. After a single thread compiles and builds the other threads use the same kernel object but setting the appropriate kernel arguments for their respective tasks hence maintaining program correctness. Besides this strategy, parallel compilation among mutiple slave threads is achieved when having different tasks with distinct kernel code are scheduled to them.

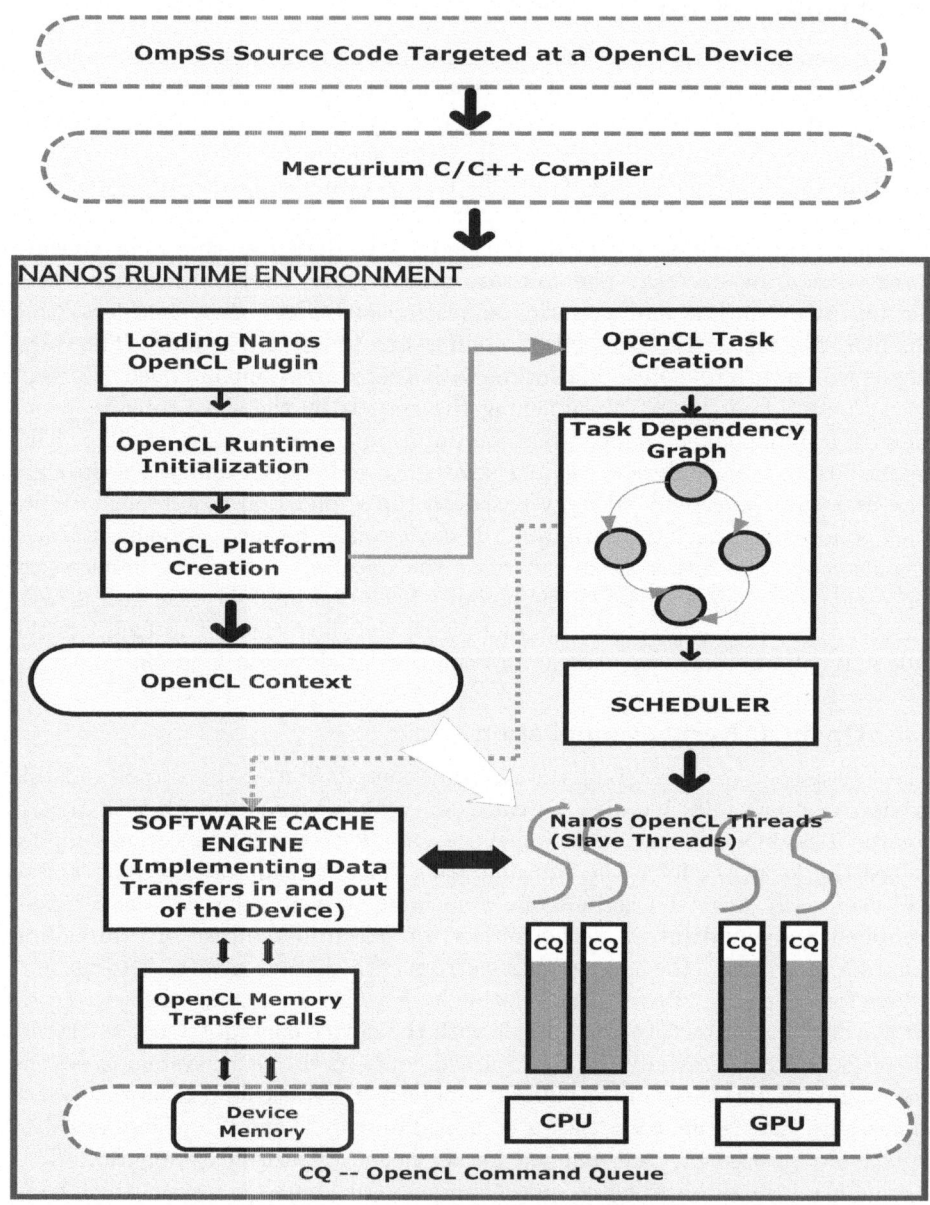

Fig. 3. Nanos-OpenCL Integration - Working Model

4.4   Device Partitioning

By definition the task parallelism offered by OpenCL uses a single OpenCL thread and hence a single compute unit which corresponds to a single core in a multicore architecture. Using clenqueueTask() for executing kernels uses only one core of the multicore machine making it a performance bottleneck. With task-parallel OpenCL behaving in this manner puts forth a hurdle to OmpSs inorder to utilize the machine to its maximum computing power. However, inorder to use all the cores of the system, each logical CPU cores of the system can be visualized into one physical processor which can be implemented using clCreateSubDevices () from OpenCL API extensions at runtime. This call can be used to partition the device into mutiple sub-devices. This allows tasks to run parallel in different sub-devices and hence providing an oppurtunity to utilize them better. Moreover device partitioning can be done inorder to use the computational resources in a much better way, enabling task parallelism being one, this feature also helps in partitioning the device based on cache sharing to leaverage data sharing and to reuse data[13]. This concept is implemented in Nanos creating sub-devices (based on cache, affinity and count) equal to the number of slave threads instantiated which can be expressed by the user as a environment variable. Each slave thread is associated to a command queue and with device partitioning feature we associate both to each sub-device. With this each slave thread enqueues tasks using its own command queue to its associated sub device. Consequently we try to use all the available cores of the device maintaining data synchrocy among the different sub-devices. This is similar in spirit to concurrent kernel execution across the multiple cores in the machine. This scheme tries to use the all the available cores and hence making the runtime more scalable. In addition it also helps to keep the user away from the tedious process of creating subdevices and programming accordingly. However this techinique is still in development stage with many hardware vendors and it is implemented as an OpenCL extension construct in the current OpenCL packages. To add to this it does not work with GPUs at all which makes it hard to do an extensive analysis of its behaviour with CPUs and GPUs in this paper and we continue our focus on the evelution of data parallel OmpSs with key benchmarks in the next section. Further we also try giving a glimpse to task parallel OmpSs performance in section 6.

5   Evaluation

We evaluate our runtime system by analyzing different benchmarks with a OmpSs version against a standard OpenCL one. The OmpSs version follows sequential programming style with annotated pragmas targetting OpenCL device. This inturn uses the Nanos runtime for executing the parallel region (kernel code). We compare the execution time of OmpSs and with the original OpenCL data parallel version. We have found comparable performance with greater ease in programmability. The benchmarks were run with different problems sizes to check scalability and also experimented with multi-kernel application. The benchmarks launch kernels in data parallel model using clEnqueueNDRangeKernel with globalworksize, localworksize and work dimensions for each kernel mentioned as a command line argument by the user, as the programmer only knows the way in which the kernel has been coded.

We have carried out our investigation in both GPUs and CPUs machines. Our CPU platform, 2 Intel Xeon CPU E5649 at 2.53GHz (12 CPU Cores/Open-CLCompute Units) and a Nvidia Tesla M2090 (20 OpenCLcomputeUnits), the GPU platform. In the CPU we use OpenCL 1.1(Intel Implementation with Auto-vectorization), however in GPU OpenCL version 1.0(Nvidia implementation) is used. Mercurium and Nanos-OpenCL runtime were retained to be the same version for both the machines. Moreover, In both the systems Nanos was confined to performance mode so as to experience maximum optimizations in executing tasks.

5.1   Benchmarks

We choose to experiment the platform using five benchmarks from various computing domains. Typical double precision dense matrix multiplication of two square matrices with varying problem size. With growing use of GPUs in scientific computing we decided to use N-Body simulation and Convolution as a benchmark for our comparison. Likewise Black scholes algorithm measuring option pricing from financial engineering is also taken for study. Further Stream benchmark with 4 different kernels namely copy-task, scale-task, triad-task and add-task doing respective vector operations with varying sizes were used to study the runtime system. Also Blocked matrix multiplication is also used to express the advantages of the nanos runtime system.

NBody simulation works with a large number of particles and in OmpSs version we create a task for all particles. OmpSs and OpenCL GPU/CPU versions are almost indistinguishable even with increase in number of particles. OmpSs version of Normal Matrix Multiplication is alike the OpenCL verision with the kernel specified as a task. The execution of a single task(kernel) completes the multiplication. OmpSs verision initialize the matrix and call the task/kernel and the rest of the process is carried out by nanos. We can see in the graph (figure 4) that for the GPU version the difference in execution time is very negligible and CPU version offering almost 90 % or more matching performance compared with the original OpenCL code. Whereas the blocked version of matrix multiplication, creates multiple tasks based on the block size with the initial tasks providing the data for latter tasks to work upon thereby benefitting on having lesser data communication. Interestingly, this can be expressed in a partitioned manner with plenty of independent data parallel tasks which makes nanos to best utilize the hardware. As we can notice blocked Matrix Mutiplication offers much better performance compared to the normal OpenCL matmul version used in the previous normal matmul example. This is predominately because the tasks are created for specified blocked data and allowing the asynchronous task parallel Nanos system[3] to take advantage hence saving on data transfer time which can be evidently seen with GPU results. This needs some effort from the programmer to understand the algorithm and partition accordingly and the remaining is well anchored by the Nanos runtime presenting better performance. In addition, this better performance is also because of the cache engine which transfers the data to the device before the task needs it. This can be realized by

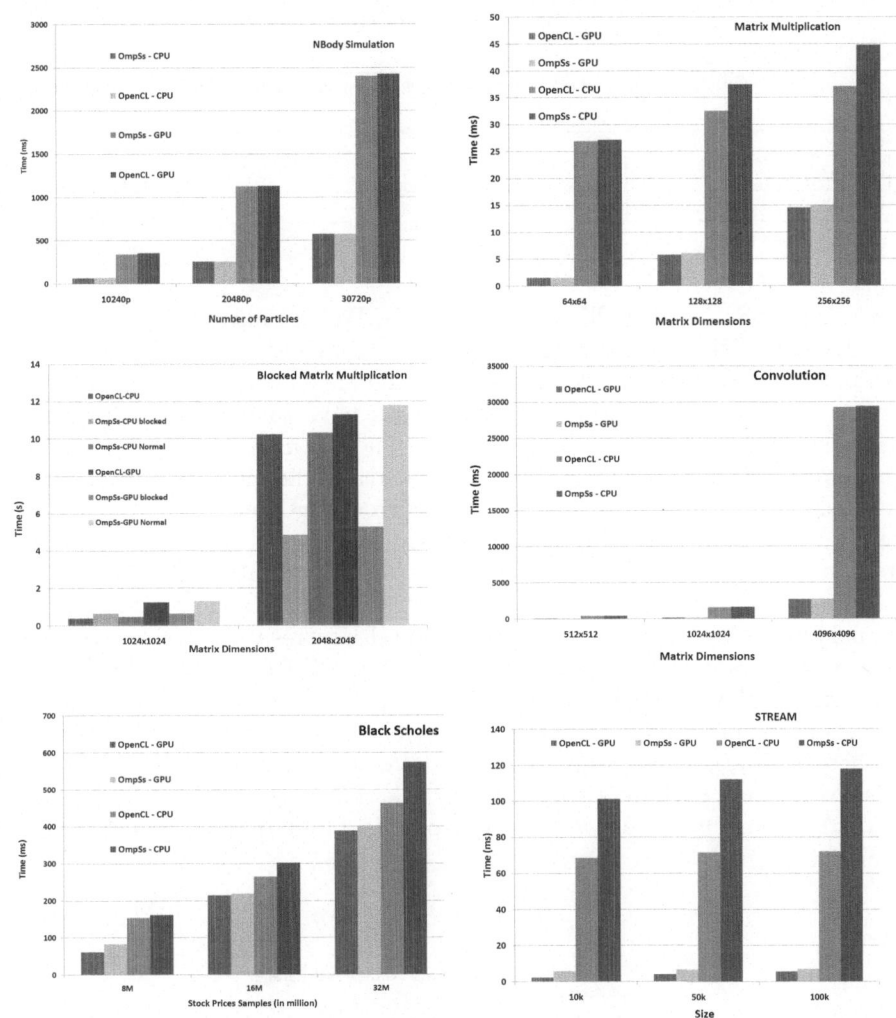

Fig. 4. Evaluation of OmpSs against OpenCL on CPUs and GPUs

having data transfers and kernel launches enqueued in different queues to make it overlapped and asynchronous. This method of partitioning data and writing OmpSs source code with many tasks transforms into runtime optimizations can be seen in the graph in figure 4. With increasing problem sizes which is with more tasks (independent data) and the OmpSs blocked version outperforms the original OpenCL version with both having identical kernel codes.

Black scholes iterates over the sample stock prices to find a optimum pricing. A task is created for the entire stock prices and the kernel is run, calculating the option pricing using floating point operations. As we can see the graph(figure 4) shows the difference is very small till 16 million stock prices and almost a second

Table 1. Lines of code

Benchmark	Matmul	Nbody	BlackScholes	Convolution	Stream	Blocked MatMul
Original OpenCL	298	308	364	312	485	298
OmpSs	51	71	58	68	87	81

slower is OmpSs for 32 million for the CPUs. We can also notice that OmpSs and OpenCL GPU versions performs almost identically.

OmpSs Stream benchmark consist of 4 different tasks doing different vector operations. This implies that 4 OmpSs tasks have to created with their descriptions and the dependency across them. These constitute majorly the nanos overhead time and hence we can see irrespective of the increase in problem size the execution time of OmpSs doesn't seem to change much as the overhead is because of the nanos task creation and dependency graph generation. In Convolution, a maskinput matrix is kept constant(65X65) for all 3 different problems sizes. From the graph (figure 4) we can see that OmpSs is almost equivalent with original OpenCL version for both CPUs and GPUs irrespective of problem sizes.

From this evaluation we can say OmpSs-OpenCL integration offers satisfactory results with very less time spent on development. An insight into the number of lines of code programmed for these benchmarks is shown in table 1. As we can see there is almost 5 fold decrease in lines of code in all applications for OmpSs verision. Stream benchmark with 4 different kernels makes the best difference in lines of code for OmpSs as we need not compile, build, do data transfer and set arguments for 4 different kernels.

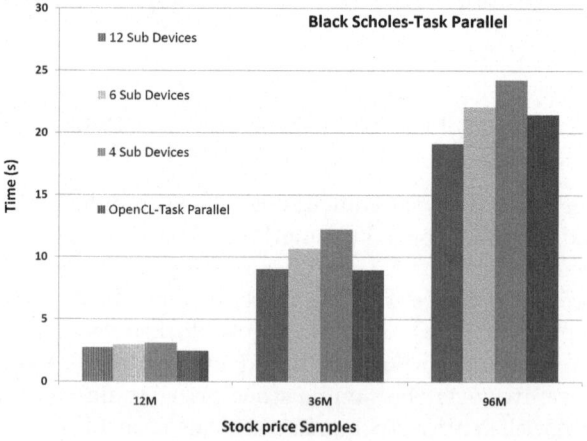

Fig. 5. Evaluation of Task-Parallel OpenCL with OmpSs Device Fissioned verision

6 Task-Parallel OpenCL

An experiment with task parallelism offered by OpenCL was done with black scholes application as is easy to partition with no inter data dependence. The sample stock prices where partitioned across different subdevices and task parallel kernels where launched on each sub device. The graph (figure 5) shows the execution time for each of the problem size and number of subdevices on the Intel 12 Core Xeon machine. This is compared with the original task-parallel OpenCL verision. Black scholes performs well with 12 subdevices on bigger problem size as the overhead involved in creation of subdevices and its corresponding nanos thread creation undermines the performance of 4,6 subdevices. With 12 count partitioning each sub device will be a single core processor and we use the complete CPU machine for the benchmark hence we can achieve better performance with bigger problem sizes. On the whole we can conclude that with increase in problem size and more subdevices, faster is the application. Our analysis of device fission for task parallel OpenCL is superficial as this is still under development with many vendors and is yet to be supported by GPUs. With the current software development scenario strongly adopting data parallel OpenCL model our results focus more on the OmpSs-OpenCL data parallel model.

7 Related Work

With hetergeneous computing coming into main stream research, several research groups and industry labs are involved in developing better programming models. OpenCL a open source programming API targetted at various architectures have inclined researchers to investigate deeper into the model aiming for better performance. In [10] a static partitioning of data parallel task are carried out for hetergeneous arhitecture. Based on prediction a portable partitioning scheme is proposed for dividing data parallel tasks for GPUs. Similarly [12] the data parallel tasks are dynamically schdeuled to a CPU or GPU based on the contention state (metadata during runtime) and historical data (during profiling). In [11] talks about Hybrid OpenCL for distributed computing. The paper proposes the combined use of OpenCL and MPI for multiple node architecture. Further in [9] supports OpenCL execution with a software cache for architectures with no cache(CELL processor). Summarizing, we find that researchers have restricted themselves to the data parallel OpenCL model and have neglected to address the laborious development time involved in it. Our approach mainly reduces the strenuous programming process in OpenCL targetting Data/Task-based OpenCL execution model.

8 Conclusion and Future Work

In this paper we propose an approach to integrate OmpSs and OpenCL programming models with an emphasis on reducing programmer effort and improving code portability and reusability. OpenCL programming model which is widely adopted as an industry standard provides a portable platform for programming heterogeneous architectures but falls short when it comes to programmability (Lot of effort is required). We present the integration of OpenCL with OmpSs programming model which can help eliminate the laborious programming process by empowering programmers with simple annotated pragmas. The approach is to use data parallel OpenCL model with asynchronous Nanos runtime system which takes advantage of the hardware. We also discuss interactions between Nanos runtime environment and OpenCL in detail. Our experiments show comparable performance with programs written only using OpenCL thereby making a strong case for using OmpSs-OpenCL model. We believe that current industry trends hold lot of promise for the proposed approach. With OpenCL 1.2 release supporting device partitioning, it would be possible to execute different tasks in each core of the machine and realize concurrent kernel execution in CPUs. In the GPU domain, product roadmaps predict GPUs with concurrent execution features by the end of the year thereby creating demand for robust programming models that offer good performance and reduces development effort. As part of future work we plan to extend the model to support multiple devices (both CPUs and GPUs) and run simultaneous tasks using both data and task parallel opencl model on hetergeneous plaforms with effective scheduling strategies.

Acknowledgement. We thankfully acknowledge the support of the European Commission through the TERAFLUX project (FP7-249013) and the HiPEAC-2 Network of Excellence (FP7/ICT 217068),the support of the Spanish Ministry of Education (TIN2007-60625, CSD2007-00050 and FI program) and the Generalitat de Catal unya (2009-SGR-980).

References

1. OpenCL programming, http://www.khronos.org/registry/cl/specs/OpenCL-1.1.pdf
2. Duran, A., Ayguadé, E., Badia, R.M., et al.: OmpSs: a Proposal for Programming Heterogeneous Multi-Core Architectures. Parallel Processing Letters, 173–193 (2011)
3. Perez, J.M., Badia, R.M., Labarta, J.: Handling task dependencies under strided and aliased references. In: Proceeding ICS 2010 Proceedings of the 24th ACM International Conference on Supercomputing (2010)
4. CUDA Programming, http://developer.download.nvidia.com/compute/cuda/4_0/toolkit/docs/CUDA_C_programming_Guide.pdf
5. CELL Programming HandBook, https://www-01.ibm.com/chips/techlib/techlib.nsf/techdocs/1741C509C5F64B3300257460006FD68D/$file/CellBE_PXCell_Handbook_v1.11_12May08_pub.pdf
6. Parallel Program Visualization and Analysis Tool, http://www.bsc.es/media/1364.pdf
7. Ayguadé, E., Badia, R.M., Igual, F.D., Labarta, J., Mayo, R., Quintana-Ortí, E.S.: An Extension of the StarSs Programming Model for Platforms with Multiple GPUs. In: Sips, H., Epema, D., Lin, H.-X. (eds.) Euro-Par 2009. LNCS, vol. 5704, pp. 851–862. Springer, Heidelberg (2009)

8. Munshi, A., Gaster, B.R., Mattson, T.G., Fung, J., Ginsburg, D.: OpenCL Programming Guide, 1st edn. Addison-Wesley Professional (July 25, 2011) ISBN-10: 0321749642
9. Lee, J., et al.: An OpenCL framework for heterogeneous multicores with local memory. In: Proceedings of the 19th International Conference on Parallel Architectures and Compilation Techniques, PACT (2010)
10. Grewe, D., O'Boyle, M.F.P.: A Static Task Partitioning Approach for Heterogeneous Systems Using OpenCL. In: Knoop, J. (ed.) CC 2011. LNCS, vol. 6601, pp. 286–305. Springer, Heidelberg (2011)
11. Aoki, R., et al.: Hybrid OpenCL: Enhancing OpenCL for Distributed Processing. In: Parallel and Distributed Processing with Applications, ISPA (2011)
12. Gregg, C., et al.: Contention-Aware Scheduling of Parallel Code for Heterogeneous Systems. In: Poster at HotPar 2010 (2010)
13. http://software.intel.com/en-us/articles/opencl-device-fission-for-cpu-performance/

Compiler Optimizations for Industrial Unstructured Mesh CFD Applications on GPUs*

C. Bertolli[1], A. Betts[1], N. Loriant[1], G.R. Mudalige[2], D. Radford[5], D.A. Ham[1,4], M.B. Giles[2,3], and P.H.J. Kelly[1]

[1] Dept. of Computing, Imperial College London
{c.bertolli,a.betts,n.loriant,david.ham,p.kelly}@imperial.ac.uk
[2] Oxford e-Research Centre, University of Oxford
gihan.mudalige@oerc.ox.ac.uk
[3] Mathematical Institute, University of Oxford
mike.giles@maths.ox.ac.uk
[4] Grantham Institute for Climate Change, Imperial College London
[5] Rolls Royce Plc.
David.Radford@Rolls-Royce.com

Abstract. Graphical Processing Units (GPUs) have shown acceleration factors over multicores for structured mesh-based Computational Fluid Dynamics (CFD). However, the value remains unclear for dynamic and irregular applications. Our motivating example is HYDRA, an unstructured mesh application used in production at Rolls-Royce for the simulation of turbomachinery components of jet engines. We describe three techniques for GPU optimization of unstructured mesh applications: a technique able to split a highly complex loop into simpler loops, a kernel specific alternative code synthesis, and configuration parameter tuning. Using these optimizations systematically on HYDRA improves the GPU performance relative to the multicore CPU. We show how these optimizations can be automated in a compiler, through user annotations. Performance analysis of a large number of complex loops enables us to study the relationship between optimizations and resource requirements of loops, in terms of registers and shared memory, which directly affect the loop performance.

Keywords: Computational Fluid Dynamics, Unstructured Meshes, Graphical Processing Units, Compilers.

1 Introduction

Unstructured mesh (or grid) applications are widely used in Computational Fluid Dynamics (CFD) simulations when complex geometries are involved. They achieve

---

* This research is partly funded by EPSRC (grant reference numbers EP/I00677X/1, EP/I006079/1), the UK Technology Strategy Board, and Rolls Royce plc through the SILOET programme. The authors gratefully acknowledge Rolls-Royce plc for providing financial support toward this research and for giving permission to publish this paper.

H. Kasahara and K. Kimura (Eds.): LCPC 2012, LNCS 7760, pp. 112–126, 2013.
© Springer-Verlag Berlin Heidelberg 2013

a higher degree of correctness by enabling critical components of the geometry to be finely discretized.

This comes at the cost of increased difficulty in achieving high memory system utilization. In structured mesh applications, compilers can leverage the topology of the mesh which is explicit in the program structure. In contrast, in unstructured mesh applications, the mesh topology is not known at compile-time. It may include elements (e.g. triangular faces) of widely different sizes to reflect the modeller's interest in specific sections of the geometry, and consequentially the adjacency relationship is non-uniform. To support this flexibility, implementations depend on indirections between adjacent mesh elements, which prevent many structured mesh compiler optimizations. A typical instance of this behaviour is when a program visits all edges of the mesh and accesses data associated to vertices. To do so, it uses a *mapping* between edges and vertices, which represents the grid structure itself and expresses a non-affine access to arrays holding mesh data.

In this paper we consider a motivating example – HYDRA, an unstructured mesh finite-volume CFD application used at Rolls Royce for the simulation of inner turbomachinery components of jet engines. It consists of 50,000 lines of code, including more than 1,000 parallel loops over the mesh, and it supports the simulation of a wide range of CFD problems, including linear, non-linear and adjoint cases.

Our research aim is the acceleration of HYDRA through both strong and weak scaling, i.e. decreasing simulation times and increasing the size of the geometries modelled. For this purpose, HYDRA has been modified to use our unstructured mesh library, called OP2, which is supported by a compiler and run-time library. OP2 supports a wide range of architectures, including clusters of CPUs and GPUs. In this paper we focus on the acceleration of HYDRA on a single GPU node.

In a preliminary optimization phase, we studied the performance of HYDRA on a single multicore node using MPI, against that of a single GPU node. Our results showed that a baseline GPU implementation, featuring only standard unstructured mesh optimizations, is not sufficient to achieve performance comparable to the execution on a single CPU. To improve this situation, we identified pathological patterns in the HYDRA code. We used three optimizations to address those patterns: loop fission, an improved colouring strategy, and loop-specific tuning of partition size and CUDA thread block size. We applied these optimizations manually to four specific loops of HYDRA having low performance on a GPU. These results are shown in Figure 1: the execution of HYDRA on Intel Westmere and Sandybridge processors, using different numbers of cores using MPI, are compared to execution on an NVIDIA Fermi C2070.

In this paper we build on the experience and techniques gathered from our preliminary optimization steps. The described optimizations are automated in the compiler by extending the OP2 language with annotations. These are used by the programmer to signal the compiler that the optimizations can be applied to the annotated loops. This reduced significantly the compiler design complexity,

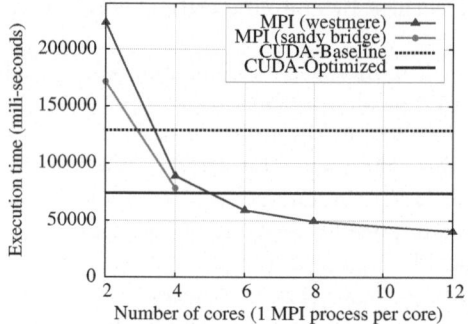

Fig. 1. Comparison of HYDRA performance on single CPU and GPU. The starting point for this paper is the lower, manually-optimised performance.

as it does not need to analyze the entire user kernel code, but only the loop parameters and annotations.

As the described optimizations are composable for the same loop, the compiler is given tools to select the best combination of optimizations to be applied to each loop. We take a step forward understanding what (composition of) optimizations actually deliver better performance. By taking advantage of the large number of complex OP2 loops available in HYDRA, we can put the performance improvement due to optimizations into relation with the loop features, and their resource requirements for GPUs. This represents a key step towards a fully-automatic optimizing compiler for unstructured mesh applications. The contributions of this paper are the following:

– We present an annotation-based scheme that allows our compiler to split complex loops over unstructured meshes in a way that optimises effective use of shared memory.
– We present performance analysis for this and other optimisations, separately and in combination, on a wide variety of OP2 loops from a substantial application case study.
– From this experimental work we characterise the properties of loops that most impact their performance. We show how OP2's access descriptors, in combination with quantitative compile-time metrics of shared-memory and register requirements, can be used to determine where these optimisations are valid and profitable.

2   Related Work

A huge literature exists related to optimisations for unstructured grid applications, or, in more general terms, for irregular applications. Most optimizations attempt to improve data locality through mesh renumbering, with the goal of improving cache usage (e.g. [1, 2]). Our run-time library is currently able to use either PT-Scotch [3], and METIS [4]. However, the performance results shown in this paper is based on well-ordered meshes. The optimisations that we present do not require the analysis of the iteration order, and they are based on input program transformations, alternative code syntheses, and run-time tuning.

The optimization strategy that we aim at developing shares similar goals with the work presented by Strout et al. in [5]. This introduces a framework for composing optimisations for irregular applications, where examples of such optimisations include iteration and data re-ordering, and loop tiling. The framework enables modelling of optimizations at compile-time in terms of undefined functions, which are then applied at run-time by analysing the mesh in the *inspection phase*. The result of the mesh inspection is the instantiation of the loop *execution phase*, with improved performance as a consequence of optimisations. The compiler framework allows sound composition of the undefined optimization functions, effectively providing an abstraction for composing optimizations.

A number of development projects include elegant abstractions for parallel computing on unstructured meshes using MPI. The most prominent research effort targeting intra-node parallelisation is theg Liszt project [6], which has many similarities with our work. Liszt is a domain specific language for programming unstructured mesh applications, and it targets performance portability across multiple different architectures. Unlike the OP2 compiler, the Liszt compiler synthesizes stencil information by analyzing user kernels, with the aim of applying platform-specific optimizations. Performance results from a range of systems (GPU, multi-core CPU, and MPI based cluster) executing a number of applications written using Liszt have been presented in [6]. We are not aware of any industrial applications developed using Liszt.

3   The OP2 Library

In this section we give a brief description of the mesh abstraction that is exposed by OP2, and we relate it to its user interface. The reader is invited to refer to [7, 8] for a full description of the interface. A mesh is modelled as a graph and it includes a collection of interconnected sets. In a typical CFD program, the mesh includes the following sets: edges, vertices, and cells. A set is a programming abstraction of the OP2 library (op_set) and it is used to build an iteration space. To declare an op_set, the user is provided with the op_decl_set call, which requires the iteration space cardinality (or size), i.e. the number of elements in the set.

The connectivity between sets expresses the mesh topology, and it specifies how a generic element of a set maps to elements in another set. For instance, the user can specify for each edge what are the incident vertices. This translates in OP2 with the op_map data structure and with a call for declaring it (op_decl_map). The call takes as input: the *from* and *to* sets of the mapping; the arity (or dimension) of the mapping, i.e. the number of elements in the *to* associated to each element in the *from* set (this number must be homogeneous for all mapped elements); an array of indices implementing the mapping.

Data in OP2 is associated to mesh sets. A dataset associates a tuple to each element of a set, and is abstracted in OP2 through the op_dat data structure

```
1    @op_inc_id(v1Data, v2Data)
2    void incrVertices (double * eData, double * v1Data, double * v2Data) {
3      ...
4      *v1Data += t;
5      *v2Data += t;
6    }
7    op_par_loop (incrVertices, edges,
8      op_arg_dat (edgeData, -1, OP_ID, OP_READ),
9      op_arg_dat (vertData, 0, edges2Verts, OP_INC),
10     op_arg_dat (vertData, 1, edges2Verts, OP_INC));
```

Fig. 2. Example of user kernel and OP2 op_par_loop. The first line is an annotation extension which we will describe in Section 4.

and declared with the op_decl_dat function. This function takes as input the set to which the op_dat is associated, the cardinality (or dimension) of the tuples (i.e. the number of data items associated to each set element, that must be homogeneous), and the array of tuples. For instance, an op_dat contains the 3D spatial coordinates for each vertex.

In OP2, computation is expressed through parallel loops, which apply a user-programmed kernels to all elements of a chosen iteration op_set. An example of a user kernel, which reads data associated to an edge and modifies the data associated with the two connected vertices, is illustrated in Figure 2. We also show the related op_par_loop call, expressing the application of the user kernel to all edges. The first two arguments of the op_par_loop are the user kernel and the iteration set. Then, the user is required to specify how datasets are accessed to instantiate actual arguments for the user kernel. For this purpose, the op_par_loop takes as input further arguments (called op_args), one for each parameter of the user kernel. For each op_arg, the user specifies:

- The dataset, or op_dat, from which the actual argument is to be retrieved (first parameter).
- If the dataset is associated with the iteration set (edges in Figure 2), then no indirection is necessary. In this case the second and third parameters assume the values -1 and OP_ID. For a given iteration, the dataset is accessed *directly* using the iteration identifier.
- If the dataset is associated to a set different from the iteration set, then an op_map is needed. The third parameter is a reference to the op_map to be used to translate iteration set identifiers to op_dat associated set identifiers. The second parameter is an integer specifying which mapped element is to be considered. For instance, for the mapping from edges to vertices the user has to specify 0 or 1, to address the first or second vertex associated to each edge.
- The access modality: read (OP_READ), write (OP_WRITE), increment (OP_INC), read and write (OP_RW). The user kernel must reflect the access modality expressed for the op_par_loop parameters.

This information is called the access descriptor and it exposes the loop's data-access pattern to the OP2 compiler. It is important to notice that an access descriptor implicitly contains information related to the cardinality of the involved op_dat and the arity of the op_map used (if any). This information is extracted by the compiler by analysing op_dat and op_map declarations, and can be used to compute the memory requirements for a specific iteration of an op_par_loop.

To maximise parallelism for op_par_loops, OP2 assumes that the loop iteration ordering does not influence the final result. Some combinations of access descriptors, i.e. when indirectly modifying a dataset, might incur data races if not properly controlled. The OP2 implementation guarantees data race avoidance when incrementing (OP_INC) a dataset accessed indirectly. For all other cases (OP_WRITE, OP_RW) it is responsibility of the user to express parallelism control by constructing and, if necessary, partitioning the mesh to ensure no conflicts exist.

3.1   Compiler and Run-Time Support

The current implementation of OP2 includes: a source-to-source translator that implements a OP2 program to multiple target languages, such as CUDA, OpenMP, OpenCL and MPI; a run-time library which performs unstructured mesh optimizations, such as mesh partitioning and coloring (see below). We give a description of the CUDA implementation of OP2.

For GPUs, the size of the mesh is constrained to be small enough to fit entirely within the GPU's memory. This means that for non-distributed memory implementations (i.e. single node) data transfer only happens at the time of data declaration, and possibly at the end of the computation. For CUDA, the compiler parallelizes an op_par_loop by partitioning its iteration set and assigning each partition to a Streaming Multiprocessor (SM)[1]. In this section we discuss two main features of the implementation: coalescing memory accesses and a coloring strategy to prevent data races. The implementation distinguishes between op_par_loops that use at least one op_map, called indirect loops, and those that do not, called direct loops.

For direct op_par_loops, we partition the iteration set in chunks of the same size, and each thread in a CUDA block works on at most $\lceil \frac{n}{m} \rceil$ elements of the partition, where m and n are the sizes of the thread block and partition. Observe that this execution model is sufficient to avoid data races because, by definition, none of the data is accessed indirectly and therefore each thread can only update data belonging to its iteration set elements. The main concern is to avoid non-coalesced accesses into device memory. This is achieved by staging data between device memory and the shared memory, in two stages. (1) Before the user kernel executes, any dataset read whose cardinality per set element exceeds one is brought into the shared memory. The rationale behind this is that unary data will be accessed during execution through a naturally coalesced transfer. (2) After the user kernel, any modified dataset is moved back from shared into device memory.

For indirect op_par_loops, we chose a different strategy, where we distinguish between op_dats accessed directly or indirectly. Indirectly accessed op_dats are staged between device and shared memory. The data can be scattered in the device memory because of mappings, even if proper renumbering algorithms are used to minimise the dispersion of data. For contiguos regions, memory accesses are coalesced. The stage in phase coalesces device memory data into shared memory locations mapping successive memory addresses into successive thread identifiers. Directly accessed op_dats are instead left in device memory. This reduces the shared memory requirements for the CUDA kernel and relies on the L1 cache.

Additionally to memory access coalescing, for indirect op_par_loops we need to avoid data races between threads. That is, allowing threads to operate on distinct elements of the iteration set does not guarantee an absence of data dependencies due to indirect accesses, as previously discussed. The implementation is based on *coloring* the iteration set in an inter- and intra-partition fashion to resolve this issue. The inter-partition coloring is used to avoid conflicts between the data shared at partition boundaries. Since the library ensures partitions with the same color do not share elements retrieved through a mapping, these can proceed in parallel. Intra-partition coloring is needed to prevent threads in the same thread block from data race conflicts. In OP2 increments are computed in a fully-parallel way by threads in the same block using local private thread variables. Colors are followed when applying the increments to the shared memory variables, to prevent conflicts.

4   Optimizations

An application programmer writing an OP2 loop is insulated from the details of the implementation on the back-end architectures which OP2 supports. As such, there is no restriction on how many sets, maps and datasets are used in the loop, their size or access pattern. Thus, given specific back-end hardware, the OP2 code transformation framework needs to take into consideration not only how an op_par_loop can be optimized, but also the limitations of the underlying hardware that degrade performance. This is a key issue that we encountered when utilizing OP2 for accelerating HYDRA.

We consider an example loop of HYDRA, called EDGECON, which is representative of the key loops that make up over 90% of the runtime in HYDRA on a GPU. EDGECON computes the gradient contribution on edges, by iterating over edges accessing datasets associated to both edges and vertices (using a mapping from edges to vertices). This scheme is common in CFD code, and its pattern is shown in Figure 2. The input of the loop includes both indirectly and directly accessed op_dats. Each iteration of the loop accesses directly 24 bytes (1 op_dat), and indirectly a total of 544 bytes (10 op_dats). Of these, two op_dats are accessed indirectly and incremented, and their total size is 384 bytes per iteration. As these incremented op_dats are allocated to shared memory and local thread variables, they represent a main source of shared memory and register pressure. The elemental user kernel used by EDGECON is made of 102 double precision floating point operations, and about 200 integer operations. The PGI compiler reports the use of 41 registers per thread, which is larger than the 31 available for double precision on the NVIDIA C2070 GPU. The largest iteration size available for execution is 64, which requires 34KB of shared memory (a Fermi GPU supports 48KB).

From this analysis it can be noted that the loop suffers from two main issues when mapped to a GPU. Firstly, as the partition size is small, the available parallelism within each SM is limited. To improve this, shared-memory requirements need to be reduced. For instance, to employ partitions of 128 iterations, we need to fit all indirectly accessed arguments into shared memory. When the iterations in a same partition do not share any data (i.e. in the worst case), this requires a partition with 64 iterations to use no more than 24KB in shared memory, as the shared memory requirements roughly double with the partition size. Conversely, an effect of high shared memory requirements is a poor CUDA block occupancy. Secondly, the registers required for each iteration are more than the maximum available on a Fermi GPU. This hardware resource shortage prevents the dynamic SM scheduler from allocating all 32 threads per warp.

4.1   Compiler Support for Loop Fission

Loop fission is an effective means to address the high register pressure and high shared memory requirements exhibited in the EDGECON loop. Splitting a loop manually requires the developer to analyze the kernel for valid splitting points and to explicitly refactor the kernel to pass data across sub-kernels. This task is tedious and error-prone.

As discussed, the EDGECON loop follows a widely used loop scheme in unstructured mesh CFD. It iterates over edges of the mesh (line 9) and increments two arguments through an indirection (lines 11 and 12). The user kernel typically computes a unique contribution value on a local function variable (*i.e.*, t), which is then used to apply the increment through the indirection to the two vertices of the edge (lines 5 and 6). This scheme is widely used in HYDRA by all performance-critical loops, which together account for the 90% of execution time. It also exists in a few variants: for example, one vertex data value is incremented while the other is unchanged or decremented.

Because this scheme is critical and opens up a natural splitting point between the contribution computation and the *dispatch* to the vertices, we extended the OP2 abstractions with annotations to categorize kernels. Using these, developers can drive the OP2 compiler as depicted in Figure 2, line 1. We extended the OP2 compiler to leverage annotated code with automatic OP2 to OP2 loop splitting. Our transformation replaces the original loop with three loops, depicted in Figure 3, with equivalent semantics:

- The first loop computes the contributions for each edge and stores them into a new op_dat associated with the edges (lines 14-16). The kernel code is obtained from the original kernel by moving the argument corresponding to the second vertex data to a local variable (line 3). In doing so, the second increment no longer has any effect and can be safely eliminated by the compiler.

```
1   void incrVerticesAlt (double * eData, double * v1Data) {
2     double v2Data [1];
3     ...
4     *v1Data += t;
5     *v2Data += t;
6   }
7   void incrVerticesCpy (double * e, double * v) {
8     *v += *eData;
9   }
10  op_par_loop ( incrVerticesAlt, edges,
11    op_arg_dat ( edgeData, -1, OP_ID, OP_READ),
12    op_arg_dat ( incrVerticesTemp, -1, OP_ID, OP_WRITE));
13  op_par_loop ( incrVerticesCpy, edges,
14    op_arg_dat ( incrVerticesTemp, -1, OP_ID, OP_READ),
15    op_arg_dat ( vertData, 0, edges2Verts, OP_INC));
16  op_par_loop ( incrVerticesCpy, edges,
17    op_arg_dat ( incrVerticesTemp, -1, OP_ID, OP_READ),
18    op_arg_dat ( vertData, 1, edges2Verts, OP_INC));
```

Fig. 3. Source to source loop fission of the example shown in Figure 2

– The second and third loops iterate over edges and apply the increment, passed in the new op_dat, to the vertices (lines 17-22). The corresponding kernel code (lines 9-12) is generated according to the kernel annotation and the types of the vertex data.

This distribution of one loop into three allows the number of op_args to be reduced for each loop w.r.t. the original loop. For the first loop, it also transforms two indirect op_arg accesses into a single directly accessed op_arg. As directly accessed op_args for indirect loops are not staged into shared memory, this reduces the shared memory requirements for the first loop. The increment loops are generally simpler loops, with a smaller number of input parameters and small kernels, and can be thus easily accelerated.

4.2 Alternative Coloring Schemes

In Section 3 we showed that OP2 guarantees absence of data races by using a two-level coloring technique. The optimization presented here provides an alternative strategy for intra-partition coloring. In the current OP2 implemention the following scheme is applied. First, the user kernel is evaluated for all iterations in the partition. The parallelism degree for this stage is the minimum between the number of iterations in the partition, and the number of threads in the CUDA block. In this phase, the increment contributions are not applied directly to the op_dat in shared memory, to prevent data races between threads, but local *private* thread variables are used to store the increments. There is one such variable for each thread and for each incremented op_dat. After executing the user kernel, the increments are applied to the shared memory by following colors.

This strategy maximizes the parallelism when evaluating the user kernel, at the cost of a larger register pressure due to the additional thread private variables.

An alternative to this is to program threads to compute and apply the increments to shared memory when executing the user kernel. The user kernel is passed a shared memory address, instead of private thread variable references. To prevent data races while executing the user kernel, the thread execution must follow colors. This reduces the amount of total parallelism when evaluating the kernel, but it also reduces the register requirements due to the eliminated private variables. The implementation of this alternative strategy is confined to the CUDA kernels synthesized for OP2 loops. This behavior can be selected by the user through annotations on the loop, similar to the ones used for fission. However, this is a short term solution, and we aim at understanding when this alternative synthesis actually delivers better performance. In Section 5 we discuss how this can be deduced by combining information from access descriptors and CUDA compiler reports.

4.3   Tuning Partition and Thread Block Size

The final optimization that we extensively applied to HYDRA loops is the tuning of the partition and thread block size. These two parameters are inter-dependent: the partition size is the number of iterations that are mapped to the same SM, while the thread block size is the number of threads that are used in the CUDA program to execute the iterations.

Both the partition and thread block size represent an upper bound on the amount of parallelism that can be achieved by a SM when executing a partition. The execution consists in the following phases, as discussed in Section 3: *(i)* stage in of input data from device to shared memory, one dataset at a time; *(ii)* execution of the user kernel; *(iii)* stage out from shared to device memory, one dataset at a time. When executing the user kernel the maximum parallelism achievable is equal to the number of iterations in the partition; in the staging phases the parallelism is instead limited by the number of elements to be staged, multiplied by the dataset cardinality. With no data re-use, this is equal to the partition size multiplied by the cardinality of the dataset. Using a larger CUDA thread block size permits more parallelism in the staging phases, without losing the coalescing property. As a general rule, a larger partition size, constrained by the shared memory size, is always preferred to provide more parallelism to the SM. However, the optimal block size depends on the size of the op_dats and the kind of access. Section 5 studies the relation between multiple loops with different access descriptors and the optimal block size.

5   Experiments

In this section we show the results of performance analysis of the optimizations described in the previous section applied to several loops in HYDRA. The simulation used is a standard CFD test problem used for validation of correctness and performance called NASA Rotor 37, that models a blade of a turbomachinery component. In our tests we replicate the blade twice to set up a mesh size including: 2.5M edges, 860K vertices, and 54K wall edges. The simulation solves the Navier-Stokes equation to evaluate the flow through one passage of the two NASA Rotor 37 blades and it is the same application used in the performance graph of Section 1. In previous tests, we also used a larger mesh, including 4 NASA Rotor 37 blades, and we obtained similar performance results of the case used here, scaled by a factor of 2.

The configuration of HYDRA required for this simulation uses 33 op_par_loops some of which are extremely complex. In our tests, we used an NVIDIA Fermi C2070 including 14 SMs (i.e. 448 CUDA cores), 6 GB of main memory and 48/16 KB of shared memory and L1 cache, respectively. The full simulation runs for tens of minutes, but we limited performance analysis to 30 time steps to reduce the total performance analysis time. To compile the CUDA code generated by the OP2 compiler we used the PGI Fortran CUDA compiler version 12.2, with CUDA 4.0, and the NVIDIA CUDA compiler version 4.0.17. The optimization options are, respectively, -O4 and -O3. The experiments focus on the effects of optimizations on all loops involved in the simulation. For each loop, there are a limited number of optimizations that can be applied, and that can be composed together. We analyze the performance of each loop when applying the optimizations individually, and in all their possible compositions. The aim of these experiments is to put into relation: (1) The features of an op_par_loop in terms of its input arguments including: the type and cardinality (or dimension) of the related op_dat ; the arity (or dimension) of the related op_map, if used. (2) The GPU resource requirements, in terms of the number of registers needed for each thread and the shared memory size required given a specific partition size. (3) The performance in terms of execution time for the CUDA kernel section.

5.1   Fission, Block Tuning and Coloring

A number of OP2 loops in NASA Rotor 37 can be subject to all the three optimizations discussed in the previous section. For space reasons, we study the following relevant loops: accumulation of contributions on edges (ACCU), gradient contribution on edges (EDGECON), viscous flux calculation (VFLUX), inviscid flux calculation (IFLUX), viscous wall flux calculation (WFFLUX), and summation of near wall edge contributions (SUMWALLS). The first five loops adhere to the requirements of the fission optimization, by incrementing equivalent amounts to two op_dats. Unlike the previous loops, the last one has a single incremented op_dat. We used this case as an experiment to understand if loop fission increases performance. This explores the general idea that smaller kernels are always better parallelized on a GPU than larger ones.

Table 1 illustrates the main features of the loops, by inspecting their access descriptors. All loops feature an average to large number of input op_dats, each with a large cardinality, resulting in a large amount of shared memory required to execute each iteration. The first four loops iterate over the largest mesh set (edges), while the last two iterate on the wall edge set that is two orders of magnitudes smaller.

Table 1. Loop properties resulting from access descriptor analysis for loops which can be subject to fission and alternative coloring

	ACCU	EDGECON	VFLUX	IFLUX	WFFLUX	SUMWALLS
Iteration set	edges	edges	edges	edges	wall edges	wall edges
No. of op_arg_dats	13	11	19	9	15	8
No. of indirect op_arg_dats	12	10	18	8	12	5
Size of op_arg_dats (bytes)	712	568	776	296	628	228
Size of increments (bytes)	200	288	96	96	96	48

This is reflected in the average performance of the loops, as we detail below. The size of the input data for each iteration can be used to define the maximum permitted partition size that a loop can use. As a partition is mapped to a single streaming multiprocessor (SM), all iteration data for that partition must fit into shared memory, i.e. into 48KB on the C2070 GPU. The run-time profiling of OP2, which analyses the mesh, computes the average data re-use, and with these results, the kernel configuration can be tuned to maximize the partition size.

Figure 4 shows the results of applying each optimization to the described loops. Table 2 shows the resource requirements for each loop when applying different optimization schemes. For each optimization, we always choose the

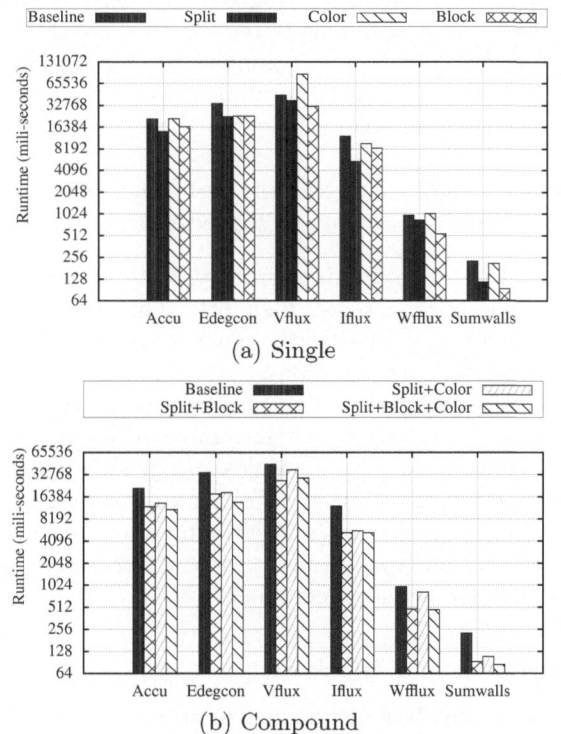

(a) Single

(b) Compound

Fig. 4. Performance results when applying optimizations alone and in composition. The Y-axis is in log-2 scale.

Table 2. Resource usage for OP2 optimizations. In 'Split' columns there are 3 values as each loop is split into 3 loops.

(a) Register Usage

Loop	Baseline, Block	Color	Split (+block)	Split + Color (+block)
ACCU	63	63	63, 28, 28	63, 18, 23
EDGEC.	41	46	37,32, 32	37, 34, 34
VFLUX	63	63	63, 27, 31	63, 29, 34
IFLUX	63	63	63, 28, 29	63, 29, 32
WFFLUX	63	63	63, 28, 28	63, 18, 18
SUMW.	37	41	34, 28	34, 15

(b) Shared Memory Usage

Loop	Baseline, Color, Block	Split (all compounds)
ACCU	43	36, 25, 25
EDGEC.	34	20, 24, 24
VFLUX	47	41, 6, 6
IFLUX	34	22, 6, 6
WFFLUX	36	30, 12, 12
SUMW.	24	18, 6

maximum partition size achievable or the one delivering better performance. For all cases, except the block tuning optimizations, the CUDA thread block size is equal to the partition size: this assigns one thread per iteration.

The analysis of the results shows:

- Splitting a loop reduces both shared memory and register pressure, and should thus be applied extensively. In some cases, it also permits larger partition sizes to be achieved, thus improving the available parallelism.
- For split loops, the alternative coloring strategy delivers slightly better performance in nearly all cases. This is related to a reduction in the average number of colors for split loops. If applied to original loops, this strategy can deliver significantly worse performance, when associated with a larger number of intra-partition colors. Thus, it should only be used in tandem with splitting.
- Block and partition tuning improves the performance for all loops, both split and original ones, and should be applied extensively.

As highlighted, the alternative coloring strategy does not necessarily reduce register usage, but it sometimes increases it slightly. This is somewhat unexpected, and we believe that it is related to the way in which the low-level CUDA compiler treats different control-flow organizations.

As expected, loop fission improves performance by a large factor, even when the user kernel includes a relatively small number of floating point operations. Also, the choice of the alternative colouring strategy should be taken when register requirements are actually reduced. We can do this by synthesizing the two versions at OP2 compile-time, with and without alternative coloring strategy, and by choosing the best one by looking at the register requirements for the two kernels as reported by the low-level compiler.

5.2   Tuning Partition and Block Size

The final optimisation involves the tuning of seven loops of NASA Rotor 37. These loops are generically small, in terms of number of input op_dats and kernel size, and their contribution to the total performance is much lower than the six loops discussed above. However, our goal is to understand what is the best configuration of these two parameters. Table 3 shows the results, including the configuration parameter values and the obtained performance. In the table, we can notice that the first four loops obtain higher performance with the largest achievable partition and block sizes (512), while the remaining three loops perform better with a lower value (128). This can be explained by analysing the access descriptors. All loops take as input a number of op_dats between 4 and 6, but only the first four loops have all input data accessed through indirection. The remaining three loops only access a single input through an indirection, while the remaining op_dats are accessed directly.

As described in Section 3, indirect op_dats are staged into shared memory for indirect loops, while directly accessed data is left in device memory. The block size parameters strongly influences the staging performance. As the first four loops spend more time in staging data than the remaining three loops, the block size increase plays a dominant role in the performance of the loops. Also, the number of data items to be staged directly depends on the number of data values per mesh element and the partition size. The first four loops have either a larger partition size, or input op_dats with larger dimension, and can thus benefit of larger block sizes.

5.3 Discussion

The analysis of the performance results shown in this section led us to the following conclusion which can be adopted as a general optimization strategy in the compiler:

- A main source of performance degradation on GPUs for OP2 loops are small partition sizes. This is a consequence of having a large number of op_dats which sum up to a large number of input data for each iteration, resulting in larger shared memory requirements. This condition — having larger shared memory requirements — can be checked at compile-time by inspecting the access descriptors. The compiler addresses this issue by splitting the loops which have been annotated by the user.
- When a loop is split, the resulting loops can be further optimized if the alternative coloring strategy actually reduces the number of registers needed per thread. This can be achieved at compile-time by first generating two versions, each using a different coloring strategy, and then choosing the best version by feeding the OP2 run-time with register pressure information returned by the CUDA compiler. This removes the burden on the programmer to annotate loops which should be implemented using the alternative coloring strategy.
- Once the partition size is optimized, a loop exposes sufficient parallelism inside its partitions. However, the real parallelism that can be obtained on a GPU

Table 3. Partition and block tuning for seven indirect loops

	$Loop_1$	$Loop_2$	$Loop_3$	$Loop_4$	$Loop_5$	$Loop_6$	$Loop_7$
Part. and Block size	(64,64)	(64,64)	(64,64)	(64,64)	(64,64)	(64,64)	(64,64)
Perf. (millisec.)	15.70	41.94	19.58	35.30	9.53	6.13	7.46
Part. and Block size	(64,512)	(128,512)	(256,512)	(256,512)	(128,128)	(128,128)	(128,128)
Perf. (millisec.)	11.52	14.67	8.66	18.99	8.68	5.44	6.64

depends on the resource constraints of each thread, in terms of register requirements. This requirement directly influences the warp allocation strategy for the SM dynamic scheduler: if each thread requires a large number of registers, then a smaller number of threads can be allocated in the same warp. This condition must be checked also for loops with relatively small input op_dats, but with high register pressure. For this kind of loop, splitting and the alternative coloring strategy can be applied to reduce register pressure.

6   Conclusion

In this paper we have demonstrated and evaluated the effect of applying three optimizations for unstructured mesh programs to a wide number of HYDRA loops. The optimizations: (1) permit transforming the input OP2 program to optimize shared memory requirements; (2) provide a kernel-tailored code synthesis minimizing register requirements; (3) tune configuration parameters to optimize data staging for each loop. We have shown how these three optimizations can be automatically implemented by the compiler by extending the OP2 language with loop annotations. This reduces significantly the compiler complexity, as it does not need analysing the user kernels associated to each loop. Finally, in the experiment section we presented a full performance analysis showing the optimization effects on the performance of the loops, and on their resource requirements. This enabled us to derive a general optimization strategy for the complier, based on the composition of the described optimizations.

References

1. Han, H., Tseng, C.-W.: A Comparison of Locality Transformations for Irregular Codes. In: Dwarkadas, S. (ed.) LCR 2000. LNCS, vol. 1915, pp. 70–84. Springer, Heidelberg (2000)
2. Burgess, D.A., Giles, M.B.: Renumbering unstructured grids to improve the performance of codes on hierarchical memory machines. Adv. Eng. Softw. 28(3), 189–201 (1997)
3. Chevalier, C., Pellegrini, F.: PT-Scotch: A tool for efficient parallel graph ordering. Parallel Comput. 34(6-8), 318–331 (2008)
4. Karypis, G., Kumar, V.: A fast and high quality multilevel scheme for partitioning irregular graphs. SIAM J. Sci. Comput. 20(1), 359–392 (1998)
5. Strout, M.M., Carter, L., Ferrante, J.: Compile-time composition of run-time data and iteration reorderings. In: Procs. of the PLDI 2003 (June 2003)
6. DeVito, Z., Joubert, N., Palacios, F., Oakley, S., Medina, M., Barrientos, M., Elsen, E., Ham, F., Aiken, A., Duraisamy, K., Darve, E., Alonso, J., Hanrahan, P.: Liszt: a domain specific language for building portable mesh-based PDE solvers. In: Procs. of SC, pp. 9:1–9:12. ACM, New York (2011)
7. Giles, M.B.: OP2 User's Manual (April 2012), http://people.maths.ox.ac.uk/gilesm/op2/user.pdf
8. Giles, M.B., Mudalige, G.R., Sharif, Z., Markall, G., Kelly, P.H.: Performance analysis and optimization of the OP2 framework on many-core architectures. The Computer Journal 55(2), 168–180 (2012)

UCIFF: Unified Cluster Assignment Instruction Scheduling and Fast Frequency Selection for Heterogeneous Clustered VLIW Cores[*]

Vasileios Porpodas and Marcelo Cintra[**]

School of Informatics, University of Edinburgh
{v.porpodas@,mc@staffmail}.ed.ac.uk

Abstract. Clustered VLIW processors are scalable wide-issue statically scheduled processors. Their design is based on physically partitioning the otherwise shared hardware resources, a design which leads to both high performance and low energy consumption. In traditional clustered VLIW processors, all clusters operate at the same frequency. Heterogeneous clustered VLIW processors however, support dynamic voltage and frequency scaling (DVFS) independently per cluster. Effectively controlling DVFS, to selectively decrease the frequency of clusters with a lot of slack in their schedule, can lead to significant energy savings.

In this paper we propose UCIFF, a new scheduling algorithm for heterogeneous clustered VLIW processors with software DVFS control, that performs cluster assignment, instruction scheduling and fast frequency selection simultaneously, all in a single compiler pass. The proposed algorithm solves the phase ordering problem between frequency selection and scheduling, present in existing algorithms. We compared the quality of the generated code, using both performance and energy-related metrics, against that of the current state-of-the-art and an optimal scheduler. The results show that UCIFF produces better code than the state-of-the-art, very close to the optimal across the mediabench2 benchmarks, while keeping the algorithmic complexity low.

Keywords: clustered VLIW, heterogeneous, DVFS, scheduling, phase-ordering.

1 Introduction

Energy consumption has become an important design constraint for microprocessors. Clustered VLIW processors were introduced with performance and energy scalability in mind: **i.** They are statically scheduled, which removes the instruction scheduling burden from the micro-architecture. **ii.** The clustered design improves energy efficiency, operating frequency and reduces design complexity[17]. Clustered VLIW processors operate at an attractive power/performance ratio point. Examples are the Texas Instrument's VelociTI, HP/ST's Lx [6], Analog's TigerSHARC [7], and BOPS' ManArray [15].

---

[*] This work was supported in part by the EC under grant ERA 249059 (FP7).
[**] Marcelo Cintra is currently on sabbatical leave at Intel Labs.

H. Kasahara and K. Kimura (Eds.): LCPC 2012, LNCS 7760, pp. 127–142, 2013.
© Springer-Verlag Berlin Heidelberg 2013

A clustered processor has its shared non-scalable resources (such as the register file which is shared among functional units) partitioned into smaller parts. Each part of the partitioned resource, along with some of the resources that communicate with it are grouped together into a cluster. For example a cluster often contains a slice of the register file along with several functional units. Within a cluster signals travel fast, faster than in the shared resource case, and energy consumption remains low, due to the improved locality. Between clusters, communication is subject to an inter-cluster delay and there is additional energy consumption on the inter-cluster interconnect.

Traditionally, all clusters of a clustered VLIW processor operate at the same frequency and voltage. Considerable energy savings can be achieved by freeing each cluster to operate at its own frequency and voltage level. The reason for this is that the cluster utilization usually varies; some clusters are fully loaded while others have a fraction of the load. It is therefore sensible to lower the frequency of the under-utilized clusters to save energy.

In this paper we raise an important issue of the existing compilation techniques for heterogeneous clustered VLIW processors. Compiling for these architectures comprises of solving two distinct but highly dependent sub-problems:

1. Selecting the frequency that each cluster should operate at.
2. Performing cluster assignment and instruction scheduling for the selected frequencies (we refer to both as "scheduling" for simplicity).

There is a **phase-ordering** issue between these two sub-problems: **A.** One cannot properly select the frequencies per cluster without scheduling and evaluating the schedule. **B.** One cannot perform scheduling without having decided on the frequencies.

State-of-the-art work in this field ([2]) treats these two sub-problems independently and solves the first (1.) before the second (2.). At first a good set of frequencies is found by estimating the scheduling outcome for each configuration (without actually scheduling). Then scheduling is performed for this set of frequencies. We will refer to this approach as the "Decoupled" one.

The problem is that the frequency decision (1.) has a great impact on the quality of scheduling (2.). We observed that the estimation of the scheduling outcome without performing the actual scheduling, as done in [2], can be inaccurate. Nevertheless, it is a critical compilation decision since selecting a non-optimal frequency set can lead to a schedule with poor performance, energy consumption or both.

In this work we provide a more concrete solution to the problem by solving both sub-problems (frequency selection and scheduling) in a single algorithm thus alleviating the phase-ordering issue altogether. The proposed scheduling algorithm for heterogeneous clustered VLIW processors performs cluster assignment, instruction scheduling and fast frequency selection, all in a unified algorithm, as a unified scheduling pass.

The algorithm can be configured to generate optimized code for any of the commonly used metrics (Energy, $Energy \times Delay$ Product (EDP) and $Energy \times Delay^2$ (ED2), Delay). The output of the algorithm is twofold: **i.** The operating frequency of each cluster such that the scheduling metric is optimized. **ii.** Fully clustered and scheduled code for the frequencies selected by (i).

In the text that follows we use the terms "frequencies per cluster", "set of frequencies" and "frequency configuration" interchangeably.

2   Motivation

2.1   Homogeneous vs Heterogeneous

This section motivates the heterogeneous clustered VLIW design by demonstrating how energy can be saved without sacrificing performance in the example of Fig.1.

Fig.1a is the Data Flow Graph (DFG) to be scheduled. Fig.1b,c show the instruction schedules that correspond to this DFG on a two-clustered machine (single-issue per-cluster). Fig.1b is the homogeneous design with both clusters operating at the same frequency (f), while Fig.1c is the heterogeneous one with ClusterB operating at half the frequency of ClusterA ($f/2$). Nevertheless both configurations have the **same performance** as the schedule length is 4 cycles for both. The heterogeneous can perform as well as the homogeneous because ClusterB was initially under-utilized (there was slack in part of the schedule).

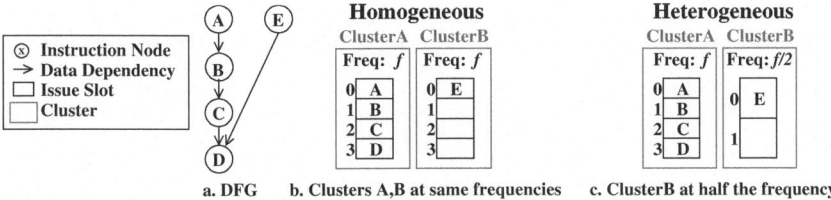

a. DFG   b. Clusters A,B at same frequencies   c. ClusterB at half the frequency

Fig. 1. Under-utilized ClusterB can have half the frequency with no performance loss

Since the target architecture is a statically scheduled clustered VLIW one, it is the job of the scheduler to find the best frequency for each cluster so that the desired metric (Energy, EDP, ED2, Delay) is optimized.

2.2   Phase Ordering

As already discussed in Section 1, there is a phase ordering issue between frequency selection and instruction scheduling. Fig.2 shows a high-level view of the scheduling algorithms for a 2-cluster processor with 3 possible frequencies per cluster (f_0, f_1, f_2).

The Decoupled algorithm (existing state-of-the-art based on [2]) is in Fig.2a. As already mentioned, there are two distinct steps:

1. The first step selects one of the many frequency configurations as the one that should be the best for the given metric (e.g. EDP). This is based on a simple estimation (before scheduling) of the schedule time ($cycles \times T$) and energy consumption that the code will have after scheduling. The exact calculations are described in detail in Section 5:*Decoupled*.

2. The second step performs scheduling on the architecture configuration selected by step 1. This includes both cluster assignment and instruction scheduling, which in an unmodified [2] are in two separate steps.

It is obvious that if step (1) makes a wrong decision (which is very likely since the decision is based on a simple estimate), then the processor will operate at a point far from the optimal one. Therefore step (2) will schedule the code for a non-optimal frequency configuration which will lead to a non-optimal result.

This phase-ordering issue is dealt with by UCIFF, the proposed unified frequency selection and scheduling algorithm (Fig.2b). The proposed algorithm solves the two sub-problems simultaneously and outputs a combined solution which is both the frequency configuration (that is the frequency for each cluster) and the scheduled code for this specific configuration.

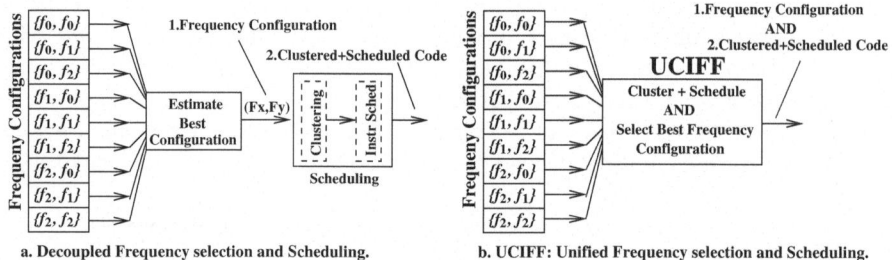

a. Decoupled Frequency selection and Scheduling.   **b. UCIFF: Unified Frequency selection and Scheduling.**

Fig. 2. The two-phase scheduling of the current state-of-the-art (a). The proposed unified approach (b) is free of this phase-ordering problem.

3   UCIFF

The proposed Unified algorithm for Cluster assignment, Instruction scheduling and Fast Frequency selection (UCIFF) can be more easily explained if two of its main ingredients are explained separately. That is: **i.** scheduling for a fixed heterogeneous processor and **ii.** unifying scheduling and frequency selection.

3.1   Scheduling for Fixed Heterogeneous Processors

An out-of-the-box scheduler for a clustered architecture can only handle the homogeneous case, where all clusters operate at the same frequency. A heterogeneous architecture on the other hand, has different frequencies across clusters. This is because schedulers work in a cycle-by-cycle manner. They schedule ready instructions on Free cluster resources and move to the next cycle. This cycle-by-cycle operation is inapplicable when clusters operate at different frequencies. The problem gets worse if cluster frequencies are not integer multiples of one another (e.g. cluster 0 operating at frequency f and cluster 1 at $1.5f$).

UCIFF introduces a scheduling methodology for heterogeneous clustered architectures with arbitrary frequencies per cluster which can be applied to existing scheduling algorithms. The idea is that the scheduler operates at a higher base

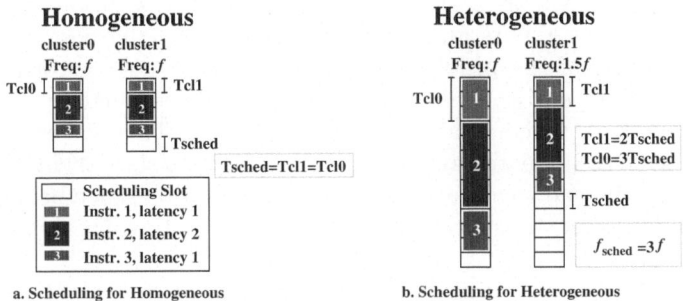

Fig. 3. The scheduler's internal clock period T_{sched} compared to the periods of the two clusters T_{cl0} and T_{cl1}, for a homogeneous (a) and a heterogeneous (b) architecture

frequency (f_{sched}) such that the clock period of any cluster is an integer multiple of the clock period of the scheduler (T_{sched}). It works in two steps:

i. The scheduler's base frequency f_{sched} is calculated as the lowest integer common multiple of all possible frequencies of all clusters. The scheduler internally works at a cycle $T_{sched} = 1/f_{sched}$, which is always an integer multiple of the cycle that each cluster operates at. For example in Fig.3b the scheduler's base cycle is T_{sched} while the cycles of cluster0 and cluster1 are $3 \times T_{sched}$ and $2 \times T_{sched}$ respectively.

ii. The instruction latencies for each cluster are increased and set to be a multiple of the original one, equal to $(T_{cluster}/T_{sched}) \times OrigLatency$. In the example of Fig.3, the instruction latencies for cluster0 are multiplied by 3 while the ones for cluster1 are multiplied by 2.

In this way the problem of scheduling for different frequencies per cluster is transformed to the problem of scheduling instructions of various latencies, which is a solved problem and is indeed supported by any decent scheduler.

3.2   Scheduling for Non-fixed Heterogeneous Processors (UCIFF)

In contrast to the existing state-of-the-art, UCIFF solves the phase-ordering problem between frequency selection and scheduling. It does so by combining them into a single unified algorithm. In addition, the scheduling algorithm performs cluster assignment and instruction scheduling together thus removing any phase ordering issues between all clustering, scheduling and frequency selection.

The UCIFF algorithm is composed of three nested layers: The driver function (Alg.1) at the outermost layer, the clustering and scheduling function (Alg.2) at the second layer and the metric calculation function (Alg.3) at the innermost.

1. The Driver: The highest level of the UCIFF algorithm (Alg.1) performs the frequency selection. It decides on a single frequency configuration for the whole scheduling region. Instead of solving the global optimization problem, of determining the optimal frequency, with a full-search over all configurations, UCIFF uses a fast hill climbing approach.

Hill climbing, in general, searches for a globally good solution by evaluating, at each point, its neighbors and by "moving" towards the best among them. Due to the nature of the problem, trying out a large number of neighbors is computationally expensive. This is because we cannot evaluate a configuration at cycle c unless we schedule all instructions up to c. This makes probabilistic algorithms (such as simulated annealing) very expensive since trying out random configurations will lead to almost the whole configuration space being scheduled to a very large extent, thus leading to a time complexity comparable to that of the full-search.

Formally, a **frequency configuration** is an ordered multiset of each cluster's frequency: $\{f_a, f_b, f_c, ...\}$. Each of $f_a, f_b, f_c, ...$ is one of the l valid frequency levels in the set $\{f_0, f_1, ..., f_{l-1}\}$. For example a valid configuration for a 2-cluster machine with 3 possible frequency levels (f_0, f_1, f_2) is $\{f_2, f_0\}$ (where clusters 0,1 operate at f_2, f_0 frequencies respectively).

The **neighbors** of a configuration c are the configurations which are close frequency-wise to c. More precisely, the configuration $\{f_{na}, f_{nb}, f_{nc}, ...\}$ is a UCIFF neighbor of $\{f_a, f_b, f_c, ...\}$ if $nx = x$ for all x except one (say y) such that $|ny - y| < NDistance$. For example, the neighbors of $\{f_1, f_1\}$ for $NDistance = 1$ are $\{f_0, f_1\}$, $\{f_2, f_1\}$, $\{f_1, f_0\}$ and $\{f_1, f_2\}$.

In UCIFF the hill climbing search is done gradually, in steps of cycles, while the code gets scheduled for the duration of the step. After each step there is an evaluation. We refer to this step-evaluation-step approach as "gradual hill climbing" and to the act of scheduling within a step as "partial scheduling". This makes UCIFF fast and accurate. The hill climbing search stops when all instructions of the best neighbors have been scheduled. All of the above will be further explained through the following example.

A high level example of the UCIFF algorithm for the 2-cluster machine of Fig.2 is illustrated in Fig.4. On the vertical axis there are all 9 possible frequency configurations. The horizontal axis represents the scheduler's cycles (of T_{sched} duration). The partial schedule of each configuration is a horizontal line that starts from the vertical axis at the configuration point and grows to the right. The evaluation (every STEP instructions) is represented by the vertical gray line.

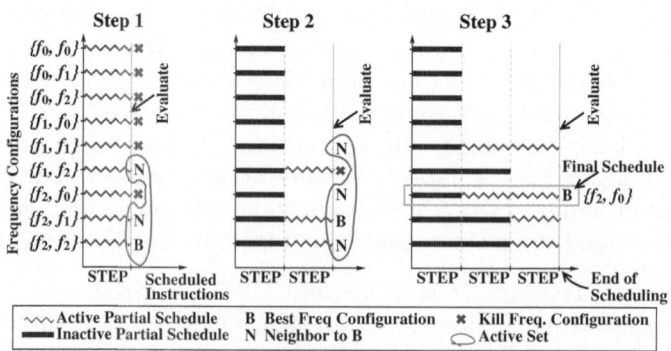

Fig. 4. Overview of the UCIFF gradual hill climbing algorithm for a schedule that consists of three steps

At first (**Step 1**) all configurations are partially scheduled for "STEP" instructions. Once partially scheduled, they are evaluated and the best configuration is found and marked as "B". At this point the neighbors of "B" are found, according to the definition given earlier. The neighbors are marked as "N". The neighbors ("N") along with the best ("B") form the active set. The configurations not in the active set are marked with a red "X".

In **Step2** the configurations in the active set get partially scheduled for another "STEP" instructions (curly red lines). They get evaluated and the best one ("B") and its neighbors ("N") are found.

In **Step3** the active set of Step2 gets partially scheduled for another "STEP" instructions. At this point it is interesting to note that $\{f_2, f_0\}$ and $\{f_1, f_1\}$ have to be scheduled for both the 2nd and 3rd "STEP". Now there are no instructions left to schedule for the active configurations, therefore the algorithm terminates. After the final evaluation, the best configuration of the active set is found ("B", $\{f_2, f_0\}$). The **full schedule** for this configuration is **returned** (gold rectangle).

Note that the bar lengths are not proportional to any metric value. They just show the progress of the algorithm while instructions get scheduled.

The detailed algorithm is listed in Alg.1. The algorithm initially performs partial scheduling of all frequency configurations for "STEP" instructions (Alg.1 lines 11, 14-20). This determines the best configuration and stores it into "BFC".

Algorithm 1. UCIFF

```
 1  /* Unified Cluster assignment Instr. Scheduling and Fast Frequency selection.
 2      In1: METRIC_TYPE that the scheduler should optimize for.
 3      In2: Schedule STEP instructions before evaluating and getting the best.
 4      In3: STEPVAR: Decrement STEP by STEPVAR upon each evaluation.
 5      In4: NEIGHBORS: The number of neighbors per cluster.
 6      Out: Scheduled Code and Best Frequency Configuration. */
 7  uciff (METRIC_TYPE, STEP, STEPVAR, NEIGHBORS)
 8  {
 9      do
10          if (BFC not set)    /* If first run */
11              NEIGHBORS_SET = all frequency configurations
12          else
13              NEIGHBORS_SET = neighbors of BFC /*up to NEIGHBORS per cluster*/
14          for FCONF in NEIGHBORS_SET
15              /* Partially schedule the ready instructions of FCONF frequency
                    ↪configuration for STEP instructions, optimizing METRIC_TYPE
                    ↪*/
16              SCORE = cluster_and_schedule (METRIC_TYPE, STEP, FCONF)
17              Store the scheduler's calculated SCORE into  SCORECARD [FCONF]
18          Decrement STEP by STEPVAR until 1. /* Variable steps (optional) */
19          BFC = Best Freq Configuration of SCORECARD, clear SCORECARD
20      while there are unscheduled instructions in active set
21      return BFC and scheduled code of BFC
22  }
```

For the rest of the algorithm, each frequency configuration in the neighboring set of "BFC" (lines 13,14) gets partially scheduled for "STEP" instructions and evaluated (lines 15,16). The best performing of the neighbors gets stored into "BFC" (line 19). The algorithm repeats until no instructions in the neighboring set of "BFC" (a.k.a. active set) are left unscheduled (line 20). Each iteration of the algorithm decreases "STEP" by "STEPVAR" (line 18) so that re-evaluation of the schedules keeps getting more frequent. This makes the algorithm track the best configuration faster.

This gradual hill-climbing process accurately selects a good configuration among many without resorting to a full-search across all frequency configurations. The end result is a fully scheduled code for the selected configuration.

It is interesting to note that partial scheduling of all neighbors could be done in parallel. This could speed up the UCIFF scheduler, to reach speeds close to those of the Oracle.

2. The Core: At one level lower lies the core of the scheduling algorithm (Alg.2). It is a unified **cluster assignment and scheduling algorithm** which shares some similarities with UAS [14] but has several unique attributes: **i.** It operates on a heterogeneous architecture where clusters operate at different frequencies (as described in Section 3.1). **ii.** It only issues an instruction to the cluster chosen by the heuristic. It does not try to issue on any other cluster if it cannot currently issue on the chosen cluster. **iii.** It is capable of performing partial scheduling for "STEP" number of instructions. **iv.** It can optimize for various metrics (not just Delay). This includes energy related ones: Energy, EDP, ED2. **v.** The start-cycle calculation is extended to work for heterogeneous clusters, which is done by adding to it the latency of the instruction on that cluster (see Alg.3 line 10).

Algorithm 2. Clustering and Scheduling for various metrics

```
1  /* In1: METRIC_TYPE: The metric type that the scheduler will optimize for.
2     In2: STEP: Num of instrs to schedule before switching to next freq. conf.
3     In3: FCONF: The architecture's current frequency configuration.
4     Out: Scheduled Code and metric value. */
5  cluster_and_schedule (METRIC_TYPE, STEP, FCONF)
6  {
7     /* Restore ready list for this frequency configuration */
8     READY_LIST = READY_LIST_ARRAY [FCONF]
9     /* Restore current cycle. CYCLE is the scheduler's internal cycle. */
10    CYCLE = LAST_CYCLE [FCONF]
11    Restore the Reservation Table state that corresponds to FCONF
12    while (instructions left to schedule && STEP > 0)
13       update READY_LIST with ready to issue at CYCLE, include deferred
14       sort READY_LIST based on list-scheduling priorities
15       while (READY_LIST not empty)
16          select INSN, the highest priority instruction from the READY_LIST
17          create LIST_OF_CLUSTERS[] that INSN can be scheduled at on CYCLE
18          BEST_CLUSTER=best of LIST_OF_CLUSTERS[] by comparing for each cluster
                ↪ calculate_heuristic(METRIC_TYPE,CLUSTER,FCONF,INSN,IPCL[])
19          /* Try scheduling INSN on the best cluster */
20          if (INSN can be scheduled on BEST_CLUSTER at CYCLE)
21             schedule INSN, occupy LATENCY[FCONF][BEST_CLUSTER][INSN] slots
22             IPCL [CLUSTER] ++  /* count number of instructions per cluster */
23             remove INSN from READY_LIST
24          /* If failed to schedule INSN on best cluster, defer to next cycle */
25          if (INSN unscheduled)
26             remove INSN from READY_LIST and re-insert it at CYCLE + 1
27       /* No instructions left in ready list for CYCLE, then CYCLE ++ */
28       CYCLE ++
29       /* If we have scheduled STEP instructions, finalize and exit */
30       if (instr. scheduled > STEP instructions)
31          Update READY_LIST_ARRAY[], LAST_CYCLE[] and Reservation Table
32          return metric value of current schedule
33 }
```

In more detail, the algorithm is a list-scheduling based one, that operates on a ready list. The scheduler performs partial scheduling on each active frequency configuration for a small window of "STEP" instructions. Once a (configuration, cycle) pair is scheduled it is never revisited. Switching among configurations requires that the scheduler maintains a private instance of its data structures (ready list, reservation table, current cycle) for each configuration. To that end, it saves and restores the snapshot of its structures upon entry and exit (Alg.2 lines 7-11, 31). The ready list gets filled in with ready and deferred instructions (line 13). Then it gets sorted based on priority (calculated on the Data Dependence Graph) (line 14) and the highest priority one is selected for scheduling (line 16). A list of candidate clusters is created (line 17) and the best cluster is found based on the values of the metric used for scheduling (line 18). The instruction is then tried on the best cluster at the current cycle (lines 19,20). If successful, then its presence in the schedule is marked on the reservation table for as many cycles as its latency as specified by LATENCY [ ] array (line 21), the IPCL (Instructions Per CLuster) counts the issued instruction (line 22), and INSN gets removed from the ready list (line 23). If unsuccessful, INSN's execution is deferred to next cycle (lines 24-26). We move to the next cycle only if the current ready list is empty (lines 27-28).

3. The Metrics: The combined clustering and scheduling algorithm used in UCIFF is a modular one. It can optimize the code not only for cycle count, but also for several other metrics that are useful in the context of a heterogeneous clustered VLIW. It supports energy-related metrics (Energy, EDP, ED2) and also execution Delay (Alg.3). The metric type controls the clustering heuristic which decides on the BEST_CLUSTER in Alg.2 line 18.

The energy-related metrics require that the scheduler have an **energy model** of the resources. The energy model is a small module in the scheduling algorithm and it is largely decoupled from the structure of the algorithm. The energy is calculated as the sum of the static and dynamic energy consumed by the clusters and the inter-cluster communication network. Static energy consumption is relative to the time period that the system is "on". Each instruction that executes on a cluster consumes dynamic energy relative to its latency. Each inter-cluster communication consumes dynamic energy as much as an instruction of the fastest cluster. The exact formulas for these calculations are in Table 1.

Table 1. Formulas for energy calculation

$E = \sum_{clusters}[E_{st}(cl) + E_{dyn}(cl)]$	
$E_{st}(cl) = P_{st} \times cycles_{cl} \times T_{cl}$	$E_{dyn}(cl) = E_{dyn,ins}(cl) + E_{dyn,icc}$
$P_{st}(cl) = C_{st} \times V_{cl}$	$E_{dyn,ins}(cl) = \sum_{ins}[P_{ins}(cl) \times Latency(ins, cl)]$
	$P_{ins}(cl) = C_{dyn} \times f_{cl} \times V_{cl}^2$
	$E_{dyn,icc} = P_{icc} \times NumICCs$
	$P_{icc} = C_{dyn} \times f_{fastest} \times V_{fastest}^2$

Algorithm 3. Heuristic calculation

```
 1  /* In1: METRIC_TYPE: The metric type that the scheduler will optimize for.
 2     In2: CLUSTER: The cluster that INSN will be tested on.
 3     In3: FCONF: The architecture's current frequency configuration.
 4     In4: INSN: The instruction currently under consideration.
 5     In5: IPCL: The Instruction count Per CLuster (for dyn energy).
 6     Out: metric value of METRIC_TYPE if INSN scheduled on CLUSTER under FCONF*/
 7  calculate_heuristic (METRIC_TYPE, CLUSTER, FCONF, INSN, IPCL[])
 8  {
 9      START_CYCLE = earliest cycle INSN can be scheduled at on CLUSTER
10      UCIFF_SC = START_CYCLE + LATENCY[FCONF][CLUSTER][INSN]
11      switch (METRIC_TYPE)
12          case ENERGY: return energy (CLUSTER, FCONF, UCIFF_SC, IPCL[])
13          case EDP: return edp (CLUSTER, FCONF, UCIFF_SC, IPCL[])
14          case ED2: return ed2 (CLUSTER, FCONF, UCIFF_SC, IPCL[])
15          case DELAY: return UCIFF_SC
16  }
```

3.3   DVFS Region

UCIFF determines the best frequency configuration at a per-scheduling-region basis. This is the natural granularity for a scheduling algorithm. This however is not the right granularity for Dynamic Voltage and Frequency Scaling (DVFS), which usually takes longer time. Therefore UCIFF's decisions on the frequency and voltage levels occur more frequently than what a real DVFS system could follow. As a result, UCIFF's per-region decisions have to be coarsened by some mapping from multiple UCIFF decisions to a single DVFS decision.

There are both hardware and software solutions to this. A possible micro-architectural solution involves pushing UCIFF's decision into a FIFO queue. Once the queue is full, a DVFS decision is made based on the average of the items in the queue, and the queue gets flushed.

A software solution is to perform sampling on the UCIFF configurations at a rate at most as high as the one supported by the system. Another way is to come up with a single DVFS point for the whole program by calculating the weighted average of the region points generated by UCIFF. A more accurate solution could be based on the control-edge probabilities. This knowledge can be acquired by profiling and can be used to form super-regions which operate at a single DVFS point.

The mapping decision for the DVFS points is completely decoupled from the UCIFF algorithm. A thorough evaluation of the possible solutions is not in the scope of this paper.

4   Experimental Setup

The target **architecture** is an IA64 (Itanium) [16] based statically scheduled clustered VLIW architecture. The architecture has 4 clusters and an issue width of 4 in total (that is 1 per cluster), similar to [2]. Each cluster's cycle time is 4, 5, 6 or 7 times a reference base cycle. Therefore the ratio of the fastest frequency to the slowest one is 7:4.

We have implemented UCIFF in the scheduling pass (haifa-sched) of GCC-4.5.0 [1] cross **compiler** for IA64.

Our experimental setup has some of its aspects deliberately idealized so that the generated code quality is isolated from external noise. **i.** Each cluster has all possible types of resource units available for all its issue slots. This alleviates any instruction bundling issues (which exist in the IA64 instruction set). **ii.** No noise from register allocation / register spills. Although the scheduler runs twice (before and after register allocation) our measurements are taken before register allocation. At this stage the compiler still considers an infinite register file. This is not far from reality though, as clustered machines have abundant register resources (each cluster has a whole register file for its own use).

We evaluated UCIFF on 6 of Mediabench II video [8] **benchmarks**. All benchmarks were compiled with optimizations enabled (-O flag).

5 Results

We evaluate UCIFF by comparing it against the Decoupled, the Oracle and the Full-Search algorithms.

The **Decoupled** scheduler is the state-of-the-art acyclic scheduler for heterogeneous clustered VLIW processors (based on the cyclic scheduler of [2]). It decouples frequency selection from instruction scheduling. The frequency selection step is done via a simple estimation of the energy consumption and the execution (schedule) time. The estimation was done as in [2]:

The schedule time is equal to the cycle count of a profiled homogeneous architecture ($cycles_{hom}$) multiplied by the arithmetic mean of the clock periods of the heterogeneous clusters: $Time = cycles_{hom} \times (\sum_{cl} T_{cl})/NumOfClusters$. The cycle count of each cluster is easily calculated as: $cycles_{cl} = Time/T_{cl}$.

The energy calculation is similar to that of UCIFF (Table 1) with two main differences:

1. The dynamic energy of a cluster is equal to a fraction of that of a homogeneous cluster, proportional to the ratio of f_{cl} to the average frequency:
   $E_{dyn,ins}(cl) = E_{dyn,ins\_hom}(cl) \times f_{cl}/[\sum_{cl}(f_{cl})/NumOfClusters]$
2. The energy of the interconnect is equal to that of the homogeneous:
   $E_{dyn,icc} = P_{icc} \times NumICCs_{homogeneous}$

The **Oracle** scheduler is a decoupled scheduler with a perfect frequency selection phase. The frequency configuration selected will always produce the best schedule with 100% accuracy. This scheduler is the upper bound (optimal) in code quality (Fig.6) and the lowest bound (optimal) in the scheduler run-time (Fig.7). It is non-implementable as it requires future knowledge.

A **Full-Search** UCIFF-based scheduler does not perform any kind of pruning on the frequency space. It is structured as UCIFF, but instead of a hill climbing search, it does a full search over the frequency configurations. This makes it the slowest (Fig.7), but in the meantime it always achieves the optimal code quality, same as that of the Oracle (Fig.6).

Although in the vanilla Decoupled ([2]) clustering and scheduling are in separate steps, in all implementations of the above algorithms, scheduling includes both cluster assignment and instruction scheduling in a unified pass as discussed in Section 3.2.Core and Alg.2. This lets us focus only on the phase ordering problem we are interested in: the one between frequency selection and scheduling.

The high-level features of these algorithms are summarized in Table 2.

Table 2. Some features of the algorithms under comparison

	Decoupled-based		UCIFF-based	
	Decoupled	Oracle	Full-Search	UCIFF
Phase-ordering problem	Yes	No	No	No
Code quality	Low	High	High	High
Algorithmic complexity	Low	Low	High	Medium
Realistic (implementable)	Yes	No	Yes	Yes

Since UCIFF unifies two otherwise distinct phases (frequency selection and scheduling), we show some results (Section 5.1) that quantify the first phase separately. This provides vital insights as to why the unified solution performs better.

5.1   Accuracy of Frequency Selection

The outcome of the Decoupled algorithm relies heavily on the accuracy of the frequency selection phase. The stand-alone frequency selection step makes its decision based on estimations of the energy consumption and the scheduled code's schedule length as in [2]. The estimations are based on the energy and cycle numbers of a homogeneous architecture and on the ratio of the clock cycle of each cluster of the heterogeneous against that of the homogeneous.

On the other hand UCIFF is not based on estimation, but rather on real partial scheduling results. Its frequency decision is therefore much more informed.

UCIFF's frequency selection superiority over the Decoupled algorithm is shown in Fig.5. The horizontal axis shows the error margins in the scheduling outcome when compared to that of the Oracle. For example, a 5% error margin includes the frequency selections that generate results at most 5% worse than that of the Oracle. The vertical axis shows the percentage of frequency selections that have the error margin shown in the horizontal axis. The Decoupled accuracy fluctuates significantly for various metrics; In ED2 it is about 5 times less accurate than in EDP. UCIFF, on the other hand, is constantly very accurate with the fluctuations being less than 10% over all error margins.

5.2   UCIFF Code Quality vs Algorithmic Complexity

The quality of the code generated by each scheduling algorithm when optimizing for various metrics (Energy, EDP, ED2 and Delay) is shown in Fig.6.

We provide an estimate of the algorithmic complexity by measuring the execution time of each algorithm based on the count of "scheduling actions" each algorithm performs. By "scheduling action" we refer to the action of scheduling an

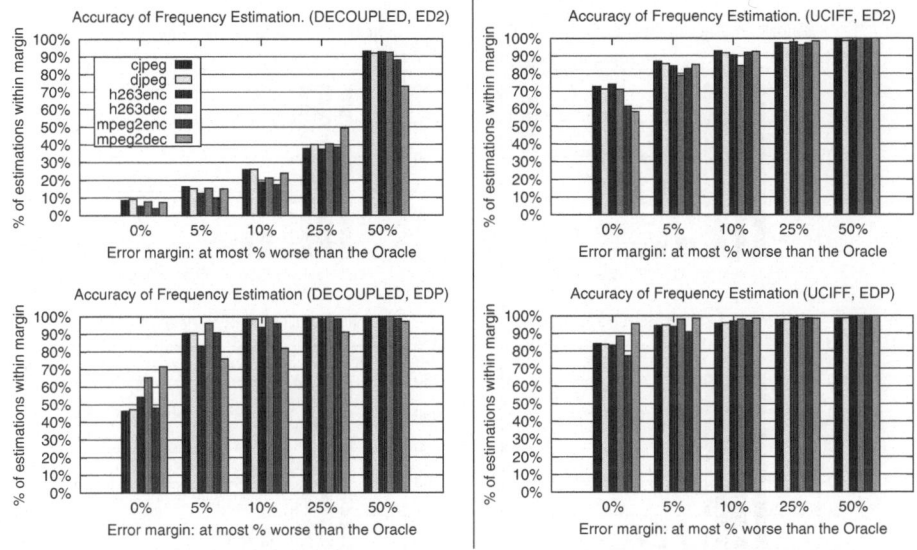

Fig. 5. The Accuracy of the Frequency Selection (Y axis) within the range from the oracle (X axis) for Decoupled (Left) and UCIFF (Right). UCIFF is tuned with STEP=8, STEPVAR=2 and NEIGHBORS=4.

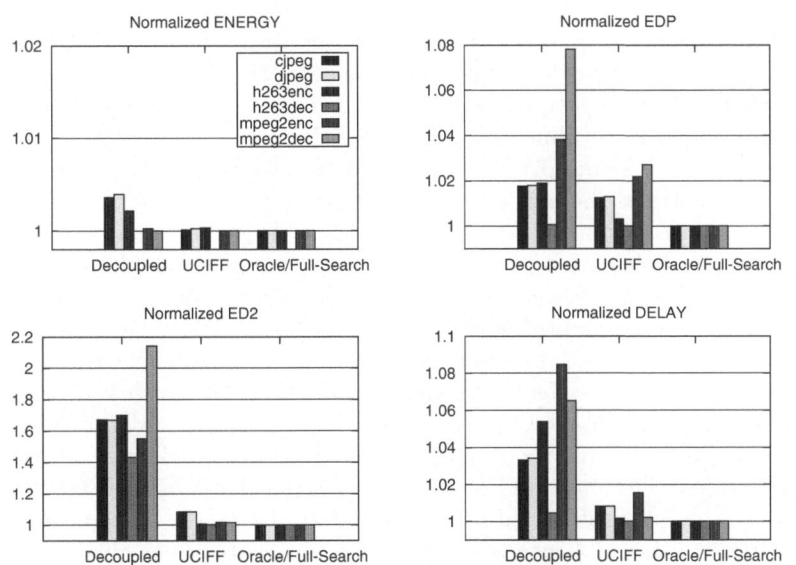

Fig. 6. Code quality (Energy, EDP, ED2, Delay) for Decoupled, UCIFF and Oracle/Full-Search(FS), over the Mediabench2 benchmarks[2] UCIFF is tuned with STEP=8, STEPVAR=2 and NEIGHBORS=4

---

[2] h263dec energy results are missing due to failure in compilation.

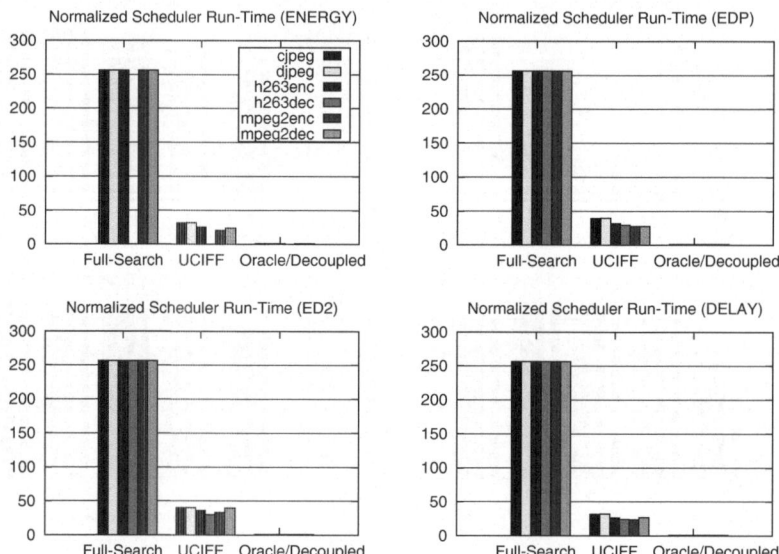

Fig. 7. The scheduler's Run-Time in terms of scheduling actions for Energy, EDP, ED2 and Delay, over the Mediabench2 benchmarks[2] normalized to the Oracle/Decoupled. UCIFF is tuned with STEP=8, STEPVAR=2 and NEIGHBORS=4.

instruction at a specific point. This is an accurate estimate of the time complexity since all algorithms share the same scheduling core. The results are shown in Fig.7.

UCIFF achieves a code quality close to that of the Oracle and the Full-Search, but with a much lower run-time than the Full-Search (Fig.7). This is because UCIFF performs a smart pruning of the frequency configuration space.

The ED2 metric is the hardest to predict at the frequency selection step. This is obvious from the code-quality results of Fig.6. It is there that the estimation of the Decoupled algorithm proves not accurate enough, being 2.15× worse than the Oracle in the worst case. UCIFF, on the other hand, is constantly more accurate than the Decoupled and very close to the Oracle.

UCIFF can be **tuned** to operate at various points in the trade-off space of code quality versus scheduling time complexity. It can get closer or even match Oracle's performance by searching more frequency configurations. There are three knobs that we can configure. In decreasing order of importance they are: NEIGHBORS, STEP and STEPVAR (see Alg.1). The NEIGHBORS variable controls the number of neighboring configurations in the neighboring set. A NEIGHBORS value of 4 means that at most 4 neighbors per cluster are in the neighboring set (that is equivalent to $NDistance = 2$ of Section 3.2). The higher its value, the more accurate the result but the longer it takes for the scheduler to run. The STEP controls the cycle distance before evaluating and re-selecting the neighbors. For very small regions STEP should be as high as the size of the region, to allow for a full-search over it. A high value of STEP however makes the algorithm less adaptive to changes. This is the job of STEPVAR.

It decreases STEP by STEPVAR until STEP reaches 1. The results shown were taken with NEIGHBORS=4, STEP=8, STEPVAR=2. A full investigation of optimally selecting these variables is beyond the scope of this paper.

6 Related Work

The vast majority of code generation related literature on clustered VLIW processors is on **homogeneous designs**.

Pioneering work on code generation for clustered architectures appeared in [5], where the Bottom-Up-Greedy (BUG) cluster-assignment algorithm was introduced. The main heuristic used is the completion-cycle, which calculates the completion cycle of an instruction on each of the possible cluster candidates.

Significant contributions to compilation for clustered VLIW machines were made in the context of the Multiflow compiler [12]. Clustering is based on Ellis' work ([5]). The various design points (heuristic tuning, order of visiting the instructions, etc.) of instruction scheduling, including the cluster assignment, are discussed in detail in this work.

[4] provides an iterative solution to cluster assignment. Each iteration of the algorithm measures the schedule length by performing instruction scheduling and by doing a fast register pressure and communication estimation. This being an iterative algorithm, it has a long run-time and its use is not practical in compilers.

The first work that combines cluster assignment and instruction scheduling was UAS [14]. Unlike BUG ([5]), this is list-scheduling based, not critical-path based solution. Several clustering heuristics are evaluated with the start-cycle heuristic (that is the first half of BUG's completion-cycle heuristic ([5])) shown to be the best one on an architecture with a 1-cycle inter-cluster delay. This work considers the inter-cluster bandwidth as a scheduling resource. UCIFF's scheduling core extends UAS, as discussed in detail in Section 3.2.

CARS ([9,10]) is a combined scheduling, clustering, and register allocation code generation framework based on list scheduling. Depth and height heuristics are used to guide the algorithm. UCIFF could be adapted to work in such a framework for architectures with small register files, where register pressure becomes a bottleneck.

The RAW clustered architecture ([11]) communicates data across clusters with send/receive instructions. The scheduler visits instructions in a topological order and uses the completion time heuristic to guide the process.

A dynamically-scheduled **heterogeneous clustered** processor was proposed in [3]. The dual-cluster design has one high-performance and one low-performance cluster. It does not support DVFS. A DVFS-capable heterogeneous clustered processor was introduced by [13]. The proposed design though is a dynamically scheduled one, and as such no contributions are made on the compiler side.

The most closely related work to UCIFF is [2]. It proposes **code generation** techniques for a heterogeneous clustered VLIW processor, very similar to ours. It proposes a loop scheduling algorithm based on modulo scheduling. This approach however, as we have discussed extensively in Section 2.2, suffers from the phase ordering issue of frequency selection and scheduling which are completely decoupled from one another. The frequency selection is done by estimating the energy and the execution time of each frequency configuration based on profiling data from a homogeneous run.

7 Conclusion

Energy efficiency is becoming a predominant design factor in high performance microprocessors. Heterogeneous clustered VLIW architectures are a viable choice under these design goals. This paper proposes a code generation algorithm for such architectures that performs cluster assignment, instruction scheduling and per-cluster fast frequency selection in a unified manner. Our evaluation shows that the proposed algorithm produces code of superior quality than the existing state-of-the-art and reaches the quality of a scheduler with an oracle frequency selector. This is achieved with a modest increase in algorithmic complexity.

References

1. Gcc: Gnu compiler collection, http://gcc.gnu.org
2. Aleta, A., Codina, J., González, A., Kaeli, D.: Heterogeneous clustered vliw microarchitectures. In: CGO, pp. 354–366 (2007)
3. Baniasadi, A., Moshovos, A.: Asymmetric-frequency clustering: a power-aware back-end for high-performance processors. In: ISLPED, pp. 255–258 (2002)
4. Desoli, G.: Instruction assignment for clustered vliw dsp compilers: A new approach. HP laboratories Technical Report HPL (1998)
5. Ellis, J.: Bulldog: A compiler for vliw architectures. Technical Report, Yale Univ., New Haven, CT, USA (1985)
6. Faraboschi, P., Brown, G., et al.: Lx: a technology platform for customizable vliw embedded processing. In: ISCA, pp. 203–213 (2000)
7. Fridman, J., Greenfield, Z.: The tigersharc dsp architecture. IEEE Micro 20(1), 66–76 (2000)
8. Fritts, J., Steiling, F., et al.: Mediabench ii video: expediting the next generation of video systems research. In: Proceedings of SPIE, vol. 5683, p. 79 (2005)
9. Kailas, K., Ebcioglu, K., Agrawala, A.: Cars: a new code generation framework for clustered ilp processors. Technical Report UMIACS-TR-2000-55 (2000)
10. Kailas, K., Ebcioglu, K., Agrawala, A.: Cars: a new code generation framework for clustered ilp processors. In: HPCA, pp. 133–143 (2001)
11. Lee, W., Barua, R., et al.: Space-time scheduling of instruction-level parallelism on a raw machine. In: ASPLOS (1998)
12. Lowney, P.G., Freudenberger, S.M., et al.: The multiflow trace scheduling compiler. Journal of Supercomputing 7, 51–142 (1993)
13. Muralimanohar, N., et al.: Power efficient resource scaling in partitioned architectures through dynamic heterogeneity. In: ISPASS, pp. 100–111 (2006)
14. Ozer, E., et al.: Unified assign and schedule: a new approach to scheduling for clustered register file microarchitectures, pp. 308–315 (1998)
15. Pechanek, G., Vassiliadis, S.: The ManArray embedded processor architecture. Euromicro 1, 348–355 (2000)
16. Sharangpani, H., Arora, H.: Itanium processor microarchitecture. IEEE Micro 20(5), 24–43 (2000)
17. Terechko, A., Corporaal, H.: Inter-cluster communication in vliw architectures. ACM Transactions on Architecture and Code Optimization (TACO) 4(2), 11 (2007)

A Study on the Impact of Compiler
Optimizations on High-Level Synthesis

Jason Cong, Bin Liu, Raghu Prabhakar, and Peng Zhang

University of California, Los Angeles
{cong,bliu,raghu,pengzh}@cs.ucla.edu

Abstract. High-level synthesis is a design process that takes an un-
timed, behavioral description in a high-level language like C and produces
register-transfer-level (RTL) code that implements the same behavior in
hardware. In this design flow, the quality of the generated RTL is greatly
influenced by the high-level description of the language. Hence it follows
that both source-level and IR-level compiler optimizations could either
improve or hurt the quality of the generated RTL. The problem of ordering compiler optimization passes, also known as the phase-ordering
problem, has been an area of active research over the past decade. In
this paper, we explore the effects of both source-level and IR optimizations and phase ordering on high-level synthesis. The parameters of the
generated RTL are very sensitive to high-level optimizations. We study
three commonly used source-level optimizations in isolation and then
propose simple yet effective heuristics to apply them to obtain a reasonable latency-area tradeoff. We also study the phase-ordering problem
for IR-level optimizations from a HLS perspective and compare it to a
CPU-based setting. Our initial results show that an input-specific order
can achieve a significant reduction in the latency of the generated RTL,
and opens up this technology for future research.

Keywords: Compiler Optimization, Design space exploration, High-level
synthesis, Phase ordering.

1 Introduction

The field of compiler optimizations has been an area of active research for more
than fifty years. Numerous optimizations have been proposed and deployed over
the course of time, each trying to optimize a certain aspect of an input program.
Optimizations play a key role in evaluating a compiler.

A well-known fact in literature [17] is that optimizations have enabling and
disabling interactions among themselves, and the best order is dependent on the
program, target and the optimization function. As the solution space is huge,
compiler researchers have tried a plethora of methods over the past decade based
on searching techniques ([7] [13] [12], [3]), analytical models ([22], [25], [20], [24]),
empirical approaches based on statistical data ([19], [18] [2]), and a mixture of
all of these ([9], [21], [16]). However, it is to be noted that all aforementioned

H. Kasahara and K. Kimura (Eds.): LCPC 2012, LNCS 7760, pp. 143–157, 2013.

approaches have been used in a CPU-based setting. In this case, decisions regarding optimization orders are implicitly or explicitly influenced by execution parameters such as the processor pipeline, size of the instruction window, presence of hardware-managed caches etc. How different would such optimization orders be if the code being optimized was not going to be 'executed' on a processor, but is a behavioral description to be synthesized into some customized hardware itself?

```
int add(int a[20], int o[2])
{
    int i;
    o[0] = 0;
    o[1] = 1;
    for(i = 1; i < 20; i++) {
        if(a[i]%2 == 0) {
            o[0] += a[i];
            o[1] *= a[i];
        }
    }
}
```
(a)

Sequence	CPU(cycles)	HLS (cycles)
gim	3903	12
img	3814	22

(b)

Fig. 1. (a) Example design. (b) CPU vs. HLS setting. CPU best sequence differs from HLS best sequence.

Consider the simple design in Fig. 1. Also, let us consider a set of three optimizations[1]: *global value numbering* (g), *memory to register promotion* (m) and *induction variable canonicalization* (i). The table in Fig. 1(b) summarizes the performance of two sequences *gim* and *img*. The CPU numbers were obtained using Simics, an out-of-order processor simulator, while HLS numbers were obtained using xPilot [4], a research tool for high-level synthesis. We can clearly observe that the sequence *gim* wins in the HLS setting while sequence *img* wins in the CPU setting. We find that *img* produces smaller code with fewer loads, because '*g*' applied after '*m*' is exposed to a greater number of opportunities, thereby performing well on CPU. However, while *img* reduced the loads by reusing computed values, it increased the length of the data dependency chain. This led to the *img* design having one extra state in its finite state machine created during scheduling due to data constraints, thus increasing its latency in the HLS setting.

This simple example shown above demonstrates that there are very subtle details and side effects that can have different impacts on CPU code and HLS designs. The impact of one optimization can be more pronounced in an HLS setting than in a CPU design. A typical CPU has many hardware features that enhance the performance of code that is being executed. For example, multiple levels of caches, out-of-order execution and load/store queues drastically reduce the cost of a single load. Branch prediction and speculative execution can hide the cost of evaluating a branch most of the times in case of loops. High-level synthesis is a different area in that way where each load corresponds to a read from a memory block, and each load costs the same number of cycles. Every branch instruction is dependent on another instruction that computes the exit condition, and branch

---

[1] We use the letters within brackets to refer to the respective optimizations in this section.

prediction mechanisms have to be specified in software manually by the designer if needed. Also, HLS can potentially exploit greater ILP limited only by the physical resources available on the target platform. On a typical processor, only the ILP available within the instruction window is exploited.

In this paper we perform an initial investigation into the impact of compiler transformations in a high-level synthesis setting (HLS). High-level synthesis is an automated design process that takes an un-timed, behavioral description of a circuit in a high-level language like C, and generates a register-transfer-level (RTL) net-list that implements the same behavior. The RTL generated by a HLS process is heavily influenced by the way the design is specified at the high level, making high-level optimizations very significant in the design flow. Works like [10] have tried solving similar problems in the HLS community in the past. We describe and use a set of simple, yet effective heuristics to quickly search the space of the described optimizations and study their effects on several benchmarks.

We also study the impact of classical IR-level optimizations on high-level synthesis. We evaluate several approaches, and suggest a new approach based on *lookahead* for optimizations. We also analyze two real-world benchmarks in a CPU-based and HLS-based setting and show how optimizations can have contrasting side effects. Our initial experiments show that latency improvements of more than 3X can be achieved by choosing the right order for an input behavioural description.

The rest of this paper is organized as follows. We provide some necessary background information regarding HLS and xPilot in Section 2. Our study on high-level optimizations is described in Section 3. We describe our methodology to search the space of IR-level optimizations in Section 4. We provide a detailed evaluation of our approaches in Section 5. We conclude with comments on future work in Section 6.

2   Background

High-level synthesis (HLS), or behavioral synthesis, is the process of automatically generating cycle-accurate RTL models from behavioral specifications. The behavioral specifications are typically in a high-level language, like C/C++/ Matlab. The generated RTL models can then be accepted by the downstream RTL synthesis flow for implementation using ASICs or FPGAs. Compared to the traditional RTL-based design flow, potential advantages of HLS include better management of design complexity, code reuse and easy design-space exploration.

HLS has been an active research topic for more than 30 years. Early attempts to deploy HLS tools began when RTL-based design flows were well adopted. In 1995, Synopsys announced Behavioral Compiler, which accepts behavioral HDL code and connects to downstream flows. Since 2000, a new generation of HLS tools have been developed in both academia and industry. Unlike many predecessors, many of them use C-based languages to capture the design. This makes them more accessible to algorithm and system designers. It also enables hardware and software to be specified in the same language, facilitating software/hardware co-design and co-verification. The use of C-based languages also makes it easy to leverage new techniques in software compilers for parallelization and optimization. As of 2012, notable commercial C-based tools include Cadence C-to-Silicon Compiler, Calypto Catapult C (formerly a product of Mentor Graphics), Synopsys Synphony C and Xilinx AutoESL (originating from the UCLA xPilot project [4]). More detailed surveys on the history and progress of HLS are available from sources such as [8] [5].

xPilot [4] is an academic HLS tool developed at UCLA. It takes as input a C function and generates an RTL Verilog module to implement the functionality. Compiler transformations are first performed on the source code using LLVM [14] to obtain an optimized IR, which can be translated to a control-data flow graph (CDFG). Scheduling is then performed on the CDFG to generate a finite-state machine with data path (FSMD) model, where each operation is assigned to a state in the FSM. Binding is then performed on the FSMD to allocate functional units, storage units and interconnects, and then the RTL net-list is decided.

For a given CDFG, the scheduler in xPilot tries to minimize worst-case latency by default, under the constraints of data dependency, control dependency, clock frequency, and resource limits [6]. The scheduler tries to insert clock boundaries on certain edges of the dependency graph, in order to guarantee that the delay and resource constraints are met. In a simplified model, operations in the same basic block are scheduled into consecutive control states; branches (including loops) are implemented as state transitions in the FSM. Thus, the resulting FSM is somewhat similar to the control-flow graph of the input function. If the control-flow graph of the input function is reducible, it is possible to estimate the worst-case latency of the module given the trip counts of loops.

3   Source-Level Optimizations

In this section, we describe our study of high-level optimization interactions. We consider three optimizations - *array partitioning, loop unrolling* and *loop pipelining*. We have chosen these optimizations as they are most commonly employed in standard high-level synthesis flow [1]. All the experiments in this section have been performed using AutoESL v1.0, 2011. [23]

3.1   Array Partitioning

Array structures in high-level design descriptions are implemented as memory blocks by default. However, mapping arrays to a single RAM resource can create resource constraints as each RAM block has only a few read and write ports. Mapping arrays to multiple RAM blocks can alleviate the resource constraint problem, provided the right number of banks are chosen. In this study, we concentrate only on cyclic distribution of array elements to different partitions. For example, consider a simple, contrived design as shown in Fig. 2(a). Fig. 2(b) shows the effect of partition factors on the latency and area. We make the observation that the best choices for the number of partitions are powers of 2. When

```
void testAP(int a[10], int i)
{
    a[i] = i;
}
```

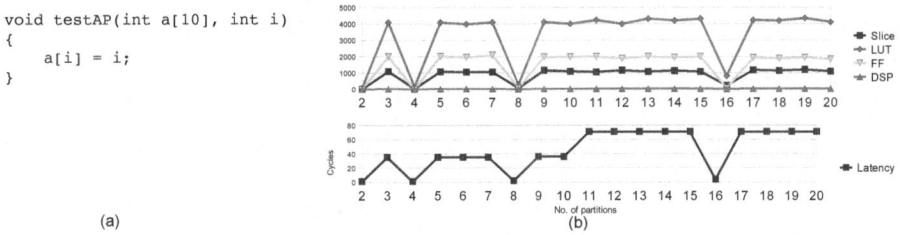

(a)   (b)

Fig. 2. (a) Example design to study array partitioning. DSP: No. of DSP blocks, FF: No. of Flip-Flops, LUT: No. of Look-up tables.(b) Comparison of latency and area numbers for different partitions for design in (a).

an array is partitioned, additional code is inserted that performs *mod* operation on the index to select the right bank. Implementing *mod* on a power-of-2 number n just involves extracting the least significant $log_2(n)$ bits in the binary representation of n and truncating the rest, while for other numbers full 32-bit *mod* operation has to be realised in hardware. Such an operation is slow and occupies a lot of area.

3.2   Loop Unrolling

Loop unrolling is a popular optimization used to reduce loop overhead and increase ILP. It also exposes more opportunities to other optimizations like scalar replacement and dead code elimination. Consider two simple kernel loops shown

```
#define N 500                              #define N 500
void daxpy(int a[N], int b[N], int k, int c)   void prefix(int a[N+1], int b[N+1], int k, int c)
{                                          {
    int i;                                     int i;
    L1:for(i=0;i<N;i++)                        L1:for(i=1;i<N+1;i++) {
    {                                              a[i] = a[i-1] + a[i];
        a[i] = b[i] * k + c;                   }
    }                                      }
}

    (a) No dependency                          (b) Dependence distance = 1
```

Fig. 3. Two simple kernels subject to loop unrolling

in Fig. 3. Fig. 4(a) and 4(b) show the latency and area numbers of the loops in Fig. 3. We make the following observations – (1) The best performing unroll factors in both the kernels considered are *2,4,5,8,10,16,20*. In general, the set of best unroll factors consists of both the factors of the loop trip-count as well as all powers of 2 lesser than the trip count. Unrolling a loop with a number that is not a factor of the trip-count adds the overhead of additional exit checks and branches. For non-power-of-2 unroll factors, the exit checks need a full *32-bit* comparators which are much slower, making them poor choices. Due to these reasons, the FSM created for this design during the scheduling phase is larger and complicated, thereby needing greater area to be implemented. (2)

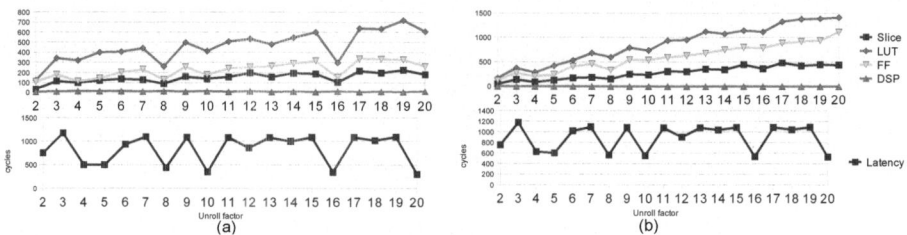

Fig. 4. Latency and area numbers for (a) Fig. 3(a) and (b) Fig. 3(b)

Area consumption increases linearly with unroll factor as it increases the size of one iteration and also the size of the FSM. (3) Unrolling loops with a carried dependency enables optimizations like scalar replacement and global value numbering. (4) Latency gain from unrolling quickly flattens out, while area does not. From the observations above, we form the following conclusions:

- The set of good unroll factors S for a loop L with a trip-count of n can be defined as follows:

$$S = \{f_i | mod(f_i, n) = 0\} \bigcup \{2^k | (k \in N) \land (2^k \le n)\} \tag{1}$$

- Starting from the lowest unroll factor s_i in S, we iterate through the unroll factors and measure the relative drop in latency as well as relative increase in area. We continue our iterative search until we arrive at an unroll factor whose slope of area increase is greater than the slope of latency decrease, and return the previous best unroll factor at this stage. We use AutoESL's estimates to steer the algorithm as it is faster and accurate enough.

3.3 Loop Pipelining

Software pipelining is another popular loop transformation that also attempts to exploit ILP by re-ordering instructions across iterations and overlapping execution of consecutive iterations. Pipelining a loop with low initiation interval yields a high throughput. However, software pipelining can be constrained by the available memory bandwidth. Consider Fig. 5(a) for instance, where resource constraints is inhibiting pipelining. With appropriate array partitioning (Fig. 5(b)), software pipelining combined with loop unrolling proves to be a powerful combination.

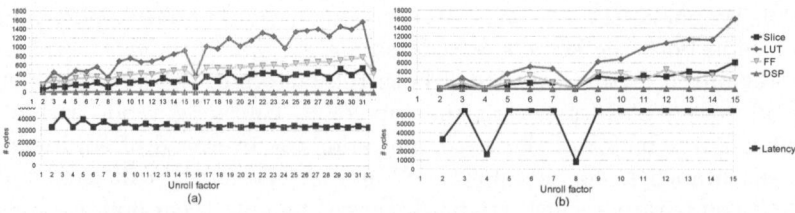

Fig. 5. Pipelining with unrolling loop in Fig. 3(a) for 65536 iterations in (a) without memory partitioning (b) with memory partitioning

3.4   Approach to Search Optimization Space

We use the algorithm described in section 3.2 to obtain the unroll factor u_i giving best performance to area. The loop is unrolled u_i number of times and then pipelined. If the II is constrained due to memory resources, the appropriate array is subjected to partitioning. The partition factor starts at 2 and is then doubled in subsequent iterations if the previous partition factor was insufficient to resolve the resource constraint. We discuss and evaluate our approach in section 5.

4   IR-Level Optimizations

In this section, we describe our study on the effects of phase-ordering of IR-level optimizations.

Optimizations Considered. By default, xPilot applies close to 250 transformations from a set of 55 unique optimizations. The optimization space is very discrete as can be seen in Fig. 6, which was obtained after evaluating 1000 random sequences of length 200 from the same optimization set. We first reduce the search domain in order to obtain greater insight. For this purpose, we randomly chose 100 sequences and examined the effect of each optimization in the sequence. Table 1 gives a brief description of all the short-listed optimizations. From here on in this paper, we restrict all our experiments to this restricted subset of optimizations.

Random Search. In our implementation of random search, we generate random sequences containing upto 25 optimizations each allowing repetitions. We generated and evaluated 5000 random sequences for each of the benchmarks considered.

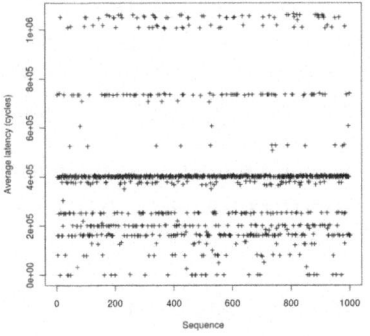

Fig. 6. Scatterplot of latencies for *matrixmul*

Genetic Algorithm. We implement a genetic algorithm to search the space of optimization sequences using latency as the minimization cost function. In our implementation, we chose to have a randomly generated initial population of 20 sequences, each of which can have upto 25 optimizations. We repeat the iterative search process for 500 generations. In each iteration, all the sequences in the population are evaluated and ranked. At the end of evaluation, sequences in the population undergo mutation and crossover. The best sequence is preserved as it is. Finally, 8 to 10 sequences are randomly chosen and mutated. Our implementation chooses sequences at the bottom with a higher probability to be mutated by changing flags randomly. Finally, duplicate sequences are replaced with random sequences. The best solution found after 500 generations is reported.

n-Lookahead   Scheme. The n-lookahead scheme attempts to construct an optimization sequence by progressively deciding on the best subsequence of length n. It is based on an observation that the number of optimizations enabled or disabled by each optimization is relatively small. We are effectively *looking ahead* by n steps and choosing the subsequence that gives the best overall benefit at each step. Therefore, a 0-lookahead scheme is a greedy ap-

Table 1. Subset of optimizations and descriptions

Name	Description
adce (a)	Aggressive dead code elimination
bitwidthmin (b)	Bitwidth minimization
condprop (p)	Conditional propagation
constprop (k)	Constant propagation
dse (e)	Dead store elimination
gcse (c)	Global common subexpression elimination
gvn (n)	Global value Numbering
indvars (v)	Canonicalize induction variables
instcombine (i)	Combine redundant instructions
inst-simplify (t)	Operator strength reduction
loop-deletion (d)	Delete dead loops
loop-preproc (o)	Loop preprocess
loop-simplify (l)	Canonicalize natural loops
mem2reg (m)	Promote memory to register
ptr-legalization (r)	Convert pointers to array indices
simplifycfg (s)	Simplify the control-flow graph
xunroll (x)	Partially unroll loops

proach that chooses the best optimization successively and an N-lookahead scheme (where N is the length of the target sequence) is an exhaustive search. The parameter n provides a tradeoff between the amount of global information considered and number of comparisons. If we have to construct a sequence of length k with n levels of look ahead, and we have N number of unique optimizations, the number of combinations to be evaluated is $(\frac{k}{n}) * N^n$. Larger values of n increases number of sequences exponentially. In section 5, we evaluate the effectiveness of 0-lookahead and 1-lookahead schemes.

MSIR. We also evaluate an approach called Multi- Start Iterative Refinement (MSIR). In this approach, we generate N random sequences. Each sequence $(a_1, a_2...a_n)$ is subjected to an iterative refinement process as follows: Starting from the first pair (a_1, a_2), we generate two sequences starting with (a_1, a_2) and (a_2, a_1) choose the better sequence. We then move to the next pair in the chosen sequence (i.e., to the second position) and perform a similar evaluation. We continue iterating through pairs as long as we see improvement. The iterative search stops when no improvement is obtained upon one iteration through the entire sequence. The best sequence obtained from all the random sequences is returned. Section 5 evaluates and compares MSIR with the other described approaches.

5   Evaluation

5.1   Experiment Design Flow

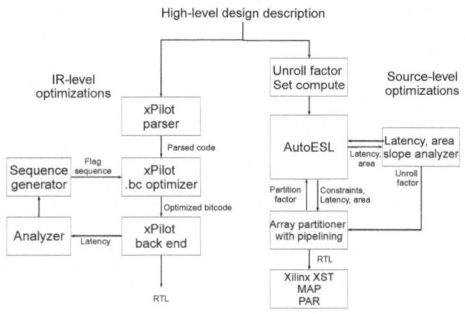

Fig. 7. Broad design flow used in all our experiments

Fig. 7 describes the architecture of our flow. Source-level transformations are studied using AutoESL. The final area numbers reported are from Xilinx's back-end tools. We use xPilot to study IR-level transformations and their impact on the latency of the RTL generated. As AutoESL is does not provide the user such fine-grained control to specify IR-level optimizations, AutoESL is not a suitable tool to study such lower level optimizations. We have modified xPilot to specify arbitrary optimization sequences. Also, as we do not study area utilization for IR-level transformations we do not go through the Xilinx back-end.

5.2   High-Level Optimizations

For purposes of evaluation, we use AutoESL v1.0, an industry-standard high-level synthesis tool. We obtain area numbers from the EDA tool-chain provided by Xilinx. The target platform we consider here is Xilinx Virtex-5.

Results. We tested our approach on five different kinds of kernels taken from the Open Accelerator repository [1] and MiBench [11]. We have hand-chosen different kernels in order to achieve a broader evaluation coverage. The benchmarks are described in Table 2. Overall, we achieve a mean reduction in latency

Table 2. Benchmarks for evaluation of high-level optimizations

Benchmark	Description
adpcm_decoder	Kernel function of the ADPCM decoding algorithm.
daxpy	kernel function performing the vector operation $A = Bk + c$
prefix	kernel function calculating prefix sum on a vector of integers
segmentation	Compute step in an image segmentation algorithm
smithwaterman	Smith-Waterman algorithm

of 50.42% over xPilot's default setting. Table 3 shows the factor obtained from our approach, number of partitions required, latency and area numbers for all benchmarks. Each benchmark is reported under three configurations: *Baseline* – where the benchmark was run without any high-level optimization; *Baseline + PP* – baseline with pipelining, where the main loop was pipelined with the

Table 3. Comparison between baseline and optimized benchmark versions against latency and area using ER

Benchmark	Unroll factor	No. of partitions	Numbers							
				Slice	LUT	FF	II	Depth	Latency	ER
adpcm_decoder	4	1	Baseline	200	588	217	-	-	2502	1
		1	Baseline + PP	224	741	234	2	5	1006	2.22
		1	U4 + PP	619	2009	471	8	11	1006	0.8035
daxpy	8	1	Baseline	21	80	62	-	-	1501	1
		1	Baseline + PP	26	92	75	1	3	504	2.405
		4	U8 + PP	89	324	315	1	3	67	5.286
prefix	8	1	Baseline	29	113	80	-	-	1501	1
		1	Baseline + PP	43	166	91	2	3	1003	1.009
		8	U8 + PP	109	307	375	2	4	130	3.072
segmentation	32	1	Baseline	31	110	65	-	-	8321	1
		1	Baseline + PP	43	153	88	1	2	4100	1.463
		16	U32 + PP	173	522	160	1	3	132	11.296
smithwaterman[2]	4	1	Baseline	26	102	46	-	-	52281	1
		1	Baseline + PP	19	73	46	2	3	11708	6.110
		1	U4 + PP	-	-	-	-	-	-	-

required number of array partitions; and $U(num) + PP$ – unroll by obtained unroll factor with pipelining along with required number of array partitions.

We define the *efficiency ratio* ER as the latency-area product, as follows:

$$ER = \frac{latency_b * area_b}{latency * area} \qquad (2)$$

Here, $latency_b$ and $area_b$ are the latency and area numbers of the baseline respectively. We use the number of slices occupied as the representative for area of a design. We make the following observations:

- *adpcm_decoder* does not benefit from unrolling due to a scalar loop-carried dependency. Due to a scalar carried constraint, unrolling the loop does not increase ILP. Hence the best result for this benchmark is when unrolling is at its minimum i.e., the loop is completely rolled.
- *Segmentation* achieves a remarkable benefit with its configuration with an ER of around 11. As the core loop is data parallel, the only constraint to achieve minimal II would be array resources, and a partitioning factor of 16 resolves all resource constraints.
- smithwaterman benefits from pipelining with an ER of 6, and also shows impressive area usage. Using our heuristics, an unroll factor of 4 was found to give the best performance to area value. However, pipelining the unrolled loop resulted in an AutoESL crash due to an internal bug in the tool.

5.3   IR-Level Optimizations

In this section, we evaluate our approaches described in section 4. Table 4 lists and describes the set of benchmarks that we consider in our evaluation process. We have chosen a few different benchmarks in this section because xPilot is not as mature a tool as AutoESL and failed to synthesize some of the benchmarks.

Random Sampling vs. xPilot. Fig. 8 shows the comparison between the results of random search and the default optimization setting in xPilot. It can be seen that there are significant gains that can be achieved with an optimization order that is benchmark-specific. Overall, we achieve a mean reduction in latency of 50.42% over xPilot's default setting.

Table 4. Benchmarks and description

Benchmark	Description
binarysearch	Iterative binary search
cftmdl	Kernel region in 1D FFT computation
chem	DSP algorithm in a chemical plant
dir	Direct implementation of 1D DCT
fft	Fast fourier tranform from MiBench [11]
honda	DSP filter application
jacobi	Jacobi method to solve linear equations
lee	Lee's algorithm for 1D DCT [15]
matrixmul	Tiled matrix multiplication
sha	SHA-1 encryption algorithm
smithwaterman	Smith-Waterman algorithm

Comparison of Approaches. We compare the performances of various approaches discussed in Section 4. We include only one small benchmark (*binarysearch*) for brevity as a representative example for all the other smaller benchmarks in all our further analyzes.

We can observe from Table 5 that random search and genetic algorithm match up to each other in most cases except *fft*. We can also observe that a similar trend exists between random search and 1-lookahead. We consider this a promising result, as we can achieve the same result as random search in lesser comparisons. We can observe that *mem2reg* is the sole critical optimization for *sha*. Also, we found that *jacobi* suffered with the default sequence due to a disabling interaction between -*scalarrepl* and -*gvn*.

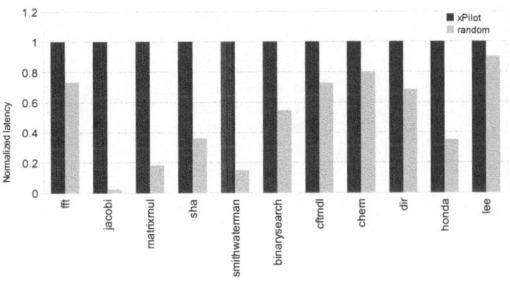

Fig. 8. Comparison of normalized latencies. *Default*: xPilot's default sequence.

Comparison with CPU Performance In order to compare the HLS setting with a CPU-based setting, we picked 200 of the randomly generated optimization sequences for two benchmarks, *sha* and *smithwaterman*. 200 executables were created, labeled with their sequence and simulated using Simics to get accurate cycle counts. Each sequence was given a *CPU rank* and an *xPilot* rank based on their execution time and latency respectively.

Fig. 9 shows the rank disparity between xPilot and CPU for the same optimization sequence. Consider a specific example. It is surprising to see that Sequence 1101 for benchmark *Sha* has an xPilot rank of 2 but a CPU rank of 175: `ldaomboptcxrp`

Our analysis shows that the HLS-specific *bitwidth* optimization was adding a lot of overhead instructions to obtain the operands of the appropriate width, thereby increasing the instruction count. Such side-effects do not exist in HLS because an operator of a specific bit-width can be realized in hardware. We

Table 5. Comparison of different approaches. The *Gen:* field shows the number of generations taken to converge. MSIR has been evaluated with N=10 random sequences. We generated 5000 sequences to evaluate random search.

Benchmark	Approach		Benchmark	Approach	
fft	Random	Latency: 2361 Sequence: srnaln	jacobi	Random	Latency: 492 Sequence: cbaemkxemsbsdtntsem
	GA Gen: 186	Latency: 1896 Sequence: kmnsosbcsenainr		GA Gen: 33	Latency: 492 Sequence: bmciensi
	0-lookAhead	Latency: 2359 Sequence: nktadnxpslbcoemns		0-lookAhead	Latency: 48358 Sequence: mxbtpsealodk
	1-lookAhead	Latency: 2339 Sequence: mnriksbtvbosknkacr		1-lookAhead	Latency: 492 Sequence: kmnsossbcsebnaiinr
	MSIR	Latency: 5359 Sequence: pmkasr		MSIR	Latency: 66116 Sequence: mxbeon
matrixmul	Random	Latency: 49 Sequence: aooeakbesmdsttvocaosa	sha	Random	Latency: 1442 Sequence: mxxasdotxrlxlbrmnt
	GA Gen: 28	Latency: 49 Sequence: mceosi		GA Gen: 1	Latency: 1442 Sequence: iiiiiiim
	0-lookAhead	Latency: 80119 Sequence: rnevxbntoldamssss		0-lookAhead	Latency: 1442 Sequence: mxnapseixrnacsmo
	1-lookAhead	Latency: 669 Sequence: rpnevxbpdeboomisiceb		1-lookAhead	Latency: 1442 Sequence: kmsipekrbrrpemoker
	MSIR	Latency: 368094 Sequence: kbrmae		MSIR	Latency: 1442 Sequence: cltpmx
smithwaterman	Random	Latency: 23 Sequence: kbvdsbbtmeosmn	binarysearch	Random	Latency: 12 Sequence: etaneb
	GA Gen: 51	Latency: 23 Sequence: inemsobs		GA Gen: 1	Latency: 12 Sequence: iiiiiiin
	0-lookAhead	Latency: 844 Sequence: kneimmissnirnxxxp		0-lookAhead	Latency: 12 Sequence: mtsnprciebvsdsak
	1-lookAhead	Latency: 23 Sequence: neamiaosaaaa		1-lookAhead	Latency: 23 Sequence: kmpkrsnciienaebmts
	MSIR	Latency: 2765 Sequence: vsamdn		MSIR	Latency: 12 Sequence: obrnxs

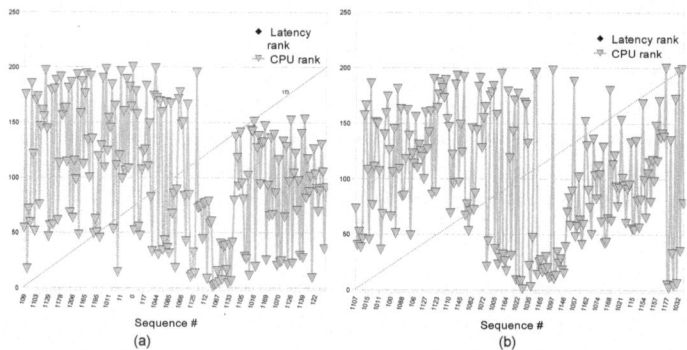

Fig. 9. Rank comparison for CPU vs xPilot. (a) Sha. (b) SmithWaterman.

generated another binary using the same sequence without the *-bitwidthmin* optimization, and observed that the CPU cycle count dropped from 70790 to 55981, which is very close to the lowest value of 48673. We also found that most of the lower-ranked sequences for CPUs had *-bitwidthmin* optimization included in them. Consider the opposite case in optimization sequence 118, which has a CPU rank of 9 and an xPilot rank of 191: npxvervadkxnrnlx

The disparity in ranks is caused due to an interesting interplay between *-gvn* and *-indvars* in the CPU-based and HLS-based settings. We performed additional experiments summarized in Table 6. We can see that the pair *-gvn*

Table 6. Comparison of CPU and HLS settings with optimization sequences involving *-gvn* and *-indvars*

Optimization sequence	xPilot latency	CPU cycle count
(none)	1844	54710
-indvars	1844	54709
-indvars -gvn	1444	54959
-gvn	1444	54958
-gvn -indvars	4024	53644

and *-indvars* affect the CPU and HLS setting in opposite ways. Intuitively *-gvn* decreases number of instructions and our simulation runs confirm that. While *-gvn* removes redundant code, it can have a potential side effect of introducing data dependency due to re-use. Also, if the data to be re-used is in memory, *-gvn* can slightly increase the number of loads in the program, as is the case in our example. The combined effect leads to an increased number of pipeline stalls which explains the increased cycle count. The *-indvars* pass increases code size and also tends to promote certain memory values to registers, thereby reducing the number of loads. Running an *-indvars* pass after *-gvn* pass effectively undoes the damage caused by *-gvn*. Hence we see that in the CPU setting, *-indvars* has a positive effect after *-gvn*.

In the HLS setting, however, there is no instruction execution pipeline. The design can be seen as a data and control-flow driven application where a finite set of instructions can be scheduled to run in every cycle. Hence, fewer instructions need fewer cycles to run. This explains the positive effect of *-gvn* on the xPilot latency. Running an *-indvars* pass after *-gvn* introduces many additional instructions and dependencies, increasing the number of FSM states and latency. We re-ran xPilot using sequence 118 without the *-indvars* option and observed that the latency dropped from 4024 to 1444.

The above experiments show convincingly that applying good transformations for a CPU may not lead to good HLS results, and HLS-specific code optimization sequences and transformations are needed.

6   Conclusions

Given the rise in popularity in high-level synthesis as a popular design choice in the system design community, we believe that having a sound compilation technology in high-level synthesis is very essential. In this paper, we have presented a first study on the impact of compiler optimization phase ordering on design space exploration and the quality of the generated RTLs. We have presented studies on three important high-level optimizations - loop unrolling, software pipelining and array partitioning. We have described simple heuristics to quickly eliminate bad choices early. We have also presented a detailed study of the IR-level optimization phase ordering on high-level synthesis where a variety of techniques were discussed and evaluated. We reported a mean reduction in

latency of 50.42% against xPilot's default setting. We compare our study to a
CPU-based setting and provide several insights into the subtle variations that
causes pairs of optimizations to have different effects.

We believe that our work opens up many interesting future directions. An
interesting direction for future work would be to consider more high-level optimizations. With the vast amount of data that we have collected, the idea of
building a predictive model using program featurs seems attractive as well. With
our promising initial results, we believe that research in this direction would benefit the high-level synthesis community.

Acknowledgements. The authors acknowledge the support of the Gigascale
Systems Research Center, one of six research centers funded under the Focus
Center Research Program (FCRP), a Semiconductor Research Corporation en-
tity, and also the support from Altera Corporation.

References

1. Open Source Accelerator Store,
   http://cadlab.cs.ucla.edu/accelerator_store.html
2. Agakov, F., Bonilla, E., Cavazos, J., Franke, B., Fursin, G., O'Boyle, M.F.P., Thomson, J., Toussaint, M., Williams, C.K.I.: Using machine learning to focus iterative
   optimization. In: Proceedings of the International Symposium on Code Generation
   and Optimization, CGO 2006, pp. 295–305. IEEE Computer Society, Washington,
   DC (2006)
3. Chabbi, M.M., Mellor-Crummey, J.M., Cooper, K.D.: Efficiently exploring compiler optimization sequences with pairwise pruning. In: Proceedings of the 1st International Workshop on Adaptive Self-Tuning Computing Systems for the Exaflop
   Era, EXADAPT 2011, pp. 34–45. ACM, New York (2011)
4. Cong, J., Fan, Y., Han, G., Jiang, W., Zhang, Z.: Platform-based behavior-level
   and system-level synthesis. In: Proc. IEEE Int. SOC Conf., pp. 199–202 (2006)
5. Cong, J., Liu, B., Neuendorffer, S., Noguera, J., Vissers, K., Zhang, Z.: High-level
   synthesis for FPGAs: From prototyping to deployment. IEEE Trans. on Computer-
   Aided Design of Integrated Circuits and Systems 30(4), 473–491 (2011)
6. Cong, J., Zhang, Z.: An efficient and versatile scheduling algorithm based on SDC
   formulation. In: Proc. Design Automation Conf., pp. 433–438 (2006)
7. Cooper, K.D., Schielke, P.J., Subramanian, D.: Optimizing for reduced code space
   using genetic algorithms. In: Proceedings of the ACM SIGPLAN 1999 Workshop
   on Languages, Compilers, and Tools for Embedded Systems, LCTES '99, pp. 1–9.
   ACM, New York (1999)
8. Coussy, P., Morawiec, A.: High-Level Synthesis: From Algorithm to Digital Circuit.
   Springer (2008)
9. Epshteyn, A., Garzarán, M.J., DeJong, G., Padua, D.A., Ren, G., Li, X., Yotov, K.,
   Pingali, K.K.: Analytic Models and Empirical Search: A Hybrid Approach to Code
   Optimization. In: Ayguadé, E., Baumgartner, G., Ramanujam, J., Sadayappan, P.
   (eds.) LCPC 2005. LNCS, vol. 4339, pp. 259–273. Springer, Heidelberg (2006),
   http://dx.doi.org/10.1007/978-3-540-69330-7_18
10. Gupta, S., Gupta, R.K., Dutt, N.D., Nicolau, A.: Coordinated parallelizing com-
    piler optimizations and high-level synthesis. ACM Trans. Design Autom. Electr.
    Syst. 9(4), 441–470 (2004)

11. Guthaus, M.R., Ringenberg, J.S., Ernst, D., Austin, T.M., Mudge, T., Brown, R.B.: Mibench: A free, commercially representative embedded benchmark suite. In: Proceedings of the Workload Characterization, WWC-4, 2001 IEEE International Workshop, pp. 3–14. IEEE Computer Society, Washington, DC (2001)
12. Kisuki, T., Knijnenburg, P.M.W., O'Boyle, M.F.P.: Combined selection of tile sizes and unroll factors using iterative compilation. In: Proceedings of the 2000 International Conference on Parallel Architectures and Compilation Techniques, PACT 2000, p. 237. IEEE Computer Society, Washington, DC (2000)
13. Kulkarni, P., Hines, S., Hiser, J., Whalley, D., Davidson, J., Jones, D.: Fast searches for effective optimization phase sequences. In: Proceedings of the ACM SIGPLAN 2004 Conference on Programming Language Design and Implementation, PLDI 2004, pp. 171–182. ACM, New York (2004)
14. Lattner, C., Adve, V.: LLVM: A compilation framework for lifelong program analysis & transformation. In: Proc. Int. Symp. on Code Generation and Optimization, p. 75 (2004)
15. Lee, B.: A new algorithm to compute the discrete cosine transform. IEEE Trans. Acoustics, Speech and Signal Processing (6), 1243–1245 (1984)
16. Pan, Z., Eigenmann, R.: Fast and effective orchestration of compiler optimizations for automatic performance tuning. In: Proceedings of the International Symposium on Code Generation and Optimization, CGO 2006, pp. 319–332. IEEE Computer Society, Washington, DC (2006)
17. Pollock, L.L.: An approach to incremental compilation of optimized code. PhD thesis, Pittsburgh, PA, USA, UMI order no. GAX86-20225 (1986)
18. Stephenson, M., Amarasinghe, S.: Predicting unroll factors using supervised classification. In: Proceedings of the International Symposium on Code Generation and Optimization, CGO 2005, pp. 123–134. IEEE Computer Society, Washington, DC (2005)
19. Stephenson, M., Amarasinghe, S., Martin, M., O'Reilly, U.-M.: Meta optimization: improving compiler heuristics with machine learning. In: Proceedings of the ACM SIGPLAN 2003 Conference on Programming Language Design and Implementation, PLDI 2003, pp. 77–90. ACM, New York (2003)
20. Tate, R., Stepp, M., Tatlock, Z., Lerner, S.: Equality saturation: a new approach to optimization. In: Proceedings of the 36th Annual ACM SIGPLAN-SIGACT Symposium on Principles of Programming Languages, POPL 2009, pp. 264–276. ACM, New York (2009)
21. Triantafyllis, S., Vachharajani, M., Vachharajani, N., August, D.I.: Compiler optimization-space exploration. In: Proceedings of the International Symposium on Code Generation and Optimization: Feedback-Directed and Runtime Optimization, CGO 2003, pp. 204–215. IEEE Computer Society, Washington, DC (2003)
22. Whitfield, D., Soffa, M.L.: An approach to ordering optimizing transformations. In: Proceedings of the Second ACM SIGPLAN Symposium on Principles & Practice of Parallel Programming, PPOPP 1990, pp. 137–146. ACM, New York (1990)
23. Zhang, Z., Fan, Y., Jiang, W., Han, G., Yang, C., Cong, J.: AutoPilot: A Platform-Based ESL Synthesis System, pp. 99–112 (2008)
24. Zhao, M., Childers, B., Soffa, M.L.: Predicting the impact of optimizations for embedded systems. In: Proceedings of the 2003 ACM SIGPLAN Conference on Language, Compiler, and Tool for Embedded Systems, LCTES 2003, pp. 1–11. ACM, New York (2003)
25. Zhao, M., Childers, B.R., Soffa, M.L.: A Framework for Exploring Optimization Properties. In: de Moor, O., Schwartzbach, M.I. (eds.) CC 2009. LNCS, vol. 5501, pp. 32–47. Springer, Heidelberg (2009)

FlowPools: A Lock-Free Deterministic Concurrent Dataflow Abstraction

Aleksandar Prokopec[1], Heather Miller[1], Tobias Schlatter[1], Philipp Haller[2], and Martin Odersky[1]

[1] EPFL, Switzerland
firstname.lastname@epfl.ch
[2] Typesafe, Inc.
firstname.lastname@typesafe.com

Abstract. Implementing correct and deterministic parallel programs is challenging. Even though concurrency constructs exist in popular programming languages to facilitate the task of deterministic parallel programming, they are often too low level, or do not compose well due to underlying blocking mechanisms. In this paper, we present the design and implementation of a fundamental data structure for composable deterministic parallel dataflow computation through the use of functional programming abstractions. Additionally, we provide a correctness proof, showing that the implementation is linearizable, lock-free, and deterministic. Finally, we show experimental results which compare our *FlowPool* against corresponding operations on other concurrent data structures, and show that in addition to offering new capabilities, FlowPools reduce insertion time by $49 - 54\%$ on a 4-core i7 machine with respect to comparable concurrent queue data structures in the Java standard library.

Keywords: dataflow, concurrent data-structure, deterministic parallelism.

1 Introduction

Multicore architectures have become ubiquitous– even most mobile devices now ship with multiple core processors. Yet parallel programming has yet to enter the daily workflow of the mainstream developer. One significant obstacle is an undesirable choice programmers must often face when solving a problem that could greatly benefit from leveraging available parallelism. Either choose a nondeterministic, but performant, data structure or programming model, or sacrifice performance for the sake of clarity and correctness.

Programming models based on *dataflow* [1, 2] have the potential to simplify parallel programming, since the resulting programs are deterministic. Moreover, dataflow programs can be expressed more declaratively than programs based on mainstream concurrency constructs, such as shared-memory threads and locks, as programmers are only required to specify data and control dependencies. This allows one to reason sequentially about the intended behavior of their program, meanwhile enabling the underlying framework to effectively extract parallelism.

H. Kasahara and K. Kimura (Eds.): LCPC 2012, LNCS 7760, pp. 158–173, 2013.

In this paper, we present the design and implementation of FlowPools, a fundamental dataflow collections abstraction which can be used as a building block for larger and more complex *deterministic* and parallel dataflow programs. Our FlowPool abstraction is backed by an efficient non-blocking data structure. As a result, our data structure benefits from the increased robustness provided by lock-freedom [12], since its operations are not blocked by delayed threads. We provide a lock-freedom proof, which guarantees progress regardless of the behavior, including the failure, of concurrent threads.

In combining lock-freedom with a functional interface, we go on to show that FlowPools are *composable*. That is, using prototypical higher-order functions such as `foreach` and `aggregate`, one can concisely form dataflow graphs, in which associated functions are executed asynchronously in a completely non-blocking way, as elements of FlowPools in the dataflow graph become available.

Finally, we show that FlowPools are able to overcome practical issues, such as out-of-memory errors, thus enabling programs based upon FlowPools to run indefinitely. By using a *builder* abstraction, instead of something like iterators or streams (which can lead to non-determinism) we are able to garbage collect parts of the data structure we no longer need, thus reducing memory consumption.

Our contributions are the following:

1. The design and Scala [19] implementation[1] of a parallel dataflow abstraction and underlying data structure that is deterministic, lock-free, & composable.
2. Proofs of lock-freedom, linearizability, and determinism.
3. Detailed benchmarks comparing the performance of our FlowPools against other popular concurrent data structures.

2 Model of Computation

FlowPools are similar to a typical collections abstraction. Operations invoked on a FlowPool are executed on its individual elements. However, FlowPools do not only act as a data container of elements. Unlike a typical collection, FlowPools also act as nodes and edges of a directed acyclic computation graph (DAG), in which the executed operations are registered with the FlowPool.

Nodes in this directed acyclic graph are data containers which are first class values. This makes it possible to use FlowPools as function arguments or to receive them as return values. Edges, on the other hand, can be thought of as combinators or higher-order functions whose user-defined functions are the previously-mentioned operations that are registered with the FlowPool. In addition to providing composability, this means that the DAG does not have to be specified at compile time, but can be generated dynamically at run time instead.

This structure allows for complete asynchrony, allowing the runtime to extract parallelism as a result. That is, elements can be asynchronously inserted, all registered operations can be asynchronously executed, and new operations can be asynchronously registered. Put another way, invoking several higher-order functions in succession on a given FlowPool does not add barriers between nodes

---

[1] See http://www.assembla.com/code/scala-dataflow/git/nodes

in the DAG, it only extends the DAG. This means that individual elements within a FlowPool can *flow* through different edges of the DAG independently.

Properties of FlowPools. In our model, FlowPools have certain properties which ensure that resulting programs are deterministic.

1. Single-assignment - an element added to the FlowPool cannot be removed.
2. No order - data elements in FlowPools are unordered.
3. Purity - traversals are side-effect free (pure), except when invoking FlowPool operations.
4. Liveness - callbacks are eventually asynchronously executed on all elements.

We claim that FlowPools are deterministic in the sense that all execution schedules either lead to some form of non-termination (*e.g.*, some exception), or the program terminates and no difference can be observed in the final state of the resulting data structures. This definition is practically useful, because in the case of non-termination it is guaranteed that on some thread an exception is thrown which aids debugging, *e.g.*, by including a stack trace. For a more formal definition and proof of determinism, see section 5.

3   Programming Interface

A FlowPool can be thought of as a concurrent pool data structure, *i.e.*, it can be used similarly to a collections abstraction, complete with higher-order functions, or combinators, for composing computations on FlowPools. In this section, we describe the semantics of several of those functional combinators and other basic operations defined on FlowPools.

Append (<<). The most fundamental of all operations on FlowPools is the concurrent thread-safe append operation. As its name suggests, it simply takes an argument of type `Elem` and appends it to a given FlowPool.

Foreach and Aggregate. A pool containing a set of elements is of little use if its elements cannot be manipulated in some manner. One of the most basic data structure operations is element traversal, often provided by iterators or streams–stateful objects which store the current position in the data structure. However, since their state can be manipulated by several threads at once, using streams or iterators can result in nondeterministic executions.

Another way to traverse the elements is to provide a higher-order `foreach` operator which takes a user-specified function as an argument and applies it to every element. For it to be deterministic, it must be called for every element that is eventually inserted into the FlowPool, rather than only on those present when `foreach` is called. Furthermore, determinism still holds even if the user-specified function contains side-effecting FlowPool operations such as <<. For `foreach` to be non-blocking, it cannot wait until additional elements are added to the FlowPool. Thus, the `foreach` operation must execute asynchronously, and be eventually applied to every element. Its signature is `def foreach[U](f: T => U): Future[Int]`, and its return type `Future[Int]` is an integer value which becomes available once `foreach` traverses all the elements added to the pool. This integer denotes the number of times the `foreach` has been called.

The `aggregate` operation aggregates the elements of the pool and has the following signature: `def aggregate[S](zero: =>S)   (cb: (S, S) => S) (op: (S, T) => S): Future[S]`, where `zero` is the initial aggregation, `cb` is an associative operator which combines several aggregations, `op` is an operator that adds an element to the aggregation, and `Future[S]` is the final aggregation of all the elements which becomes available once all the elements have been added. The `aggregate` operator divides elements into subsets and applies the aggregation operator `op` to aggregate elements in each subset starting from the `zero` aggregation, and then combines different subset aggregations with the `cb` operator. In essence, the first part of `aggregate` defines the commutative monoid and the functions involved must be non-side-effecting. In contrast, the operator `op` is guaranteed to be called only once per element and it can have side-effects.

While in an imperative programming model, `foreach` and `aggregate` are equivalent in the sense that one can be implemented in terms of the other, in a single-assignment programming model `aggregate` is more expressive. The `foreach` operation can be implemented using `aggregate`, but not vice versa.

Builders. The FlowPool described so far must maintain a reference to all the elements at all times to implement the `foreach` operation correctly. Since elements are never removed, the pool may grow indefinitely and run out of memory. However, it is important to note that appending new elements does not necessarily require a reference to any of the existing elements. This observation allows us to move the `<<` operation out of the FlowPool and into a different abstraction called a `builder`. Thus, a typical application starts by registering all the `foreach` operations, and then it releases the references to FlowPools, leaving only references to builders. In a managed environment, the GC then can automatically discard the no longer needed objects.

Seal. After deciding that no more elements will be added, further appends can be disallowed by calling `seal`. This has the advantage of discarding the registered `foreach` operations. More importantly, the `aggregate` can complete its future– this is only possible once it is known there will be no more appends.

Simply preventing append calls after the point when `seal` is called, however, yields a nondeterministic programming model. Imagine a thread that attempts to seal the pool executing concurrently with a thread that appends an element. In one execution, the append can precede the seal, and in the other the append can follow the seal, causing an error. To avoid nondeterminism, there has to be an agreement on the current state of the pool. A convenient and sufficient way to make `seal` deterministic is to provide the expected pool size as an argument. The semantics of `seal` is such that it fails if the pool is already sealed with a different size or the number of elements is greater than the desired size. Note that we do not guarantee that the same exception always occurs on the same thread– rather, if *any* thread throws *some* exception in *some* execution schedule, then in *all* execution schedules *some* thread will throw *some* exception.

Higher-Order Operators. We now show how these basic abstractions can be used to build higher-order abstractions. To start, it is convenient to have generators that create certain pool types. In a dataflow graph, FlowPools created by generators can be thought of as source nodes. As an example, tabulate (below) creates a sequence of elements by applying a user-specified function f to natural numbers. One can imagine more complex generators, which add elements from a network socket or a file, for example.

```scala
def tabulate[T]
  (n: Int, f: Int => T)
  val p = new FlowPool[T]
  val b = p.builder
  def recurse(i: Int) {
    b << f(i)
    if i < n recurse(i + 1)
  }
  future { recurse(0) }
  p
```

```scala
def map[S](f: T => S)
  val p = new FlowPool[S]
  val b = p.builder
  for (x <- this) {
    b << f(x)
  } map {
    sz => b.seal(sz)
  }
  p
```

```scala
def foreach[U](f: T => U)
  aggregate(0)(_ + _) {
    (acc, x) =>
      f(x)
      acc + 1
  }
```

The tabulate generator starts by creating a FlowPool of an arbitrary type T and creating its builder instance. It then starts an asynchronous computation using the future construct (see the companion technical report [20] for explanation and examples), which recursively applies f to each number and adds it to the builder. The reference to the pool p is returned *immediately*, before the asynchronous computation completes.

A typical higher-order collection operator map is used to map each element of a dataset to produce a new dataset. This corresponds to chaining or pipelining the dataflow graph nodes. Operator map traverses the elements of this FlowPool and appends each mapped element to the builder. The for loop is syntactic sugar for calling the foreach method on this. We assume that the foreach return type Future[Int] has map and flatMap operations, executed once the future value becomes available. The Future.map above ensures that once the current pool (this) is sealed, the mapped pool is sealed to the appropriate size.

As argued before, foreach can be expressed in terms of aggregate by accumulating the number of elements and invoking the callback f each time. However, some patterns cannot be expressed in terms of foreach. The filter combinator filters out the elements for which a specified predicate does not hold. Appending the elements to a new pool can proceed as before, but the seal needs to know the exact number of elements added– thus, the aggregate accumulator is used to track the number of added elements.

```scala
def filter
  (pred: T => Boolean)
  val p = new FlowPool[T]
  val b = p.builder
  aggregate(0)(_ + _) {
    (acc, x) => if pred(x) {
      b << x
      1
    } else 0
  } map { sz => b.seal(sz) }
  p
```

```scala
def flatMap[S]
  (f: T => FlowPool[S])
  val p = new FlowPool[S]
  val b = p.builder
  aggregate(future(0))(add) {
    (af, x) =>
      val sf = for (y <- f(x))
        b << y
      add(af, sf)
  } map { sz => b.seal(sz) }
  p
```

```scala
def union[T]
  (that: FlowPool[T])
  val p = new FlowPool[T]
  val b = p.builder
  val f = for (x <- this) b << x
  val g = for (y <- that) b << y
  for (s1 <- f; s2 <- g)
    b.seal(s1 + s2)
  p
```

```scala
def add(f: Future[Int], g: Future[Int]) =
  for (a <- f; b <- g) yield a + b
```

```
type Terminal {                    type Block {                      type FlowPool {
  sealed: Int                        array: Array[Elem]                start: Block
  callbacks: List[Elem => Unit]      next: Block                       current: Block
}                                    index: Int                       }
                                     blockindex: Int                  LASTELEMPOS = BLOCKSIZE - 2
type Elem                          }                                  NOSEAL = -1
```

Fig. 1. FlowPool data-types

The `flatMap` operation retrieves a pool for each element of `this` pool and adds its elements to the resulting pool. Given two FlowPools, it can be used to generate the Cartesian product of their elements. The implementation is similar to that of `filter`, but we reduce the size on the future values of the sizes– each intermediate pool may not yet be sealed. The operation q `union` r, as one might expect, produces a new pool which has elements of both pool q and pool r.

The last two operations correspond to joining nodes in the dataflow graph. Note that if we could somehow merge the two different `foreach` loops to implement the third join type `zip`, `zip` would be nondeterministic. The programming model does not allow us to do this, however. The `zip` function is better suited for data structures with deterministic ordering, such as Oz streams, which would in turn have a nondeterministic `union`.

4   Implementation

We now describe the FlowPool and its basic operations. In doing so, we omit the details not relevant to the algorithm[2] and focus on a high-level description of a non-blocking data structure. One straightforward way to implement a growing pool is to use a linked list of nodes that wrap elements. Since we are concerned about the memory footprint and cache-locality, we store the elements into arrays instead, which we call blocks. Whenever a block becomes full, a new block is allocated and the previous block is made to point to the `next` block. This way, most writes amount to a simple array-write, while allocation occurs only occasionally. Each block contains a hint `index` to the first free entry in the array, i.e. one that does not contain an element. An `index` is a hint, since it may actually reference an entry that comes earlier than the first free entry. Additionally, a FlowPool also maintains a reference to the first block called `start`. It also maintains a hint to the last block in the chain of blocks, called `current`. This reference may not always be up-to-date, but it always points to some block in the chain.

Each FlowPool is associated with a list of callbacks which have to be called in the future as new elements are added. Each FlowPool can also be in a sealed state, meaning there is a bound on the number of elements it can have. This information is stored as a `Terminal` value in the first free array entry. At all times, we maintain the invariant that the array in each block starts with a sequence of elements, followed by a `Terminal` delimiter. From a higher-level perspective, appending an element starts by copying the `Terminal` value to the next entry and then overwriting the current entry with the element being appended.

---

[2] Specifically the builder abstraction and the `aggregate` operation. The `aggregate` can be implemented using `foreach` with a side-effecting accumulator.

```
 1 def create()
 2   new FlowPool {
 3     start = createBlock(0)
 4     current = start
 5   }
 6
 7 def createBlock(bidx: Int)
 8   new Block {
 9     array = new Array(BLOCKSIZE)
10     index = 0
11     blockindex = bidx
12     next = null
13   }
14
15 def append(elem: Elem)
16   b = READ(current)
17   idx = READ(b.index)
18   nexto = READ(b.array(idx + 1))
19   curo = READ(b.array(idx))
20   if check(b, idx, curo) {
21     if CAS(b.array(idx+1), nexto, curo) {
22       if CAS(b.array(idx), curo, elem) {
23         WRITE(b.index, idx + 1)
24         invokeCallbacks(elem, curo)
25       } else append(elem)
26     } else append(elem)
27   } else {
28     advance()
29     append(elem)
30   }
31
32 def check(b: Block, idx:Int, curo:Object)
33   if idx > LASTELEMPOS return false
34   else curo match {
35     elem: Elem =>
36       return false
37     term: Terminal =>
38       if term.sealed = NOSEAL return true
39       else {
40         if totalElems(b,idx)<term.sealed
41           return true
42         else error("sealed")
43       }
44     null =>
45       error("unreachable")
46   }
47
48 def advance()
49   b = READ(current)
50   idx = READ(b.index)
51   if idx > LASTELEMPOS
52     expand(b, b.array(idx))
53   else {
54     obj = READ(b.array(idx))
55     if obj is Elem WRITE(b.index, idx + 1)
56   }
57
58 def expand(b: Block, t: Terminal)
59   nb = READ(b.next)
60   if nb is null {
61     nb = createBlock(b.blockindex + 1)
62     nb.array(0) = t
63     if CAS(b.next, null, nb)
64       expand(b, t)
65   } else {
66     CAS(current, b, nb)
67   }
```

```
 68 def totalElems(b: Block, idx: Int)
 69   return b.blockindex * (BLOCKSIZE - 1) + idx
 70
 71 def invokeCallbacks(e: Elem, term: Terminal)
 72   for (f <- term.callbacks) future {
 73     f(e)
 74   }
 75
 76 def seal(size: Int)
 77   b = READ(current)
 78   idx = READ(b.index)
 79   if idx <= LASTELEMPOS {
 80     curo = READ(b.array(idx))
 81     curo match {
 82       term: Terminal =>
 83         if ¬tryWriteSeal(term, b, idx, size)
 84           seal(size)
 85       elem: Elem =>
 86         WRITE(b.index, idx + 1)
 87         seal(size)
 88       null =>
 89         error("unreachable")
 90     }
 91   } else {
 92     expand(b, b.array(idx))
 93     seal(size)
 94   }
 95
 96 def tryWriteSeal(term: Terminal, b: Block,
 97   idx: Int, size: Int)
 98   val total = totalElems(b, idx)
 99   if total > size error("too many elements")
100   if term.sealed = NOSEAL {
101     nterm = new Terminal {
102       sealed = size
103       callbacks = term.callbacks
104     }
105     return CAS(b.array(idx), term, nterm)
106   } else if term.sealed ≠ size {
107     error("already sealed with different size")
108   } else return true
109
110 def foreach(f: Elem => Unit)
111   future {
112     asyncFor(f, start, 0)
113   }
114
115 def asyncFor(f:Elem => Unit, b:Block, idx:Int)
116   if idx <= LASTELEMPOS {
117     obj = READ(b.array(idx))
118     obj match {
119       term: Terminal =>
120         nterm = new Terminal {
121           sealed = term.sealed
122           callbacks = f ∪ term.callbacks
123         }
124         if ¬CAS(b.array(idx), term, nterm)
125           asyncFor(f, b, idx)
126       elem: Elem =>
127         f(elem)
128         asyncFor(f, b, idx + 1)
129       null =>
130         error("unreachable")
131     }
132   } else {
133     expand(b, b.array(idx))
134     asyncFor(f, b.next, 0)
135   }
```

Fig. 2. FlowPool operations pseudocode

The `append` operation starts by reading the `current` block and the `index` of the free position. It then reads `nexto` after the first free entry, followed by a read of the `curo` at the free entry. The `check` procedure checks the conditions of the bounds, whether the FlowPool was already sealed or if the current array entry contains an element. In either of these events, the `current` and `index` values need to be set– this is done in the `advance` procedure. We call this the **slow path** of the `append` method. Notice that there are several situations which trigger the slow path. For example, if some other thread completes the `append` method but is preempted before updating the value of the hint `index`, then the `curo` will have the type `Elem`. The same happens if a preempted thread updates the value of the hint `index` after additional elements have been added, via unconditional write in line 23. Finally, reaching an end of block triggers the slow path.

Otherwise, the operation executes the **fast path** and appends an element. It first copies the `Terminal` value to the next entry with a CAS instruction in line 21, with `nexto` being the expected value. If it fails (e.g. due to a concurrent CAS), the append operation is restarted. Otherwise, it proceeds by writing the element to the current entry with a CAS in line 22, the expected value being `curo`. On success, it updates the `b.index` value and invokes all the callbacks (present when the element was added) with the `future` construct. In the implementation, we do not schedule an asynchronous computation for each element. Instead, the callback invocations are batched to avoid the scheduling overhead– the array is scanned for new elements until the first free entry is reached.

Interestingly, note that inverting the order of the reads in lines 18 and 19 would cause a race in which a thread could overwrite a `Terminal` value with some older `Terminal` value if some other thread appended an element in between.

The `seal` operation continuously increases the `index` in the block until it finds the first free entry. It then tries to replace the `Terminal` value there with a new `Terminal` value which has the seal size set. An error occurs if a different seal size is set already. The `foreach` operation works in a similar way, but is executed asynchronously. Unlike `seal`, it starts from the first element in the pool and calls the callback for each element until it finds the first free entry. It then replaces the `Terminal` value with a new `Terminal` value with the additional callback. From that point on the `append` method is responsible for scheduling that callback for subsequently added elements. Note that all three operations call `expand` to add an additional block once the current block is empty, to ensure lock-freedom.

Multi-lane FlowPools. Using a single block sequence (i.e. lane) to implement a FlowPool does not take full advantage of the lack of ordering guarantees and may cause slowdowns due to collisions when multiple concurrent writers are present. Multi-Lane FlowPools overcome this limitation by having a lane for each CPU, where each lane has the same implementation as the normal FlowPool.

This has several implications. First of all, CAS failures during insertion are avoided to a high extent and memory contention is decreased due to writes occurring in different cache-lines. Second, `aggregate` callbacks are added to each lane individually and aggregated once all of them have completed. Finally, `seal` needs to be globally synchronized in a non-blocking fashion.

Once `seal` is called, the remaining free slots are split amongst the lanes equally. If a writer finds that its lane is full, it writes to some other lane instead. This raises the frequency of CAS failures, but in most cases happens only when the FlowPool is almost full, thus ensuring that the `append` operation scales.

5   Correctness

We give an outline of the correctness proof here. More formal definitions, and a complete set of lemmas and proofs can be found in the tech report [20].

We define the notion of an abstract pool $\mathbb{A} = (elems, callbacks, seal)$ of elements in the pool, callbacks and the seal size. Given an abstract pool, abstract pool operations produce a new abstract pool. The key to showing correctness is to show that an abstract pool operation corresponds to a FlowPool operation—that is, it produces a new abstract pool corresponding to the state of the FlowPool after the FlowPool operation has been completed.

Lemma 5.1. Given a FlowPool consistent with some abstract pool, CAS instructions in lines 21, 63 and 66 do not change the corresponding abstract pool.

Lemma 5.2. Given a FlowPool consistent with an abstract pool $(elems, cbs, seal)$, a successful CAS in line 22 changes it to the state consistent with an abstract pool $(\{elem\} \cup elems, cbs, seal)$. There exists a time $t_1 \geq t_0$ at which every callback $f \in cbs$ has been called on $elem$.

Lemma 5.3. Given a FlowPool consistent with an abstract pool $(elems, cbs, seal)$, a successful CAS in line 124 changes it to the state consistent with an abstract pool $(elems, (f, \emptyset) \cup cbs, seal)$ There exists a time $t_1 \geq t_0$ at which f has been called for every element in $elems$.

Lemma 5.4. Given a FlowPool consistent with an abstract pool $(elems, cbs, seal)$, a successful CAS in line 105 changes it to the state consistent with an abstract pool $(elems, cbs, s)$, where either $seal = -1 \wedge s \in \mathbb{N}_0$ or $seal \in \mathbb{N}_0 \wedge s = seal$.

Theorem 5.5. [Safety] Operations `append`, `foreach` and `seal` are consistent with the abstract pool semantics.

Theorem 5.6. [Linearizability] Operations `append` and `seal` are linearizable.

Lemma 5.7. After invoking a FlowPool operation `append`, `seal` or `foreach`, if a non-consistency changing CAS in lines 21, 63, or 66 fails, they must have already been completed by another thread since the FlowPool operation began.

Lemma 5.8. After invoking a FlowPool operation `append`, `seal` or `foreach`, if a consistency changing CAS in lines 22, 105, or 124 fails, then some thread has successfully completed a consistency changing CAS in a finite number of steps.

Lemma 5.9. After invoking a FlowPool operation `append`, `seal` or `foreach`, a consistency changing instruction will be completed after a finite number of steps.

$$t ::= \qquad\qquad \text{terms} \qquad\qquad p \in \{(vs, \sigma, cbs) \mid vs \subseteq Elem, \sigma \in \{-1\} \cup \mathbb{N},$$

create p	pool creation	$cbs \subset Elem \Rightarrow Unit\}$
$p << v$	append	$v \in Elem$
p foreach f	foreach	$f \in Elem \Rightarrow Unit$
p seal n	seal	$n \in \mathbb{N}$
t_1 ; t_2	sequence	

Fig. 3. Syntax

Theorem 5.10. [Lock-freedom] FlowPool operations append, foreach and seal are lock-free.

Determinism. We claim that the FlowPool abstraction is *deterministic* in the sense that a program computes the same result (possibly an error) regardless of the interleaving of execution steps. Here we give an outline of the determinism proof. A complete formal proof can be found in the technical report [20].

The following definitions and the determinism theorem are based on the language shown in Figure 3. The semantics of our core language is defined using reduction rules which define transitions between *execution states*. An execution state is a pair $T \mid P$ where T is a set of concurrent threads and P is a set of Flow-Pools. Each thread executes a *term* of the core language (typically a sequence of terms). State of a thread is represented as the (rest of) the term that it still has to execute; this means there is a one-to-one mapping between threads and terms. For example, the semantics of append is defined by the following reduction rule (a complete summary of all the rules can be found in the appendix):

$$\frac{t = p << v \; ; \; t' \quad p = (vs, cbs, -1) \quad p' = (\{v\} \cup vs, cbs, -1)}{t, T \mid p, P \; \longrightarrow \; t', T \mid p', P} \text{(Append1)}$$

Append simply adds the value v to the pool p, yielding a modified pool p'. Note that this rule can only be applied if the pool p is not sealed (the seal size is -1). The rule for *foreach* modifies the set of callback functions in the pool:

$$\frac{t = p \text{ foreach } f \; ; \; t' \quad p = (vs, cbs, n)}{T' = \{g(v) \mid g \in \{f\} \cup cbs, v \in vs\} \quad p' = (vs, \{f\} \cup cbs, n)}{t, T \mid p, P \; \longrightarrow \; t', T, T' \mid p', P} \text{(Foreach2)}$$

This rule only applies if p is sealed at size n, meaning that no more elements will be appended later. Therefore, an invocation of the new callback f is scheduled for each element v in the pool. Each invocation creates a new thread in T'.

Programs are built by first creating one or more FlowPools using create. Concurrent threads can then be started by (a) appending an element to a FlowPool, (b) sealing the FlowPool and (c) registering callback functions (foreach).

Definition 5.11. [Termination] A term t terminates with result P if its reduction ends in execution state $\{t : t = \{\epsilon\}\} \mid P$.

Definition 5.12. [Interleaving] Consider the reduction of a term t: $T_1 \mid P_1 \longrightarrow T_2 \mid P_2 \longrightarrow \ldots \longrightarrow \{t : t = \{\epsilon\}\} \mid P_n$. An *interleaving* is a reduction of t starting in $T_1 \mid P_1$ in which reduction rules are applied in a different order.

Definition 5.13. [Determinism] The reduction of a term t is *deterministic iff* either (a) t does not terminate for any interleaving, or (b) t always terminates with the same result for all interleavings.

Theorem 5.14. [FlowPool Determinism] Reduction of terms t is deterministic.

6   Evaluation

We evaluate our implementation (single-lane and multi-lane FlowPools) against the LinkedTransferQueue [14] for all benchmarks and the ConcurrentLinkedQueue [17] for the insert benchmark, both found in JDK 1.7, on three different architectures; a quad-core 3.4 GHz i7-2600, 4x octa-core 2.27 GHz Intel Xeon x7560 (both with hyperthreading) and an octa-core 1.2GHz UltraSPARC T2 with 64 hardware threads. In this section, we focus on the scaling properties of the above-mentioned data structures, Figures 4 & 5.

In the *Insert* benchmark, Figure 4, we evaluate concurrent insert operations, by distributing the work of inserting N elements into the data structure concurrently across P threads. In Figure 4, it's evident that both single-lane FlowPools and concurrent queues do not scale well with the number of concurrent threads, particularly on the i7 architecture. They quickly slow down, likely due to cache line collisions and CAS failures. On the other hand, multi-lane FlowPools scale well, as threads write to different lanes, and hence different cache lines, meanwhile also avoiding CAS failures. This appears to reduce execution time for insertions up to 54% on the i7, 63% on the Xeon and 92% on the UltraSPARC.

The performance of higher-order functions is evaluated in the *Reduce, Map* (both in Figure 4) and *Histogram* benchmarks (Figure 5). It's important to note that the *Histogram* benchmark serves as a "real life" example, which uses both the map and reduce operations that are benchmarked in Figure 4. Also note that in all of these benchmarks, the time it takes to insert elements into the FlowPool is also measured, since the FlowPool programming model allows one to insert elements concurrently with the execution of higher-order functions.

In the *Histogram* benchmark, Figure 5, P threads produce a total of N elements, adding them to the FlowPool. The `aggregate` operation is then used to produce 10 different histograms concurrently with a different number of bins. Each separate histogram is constructed by its own thread (or up to P, for multi-lane FlowPools). A crucial difference between queues and FlowPools here, is that with FlowPools, multiple histograms are produced by invoking several `aggregate` operations, while queues require writing each element to several queues– one for each histogram. Without additional synchronization, reading a single queue is not an option, since elements have to be removed from the queue eventually, and it is not clear to each reader when to do this. With FlowPools, elements are automatically garbage collected when no longer needed.

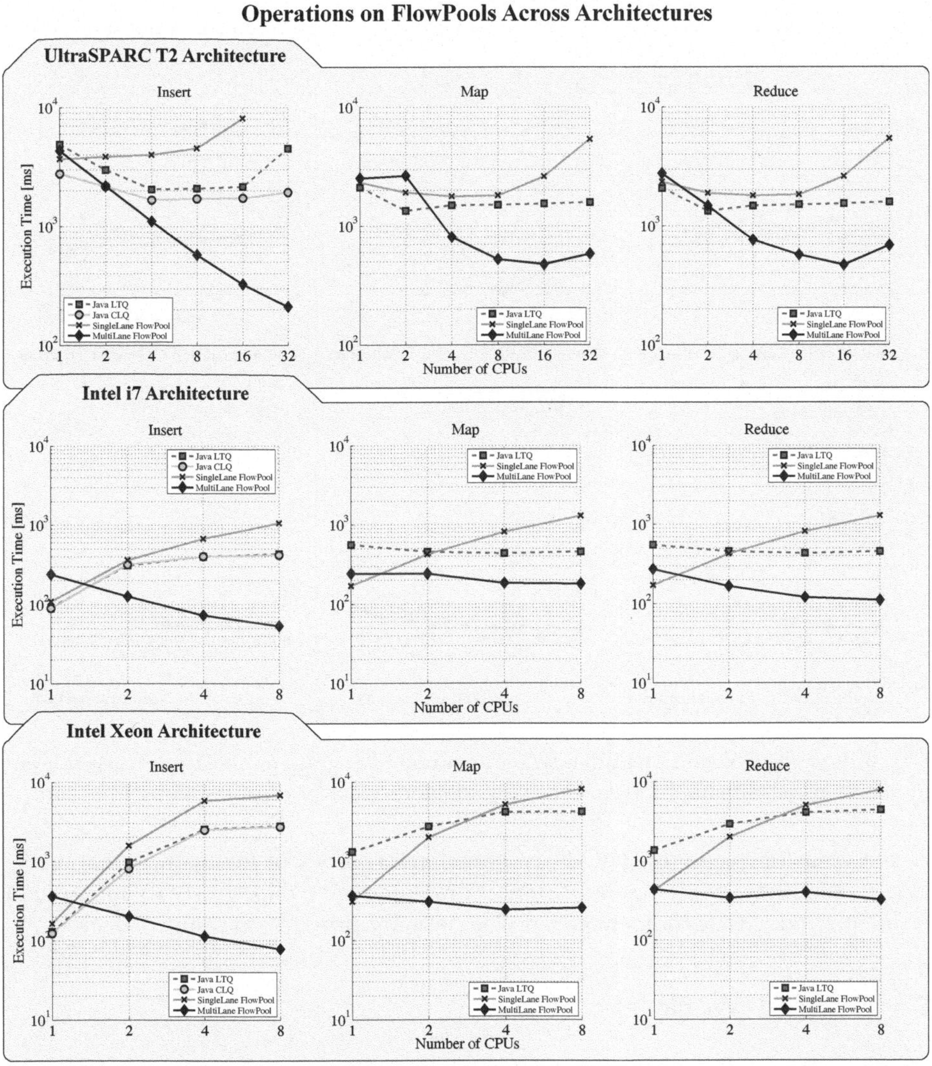

Operations on FlowPools Across Architectures

Fig. 4. Execution time vs parallelization across three different architectures on three important FlowPool operations; insert, map, reduce

Finally, to validate the last claim of garbage being automatically collected, in the *Communication/Garbage Collection* benchmark, Figure 5, we create a pool in which a large number of elements N are added concurrently by P threads. Each element is then processed by one of P threads through the use of the `aggregate` operation. We benchmark against linked transfer queues, where P threads concurrently remove elements from the queue and process it. For each run, we vary the size of the N and examine its impact on the execution time. Especially in the cases of the Intel architectures, the multi-lane FlowPools perform considerably better than the linked transfer queues. As a matter of fact, the

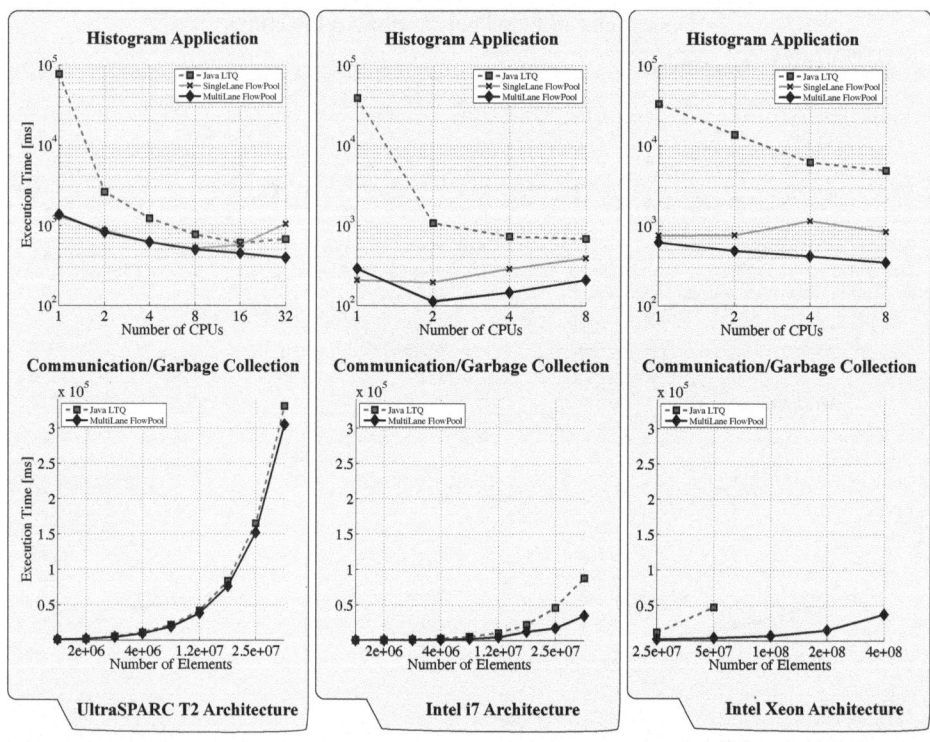

Fig. 5. Execution time vs parallelization on a real histogram application (top), & communication benchmark (bottom) showing memory efficiency, across all architectures.

linked transfer queue on the Xeon benchmark ran out of memory, and was unable to complete, while the multi-lane FlowPool scaled effortlessly to 400 million elements, indicating that unneeded elements are properly garbage collected.

7   Related Work

An introduction to linearizability and lock-freedom is given by Herlihy and Shavit [13]. A detailed overview of concurrent data structures is given by Moir and Shavit [18]. To date, concurrent data structures remain an active area of research– we restrict this summary to those relevant to this work.

Concurrently accessible queues have been present for a while, an implementation is described by [16]. Non-blocking concurrent linked queues are described by Michael and Scott [17]. This CAS-based queue implementation is cited and used widely today, a variant of which is present in the Java standard library. More recently, Scherer, Lea and Scott [14] describe synchronous queues which internally hold both data and requests. Both approaches above entail blocking (or spinning) at least on the consumer's part when the queue is empty.

While the abstractions above fit well in the concurrent imperative model, they have the disadvantage that the programs written using them are inherently nondeterministic. Roy and Haridi [21] describe the Oz programming language, a subset of which yields programs deterministic by construction. Oz dataflow streams are built on top of single-assignment variables and are deterministically ordered. They allow multiple consumers, but only one producer at a time. Oz has its own runtime which implements blocking using continuations.

The concept of single-assignment variables is used to provide logical variables in concurrent logic programming languages [23]. It is also embodied in futures proposed by Baker and Hewitt [11], and promises first mentioned by Friedman and Wise [7]. Futures were first implemented in MultiLISP [10], and have been employed in many languages and frameworks since. Scala 2.10 futures [9] and Twitter futures [6] are of interest, because they define monadic operators and a number of high-level combinators that create new futures. These APIs avoid blocking. Futures have been generalized to data-driven futures, which provide additional information to the scheduler [24]. Many frameworks have constructs that start an asynchronous computation and yield a future holding its result, for example, Habanero Java [3] (`async`) and Scala [19] (`future`).

A number of other models and frameworks recognized the need to embed the concept of futures into other data-structures. Single-assignment variables have been generalized to I-Structures [1] which are essentially single-assignment arrays. CnC [4, 2] is a parallel programming model influenced by dynamic dataflow, stream-processing and tuple spaces [8]. In CnC the user provides high-level operations along with the ordering constraints that form a computation dependency graph. FlumeJava [5] is a distributed programming model which relies heavily on the concept of collections containing futures. An issue that often arises with dataflow programming models are unbalanced loads. This is often solved using bounded buffers which prevent the producer from overflowing the consumer.

Opposed to the correct-by-construction determinism described thus far, a type-systematic approach can also ensure that concurrent executions have deterministic results. Recently, work on Deterministic Parallel Java showed that a region-based type system can ensure determinism [15]. X10's constrained-based dependent types can similarly ensure determinism and deadlock-freedom [22].

8 Conclusion

The abstraction for concurrent dataflow programming we presented provides a composable deterministic programming model. It can be implemented in a provably non-blocking manner and is efficient as well, as shown in experiments.

As future work, we plan developing other concurrent collection types with deterministic semantics, which enrich the correct-by-construction single-assignment model, such as bounded buffers, streams and maps. On the implementation level, we anticipate the need of embedding the callbacks within the data-structure itself, as is the case with callback-based futures and FlowPools – this has a particular benefit on platforms which do not support efficient continuations.

References

1. Arvind, Nikhil, R.S., Pingali, K.K.: I-structures: Data structures for parallel computing. ACM Trans. Prog. Lang. and Sys. 11(4), 598–632 (1989)
2. Budimlic, Z., Burke, M.G., Cavé, V., Knobe, K., Lowney, G., Newton, R., Palsberg, J., Peixotto, D.M., Sarkar, V., Schlimbach, F., Tasirlar, S.: Concurrent collections. Scientific Programming 18(3-4), 203–217 (2010)
3. Budimlic, Z., Cavé, V., Raman, R., Shirako, J., Tasirlar, S., Zhao, J., Sarkar, V.: The design and implementation of the Habanero-Java parallel programming language. In: OOPSLA Companion, pp. 185–186 (2011)
4. Burke, M.G., Knobe, K., Newton, R., Sarkar, V.: Concurrent collections programming model. In: Encyclopedia of Parallel Computing, pp. 364–371 (2011)
5. Chambers, C., Raniwala, A., Perry, F., Adams, S., Henry, R.R., Bradshaw, R., Weizenbaum, N.: FlumeJava: easy, efficient data-parallel pipelines. ACM SIGPLAN Notices 45(6), 363–375 (2010)
6. Eriksen, M., Kallen, N.: Twitter Finagle: Futures,
   http://twitter.github.com/finagle/
7. Friedman, D., Wise, D.: The impact of applicative programming on multiprocessing. In: International Conference on Parallel Processing (1976)
8. Gelernter, D.: Generative communication in Linda. ACM Transactions on Programming Languages and Systems 7(1), 80–112 (1985)
9. Haller, P., Prokopec, A., Miller, H., Klang, V., Kuhn, R., Jovanovic, V.: Scala improvement proposal: Futures and promises, SIP-14 (2012),
   http://docs.scala-lang.org/sips/pending/futures-promises.html
10. Halstead, J.R.H.: MultiLISP: A language for concurrent symbolic computation. ACM Trans. Prog. Lang. and Sys. 7(4), 501–538 (1985)
11. Henry, J., Baker, C., Hewitt, C.: The incremental garbage collection of processes. In: Proc. Symp. on Art. Int. and Prog. Lang. (1977)
12. Herlihy, M.: A methodology for implementing highly concurrent data structures. In: PPoPP, pp. 197–206 (1990)
13. Herlihy, M., Shavit, N.: The Art of Multiprocessor Programming (April 2008)
14. Scherer III, W.N., Lea, D., Scott, M.L.: Scalable synchronous queues. Commun. ACM 52(5), 100–111 (2009)
15. Bocchino Jr., R.L., Adve, V.S., Dig, D., Adve, S.V., Heumann, S., Komuravelli, R., Overbey, J., Simmons, P., Sung, H., Vakilian, M.: A type and effect system for deterministic parallel Java. In: OOPSLA, pp. 97–116 (2009)
16. Mellor-Crummey, J.M.: Concurrent queues: Practical fetch-and-Φ algorithms (1987)
17. Michael, M.M., Scott, M.L.: Simple, fast, and practical non-blocking and blocking concurrent queue algorithms. In: PODC, pp. 267–275 (1996)
18. Moir, Shavit: Concurrent data structures. In: Mehta, Sahni (eds.) Handbook of Data Structures and Applications, Chapman & Hall/CRC (2005)
19. Odersky, M., Spoon, L., Venners, B.: Programming in Scala. Artima Press, Mountain View (2010)
20. Prokopec, A., Miller, H., Schlatter, T., Haller, P., Odersky, M.: Flowpools: A lock-free deterministic concurrent dataflow abstraction– proofs. Technical Report EPFL-REPORT-181098, EPFL, Lausanne (June 2012)

21. Roy, P.V., Haridi, S.: Concepts, Techniques, and Models of Computer Programming. MIT Press (2004)
22. Saraswat, V.A., Sarkar, V., von Praun, C.: X10: concurrent programming for modern architectures. In: PPOPP, p. 271 (2007)
23. Shapiro, E.: The family of concurrent logic programming languages. ACM Computing Surveys 21(3), 412 (1989)
24. Tasirlar, S., Sarkar, V.: Data-driven tasks and their implementation. In: ICPP, pp. 652–661 (2011)

Task Parallelism and Data Distribution: An Overview of Explicit Parallel Programming Languages

Dounia Khaldi, Pierre Jouvelot, Corinne Ancourt, and François Irigoin

CRI, Mathématiques et systèmes, MINES ParisTech
35 rue Saint-Honoré, 77300 Fontainebleau, France
`firstname.lastname@mines-paristech.fr`

Abstract. Efficiently programming parallel computers would ideally require a language that provides high-level programming constructs to avoid the programming errors frequent when expressing parallelism. Since task parallelism is considered more error-prone than data parallelism, we survey six popular parallel language designs that tackle this difficult issue: Cilk, Chapel, X10, Habanero-Java, OpenMP and OpenCL. Using the parallel computation of the Mandelbrot set as running example, this paper describes how the fundamentals of task parallel programming are dealt with in these languages. Our study suggests that, even though there are many keywords and notions introduced by these languages, they boil down, as far as control issues are concerned, to three key task concepts: creation, synchronization and atomicity. These languages adopt one of three memory models: shared, message passing and Partitioned Global Address Space. The paper is designed to give users and language and compiler designers an up-to-date comparative overview of current parallel languages.

Keywords: Parallel language, Task parallelism, Mandelbrot set, Cilk, Chapel, X10, Habanero-Java, OpenMP, OpenCL.

1 Introduction

Parallel computing is about 50 years old. The market dominance of multi- and many-core processors and the growing importance and the increasing number of clusters in the Top500 list (`top500.org`) are making parallelism a key concern when implementing current applications such as weather modeling [10] or nuclear simulations [9]. These important applications require large computational power and thus need to be programmed to run on powerful parallel supercomputers. Programming languages adopt one of two ways to deal with this issue: (1) high-level languages hide the presence of parallelism at the software level, thus offering a code easy to build and port, but the performance of which is not guaranteed, and (2) low-level languages use explicit constructs for communication patterns and specifying the number and placement of threads, but the resulting code is difficult to build and not very portable, although usually efficient.

Recent programming models explore the best trade-offs between expressiveness and performance when addressing parallelism. Traditionally, there are two general ways to break an application into concurrent parts in order to take advantage of a parallel computer and execute them simultaneously on different CPUs: data and task parallelisms.

H. Kasahara and K. Kimura (Eds.): LCPC 2012, LNCS 7760, pp. 174–189, 2013.

In data parallelism, the same instruction is performed repeatedly and simultaneously on different data. In task parallelism, the execution of different processes (threads) is distributed across multiple computing nodes. Task parallelism is often considered more difficult to specify than data parallelism, since it lacks the regularity present in the latter model; processes (threads) run simultaneously different instructions, leading to different execution schedules and memory access patterns. Task management must address both control and data issues, in order to optimize execution and communication times.

This paper describes how six popular and efficient parallel programming language designs tackle the issue of task parallelism specification: Cilk, Chapel, X10, Habanero-Java, OpenMP and OpenCL. They are selected based on the richness of their functionality and their popularity; they provide simple high-level parallel abstractions that cover most of the parallel programming language design spectrum. We use a popular parallel problem (the computation of the Mandelbrot set [1]) as a running example. We consider this an interesting test case, since it exhibits a high-level of embarrassing parallelism while its iteration space is not easily partitioned, if one wants to have tasks of balanced run times. Since our focus is here the study and comparison of the expressiveness of each language's main parallel constructs, we do not give performance measures for these implementations.

Our paper is useful to (1) programmers, to choose a parallel language and write parallel applications, (2) language designers, to compare their ideas on how to tackle parallelism in new languages with existing proposals, and (3) designers of optimizing compilers, to develop automatic tools for writing parallel programs. Our own goal was to use this case study for the design of SPIRE [11], a sequential to parallel intermediate representation extension of the intermediate representations used in compilation frameworks, in order to upgrade their existing infrastructure to address parallel languages.

After this introduction, Section 2 presents our running example. We discuss the parallel language features specific to task parallelism, namely task creation, synchronization and atomicity, and also how these languages distribute data over different processors in Section 3. In Section 4, a selection of current and important parallel programming languages are described: Cilk, Chapel, X10, Habanero Java, OpenMP and OpenCL. For each language, an implementation of the Mandelbrot set algorithm is presented. Section 5 compares and discusses these languages. We conclude in Section 6.

2   Mandelbrot Set Computation

The Mandelbrot set is a fractal set. For each complex $c \in \mathbb{C}$, the set of complex numbers $z_n(c)$ is defined by induction as follows: $z_0(c) = c$ and $z_{n+1}(c) = z_n^2(c) + c$. The Mandelbrot set M is then defined as $\{c \in \mathbb{C}/\lim_{n \to \infty} z_n(c) < \infty\}$; thus, M is the set of all complex numbers c for which the series $z_n(c)$ converges. One can show [1] that a finite limit for $z_n(c)$ exists only if the modulus of $z_m(c)$ is less than 2, for some positive m. We give a sequential C implementation of the computation of the Mandelbrot set in Figure 2. Running this program yields Figure 1, in which each complex c is seen as a pixel, its color being related to its convergence property: the Mandelbrot set is the black shape in the middle of the figure.

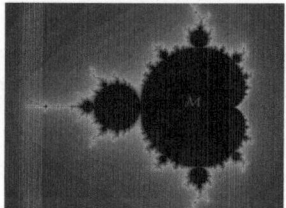

Fig. 1. Result of the Mandelbrot set

```
unsigned  long  min_color = 0,  max_color = 16777215;
unsigned  int  width = NPIXELS, height = NPIXELS, N = 2, maxiter = 10000;
double  r_min = −N, r_max = N, i_min = −N, i_max = N;
double  scale_r = (r_max − r_min)/ width ;
double  scale_i = (i_max − i_min)/ heigth ;
double  scale_color = ( max_color − min_color )/ maxiter ;
Display *display; Window win; GC gc;
for  (row = 0; row < height ; ++row) {
  for  (col = 0; col < width; ++col) {
    z.r = z.i = 0;
    /* Scale c as display coordinates of current point */
    c.r = r_min + ((double) col ∗ scale_r);
    c.i = i_min + (( double ) ( height−1−row) ∗ scale_i );
    /* Iterates z = z∗z+c while |z| < N, or maxiter is reached */
    k = 0;
    do {
      temp = z.r∗z.r − z.i∗z.i + c.r;
      z.i = 2∗z.r∗z.i + c.i; z.r = temp;
      ++k;
    } while (z.r∗z.r + z.i∗z.i < (N∗N) && k < maxiter );
    /* Set color and display point */
    color = (ulong) ((k−1) ∗ scale_color) + min_color;
    XSetForeground (display , gc, color );
    XDrawPoint (display , win, gc, col, row);
  }
}
```

Fig. 2. Sequential C implementation of the Mandelbrot set

We use this base program as our test case in our parallel implementations, in Section 4, for the parallel languages we selected. This is an interesting case for illustrating parallel programming languages: (1) it is an embarrassingly parallel problem, since all computations of pixel colors can be performed simultaneously, and thus is obviously a good candidate for expressing parallelism, but (2) its efficient implementation is not obvious, since good load balancing cannot be achieved by simply grouping localized pixels together because convergence can vary widely from one point to the next, due to the fractal nature of the Mandelbrot set.

3   Task Parallelism Issues

Among the many issues related to parallel programming, the questions of task creation, synchronization, atomicity and memory model are particularly acute when dealing with task parallelism, our focus in this paper.

3.1 Task Creation

In this paper, a task is a static notion, i.e., a list of instructions, while processes and threads are running instances of tasks. Creation of system-level task instances is an expensive operation, since its implementation, via processes, requires allocating and later possibly releasing system-specific resources. If a task has a short execution time, this overhead might make the overall computation quite inefficient. Another way to introduce parallelism is to use lighter, user-level tasks, called threads. In all languages addressed in this paper, task management operations refer to such user-level tasks. The problem of finding the proper size of tasks, and hence the number of tasks, can be decided at compile or run times, using heuristic means.

In our Mandelbrot example, the parallel implementations we provide below use a static schedule that allocates a number of iterations of the loop `row` to a particular thread; we interleave successive iterations into distinct threads in a round-robin fashion, in order to group loop body computations into chunks, of size $\mathtt{height}/P$, where P is the (language-dependent) number of threads. Our intent here is to try to reach a good load balancing between threads.

3.2 Synchronization

Coordination in task-parallel programs is a major source of complexity. It is dealt with using synchronization primitives, for instance when a code fragment contains many phases of execution where each phase should wait for the precedent ones to proceed. When a process or a thread exits before synchronizing on a barrier that other processes are waiting on or when processes operate on different barriers using different orders, a deadlock occurs. Programs must avoid these situations (and be deadlock-free). Different forms of synchronization constructs exist, such as mutual exclusion when accessing shared resources using locks, join operations that terminate child threads, multiple synchronizations using barriers[1], and point-to-point synchronization using counting semaphores [18].

In our Mandelbrot example, we need to synchronize all pixel computations before exiting; one also needs to use synchronization to deal with the atomic section (see next subsection). Even though synchronization is rather simple in this example, caution is always needed; an example that may lead to deadlocks is mentioned in Section 5.

3.3 Atomicity

Access to shared resources requires atomic operations that, at any given time, can be executed by only one process or thread. Atomicity comes in two flavors: weak and strong [13]. A weak atomic statement is atomic only with respect to other explicitly atomic statements; no guarantee is made regarding interactions with non-isolated statements (not declared as atomic). By opposition, strong atomicity enforces non-interaction of atomic statements with all operations in the entire program. It usually

---

[1] The term "barrier" is used in various ways by authors [17]; we consider here that barriers are synchronization points that wait for the termination of sets of threads, defined in a language-dependent manner.

requires specialized hardware support (e.g., atomic "compare and swap" operations), although a software implementation that treats non-explicitly atomic accesses as implicitly atomic single operations (using a single global lock) is possible.

In our Mandelbrot example, display accesses require connection to the X server; drawing a given pixel is an atomic operation since GUI-specific calls need synchronization. Moreover, two simple examples of atomic sections are provided in Section 5.

3.4 Memory Models

The choice of a proper memory model to express parallel programs is an important issue in parallel language design. Indeed, the ways processes and threads communicate using the target architecture and impact the programmer's computation specification affect both performance and ease of programming. There are currently three main approaches.

Message Passing. This model uses communication libraries to allow efficient parallel programs to be written for distributed memory systems. These libraries provide routines to initiate and configure the messaging environment as well as sending and receiving data packets. Currently, the most popular high-level message-passing system for scientific and engineering applications is MPI (Message Passing Interface) [14]. OpenCL [15] uses a variation of the message passing memory model.

Shared Memory. Also called global address space, this model is the simplest one to use [4]. There, the address spaces of the threads are mapped onto the global memory; no explicit data passing between threads is needed. However, synchronization is required between the threads that are writing and reading data to and from the shared memory. OpenMP [16] and Cilk [5] use the shared memory model.

Partitioned Global Address Space. PGAS-based languages combine the programming convenience of shared memory with the performance control of message passing by partitioning logically a global address space; each portion is local to each thread. From the programmer's point of view programs have a single address space and one task of a given thread may refer directly to the storage of a different thread. The three other programming languages in this paper use the PGAS memory model.

4   Parallel Programming Languages

We present here six parallel programming language designs and describe how they deal with the concepts introduced in the previous section. Given the large number of parallel languages that exist, we focus primarily on languages that are in current use and popular and that support simple high-level task-oriented parallel abstractions.

4.1   Cilk

Cilk [5], developed at MIT, is a multithreaded parallel language based on C for shared memory systems. Cilk is designed for exploiting dynamic and asynchronous parallelism. A Cilk implementation of the Mandelbrot set is provided in Figure 3[2].

---

[2] From now on, variable declarations are omitted, unless required for the purpose of our presentation.

```
{
  cilk_lock_init ( display_lock );
  for (m = 0; m < P; m++)
    spawn compute_points (m);
  sync;
}
cilk void compute_points ( uint m) {
  for (row = m; row < height; row +=P)
    for (col = 0; col < width; ++col) {
      // Initialization of c, k and z
      do {
        temp = z.r*z.r - z.i*z.i + c.r;
        z.i = 2*z.r*z.i + c.i; z.r = temp;
        ++k;
      } while (z.r*z.r + z.i*z.i < (N*N) && k < maxiter);
      color = (ulong) ((k-1) * scale_color) + min_color;
      cilk_lock ( display_lock );
      XSetForeground (display, gc, color);
      XDrawPoint (display, win, gc, col, row);
      cilk_unlock ( display_lock );
    }
}
```

Fig. 3. Cilk implementation of the Mandelbrot set (`--nproc P`)

Task Parallelism. The `cilk` keyword identifies functions that can be spawned in parallel. A Cilk function may create threads to execute functions in parallel. The `spawn` keyword is used to create child tasks, such as *compute_points* in our example, when referring to Cilk functions.

Cilk introduces the notion of inlets [2], which are local Cilk functions defined to take the result of spawned tasks and use it (performing a reduction). The result should not be put in a variable in the parent function. All the variables of the function are available within an inlet. `Abort` allows to abort a speculative work by terminating all of the already spawned children of a function; it must be called inside an inlet. Inlets are not used in our example.

Synchronization. The `sync` statement is a local barrier, used in our example to ensure task termination. It waits only for the spawned child tasks of the current procedure to complete, and not for all tasks currently being executed.

Atomic Section. Mutual exclusion is implemented using locks of type `cilk_lockvar`, such as *display_lock* in our example. The function `cilk_lock` is used to test a lock and block if it is already acquired; the function `cilk_unlock` is used to release a lock. Both functions take a single argument which is an object of type `cilk_lockvar`. `cilk_lock_init` is used to initialize the lock object before it is used.

Data Distribution. In Cilk's shared memory model, all variables declared outside Cilk functions are shared. To avoid possible non-determinism due to data races, the programmer should avoid the situation when a task writes a variable that may be read or written concurrently by another task, or use the primitive `cilk_fence` that ensures that all memory operations of a thread are committed before the next operation execution.

4.2   Chapel

Chapel [7], developed by Cray, supports both data and control flow parallelism and is designed around a multithreaded execution model based on PGAS for shared and distributed-memory systems. A Chapel implementation of the Mandelbrot set is provided in Figure 4.

```
coforall loc in Locales do
  on loc {
    for row in loc.id..height by numLocales do {
      for col in 1..width do {
        // Initialization of c, k and z
        do {
          temp = z.r*z.r − z.i*z.i + c.r;
          z.i = 2*z.r*z.i + c.i; z.r = temp;
          k = k+1;
        } while (z.r*z.r + z.i*z.i < (N*N) && k < maxiter);
        color = (ulong) ((k−1) * scale_color) + min_color;
        atomic {
          XSetForeground (display, gc, color);
          XDrawPoint (display, win, gc, col, row);
        }
}}}
```

Fig. 4. Chapel implementation of the Mandelbrot set

Task Parallelism. Chapel provides three types of task parallelism [3], two structured ones and one unstructured. cobegin{*stmts*} creates a task for each statement in *stmts*; the parent task waits for the *stmts* tasks to be completed. coforall is a loop variant of the cobegin statement, where each iteration of the coforall loop is a separate task and the main thread of execution does not continue until every iteration is completed. Finally, in begin{*stmt*}, the original parent task continues its execution after spawning a child running *stmt*.

Synchronization. In addition to cobegin and coforall, used in our example, which have an implicit synchronization at the end, synchronization variables of type sync can be used for coordinating parallel tasks. A sync [3] variable is either empty or full, with an additional data value. Reading an empty variable and writing in a full variable suspends the thread. Writing to an empty variable atomically changes its state to full. Reading a full variable consumes the value and atomically changes the state to empty.

Atomic Section. Chapel supports atomic sections; atomic{*stmt*} executes *stmt* atomically with respect to other threads. The precise semantics is still ongoing work.

Data Distribution. Chapel introduces a type called locale to refer to a unit of the machine resources on which a computation is running. A locale is a mapping of Chapel data and computations to the physical machine. In Figure 4, Array Locales represents the set of locale values corresponding to the machine resources on which this code is running; numLocales refers to the number of locales. Chapel also introduces new domain types to specify array distribution; they are not used in our example.

4.3   X10 and Habanero-Java

X10 [8], developed at IBM, is a distributed asynchronous dynamic parallel programming language for multi-core processors, symmetric shared-memory multiprocessors (SMPs), commodity clusters, high end supercomputers, and even embedded processors like Cell. A X10 implementation of the Mandelbrot set is provided in Figure 5.

Habanero-Java [6], under development at Rice University, is derived from X10 [8], and introduces additional synchronization and atomicity primitives surveyed below.

```
finish {
  for (m = 0; m < place.MAX_PLACES; m++) {
    place pl_row = place.places(m);
    async at (pl_row) {
      for (row = m; row < height; row+=place.MAX_PLACES) {
        for (col = 0; col < width; ++col) {
          // Initialization of c, k and z
          do {
            temp = z.r*z.r - z.i*z.i + c.r;
            z.i = 2*z.r*z.i + c.i; z.r = temp;
            ++k;
          } while (z.r*z.r + z.i*z.i < (N*N) && k < maxiter);
          color = (ulong) ((k-1) * scale_color) + min_color;
          atomic {
            XSetForeground (display, gc, color);
            XDrawPoint (display, win, gc, col, row);
          }
}}}}}
```

Fig. 5. X10 implementation of the Mandelbrot set

Task Parallelism. X10 provides two task creation primitives: (1) the `async` *stmt* construct creates a new asynchronous task that executes *stmt*, while the current thread continues, and (2) the `future` *exp* expression launches a parallel task that returns the value of *exp*.

Synchronization. With `finish` *stmt*, the current running task is blocked at the end of the `finish` clause, waiting till all the children spawned during the execution of *stmt* have terminated. The expression `f.force()` is used to get the actual value of the "future" task `f`.

X10 introduces a new synchronization concept: the clock. It acts as a barrier for a dynamically varying set of tasks [19] that operate in phases of execution where each phase should wait for previous ones before proceeding. A task that uses a clock must first register with it (multiple clocks can be used). It then uses the statement `next` to signal to all the tasks that are registered with its clocks that it is ready to move to the following phase, and waits until all the clocks with which it is registered can advance. A clock can advance only when all the tasks that are registered with it have executed a `next` statement.

Habanero-Java introduces phasers to extend this clock mechanism. A phaser is created and initialized to its first phase using the function `new`. The scope of a phaser is limited to the immediately enclosing `finish` statement. A task can be registered with zero or more phasers, using one of four registration modes: the first two are the traditional SIG and WAIT signal operations for producer-consumer synchronization;

the SIG_WAIT mode implements barrier synchronization, while SIG_WAIT_SINGLE ensures, in addition, that its associated statement is executed by only one thread. As in X10, a `next` instruction is used to advance each phaser that this task is registered with to its next phase, in accordance with this task's registration mode, and waits on each phaser that task is registered with, with a WAIT submode. We illustrate the use of clocks and phasers in Figure 8; note that they are not used in our Mandelbrot example, since a collective barrier based on the `finish` statement is sufficient.

Atomic Section. When a thread enters an `atomic` statement, no other thread may enter it until the original thread terminates it.

Habanero-Java supports weak atomicity using the `isolated` *stmt* primitive for mutual exclusion and isolation. The Habanero-Java implementation takes a single-lock approach to deal with isolated statements.

Data Distribution. In order to distribute work across processors, X10 and HJ introduce a type called `place`. A place is an address space within which a task may run; different places may however refer to the same physical processor and share physical memory. The program address space is partitioned into logically distinct places. `Place.MAX_PLACES`, used in Figure 5, is the number of places available to a program.

4.4   OpenMP

OpenMP [16] is an application program interface providing a multi-threaded programming model for shared memory parallelism; it uses directives to extend sequential languages. A C OpenMP implementation of the Mandelbrot set is provided in Figure 6.

```
P = omp_get_num_threads ();
#pragma omp parallel shared(height, width, scale_r,\
        scale_i, maxiter, scale_color, min_color, r_min, i_min)\
        private(row, col, k, m, color, temp, z, c)
#pragma omp single
{
   for (m = 0; m < P; m++)
#pragma omp task
     for (row = m; row < height; row+=P) {
       for (col = 0; col < width; ++col) {
         // Initialization of c, k and z
         do {
           temp = z.r*z.r - z.i*z.i + c.r;
           z.i = 2*z.r*z.i + c.i; z.r = temp;
           ++k;
         } while (z.r*z.r + z.i*z.i < (N*N) && k < maxiter);
         color = (ulong) ((k-1) * scale_color) + min_color;
#pragma omp critical
         {
           XSetForeground (display, gc, color);
           XDrawPoint (display, win, gc, col, row);
         }
}}}
```

Fig. 6. C OpenMP implementation of the Mandelbrot set

Task Parallelism. OpenMP allows dynamic (`omp task`) and static (`omp section`) scheduling models. A task instance is generated each time a thread (the encountering thread) encounters a `omp task` directive. This task may either be scheduled immediately on the same thread or deferred and assigned to any thread in a thread team, which is the group of threads created when an `omp parallel` directive is encountered. The `omp sections` directive is a non-iterative work-sharing construct. It specifies that the enclosed sections of code, declared with `omp section`, are to be divided among the threads in the team; these sections are independent blocks of code that the compiler can execute concurrently.

Synchronization. OpenMP provides synchronization constructs that control the execution inside a team thread: `barrier` and `taskwait`. When a thread encounters a `barrier` directive, it waits until all other threads in the team reach the same point; the scope of a barrier region is the innermost enclosing parallel region. The `taskwait` construct is a restricted barrier that blocks the thread until all child tasks created since the beginning of the current task are completed. The `omp single` directive identifies code that must be run by only one thread.

Atomic Section. The `critical` and `atomic` directives are used for identifying a section of code that must be executed by a single thread at a time. The `atomic` directive works faster than `critical`, since it only applies to single instructions, and can thus often benefit from hardware support. Our implementation of the Mandelbrot set in Figure 6 uses `critical`.

Data Distribution. OpenMP variables are either global (`shared`) or local (`private`); see Figure 6 for examples. A shared variable refers to one unique block of storage for all threads in the team. A private variable refers to a different block of storage for each thread. More memory access modes exist, such as `firstprivate` or `lastprivate`, that may require communication or copy operations.

4.5 OpenCL

OpenCL (Open Computing Language) [15] is a standard for programming heterogeneous multiprocessor platforms where programs are divided into several parts: some called "the kernels" that execute on separate devices, e.g., GPUs, with their own memories and the others that execute on the host CPU. The main object in OpenCL is the command queue, which is used to submit work to a device by the enqueueing of OpenCL commands to be executed. An OpenCL implementation of the Mandelbrot set is provided in Figure 7.

Task Parallelism. OpenCL provides the parallel construct `clEnqueueTask`, which enqueues a command requiring the execution of a kernel on a device by a work item (OpenCL thread). OpenCL uses two different models of execution of command queues: in-order, used for data parallelism, and out-of-order. In an out-of-order command queue, commands are executed as soon as possible, and no order is specified, except for wait and barrier events. We illustrate the out-of-order execution mechanism in Figure 7, but currently this is an optional feature and is thus not supported by many devices.

```
__kernel void kernel_main(complex c, uint maxiter, double scale_color,
                          uint m, uint P, ulong color[NPIXELS][NPIXELS]) {
  for (row = m; row < NPIXELS; row+=P)
    for (col = 0; col < NPIXELS; ++col) {
      // Initialization of c, k and z
      do {
        temp = z.r*z.r−z.i*z.i+c.r;
        z.i = 2*z.r*z.i+c.i; z.r = temp;
        ++k;
      } while (z.r*z.r+z.i*z.i<(N*N) && k<maxiter);
      color[row][col] = (ulong) ((k−1)*scale_color);
    }
}
cl_int ret = clGetPlatformIDs(1, &platform_id, &ret_num_platforms);
ret = clGetDeviceIDs(platform_id, CL_DEVICE_TYPE_DEFAULT, 1,
                     &device_id, &ret_num_devices);
cl_context context = clCreateContext( NULL, 1, &device_id, NULL, NULL, &ret);
cQueue=clCreateCommandQueue(context, device_id, OUT_OF_ORDER_EXEC_MODE_ENABLE, NULL);
P = CL_DEVICE_MAX_COMPUTE_UNITS;
memc = clCreateBuffer(context, CL_MEM_READ_ONLY , sizeof(complex), c);
// ... Create read−only buffers with maxiter, scale_color and P too
memcolor = clCreateBuffer(context, CL_MEM_WRITE_ONLY,
                          sizeof(ulong)*height*width ,NULL,NULL);
clEnqueueWriteBuffer (cQueue, memc, CL_TRUE, 0, sizeof(complex),&c ,0 ,NULL,NULL);
// ... Enqueue write buffer with maxiter, scale_color and P too
program = clCreateProgramWithSource(context, 1, &program_source, NULL, NULL);
err = clBuildProgram(program, 0, NULL, NULL, NULL, NULL);
kernel = clCreateKernel(program, "kernel_main", NULL);
clSetKernelArg(kernel, 0, sizeof(cl_mem),(void *)&memc);
// ... Set kernel argument with memmaxiter, memscale_color, memP and memcolor too
for(m = 0; m < P; m++) {
  memm = clCreateBuffer(context, CL_MEM_READ_ONLY , sizeof(uint), m);
  clEnqueueWriteBuffer(cQueue, memm, CL_TRUE, 0, sizeof(uint), &m, 0, NULL, NULL);
  clSetKernelArg(kernel, 0, sizeof(cl_mem),(void *)&memm);
  clEnqueueTask(cQueue, kernel, 0, NULL, NULL);
}
clFinish(cQueue);
clEnqueueReadBuffer(cQueue, memcolor ,CL_TRUE,0 ,space ,color ,0 ,NULL,NULL);
for (row = 0; row < height; ++row)
  for (col = 0; col < width; ++col) {
    XSetForeground (display, gc, color[col][row]);
    XDrawPoint (display, win, gc, col, row);
  }
```

Fig. 7. OpenCL implementation of the Mandelbrot set

Synchronization. OpenCL distinguishes between two types of synchronization: coarse and fine. Coarse grained synchronization, which deals with command queue operations, uses the construct `clEnqueueBarrier`, which defines a barrier synchronization point. Fine grained synchronization, which covers synchronization at the GPU function call granularity level, uses OpenCL events via `ClEnqueueWaitForEvents` calls.

Data transfers between the GPU memory and the host memory, via functions such as `clEnqueueReadBuffer` and `clEnqueueWriteBuffer`, also induce synchronization between blocking or non-blocking communication commands. Events returned by `clEnqueue` operations can be used to check if a non-blocking operation has completed.

Atomic Section. Atomic operations are only supported on integer data, via functions such as `atom_add` or `atom_xchg`. Currently, these are only supported by some devices as part of an extension of the OpenCL standard. OpenCL lacks support for general atomic sections, thus the drawing function is executed by the host in Figure 7.

Data Distribution. Each work item can either use (1) its private memory, (2) its local memory, which is shared between multiple work items, (3) its constant memory, which is closer to the processor than the `__global` memory, and thus much faster to access, although slower than `__local` memory, and (4) global memory, shared by all work items. Data is only accessible after being transferred from the host, using functions such as `clEnqueueReadBuffer` and `clEnqueueWriteBuffer` that move data in and out of a device.

5   Discussion and Comparison

This section discusses the salient features of our surveyed languages. More specifically, we look at their design philosophy and the new concepts they introduce, how point-to-point synchronization is addressed in each of these languages, the various semantics of atomic sections and the data distribution issues. We end up summarizing the key features of all the languages covered in this paper.

Design Paradigms. Our overview study, based on a single running example, namely the computation of the Mandelbrot set, is admittedly somewhat biased, since each language has been designed with a particular application framework in mind, which may, or may not, be well adapted to a given application. Cilk is well suited to deal with divide-and-conquer strategies, something not put into practice in our example. On the contrary, X10, Chapel and Habanero-Java are high-level Partitioned Global Address Space languages that offer abstract notions such as places and locales, which were put to good use in our example. OpenCL is a very low-level, verbose language that works across GPUs and CPUs; our example clearly illustrates that this approach is not providing much help here in terms of shrinking the semantic gap between specification and implementation. The OpenMP philosophy is to add compiler directives to parallelize parts of code on shared-memory machines; this helps programmers move incrementally from a sequential to a parallel implementation.

New Concepts. Even though this paper does not address data parallelism per se, note that Cilk is the only language that does not provide special support for data parallelism; yet, spawned threads can be used inside loops to simulate SIMD processing. Also, Cilk adds a facility to support speculative parallelism, enabling spawned tasks abort operations via the `abort` statement. Habanero-Java introduces the `isolated` statement to specify the weak atomicity property. Phasers, in Habanero-Java, and clocks, in X10, are new high-level constructs for collective and point-to-point synchronization between varying sets of threads.

Point-to-Point Synchronization. We illustrate the way our surveyed languages address the difficult issue of point-to-point synchronization via a simple example, a hide-and-seek game in Figure 8. X10 clocks or Habanero-Java phasers help express easily the different phases between threads. The notion of point-to-point synchronization cannot be expressed easily using OpenMP or Chapel. We were not able to implement this game using Cilk high-level synchronization primitives, since `sync`, the only synchronization construct, is a local barrier for recursive tasks: it synchronizes only threads spawned in the current procedure, and thus not the two searcher and hider tasks. As mentioned above, this is not surprising, given Cilk's approach to parallelism.

```
finish  async {              finish  async{               cilk void searcher () {
  clock  cl = clock.make();    phaser ph = new phaser ();   count_to_a_number ();
  async clocked(cl) {          async phased(ph) {           point_to_point_sync (); // missing
    count_to_a_number ();        count_to_a_number ();      start_searching ();
  next;                        next;                        }
    start_searching ();          start searching ();        cilk void hidder () {
  }                            }                              hide_oneself ();
  async clocked(cl) {          async phased(ph) {           point_to_point_sync (); // missing
    hide_oneself ();             hide_oneself ();             continue_to_be_hidden ();
  next;                        next;                        }
    continue_to_be_hidden ();    continue_to_be_hidden ();  void main () {
  }                            }                              spawn searcher ();
}                            }                                spawn hidder ();
                                                            }
```

Fig. 8. A hide-and-seek game (X10, HJ, Cilk)

Atomic Section. The semantics and implementations of the various proposals for dealing with atomicity are rather subtle.

Atomic operations, which apply to single instructions, can be efficiently implemented, e.g. in X10, using non-blocking techniques such as `compare-and-swap` instructions. In OpenMP, the atomic directive can be made to work faster than the critical directive, when atomic operations are replaced with processor commands such as GLSC [12]; therefore, it is better to use this directive when protecting shared memory during elementary operations. Atomic operations can be used to update different elements of a data structure (arrays, records) in parallel without using many explicit locks. In the example of Figure 9, the updates of different elements of Array x are allowed to occur in parallel. General atomic sections, on the other hand, serialize the execution of updates to elements via one lock.

```
#pragma omp parallel for shared(x, index, n)
for (i=0; i<n; i++) {
#pragma omp atomic
    x[index[i]] += f(i);        // index is supposed injective
}
```

Fig. 9. Example of an atomic directive in OpenMP

With the weak atomicity model of Habanero-Java, the `isolated` keyword is used instead of `atomic` to make explicit the fact that the construct supports weak rather than strong isolation. In Figure 10, Threads 1 and 2 may access to `ptr` simultaneously; since weakly atomic accesses are used, an atomic access to `temp->next` is not enforced.

```
// Thread 1                                    // Thread 2
ptr = head; //non isolated statement           isolated {
isolated {                                       if (ready)
  ready = true;                                    temp->next = ptr;
}                                              }
```

Fig. 10. Data race on `ptr` with Habanero-Java

Data Distribution. PGAS languages offer a compromise between the fine level of control of data placement provided by the message passing model and the simplicity of the shared memory model. However, the physical reality is that different PGAS portions, although logically distinct, may refer to the same physical processor and share physical memory. Practical performance might thus not be as good as expected.

Regarding the shared memory model, despite its simplicity of programming, programmers have scarce support for expressing data locality, which could help improve performance in many cases. Debugging is also difficult when data races occur.

Finally, the message passing memory model, where processors have no direct access to the memories of other processors, can be seen as the most general one, in which programmers can both specify data distribution and control locality. Shared memory (where there is only one processor managing the whole memory) and PGAS (where one assumes that each portion is located on a distinct processor) models can be seen as particular instances of the message passing model, when converting implicit write and read operations with explicit send/receive message passing constructs.

Summary Table. We collect in Table 1 the main characteristics of each language addressed in this paper. Even though we have not discussed the issue of data parallelism in this paper, we nonetheless provide, for the interested reader, the main constructs used in each language to launch data parallel computations.

Table 1. Summary of parallel languages constructs

Language	Task creation	Synchronization			Data parallelism	Memory model
		Task join	Point-to-point	Atomic section		
Cilk (MIT)	spawn	sync abort	—	cilk_lock	—	*Shared*
Chapel (Cray)	begin cobegin	—	sync	sync atomic	forall coforall	*PGAS (Locales)*
X10 (IBM)	async future	finish	next force	atomic	foreach	*PGAS (Places)*
Habanero-Java (Rice)	async future	finish	next get	atomic isolated	foreach	*PGAS (Places)*
OpenMP	omp task omp section	omp taskwait omp barrier	—	omp critical omp atomic	omp for	*Shared*
OpenCL	EnqueueTask	Finish EnqueueBarrier	*events*	atom_add, ...	EnqueueND-RangeKernel	*Message Passing*

6   Conclusion

This paper presents, using the Mandelbrot set computation as a running example, an up-to-date comparative overview of six parallel programming language designs: Cilk, Chapel, X10, Habanero-Java, OpenMP and OpenCL. These languages are in current use, popular, offer rich and highly abstract functionalities, and most support both data and task parallel execution models. The paper describes how, in addition to data distribution and locality, the fundamentals of task parallel programming, namely task creation, collective and point-to-point synchronization and mutual exclusion are dealt with in these languages.

This paper can be of use to (1) programmers, by providing a taxonomy of parallel language designs useful when deciding which language is more appropriate for a given project, (2) language designers, by presenting design solutions already field-tested in previous languages, and (3) implementors of automatic program conversion tools, by helping them narrow down the issues that need to be tackled when dealing with parallel execution and memory models.

This case study served as the basis of our design of SPIRE [11], a sequential to parallel intermediate representation extension that can be used to upgrade the intermediate representations of compilation frameworks to represent task concepts in parallel languages. SPIRE is simple and generic enough to describe, to our knowledge, all parallel languages, even though the intricacies of the various existing synchronization models, exhibited by this study, require low-level representation support.

References

1. The Mandelbrot Set, http://warp.povusers.org/Mandelbrot/
2. Cilk 5.4.6 Reference Manual. Supercomputing Technologies Group, MIT Laboratory for Computer Science (1998), http://supertech.lcs.mit.edu/cilk
3. Chapel Language Specification 0.796. Cray Inc., 901 Fifth Avenue, Suite 1000, Seattle, WA 98164 (October 21, 2010)
4. Adve, S.V., Gharachorloo, K.: Shared Memory Consistency Models: A Tutorial. IEEE Computer 29, 66–76 (1996)
5. Blumofe, R.D., Joerg, C.F., Kuszmaul, B.C., Leiserson, C.E., Randall, K.H., Zhou, Y.: Cilk: An Efficient Multithreaded Runtime System. Journal of Parallel and Distributed Computing, 207–216 (1995)
6. Cavé, V., Zhao, J., Sarkar, V.: Habanero-Java: the New Adventures of Old X10. In: 9th International Conference on the Principles and Practice of Programming in Java (PPPJ) (August 2011)
7. Chamberlain, B., Callahan, D., Zima, H.: Parallel Programmability and the Chapel Language. Int. J. High Perform. Comput. Appl. 21, 291–312 (2007)
8. Charles, P., Grothoff, C., Saraswat, V., Donawa, C., Kielstra, A., Ebcioglu, K., von Praun, C., Sarkar, V.: X10: An Object-Oriented Approach to Non-Uniform Cluster Computing. SIGPLAN Not. 40, 519–538 (2005)
9. Cuevas, E., Garcia, A., Fernandez, F.J.J., Gadea, R.J., Cordon, J.: Importance of Simulations for Nuclear and Aeronautical Inspections with Ultrasonic and Eddy Current Testing. Simulation in NDT (September 2010), Online Workshop, http://www.ndt.net
10. Dennis, J.B., Gao, G.R., Todd, K.W.: Modeling The Weather With a Data Flow Supercomputer. IEEE Trans. Computers, 592–603 (1984)

11. Khaldi, D., Jouvelot, P., Ancourt, C., Irigoin, F.: SPIRE: A Sequential to Parallel Intermediate Representation Extension. Technical Report CRI/A-487, MINES ParisTech (2012)
12. Kumar, S., Kim, D., Smelyanskiy, M., Chen, Y.-K., Chhugani, J., Hughes, C.J., Kim, C., Lee, V.W., Nguyen, A.D.: Atomic Vector Operations on Chip Multiprocessors. SIGARCH Comput. Archit. News 36(3), 441–452 (2008)
13. Larus, J., Kozyrakis, C.: Transactional Memory. Commun. ACM 51, 80–88 (2008)
14. MPI. Message Passing Interface, `http://www-unix.mcs.anl.gov/mpi`
15. OpenCL. The Open Standard for Parallel Programming of Heterogeneous Systems, `http://www.khronos.org/opencl`
16. OpenMP. Specifications, `http://openmp.org/wp/openmp-specifications/`
17. Padua, D.A. (ed.): Encyclopedia of Parallel Computing. Springer (2011)
18. Sarkar, V.: Synchronization Using Counting Semaphores. In: ICS 1988, pp. 627–637 (1988)
19. Shirako, J., Peixotto, D.M., Sarkar, V., Scherer, W.N.: Phasers: A Unified Deadlock-Free Construct for Collective and Point-To-Point Synchronization. In: ICS 2008, pp. 277–288. ACM, New York (2008)

A Fast Parallel Graph Partitioner
for Shared-Memory
Inspector/Executor Strategies

Christopher D. Krieger and Michelle Mills Strout

Colorado State University, Fort Collins CO 80523, USA
{krieger,mstrout}@cs.colostate.edu

Abstract. Graph partitioners play an important role in many parallel work distribution and locality optimization approaches. Surprisingly, however, to our knowledge there is no freely available parallel graph partitioner designed for execution on a shared memory multicore system. This paper presents a shared memory parallel graph partitioner, ParCubed, for use in the context of sparse tiling run-time data and computation reordering. Sparse tiling is a run-time scheduling technique that schedules groups of iterations across loops together when they access the same data and one or more of the loops contains indirect array accesses. For sparse tiling, which is implemented with an inspector/executor strategy, the inspector needs to find an initial seed partitioning of adequate quality very quickly. We compare our presented hierarchical clustering partitioner, ParCubed, with GPart and METIS in terms of partitioning speed, partitioning quality, and the effect the generated seed partitions have on executor speed. We find that the presented partitioner is 25 to 100 times faster than METIS on a 16 core machine. The total edge cut of the partitioning generated by ParCubed was found not to exceed 1.27x that of the partitioning found by METIS.

Keywords: inspector/executor strategies, graph partitioning, irregular applications, sparse tiling.

1 Introduction

Computations involving irregular data access patterns figure prominently in many important scientific applications. These include solving partial differential equations over irregular grids, molecular dynamics simulations, and computations over sparse matrices. Often, key loops in these computations are largely free of loop carried dependencies and can be performed using doall parallelism across all or a subset of elements. Additionally, loops performing reductions can often be parallelized. Unfortunately, in many cases these straightforward parallelization strategies encounter performance problems due to the irregularity of the data accesses. Irregular accesses that jump around in memory decrease the efficiency of caching and data prefetching and therefore increase the demand on memory bandwidth.

H. Kasahara and K. Kimura (Eds.): LCPC 2012, LNCS 7760, pp. 190–204, 2013.
© Springer-Verlag Berlin Heidelberg 2013

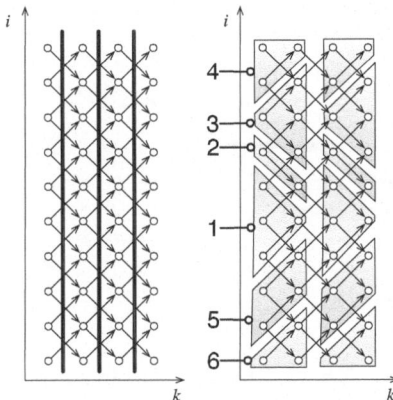

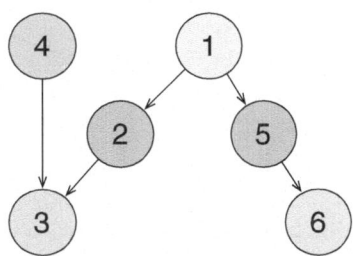

(a) At left, the Jacobi iteration space for a tri-diagonal sparse matrix with a doall parallelization. On the right, a full sparse tiling of the computation.

(b) Task graph for the full sparse tiled Jacobi computation

Fig. 1. Transformation of Jacobi computation from doall to task graph parallelism

To avoid memory bandwidth bottlenecks, these algorithms are modified by performance programmers to improve the algorithm's temporal and spatial locality. These optimization techniques include irregular cache blocking [5], full sparse tiling [11], and communication avoiding algorithms [10].

The benefits realized by these approaches can be illustrated by applications as simple as a sparse Jacobi solver, which has the common nearest neighbor dependence structure that can be found in many irregular or sparse applications. The sparse Jacobi solver algorithm is an iterative algorithm for determining solutions to a system of linear equations. Given a sparse matrix A, and two vectors u and f related by $Au = f$, one iteration of the sparse Jacobi method produces an approximation to the unknown vector u. This method is known to converge if A is strictly diagonally dominant. The recurrence equation that describes Jacobi is as follows:

$$u_i^{(k)} = \frac{1}{A_{ii}} \left(f_i - \sum_{j \neq i} A_{ij} * u_j^{(k-1)} \right)$$

While the Jacobi method admits a straightforward doall parallel solution on the i loop, this approach quickly hits scalability issues due to memory bandwidth demands. Figure 1(a) shows the iteration space for sparse Jacobi when the matrix is tri-diagonal so the matrix graph is a line. The left-side of Figure 1(a) shows a doall parallelization with barriers between each iteration of the outer k loop. The right side of Figure 1(a) shows a possible sparse tiling of Jacobi. That tiling

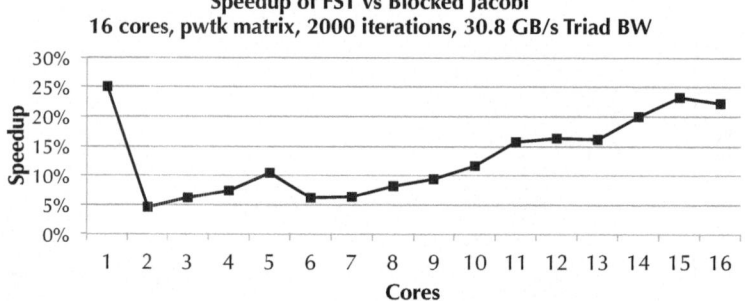

Fig. 2. Performance difference between full sparse tiled and blocked Jacobi solvers

results in the task graph shown in Figure 1(b). Figure 2 shows a comparison of the execution time between a doall parallelized Jacobi solver and a full sparse tiled [11,12] version as threads are increased from one to sixteen on the 16 core machine (described in Section 4). The benefit ranges from 5% to 25% as cores are added and memory bandwidth demand increases.[1]

A common theme among optimization approaches such as full sparse tiling is the reduction of communication or data sharing between execution units through the aggregation of computation that accesses common data. As such, it is common to create a graph where each node represents some computation (e.g. an iteration point in 1(a)) and edges between such points represent that those computations share data. For example, the matrix graph for a sparse matrix, where each row/column is a node and there is an edge between nodes i and j if $A_{ij} \neq 0$, can be partitioned to create a seed partitioning for growing sparse tiles.

The graph partitioning problem is to divide a graph $G = (V, E)$ with $|V| = n$ into k partitions V_i such that $\bigcup_{i=1}^{k} V_i = V$ and $\bigcap_{i=1}^{k} V_i = \emptyset$ with the added constraint that the *edge cut*, the number of edges whose incident vertices are in different partitions, is minimized.

Given the importance of graph partitions, we were surprised to find no freely available parallel graph partitioner designed for execution on a shared memory multicore system. Therefore in this paper we present a shared memory parallel graph partitioner called *ParCubed* (Par Parallel Partitioner or PAR[3]), emphasizing that the algorithm is parallel and produces results roughly on par with other partitioners. Section 2 presents the graph partitioning algorithm, and Section 3 describes how the algorithm is efficiently implemented. We evaluate the new partitioner by comparing it with METIS and GPart in Section 4. Section 5 presents related work, and Section 6 concludes the paper.

---

[1] Performance monitoring hardware indicates that the drop from one core to two cores is due to a doubling of last level cache available as a second 24MB shared cache on a second socket entered into use.

```
Inflate(initialNodeID , maxSize)
{
 // initialization
 enqueue initialNodeID into FIFO
 initialize currentSize to 1

 // main inflation loop
  while ( (currentSize < maxSize) && FIFO not empty )
  {
    dequeue nodeID from front of FIFO
    if (size of partition containing nodeID is 1)
    {
        if ( (currentSize + 1) <= maxSize )
        {
            // merge this node into the partition
            merge nodeID and initialNodeID partitions
            increment currentSize by one

            // add next generation of adjacent nodes to the FIFO
            foreach (node adjacent to node nodeID)
            {
                enqueue adjacent node at back of FIFO
            }
} } } }
```

Fig. 3. Pseudocode of the inflation phase used to create partitions from starting nodes

2 Overview of the *ParCubed* Graph Partitioning Algorithm

In this section, we present an overview of our graph partitioning approach, Par-Cubed. At the highest level, the partitioning processing consists of three phases: *inflate*, *join*, and *fold*. First, single vertices are used as seeds for partitions. These partitions are *inflated* by adding adjacent vertices using a layered approach. In the second phase, these subpartitions are *joined* together to create fewer, but larger, partitions. Finally, if the generated number of partitions still exceeds the desired number, the excess partitions are *folded* into other partitions to bring the partition count down to the target number. In this section we detail each of these phases, and in Section 3 we parallelize the overall ParCubed partitioning algorithm.

2.1 Description of the Inflation Phase

The inflation subroutine is expressed in pseudocode in Figure 3. It is essentially a breadth first growth. The algorithm arbitrarily selects a node from the graph to serve as the seed of a partition. It then adds all of that node's adjacent neighbors, reducing the edge cut contribution from the original node as much as possible, ideally to zero. It then proceeds to add all the neighbors of each of the original node's neighbors, and so forth, until the partition size limit is reached.

As the partition is inflated, neighbors may be encountered that are already in another partition. In that case, the inflation stops expanding in that direction, yielding to the other partition. Because of this, it is sometimes impossible to reduce the edge cut contribution of a layer to zero.

```
GPartJoin(initialVertex , maxSize)
{
  currentPar = partition that contains initialVertex
  currentSize = size of currentPar

  foreach neighbor neighborVertex of initialVertex
  {
    neighborPar = partition that contains vertex neighborVertex
    neighborSize = size of neighborPar
    if (neighborSize + currentSize <= maxSize)
    {
      merge currentPar and neighborPar
      currentSize += neighborSize
  } } }
```

Fig. 4. Pseudocode of the GPart-like join phase

If at any time a growing partition cannot expand, such as when it is surrounded by other partitions, the process stops for this initial node. The algorithm then continues with another node taken as the seed of another subpartition.

2.2   Description of the Join Phase

It is possible that a large number of small partitions may result from the inflation process. To deal with this, the partitioner follows up the inflation step with a hierarchical partition joining step similar to GPart [7]. This phase is expressed in pseudocode in Figure 4. During this phase, each node is visited once again. If any neighbor of that node is found to be in a partition that is small enough that merging it with the currently visited node's partition would not exceed the maximum partition size, the two partitions are merged. This differs from inflation in that entire subpartitions are being merged, rather than single vertices being added to a partition.

2.3   Description of the Folding Phase

Commonly, the first two phases produce more partitions than are desired. A third, final step is used to trim the number of partitions. During the *folding* step, the partitions are ordered by partition size from smallest to largest. If k partitions are desired, then the *adopting partition* P_k and *extra partition* P_{k-1} are merged, P_{k+1} and P_{k-2} are merged, and so forth. This combines increasingly smaller extra partitions with increasingly larger adopting partitions. If more than twice the desired number of partitions was originally found, the folding process functions in a modulo fashion, wrapping as needed.

Extra and adopting partitions are matched solely based on size. Due to this fact, unconnected partitions can be created. If the matching process between adopting and extra partitions were to consider adjacency, higher quality partitions may be produced. In the interest of reducing runtime, adjacency is currently ignored.

Also note that during folding, the maximum partition size is ignored, so partitions that exceed the desired size can be produced. In practice, we saw

```
Fold(partNums : array of partition numbers
{
  origNumFoundPartitions = number of found partitions
  numberExtraPartitions = origNumFoundPartitions − num desired partitions;
  firstAdoptingPartitionIndex = numberExtraPartitions

  // figure out the point at which to fold
  adoptingPartitionIndex = firstAdoptingPartitionIndex;
  extraPartitionIndex = firstAdoptingPartitionIndex −1;

  // merge the partitions
  foreach extra partition
  {
    extraPartition = partNums[extraPartitionIndex−−]
    adoptingPartition = partNums[adoptingPartitionIndex++]

    // do modulo wrap
    if (adoptingPartitionIndex >= origNumFoundPartitions)
    {
      adoptingPartitionIndex = numberExtraPartitions;
    }

    // merge
    merge extraPartition and adoptingPartition
}
```

Fig. 5. Pseudocode of the folding step

approximately 5% of the partitions to be oversized. In general, the oversized partitions were within 15% of the target size, but a handful of extreme outliers were observed that were as large as 150% of the target.

3 Parallel Implementation of the Partitioner

Having provided an overview of our graph partitioning algorithm, we now turn to the details of how the algorithm can be efficiently implemented for parallel execution.

3.1 Parallel Disjoint Set Data Structure

Since much of the algorithm consists of identifying which partition a node is in, adding nodes to partitions, or merging two partitions, having an efficient way to do these operations in parallel is critical. The backbone of our implementation is therefore a parallel implementation of a disjoint set data structure. This structure is also known as a *union-find* data structure because of its efficient support for those two operations. It provides an $O(n)$, where n is the number of graph nodes, determination of which set contains a particular node and an $O(1)$ set merge operation.

The disjoint set data structure is built on the concept of a *forest of trees*. Each element of the disjoint set is either a top level root or else points to another element in the structure, indicating membership in that set. The element at which it points may be a root or may in turn point at another element, creating a hierarchy. To perform a merging of two sets, the root of one set is pointed to any element of the other set, usually the root.

Determining the set to which any given element belongs is a find operation. In a find on a given element, that element is visited. If it is a root, then the element belongs to that set. If it is not a root, the node at which it points is recursively visited until a root is reached.

While the merge operation is very efficient, it can lead to deep trees that must be traversed repeatedly during find operations. A find operation is always $O(n)$, but several optimizations can reduce the runtime cost in practice. *Path halving* involves linking each node to its grandparent during a find operation, effectively halving each node's depth. *Path flattening* is similar, but finds the root node for a given node, then points all elements between the initial node and the root node directly to the root node. As explained below, our approach does not use either optimization.

Our disjoint set structure was originally taken from Berman's thesis [2]. We subsequently modified that implementation to better suit our application. Our implementation consists of a one dimensional array of integers sized to hold one array element for each vertex in the adjacency graph. The value of each array element can represent one of two things. If the value is negative, then this element is a root of a set and the absolute value of the stored value is the size of the set. If the value is positive, it represents the array index of the parent of this element.

In general, disjoint set structures are not safe for parallel operation. To resolve this, we made a number of straightforward modifications to the standard disjoint set structure and its usage. First, find operations can proceed in parallel without any synchronization. This allows for many concurrent find operations to occur without the overhead of locking. A detrimental effect is that find operations cannot perform path flattening or path halving optimizations. However, these optimizations are largely unneeded by our algorithm. During the inflation process, we merge the original seed set only with nodes that are not yet merged with any other nodes. As a result, each of these other nodes is the root in its own set. When it is merged with the seed set, it creates a tree with depth two. When the inflation step completes, the entire disjoint set structure has maximum depth two and cannot be flattened further. During the join step, the disjoint set depth can grow, but since it is starting with a very shallow tree the depth typically does not exceed a depth of four, with depth eight being the greatest observed in our testing.

On a merge operation, a lock is acquired for both root nodes in the merge. Since a node's set may change after a find operation has returned its set, set membership information may be stale. To handle this, after locking the nodes passed to a merge, they are checked to see if they are still truly root nodes. If not, their locks are released and the nodes' paths are traversed until a root is again found. Those roots are locked and once again checked to determine if they are root nodes. This continues until both nodes are locked and are roots. The two sets are then merged and the locks are released.

The performance and scalability of the inflation step proved to be sensitive to the number of locks used by the disjoint set. If too coarse grained locks were used, lock contention hurt performance. If too fine grained locks were used, performance suffered in some cases because the locks were polluting the per-core caches and creating memory traffic. Time to initialize the locks also contributed significantly to total algorithm runtime when excessive locks were used.

To tune the number of locks, we used a process of gradual lock refining. We varied the number of locks and swept the thread count. At each point, we measured the amount of time spent in the merge algorithm as a rough proxy for lock contention. We also examined total partitioner runtime. Based on these data, we determine the lock count using a simple linear function of thread count and graph node count. The average degree of nodes in the adjacency graph had a secondary effect but is ignored in our current lock count calculation.

3.2 Overview of Partitioner Parallelization

The general parallelization strategy used for partitioning is a straightforward SPMD approach. Each thread is assigned a block of nodes.

Each thread immediately begins inflating from nodes in its block. As they grow, partitions can pull in nodes outside the thread's range, but because all operations done during the inflate phase use the disjoint set structure described above, they require no additional synchronization. There is, however, a barrier between the inflate and the join phases of our algorithm.

As with the inflate phase, any operation on shared data during the join phase consists entirely of disjoint set operations. Each thread attempts to join partitions within its chunk with adjacent partitions.

The final folding phase is currently done serially. It could be parallelized, but at present takes between 1% - 4% of the total algorithm runtime on a 16 core machine.

This approach to parallelization results in non-deterministic partitionings. The order in which nodes are initially inflated, and in which they are joined, impacts the final partitioning results. This order depends on several factors. First, the number of threads directly impacts the visitation ordering. A node that is visited first by some core when using N threads will most likely not be visited first when using $N + 1$ threads, simply because it will no longer be the first node in a block. Also, slight differences in operating system scheduler behavior cause different interleavings between threads, resulting in a different global ordering of node visitation.

4   Evaluation

There are several aspects of performance that were considered when evaluating the ParCubed graph partitioner. We first wanted to evaluate the usefulness of each of the three distinct phases. In the context of a shared memory inspector, the runtime of the partitioner is crucial and was evaluated. Lastly, the edge cut

Table 1. Characteristics of sparse matrices used in the performance evaluation

Name	Rows	Avg Nonzeroes/Row	Memory (MB)
xenon2	157464	24	48
thermal2	1228045	7	130
pwtk	217918	53	138
nd24k	72000	399	345
audikw_1	943695	82	913

of the partitioning is one well understood measure of the partitioning quality. We supplement edge cut results by also measuring the runtime of the executor phase while performing a full sparse tiling inspector/executor strategy. This runtime is the bottom line measure of partitioning quality.

The tiled computation used in this performance evaluation is a sparse Jacobi solver. The Jacobi algorithm is described in detail in Section 1. In these tests, the Jacobi kernel is tiled across two convergence iterations of the main loop. Each tile was sized to access approximately 200kB of data, so as to fit within the mid-level cache of the processors used.

All of the sparse matrices were drawn from the University of Florida Matrix Market and are listed in Table 1. The tests were run on a two socket 16 core Xeon E7-4830 server with 256kB mid level data caches per core and 24 MB of shared last level cache per socket. The Intel icpc compiler, version 12.1.2 (20111128) was used at optimization level -O3.

The GPart algorithm used for comparison purposes was run in three passes. The first pass created partitions of up to 50% the size of the final maximum partition size. The second pass permits partitions up to 75% of the final size, while the third pass accepts partitions up to 125% of the maximum size. We experimented with a variety of different size progressions and found this progression to give the lowest geometric mean of edge cuts across all input graphs. Also note that GPart typically does not generate the desired number of partitions. Using this progression, GPart on average returned a number of partitions equal to 97.5% of the requested number.

The serial METIS algorithm is the METIS_PartGraphKway() algorithm, with the partition size as the only balance constraint. Neither edge nor vertex weights were used and the objective function was set to minimize edge cut rather than communication volume.

4.1   Benefit Derived from Each Phase of the Partitioning Process

As seen in Figure 6, the number of partitions affected by each of the three phases (inflation, joining, folding) varies greatly between sparse matrices. The figure shows how many partitions exist after each phase of the algorithm. The requested number of partitions is always reached after folding.

In general, if the input matrix is sufficiently connected, meaning that it has a relatively high number of non-zero elements per row, than the inflation phase

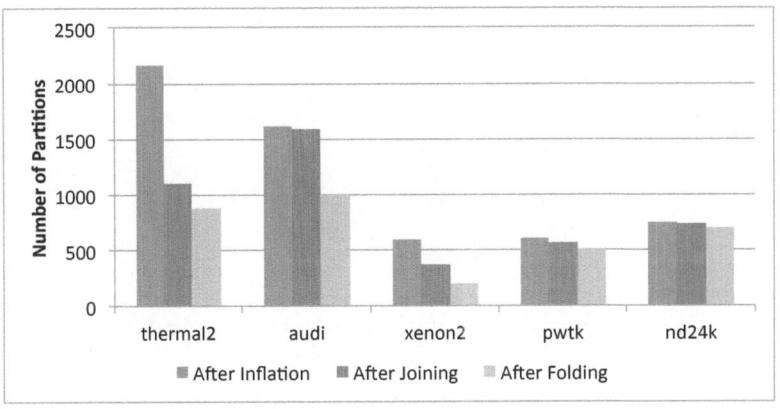

Fig. 6. Number of partitions after each phase

is able to do a good job of generating partitions. In these cases, the hierarchical joining phase provides little benefit. However, when the matrix is more sparse, such as the thermal2 matrix in this evaluation, the join step is able to combine smaller partitions and bring the total number of partitions more in line with the target. The audikw_1 matrix results shows a large number of partitions being combined during folding, demonstrating the value of the folding step. Note that METIS always generates the desired number of partitions for these input sets, while GPart regularly produces more or fewer partitions than requested.

4.2 Speed of Partitioner Compared with METIS and GPart

A major requirement for partitioners in a shared memory multicore environment is extremely low runtime. In Figure 7, we compare the total partitioning time of 16 core multithreaded ParCubed, single threaded ParCubed, serial METIS, and serial GPart on the five different sparse matrices in our test suite. All times are normalized to the METIS time. METIS is consistently the slowest algorithm, on the order of 5 to 30 times slower than serial ParCubed and 25 to 100 times slower than 16 thread ParCubed.

A full comparative study of parallel ParMETIS performance is a work in progress. However, due to the time required to either read in sparse matrix data on each rank or communicate portions of the data between ranks, the performance will not be comparable. For example, partitioning a trivial matrix using ParMETIS on a multicore machine using a shared memory MPI transport took 1.025 seconds. By comparison, 16 thread ParCubed on a similar machine took just 0.18 seconds to fully partition the audikw_1 matrix, the largest in our study.

4.3 Comparison of Total Partitioning Edge Cut

One common metric of graph partitioning quality is the edge cut of the set of partitions. Figure 8 shows the edge cuts that were obtained using 16 way parallel

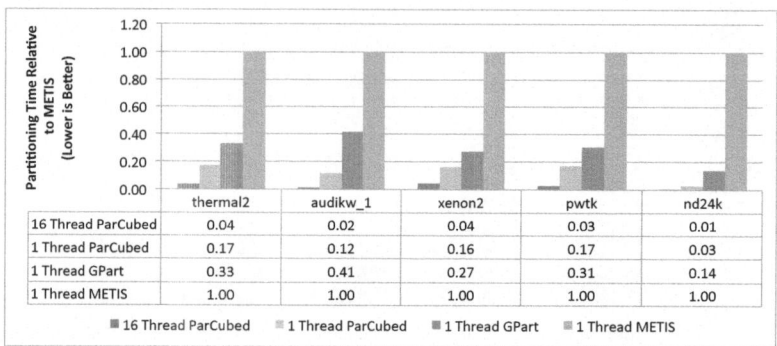

Fig. 7. Runtimes of different partitioning algorithms relative to serial METIS

ParCubed, serial ParCubed, GPart, and METIS. As explained earlier, in parallel ParCubed, the order in which nodes are visited varies with the number of threads used. As these results show, the quality of the partitioning is not greatly impacted by this effect in general, with results varying slightly in either direction.

When comparing the edge cut, note that METIS always generated the desired number of partitions for these input sets, while GPart regularly produced more partitions than requested.

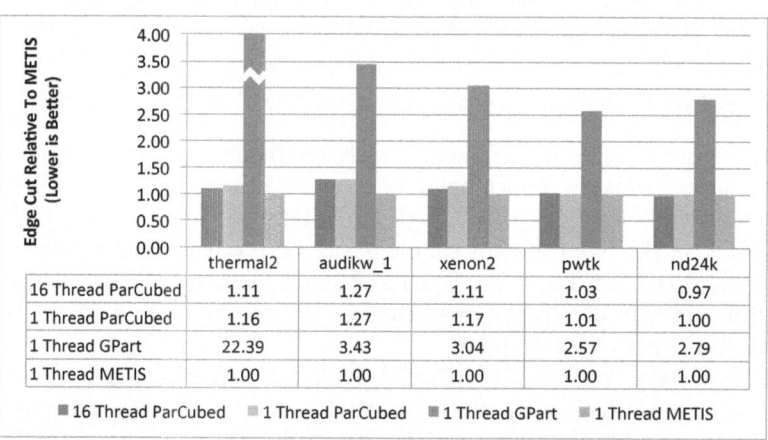

Fig. 8. Relative edge cuts achieved by different partitioning algorithms. Bars are normalized to METIS edge cut values. For thermal2, the GPart value of 22.39x is off the top of the chart. Lower values are better.

4.4   Executor Runtime

The ultimate purpose of partitioning the executor work is to reduce runtime. The runtime of the executor when run with 16 threads is shown in Figure 9.

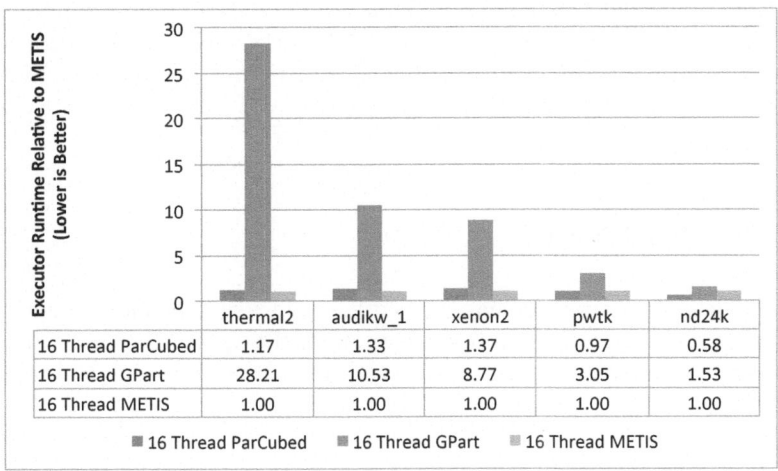

	thermal2	audikw_1	xenon2	pwtk	nd24k
16 Thread ParCubed	1.17	1.33	1.37	0.97	0.58
16 Thread GPart	28.21	10.53	8.77	3.05	1.53
16 Thread METIS	1.00	1.00	1.00	1.00	1.00

■ 16 Thread ParCubed   ■ 16 Thread GPart   ■ 16 Thread METIS

Fig. 9. Relative performance of the Jacobi executor. Bars are normalized to METIS executor runtime values. Lower values are better.

The results largely track the edge cut results of Figure 8, as expected. The nd24k sparse matrix is an exception. That matrix is the most highly connected in our test suite. It also exhibits the largest run to run variation in executor runtime. We believe that because of the large amount of shared data, it is very sensitive to task placement within the machine. If two tiles that share significant amounts of data are executed back to back on the same core, that core's cache will contain some of the shared data. This means that the assumption that each edge between partitions is equally costly does not always hold true. If communication between tiles requires accessing main memory, it is more expensive than data cache accesses. We believe that this effect partially explains the miscorrelation between edge cut and executor performance in this case.

5   Related Work

The ParCubed graph partitioner presented in this paper depends on a parallel union-find data structure, therefore we summarize some of the work related to such data structures. Additionally we summarize other graph partitioners with similar approaches to the ParCubed graph partitioner, but that are not parallel or are only parallelized for distributed memory machines.

5.1   Parallel Union Find Algorithms and Data Structures

A major enabler of the algorithm presented here is the *disjoint set* or *union-find* data structure. A number of different implementations have been developed for use in parallel applications. Wait-free implementations are described in [1] and rely on atomic compare and exchange operations for correctness. Additional methods of implementing parallel disjoint set data structures are presented in [4]. In [2], the code complexity of a number of different parallel implementations of union-find is surveyed from a software engineering perspective. This work includes software transactional memory, coarse and fine grained locking, and wait free approaches.

5.2   Graph Partitioners

The field of graph partitioning has been extensively researched for decades. While many different techniques have been developed, the approaches most related to this research focus either on multi-level graph partitioning or on hierarchical partitioning.

Multi-level graph partitioners
Multi-level graph partitioners, such as the METIS [9] algorithm that was used in our comparison above, deliver high quality partitions. They typically involve a coarsening phase in which the graph is reduced, or coarsened, by combining multiple nodes into clusters or supernodes. This step is followed by a direct partitioning of the coarse graph. The results of the partitioning are then projected back onto the original graph. Multi-level partitioners differentiate themselves in the method used to perform each of these phases and in additional refinement steps added to improve the quality of the final partitioning.

To speed up the partitioning process, many multi-level partitioners have been parallelized. ParMETIS [8] is a set of multi-level parallel partitioning algorithms related to METIS. It is parallelized using MPI and is designed for use in distributed memory environments. METIS has also been parallelized for use on shared memory machines using the Galois system, but that implementation is presently slower than ParMETIS [13].

Jostle [14] is another MPI parallelized multi-level graph partitioner. Published results show that it can produce partitionings equal to or better than ParMETIS, but it is typically slower. Another multi-level graph partitioner, PT-Scotch [3], is also parallelized using MPI and likewise is slower than ParMETIS.

Hierarchical clustering or growth based partitioners
Another general approach to graph partitioning is to combine graph nodes together into clusters. These clusters are then combined to form larger clusters and so on until the desired partition size has been achieved.

GPart [7] is a hierarchical clustering partitioner that is significantly faster than METIS, but to the best of our knowledge it has not been parallelized. Its use has focused more on data reordering to improve locality [6] and it has features that allow the partitioning to target multiple levels of cache. The join phase of our partitioner is essentially a slight variation on the GPart technique. TLayout [15] is a growth based parallel graph partitioner, but it is specifically designed for execution on a GPGPU and performs poorly on multicore CPUs.

6   Conclusions and Future Work

ParCubed is a fast, parallel graph partitioner for shared memory systems. It delivers results comparable to those of METIS in a fraction of the runtime. This makes it an attractive option for applications such as inspector/executor optimizations in which the execution time of the partitioner must be minimized, even at the cost of a slight increase in graph partition edge cut.

Work on the ParCubed partitioner is ongoing. We are currently investigating the optimal settings for parameters such as target partition sizes used in each step. Setting the target size to less than the final desired partition size during inflation, then setting it to slightly larger than the target size during the join phase has shown some promise. Testing on a larger variety of sparse matrices continues as well. We are also investigating improvements to the inflation phase of the algorithm, searching for techniques to further reduce the total edge cut of the partitioning. We will also compare the partitioning times of this algorithm with those of ParMETIS running a shared memory based MPI communication layer on a multicore system.

Future work will include using the partitioner on problems from additional problem domains, such as molecular dynamics. In these cases, the adjacency graph is not based on a sparse matrix, but comes from an earlier phase of the inspector that determines adjacency based on physical proximity of atoms in the simulation space.

Acknowledgments. We thank Xipeng Shen and Bo Wu of the College of William and Mary for their help with the TLayout partitioner.

This project is supported by a Department of Energy Early Career Grant DE-SC0003956, by a National Science Foundation CAREER grant CCF 0746693, and by the Department of Energy CACHE Institute grant DE-SC04030.

References

1. Anderson, R.J., Woll, H.: Wait-free parallel algorithms for the union-find problem. In: Proceedings of the Twenty-Third Annual ACM Symposium on Theory of Computing, STOC 1991, pp. 370–380. ACM, New York (1991)
2. I. Berman. Multicore programming in the face of metamorphosis: Union-find as an example. Master's thesis, Tel-Aviv University, July 2010.
3. Chevalier, C., Pellegrini, F.: PT-Scotch: A tool for efficient parallel graph ordering. Parallel Comput. 34(6-8), 318–331 (2008)
4. Cybenko, G., Allen, T.G., Polito, J.E.: Practical parallel union-find algorithms for transitive closure and clustering. Int. J. Parallel Program 17(5), 403–423 (1989)
5. Douglas, C.C., Hu, J., Kowarschik, M., Rüde, U., Weiss, C.: Cache optimization for structured and unstructured grid multigrid. Electronic Tranactions on Numerical Analysis 10, 21–40 (2000)
6. Han, H., Tseng, C.-W.: A Comparison of Locality Transformations for Irregular Codes. In: Dwarkadas, S. (ed.) LCR 2000. LNCS, vol. 1915, pp. 70–84. Springer, Heidelberg (2000)

7. Han, H., Tseng, C.-W.: Improving Locality for Adaptive Irregular Scientific Codes. In: Midkiff, S.P., Moreira, J.E., Gupta, M., Chatterjee, S., Ferrante, J., Prins, J.F., Pugh, B., Tseng, C.-W. (eds.) LCPC 2000. LNCS, vol. 2017, pp. 173–188. Springer, Heidelberg (2001)
8. Karypis, G., Kumar, V.: Parallel multilevel k-way partitioning scheme for irregular graphs. In: Proceedings of the 1996 ACM/IEEE Conference on Supercomputing (CDROM), Supercomputing 1996, IEEE Computer Society, Washington, DC (1996)
9. Karypis, G., Kumar, V.: A fast and high quality multilevel scheme for partitioning irregular graphs. SIAM J. Sci. Comput. 20(1), 359–392 (1998)
10. Mohiyuddin, M., Hoemmen, M., Demmel, J., Yelick, K.: Minimizing communication in sparse matrix solvers. In: Proceedings of the Conference on High Performance Computing Networking, Storage and Analysis, SC 2009, pp. 36:1–36:12. ACM, New York (2009)
11. Strout, M.M., Carter, L., Ferrante, J., Freeman, J., Kreaseck, B.: Combining Performance Aspects of Irregular Gauss-Seidel Via Sparse Tiling. In: Pugh, B., Tseng, C.-W. (eds.) LCPC 2002. LNCS, vol. 2481, pp. 90–110. Springer, Heidelberg (2005)
12. Strout, M.M., Carter, L., Ferrante, J., Kreaseck, B.: Sparse tiling for stationary iterative methods. International Journal of High Performance Computing Applications 18(1), 95–114 (2004)
13. Sui, X., Nguyen, D., Burtscher, M., Pingali, K.: Parallel Graph Partitioning on Multicore Architectures. In: Cooper, K., Mellor-Crummey, J., Sarkar, V. (eds.) LCPC 2010. LNCS, vol. 6548, pp. 246–260. Springer, Heidelberg (2011)
14. Walshaw, C., Cross, M.: Parallel optimisation algorithms for multilevel mesh partitioning. Parallel Comput. 26(12), 1635–1660 (2000)
15. B. Wu, E. Z. Zhang, and X. Shen. Enhancing data locality for dynamic simulations through asynchronous data transformations and adaptive control. In Proceedings of the 2011 International Conference on Parallel Architectures and Compilation Techniques, PACT 2011, pp. 243–252. IEEE Computer Society, Washington, DC (2011)

A Software-Based Method-Level Speculation Framework for the Java Platform*

Ivo Anjo and João Cachopo

ESW
INESC-ID Lisboa/Instituto Superior Técnico/Universidade Técnica de Lisboa
Rua Alves Redol 9, 1000-029 Lisboa, Portugal
{ivo.anjo,joao.cachopo}@ist.utl.pt

Abstract. With multicore processors becoming ubiquitous on computing devices, the need for both parallelizing existing sequential applications and designing new parallel applications is greatly intensified. With our work, we intend to tackle the former issue.

In this paper, we present the design of a software-based automatic parallelization framework for sequential applications that run on the Java platform: the JaSPEx-MLS framework.

Our framework employs Method-Level Speculation: It uses method invocations as fork points and converts those invocations to return futures that can be stored in local variables in place of the original values. The support for speculative execution is provided by automatically modifying application bytecode to use a custom lightweight Software Transactional Memory (STM), and we present a novel approach to integrate futures representing speculative executions with the STM. Thread state transfer is done by employing a Java Virtual Machine that provides support for first-class continuations.

We present preliminary results from our implementation of the proposed techniques on the JaSPEx-MLS framework, which works on top of the OpenJDK Hotspot VM.

Keywords: Automatic Parallelization, Method Level-Speculation, Software Transactional Memory, Continuations, OpenJDK Hotspot JVM.

1 Introduction

With the move to multicore processors, many new applications are being developed with concurrent architectures in mind. Yet, many existing applications are still sequential, and fail to take advantage of the full computing potential promised by the multicore age.

Unfortunately, it is not feasible for a vast majority of sequential applications to be rewritten to work in parallel within a reasonable time frame. Thus, an enticing option is to use an automatic approach to parallelization.

---

* This work was supported by FCT (INESC-ID multiannual funding) through the PID-DAC Program funds and by the RuLAM project (PTDC/EIA-EIA/108240/2008).

H. Kasahara and K. Kimura (Eds.): LCPC 2012, LNCS 7760, pp. 205–219, 2013.

Parallelizing compilers [4, 19] are one such approach that attempts to extract concurrency from sequential programs automatically by proving that parts of an application can be safely executed in parallel. The problem is that they fail to parallelize many irregular applications [8, 9, 12] that employ dynamic data structures, loops with complex dependences and control flows, and polymorphism, which are very hard or even impossible to analyze in a fully static way.

Thread-level speculation (TLS) systems [5, 10, 11, 13, 15, 21] attempt to work around this issue by optimistically running parts of the application in parallel, even if the TLS system is not able to prove statically that there will be no dependences. Instead, correctness is dynamically ensured at runtime, during or after execution of the parallel tasks. Incorrect operations and memory changes are prevented by buffering and tracking the execution of such operations, followed by validation before they are propagated to the global program state.

There are multiple ways of identifying tasks from a sequential application to be executed in parallel. Most TLS proposals concentrate only on loops [5, 10, 11, 15], whereas on our system we chose to use method calls as spawning points, as proposed by [6, 12, 13, 18].

In this paper, we present the design of our method-based speculation system, which was implemented on top of the JaSPEx [1, 2] speculative parallelization framework. Our system needs no special hardware extensions, instead relying on Software Transactional Memory (STM) for transactional support, and it works on top of a modified version of the OpenJDK Hotspot Java Virtual Machine (JVM), allowing it to benefit from a state-of-the-art, production-level managed runtime with dynamic optimization, garbage collection, and support for Java 6.

The rest of this paper is organized as follows. Section 2 introduces the Method-Level Speculation technique, and Section 3 introduces the JaSPEx-MLS parallelization framework. The static modifications done by the JaSPEx-MLS classloader are described in Section 4, whereas in Section 5 we detail the runtime creation and coordination of speculative tasks. Section 6 presents preliminary experimental results for our system. Section 7 discusses the related work, and we finish in Section 8 by presenting conclusions and future research directions.

2   Method-Level Speculation

Method-level speculation (MLS) is a speculative parallelization strategy first discussed in the context of Java by [6], and shown to be a promising source for parallelism by [12, 13, 18]. This technique works by speculatively executing the code that follows the return of a method call — its continuation — in parallel with the method call itself.

An example of method-level speculation is shown in Figure 1. When the `computeValue()` method call is reached, the current thread (T1) begins executing it, while at the same time triggering the speculative execution (by T2) of the code following the return of that method.

In this example, both the original parent thread and the speculative child thread have to join to produce the result of the method. If the value of the

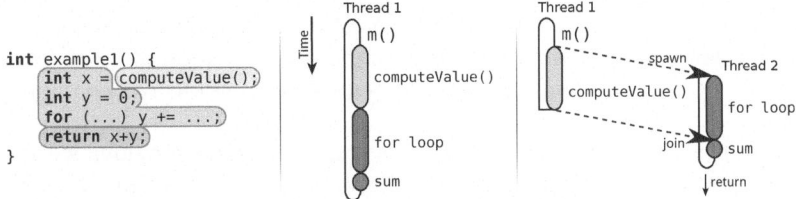

Fig. 1. Execution of `example1()` method when run normally (center) and parallelized with MLS (right)

variable x was never used, it would be possible to speculate past the return of `example1()`, and continue execution of the method that invoked it.

Alternatively, even if x's value is needed to proceed with the execution, we can employ return value prediction [7, 14] to guess a probable value of x, and continue speculation using this assumption.

3   The JaSPEx-MLS Parallelization Framework

JaSPEx-MLS is a fully software-based speculative parallelization framework that provides both a Java classloader that modifies application code as it is requested by the virtual machine, and a runtime Java library that orchestrates speculative execution. It is based on the JaSPEx framework [1, 2], but with both an entirely new MLS-based speculation model, and a new transactional backend.

The JaSPEx-MLS classloader (Section 4) is responsible for preparing application code for speculative parallelization. This includes transactifying the code, adding hooks to allow the framework to correctly handle non-transactional operations, and inserting into the application the spawn points that will be used at runtime to create speculative tasks.

The runtime orchestration library (Section 5) is responsible for controlling the creation of speculative tasks, establishing the commit order for the underlying transactional system, deciding when to validate and to commit speculative tasks, correctly handling aborting and retrying, and controlling the execution of non-transactional operations. Speculative work is submitted to a thread pool, which we attempt to keep busy at all times. Nested speculation is supported.

Almost all of JaSPEx-MLS is implemented in Java, and modifications to applications are done via bytecode rewriting.[1] The lone exception to this is that JaSPEx-MLS relies on having first-class continuation support, which is provided by a modified version of the OpenJDK virtual machine.

The OpenJDK VM is the result of the open-sourcing of Oracle's Java technology, including the Hotspot JVM. By working on top of OpenJDK, JaSPEx-MLS has access to all the features and optimizations of a modern production JVM: just-in-time compilation and adaptive optimization, state-of-the-art garbage collection algorithms, support for Java 6 and optimized concurrency primitives.

---

[1] To simplify presentation, the examples in this paper instead appear in Java.

We believe that the combination of software-only speculation on top of a modern production JVM sets our system apart from previous work: Our approach can work on commonly available modern hardware, and on top of the same codebase regularly used to run the sequential versions of the applications that we are targeting.

Our first-class continuation implementation is based on previous work by Yamauchi [20], which itself was based on the work of Stadler et al. [16]. We have developed a library that currently includes backends for two different JVM implementations of first-class continuations, and that will allow JaSPEx-MLS to easily adapt to future developments in this area.

4   JaSPEx-MLS Classloader: Static Code Preparation

As introduced in Section 3, the JaSPEx-MLS classloader handles the static preparation of classes for speculative parallelism. An important assumption that we make is that any class that is prepared and loaded by this classloader is fully safe to invoke with transactional semantics. The modifications described in the following subsections allow a class to fulfill this assumption.

4.1   Transactification

The first part of static application processing is concerned with allowing application code to run with transactional semantics. This allows JaSPEx-MLS to control memory read and write operations during speculative execution, to have a means of validating them, and to decide if they should be kept or not.

Rather than modifying the virtual machine to obtain this transactional support, we intercept any Java bytecodes that may access and mutate heap-allocated memory locations—that is, accesses to object slots and to array elements.

As such, an application is modified to use an STM-like API whenever it must read or write to slots and arrays.[2] This API is very lightweight, type-specific, and static, allowing the JVM to easily inline it into hot paths of the code.

4.2   Handling Non-transactional Operations

In any transactional system, there are always some operations that cannot be made to behave transactionally, as they are outside the control of the system.

For JaSPEx-MLS, and in the JVM platform, we consider as non-transactional two types of operations: (1) native methods, which are implemented with pre-compiled binary code, making them hard to analyze and transactify; and (2) code belonging to the JDK (any classes in the java.* package namespace).

Code belonging to the JDK is considered to be non-transactional because the OpenJDK JVM, like Oracle's JVM, does not allow alternative versions of JDK classes to be loaded at runtime. To reduce the number of non-transactional operations resulting from this limitation, we use a semi-manually–compiled whitelist

---

[2] An exception is the access to final fields, which do not change after initialization.

```
java.util.List l = ...;
if (!(l instanceof Transactional)) nonTransactionalActionAttempted();
l.clear();
```

Listing 1.1. Runtime check for `Transactional` instances

that includes immutable classes and methods that do not change any state, and that do not access state from non-transactional classes nor arrays. Yet, in the future, we intend to explore either the feasibility of modifying the VM to remove this restriction, or a more limited offline modification of these base classes before they are loaded.

To protect an application from executing a non-transactional operation while performing speculative execution, we prepend any such operation with a call to the framework method `nonTransactionalActionAttempted()`, which validates the current speculation, waiting if needed, before allowing the operation to proceed, or aborts the execution if the speculation is not valid.

In addition, as it is not always possible to distinguish statically when, for instance, a reference `l` of type `java.util.List` refers to a user-provided `MyList` or a non-transactional `java.util.ArrayList`, a runtime test is added. This runtime test relies on the fact that any class processed by our classloader implements the `Transactional` interface, and thus, at runtime, we can avoid stopping speculation unless really needed, as shown in Listing 1.1.

4.3   Modifications for MLS

Whereas the previous modification steps of the JaSPEx-MLS classloader prepared application code to run with transactional semantics, the final step readies the code for MLS.

To add support for MLS, JaSPEx-MLS replaces normal method calls with a call to a special `spawnSpeculation()` method. This method receives a `Callable` object, representing the original method invocation and its arguments, and returns a `Future`, representing the value that will be returned by the target method.

The `Callable` object is an instance of an automatically generated class that includes slots for each argument to the method call. When the `call()` method is invoked, it proceeds to call the original method.

The most complex part of the insertion of `spawnSpeculation()` is dealing with the returned future. The main objective of the transformation performed is to delay to as late as possible the retrieval of the result from the future, as it would entail waiting if the value is not yet computed. Thus, the trivial case where the future is immediately needed is not useful,[3] as nothing would be gained from just transferring execution to another thread, and so JaSPEx-MLS rejects this case. The other trivial case, where the value returned from the method is discarded, or the method is `void`, is useful, but needs no further modifications other that popping the future off the stack.

---

[3] JaSPEx-MLS currently does not employ return value prediction [7, 14].

```
void example() {
  int x = 0;
  if (condition) {
    Future f0 = spawnSpeculation(...); // original method: compute()
    x = f0;
  }
  int y = x + 1; // error: is x an int or a future ???
  { ... code that uses y ... }
}
```

Listing 1.2. Example of problematic replacement of a returned value with a future

```
void example() {
  int x = 0;
  if (condition) {
    Future f0 = spawnSpeculation(...); // original method: compute()
    x = f0;
    goto x_is_a_Future;
  }
  int y = x + 1; // x is an int
rest_of_the_method:
  { ... code that uses y ... }
  return;
x_is_a_Future:
  int y = x.get() + 1; // x is a future
  goto rest_of_the_method;
}
```

Listing 1.3. Valid version of the code from Listing 1.2, obtained by duplicating part of the method

A more interesting case however, is the common pattern of saving the result of a method on a local variable for later use. The JVM bytecode specification allows any type to be stored in any local variable (and this type can change during execution of a method), so we are allowed to write the future to the same local variable as the original return value would have.

The problem with this substitution is what happens when the return value is accessed. Consider for instance the code shown in Listing 1.2: This transformation is not valid, because the x local variable may be of type int in a possible path through the method, and of type Future on another path.

To solve this problem, we construct the control flow graph of the method and duplicate code blocks where both a future and the original return type may be present. As an example, Listing 1.3 shows the correct version of the transformation shown in Listing 1.2.

To avoid spawning speculative executions that would run only a small number of instructions before needing to synchronize with other threads, JaSPEx-MLS does a number of passes that perform simple analysis to try to avoid these cases. In addition, the MLS modification pass can use a list of methods that are known not to be profitable for speculation: This list may either be manually provided, or be the result of profiling performed on the application.

4.4   STM Support for Futures

To further delay the moment when we need to obtain the return value from the future, we added to our STM support for writing futures to memory locations.

```
// Original Method
void doCompute(Object[] results) {
  for (int i = 0; i < results.length; i++) {
    results[i] = compute(i);
  }}

// Attempted parallelization
void doCompute(Object[] results) {
  for (int i = 0; i < results.length; i++) {
    Future f0 = spawnSpeculation(...); // original method: compute(i)
    TM.storeObjectArray(results, i, f0.get()); // get() called immediately
  }}
```

Listing 1.4. Unsuccessful parallelization of doCompute()

```
void doCompute(Object[] results) {
  for (int i = 0; i < results.length; i++) {
    Future f0 = spawnSpeculation(...); // original method: compute(i)
    TM.storeFutureObjectArray(results, i, f0); // f0 is handed to the STM
  }}
```

Listing 1.5. Successful parallelization of doCompute(), with the added support for futures in the STM

Consider, for instance, Listing 1.4: In this case, the transformation performed in Section 4.3 to add the spawnSpeculation() call would not be useful, as the resulting code would immediately obtain the return value from the future, so that it can be written into the array.

In reality, due to the transactification step performed in Section 4.1, the write to the array is not done directly, but instead the value to be written is handed over to the STM. We can take advantage of this behavior to extend the STM with support for futures, allowing the resulting code to behave as shown in Listing 1.5.

Note that if each execution of compute() that is being replaced by spawnSpeculation() is fully independent, the example method (and the loop contained therein) has gone from not being parallelizable, to being fully parallel, as the entire loop can be executed without stopping speculation, and the do-Compute() method can even return to its caller, allowing other work to be done, while the computation of the values proceeds in parallel.

5   Runtime Orchestration of Speculative Executions

The JaSPEx-MLS runtime library is responsible for the creation and coordination of speculative executions.

A speculative execution starts when an application reaches a call to the spawnSpeculation() method, which was previously inserted by the JaSPEx-MLS classloader as a replacement for a normal method call. Inside this method, the framework dynamically decides weather a new speculation should be spawned by taking into account the current workload of the system. Because in our system nested speculations are supported, speculative executions can spawn further speculative executions.

If JaSPEx-MLS chooses to spawn a speculation, it starts by capturing a first-class continuation representing the stack and execution state of the current thread. Remember from Figure 1 in Section 2 that this execution state will be resumed on another thread, while the current thread will continue by executing the method call contained in the `Callable` received by `spawnSpeculation()`. To represent the task being spawned, JaSPEx-MLS creates a new instance of `SpeculationTask` and submits it for execution by the thread pool.

The created `SpeculationTask` instance is the link between the *parent* task — the task that reached the call to `spawnSpeculation()` — and the *child* task, which will resume the continuation and start its execution of the code following the call to `spawnSpeculation()`. This parent/child relation implicitly imposes a global order on all tasks on the system that mirrors the original order on the sequential application.

After submitting the child `SpeculationTask` for execution, the parent task cleans its current thread's stack by resuming an empty continuation, and proceeds to execute the method represented by the `Callable`. When the method returns, its return value is stored inside the child `SpeculationTask`, so that the child task will be able to retrieve it, and the thread running the parent task returns to the thread pool.

When the child `SpeculationTask` is picked up for execution by a thread, we first test if the task's parent already finished by checking if its result is available. If it is not, a new STM transaction is started, otherwise, because its parent already committed, no transaction is started and the task is executed in program-order mode. The thread then resumes the first-class continuation captured by the parent task: Upon resuming the continuation, execution restarts inside the `spawnSpeculation()` method, and JaSPEx-MLS returns a future to the caller method — representing the promise of a return value from the parent task — and the child task continues its execution.

This design where the thread that reaches the `spawnSpeculation()` throws away its stack and executes the parent task, while the child task will start by restoring the very same stack was chosen so as to allow tasks to be queued even when there are no free threads to execute them. The inverse option, where the thread that reaches the `spawnSpeculation()` would execute the child task and queue the parent for execution could in many cases delay the application, as the child task would not be able to commit its work before its parent was finished.

5.1   Committing a Speculation

There are three conditions that trigger the commit of a speculative task:

1. The task completed its work
2. The task needed to obtain a result from a future, and noticed that it was the oldest-running task in the system
3. The task attempted to execute a non-transactional operation

A speculative task is allowed to commit its work only if it is the oldest-running task in the system. In our design, every task has a parent that spawned it, and that parent is responsible for writing its result onto the child's `SpeculationTask`. Every parent commits before its child task and before passing its result to the child. Thus, when a child receives the result from its parent, it can also commit because it is guaranteed that its parent has finished its work.

When a task wants to commit, but no result from its parent is available, it waits on its own `SpeculationTask` for this value to arrive. Note that it may be possible that its parent is in the same situation, and that a sequence of speculative executions are all waiting for their own parents. When a parent sets its value on the child, it wakes up the child, so that the child can resume working.

After a child task receives the result from its parent, we first check for two special cases: an exception and an order to abort. If the result from the parent is an exception, then whatever work the current speculative task has done is invalid: In the original application, this code would never run, because the exception would be thrown before the code was reached. So, when this happens, the child task aborts its current STM transaction, signals its own child speculation (if any) that it should abort, and retries execution by re-resuming the continuation (which re-initializes the current execution stack back inside the `spawnSpeculation()` method) and by re-throwing the exception thrown by the parent. This scheme simulates the way the exception would appear in the original application. In case the speculation receives an order to abort, either because its parent (or any grandparent) aborted due to an exception or because a mis-speculation was detected by the STM, the current task aborts its own transaction, signals its child (if any) to abort also, and the thread is returned to the thread pool. Any computation done was wasted, because it was based on invalid assumptions.

When a thread attempts to commit, but the validation of the STM transaction fails, the transaction is aborted, and the task is retried by re-resuming the continuation received from the parent. For the re-execution, no transaction is started, as the task will be running in program-order, rather than speculatively.

Finally, whenever a task finishes its work and is able to commit successfully its STM transaction, it writes its return value on its child `SpeculationTask` and the thread hosting it is returned to the thread pool.

5.2 Custom Relaxed STM Model

The STM used in JaSPEx-MLS was designed to be very lightweight, so as to impose minimal overheads on the transactified application. It clearly distinguishes between two modes of execution: program-order mode and speculation mode.

A task that is executing in program-order mode always reads from and writes to memory directly, with no additional validation nor synchronization: At any given time, only one task is working in program-order; any other threads executing tasks are performing speculative execution.

When the program-order task attempts to write a future into a memory location, the return value from the future is immediately retrieved as, per the structure imposed by the method-level speculation scheme, that future represents the result of a previous speculation that must already have finished.

Like most STMs, for tasks running in speculative mode, JaSPEx-MLS keeps both a (value-based) read-set, which contains each heap-allocated memory location read by the transaction and its value at the time, and a write-set, which maps memory locations to values to be written to them upon commit.

In our STM model, tasks running speculatively always read directly from the requested memory location, and may observe changes being done concurrently by a task running in program-order mode. This strategy can, of course, cause inconsistent reads, but unlike normal applications that use STM, inconsistent reads are always present in the execution model, and are handled by the framework.

When a read of a memory location is attempted, and there is already an entry in the write-set for that location, the value from the write-set is returned. If the entry in the write-set contained a future in place of the real value, the result from the future is first retrieved (by waiting, if necessary), and then returned.

Whenever a speculative task wants to perform a write, a new mapping is added/updated to the write-set: a pair $(location, newvalue)$ for normal values, and a pair $(location, future)$ for futures.

Because the task coordination part of JaSPEx-MLS always commits transactions in the same order as the original sequential application, only one transaction will be trying to commit at any one time, dismissing the need for synchronization during the commit operation. As such, the commit operation consists of only two simple steps: (1) validating the the read-set by re-reading the values from the memory locations and comparing them to the ones originally read and kept in the read-set; and (2) performing the write-back of values from the write-set to the memory locations, including retrieving and writing the results from any futures.

5.3   Thread and Task Management

When a new speculative task is created, JaSPEx-MLS submits it for execution to a thread pool. The current design of the thread pool allocates a limited number of threads based on the number of CPUs on the machine, and accepts speculations only when there are idle threads.

This design is very simple, and we intend to improve it in the future in two ways: (1) by returning threads to the pool instead of waiting; and (2) by integrating a task scheduler.

The idea of returning threads to the pool instead of waiting is applicable when there is a great imbalance between the size of speculative tasks that threads are working on. If, for instance, the oldest task in the system is executing a very long-running code section, and all the other threads have, in the meantime, finished their work, and are waiting for permission to commit, no further speculations are accepted, and the application would be executing sequentially. Instead, we plan to have waiting threads capture a first-class continuation with their current state, which would then be associated with their parent. Then, when the thread running the parent task finishes its work, instead of immediately returning to the thread pool it would switch to and finish execution of its child task. This way, waiting threads would be free to return to the thread pool, where they may accept new

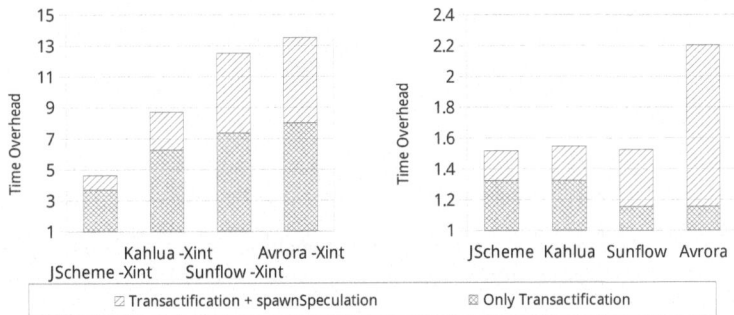

Fig. 2. Slowdown introduced by the bytecode modifications performed by JaSPEx-MLS (speculation was disabled) with the JVM in interpreter-only mode (left), and normal optimizing mode (right). *Only transactification* accounts for the modifications described in Sections 4.1-4.2, whereas *Transactification + spawnSpeculation* accounts for all bytecode modifications. Results were normalized to the runtimes of the unmodified applications.

speculative tasks that are submitted by the very busy thread, speeding up its execution once again.

Baptista [3] was able to integrate a conflict-aware scheduler into an older version of the JaSPEx framework. His work shows promising results, and we intend to adapt it to JaSPEx-MLS in the future.

6 Experimental Results

In this Section, we present preliminary experimental results obtained with the JaSPEx-MLS framework. We tested our prototype on an Intel Core i5 750 machine with 8GB of RAM, running Ubuntu Linux 12.04 64-bit, and our modified OpenJDK VM.

We tested several JVM applications: the JScheme R4RS Scheme implementation, the Sunflow ray tracing engine, the Avrora hardware simulator and analysis framework, the Kahlua Lua scripting language interpreter, and some benchmarks from the the Java Grande Forum (JGF) benchmark suite. Apart from Sunflow, the chosen benchmarks are single-threaded, although some of them employed locking and thread-local variables in some places, which we removed; we modified Sunflow to use only the single main thread to perform its rendering work.

We first measured the overheads imposed by our system when speculation is disabled. Figure 2 shows the overhead we measured, when comparing our system to the original sequential application runtime, in two cases: (1) running the JVM in interpreter-only mode (-Xint mode), and (2) with the full Hotspot VM optimizations enabled. Using only the interpreter, our bytecode modifications impose heavy overheads, but when running with optimizations enabled, we can see that the VM is successfully able to optimize away many of the added indirections, showing that our lightweight STM imposes minimal overhead on application code running in program-order. The results also show that blind conversion of normal

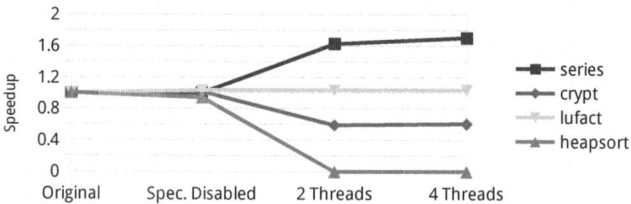

Fig. 3. Results from benchmarking with JGF benchmarks, normalized to the original application runtimes. Values above 1 correspond to a speedup, whereas below 1 correspond to a slowdown.

method calls into `spawnSpeculation()` also imposes non-trivial overheads, suggesting the importance of the integration of a profiling pass to remove unprofitable calls in our framework.

Results from testing with benchmarks from the JGF benchmark suite are shown in Figure 3. The input applications were not modified, but some manual profiling was done and a blacklist of methods unsuitable for speculation was provided to JaSPEx-MLS. The `series` benchmark was able to obtain a speedup of 1.7x, `lufact` was not able to perform any meaningful speculation, `crypt` was not able to extract speedup from the speculation done, `heapsort` had an overwhelming number of aborted transactions, and both `sor` and `sparsemult` (not shown) are not suitable for MLS parallelization as all their computation is done in a single method. These results again underline the need for a semi-automatic profiling pass that can avoid unprofitable executions, but also that it is possible to extract parallelism using JaSPEx-MLS.

7   Related Work

Many TLS proposals depend on some kind of hardware transactional support; unfortunately, while such support remains absent from common architectures these systems remain impractical. Jrpm [5] is a Java VM that does speculative loop parallelization on a multiprocessor with hardware support for profiling and speculative execution. At runtime, applications are profiled to find speculative buffer requirements and inter-thread dependences; once sufficient data is collected, the chosen loops are dynamically recompiled to run in parallel. Helper Transactions [21] rely on special hardware support to perform method-level speculation. The authors introduce the concept of implicit commit, allowing a thread that finished working to signal its sibling speculation to commit; this sibling speculation should then validate itself, commit its current work and continue executing non-speculatively. The advantage of this approach is that the oldest speculation in the system automatically switches off speculative execution as soon as possible, lowering execution overheads.

Because executing code transactionally can impose very large overheads, recent TLS proposals, similarly to JaSPEx-MLS, try to optimize the transactification and transactional model as much as possible: Oancea, Mycroft and Harris [11] proposed SpLIP, a software speculation system that targets mostly-parallel loops. The authors concentrated on avoiding performance pitfalls present on other software TLS proposals by having speculations commit their work in parallel, and using in-place updates. This contrasts with our approach of keeping changes in the write-set until commit, and increases the penalty for bad speculation decisions, which involve costly rollback operations, prompting a very careful analysis when choosing loops to parallelize. In [10] the authors propose STMlite, a lighter STM model targeting loop parallelization. STMlite aims at using a small number (2-8) of speculative threads to extract parallelism from loops, avoiding the need to transactify the whole program. During execution, transactional read and write operations are encoded using hash-based signatures that are then checked by a central bookkeeping and commit thread. Fastpath [15] is also aimed at extracting parallelism from loops using speculation. The transactional system distinguishes between the thread running in program order, and other speculative threads: The lead thread always commits its work, and has minimal overhead, whereas speculative threads suffer from higher overheads and may abort. The authors also propose two different STM-inspired algorithms for conflict detection: value and signature-based. In both conflict detection algorithms, the lead thread is always allowed to change memory locations in-place. The Fastpath system as presented did not yet support automatic parallelization; results from a hand-instrumented benchmark showed that the value-based algorithm presented the best results. The JaSPEx-MLS relaxed STM model is very similar to the Fastpath value-based algorithm, the biggest difference being our inclusion of support for futures in the STM.

The idea of using futures in Java coupled with speculative execution was also explored in a different context by Welc et al. [17]: In their work on safe futures for Java, the authors extend Java with support for futures that are guaranteed to respect serial execution semantics. Because of this, futures can be thought of as semantically transparent annotations on methods: Execution of a method can be replaced with the execution of a future, the safe future model guaranteeing that sequential semantics is respected. In contrast with our automatic approach, to use safe futures programmers manually change their code to employ futures instead of normal method calls, including solving cases where the return value from a method is used immediately. Zhang and Krintz's Safe DBLFutures [22] also support a similar approach, and includes safe handling of exceptions that respect sequential semantics.

SableSpMT [13] is a Java MLS-based automatic parallelization framework. To allow speculation even when the return value of a function call is needed immediately, SableSpMT employs return value prediction [14]. Nested speculation is not allowed, limiting some of the achievable parallelism: Although the main thread is allowed to spawn multiple speculative tasks, the tasks themselves cannot spawn further speculative tasks. Before running an application, SableSpMT performs a static analysis and modification pass on the input application: This pass inserts fork points into the application bytecode, and gathers information to be used by the return value predictor. SableSpMT is based on the SableVM virtual machine, which is a research VM, employing only an interpreter and a simpler garbage collection algorithm. The system was benchmarked using the SPECjvm98 benchmark suite on a quad-cpu machine, but no speedup was achieved over the original application runtimes due to the added overheads. In further testing with fork and join overheads factored out by considering a baseline execution where every speculation fails to commit at the end, SableSpMT was able to achieve a mean relative speedup of 1.34x. In contrast with SableSpMT, JaSPEx-MLS fully supports nested speculation, and in our system the garbage collector works normally, whereas in SableSpMT it invalidates all running speculations. The base SableVM is also a much simpler VM, with no support for Java 6 and none of the advantages of OpenJDK as introduced in Section 3.

8   Conclusions and Future Work

In this paper, we introduced the design of JaSPEx-MLS, an automatic parallelization framework for the Java platform. Our framework needs no hardware transactional support, and works atop a modern production-quality managed runtime supporting JIT compilation and advanced garbage collection facilities: the OpenJDK Hotspot virtual machine.

We described how the JaSPEx-MLS classloader transactifies applications, and also how it converts method calls into speculation spawn points. We also presented a novel approach to enable further speculation by integrating support for the futures returned at spawn points into the STM, allowing the application to behave as if the future itself was written to a memory location. We then described how speculative tasks are orchestrated at runtime, and the design of our lightweight relaxed STM model.

Our preliminary results show that an optimizing VM can hide much of the overhead introduced by our static bytecode preparation, and also that JaSPEx-MLS is already able to extract parallelism in some benchmarks.

In the future, we intend to lift some of the limitations imposed by our handling of non-transactional operations, to add support for a profiling pass that gathers information on the most profitable methods for speculation, and to improve the runtime scheduling of tasks and reuse of threads in the thread pool.

References

1. Anjo, I.: JaSPEx: Speculative Parallelization on the Java Platform. Master's thesis, Instituto Superior Técnico (2009)
2. Anjo, I., Cachopo, J.: JaSPEx: Speculative parallel execution of Java applications. In: Proceedings of the Simpósio de Informática (INFORUM 2009). Faculdade de Ciências da Universidade de Lisboa (2009)
3. Baptista, D.: Task Scheduling in Speculative Parallelization. Master's thesis, Instituto Superior Técnico (2011)
4. Blume, W., Doallo, R., Eigenmann, R., Grout, J., Hoeflinger, J., Lawrence, T.: Parallel programming with Polaris. Computer 29(12), 78–82 (1996)
5. Chen, M., Olukotun, K.: The Jrpm system for dynamically parallelizing Java programs. ACM SIGARCH Computer Architecture News 31(2), 434–446 (2003)

6. Chen, M., Olukotun, K.: Exploiting method-level parallelism in single-threaded Java programs. In: 7th International Conference on Parallel Architectures and Compilation Techniques (PACT-1998), pp. 176–184. IEEE (1998)
7. Hu, S., Bhargava, R., John, L.: The role of return value prediction in exploiting speculative method-level parallelism. Journal of Instruction-Level Parallelism 5(1) (2003)
8. Kulkarni, M., Burtscher, M., Inkulu, R., Pingali, K., Cascaval, C.: How much parallelism is there in irregular applications? ACM SIGPLAN Notices 44(4), 3–14 (2009)
9. Lam, M., Wilson, R.: Limits of control flow on parallelism. ACM SIGARCH Computer Architecture News 20(2), 46–57 (1992), http://doi.acm.org/10.1145/146628.139702
10. Mehrara, M., Hao, J., Hsu, P., Mahlke, S.: Parallelizing sequential applications on commodity hardware using a low-cost software transactional memory. ACM SIGPLAN Notices 44(6), 166–176 (2009)
11. Oancea, C., Mycroft, A., Harris, T.: A lightweight in-place implementation for software thread-level speculation. In: Proceedings of the 21st Annual Symposium on Parallelism in Algorithms and Architectures (SPAA 2009), pp. 223–232. ACM Press (2009)
12. Oplinger, J., Heine, D., Lam, M.: In search of speculative thread-level parallelism. In: 8th International Conference on Parallel Architectures and Compilation Techniques (PACT-1999), pp. 303–313. IEEE (1999)
13. Pickett, C.J.F., Verbrugge, C.: Software Thread Level Speculation for the Java Language and Virtual Machine Environment. In: Ayguadé, E., Baumgartner, G., Ramanujam, J., Sadayappan, P. (eds.) LCPC 2005. LNCS, vol. 4339, pp. 304–318. Springer, Heidelberg (2006)
14. Pickett, C.J.F., Verbrugge, C.: Return value prediction in a Java virtual machine. In: Proceedings of the 2nd Value-Prediction and Value-Based Optimization Workshop (VPW2), pp. 40–47 (2004)
15. Spear, M.F., Kelsey, K., Bai, T., Dalessandro, L., Scott, M.L., Ding, C., Wu, P.: Fastpath Speculative Parallelization. In: Gao, G.R., Pollock, L.L., Cavazos, J., Li, X. (eds.) LCPC 2009. LNCS, vol. 5898, pp. 338–352. Springer, Heidelberg (2010)
16. Stadler, L., Wimmer, C., Würthinger, T., Mössenböck, H., Rose, J.: Lazy continuations for Java virtual machines. In: 7th International Conference on Principles and Practice of Programming in Java (PPPJ 2009), pp. 143–152. ACM Press (2009)
17. Welc, A., Jagannathan, S., Hosking, A.: Safe futures for Java. ACM SIGPLAN Notices 40(10), 439–453 (2005), http://doi.acm.org/10.1145/1103845.1094845
18. Whaley, J., Kozyrakis, C.: Heuristics for profile-driven method-level speculative parallelization. In: Proceedings of the 2005 International Conference on Parallel Processing (ICPP 2005), pp. 147–156. IEEE Computer Society (2005)
19. Wilson, R., French, R., Wilson, C., Amarasinghe, S., Anderson, J., Tjiang, S., Liao, S., Tseng, C., Hall, M., Lam, M., Hennessy, J.: SUIF: An infrastructure for research on parallelizing and optimizing compilers. ACM SIGPLAN Notices 29(12), 31–37 (1994)
20. Yamauchi, H.: Continuations in servers. In: JVM Language Summit 2010 (2010)
21. Yoo, R., Lee, H.: Helper transactions: Enabling thread-level speculation via a transactional memory system. In: 2008 Workshop on Parallel Execution of Sequential Programs on Multi-core Architectures (PESPMA 2008), pp. 63–71 (2008)
22. Zhang, L., Krintz, C.: As-if-serial exception handling semantics for Java futures. Science of Computer Programming 74(5-6), 314–332 (2009), http://dx.doi.org/10.1016/j.scico.2009.01.006

Ant: A Debugging Framework
for MPI Parallel Programs*

Jae-Woo Lee, Leonardo R. Bachega, Samuel P. Midkiff, and Y.C. Hu

School of Electrical and Computer Engineering
Purdue University, West Lafayette, IN 47907
{jaewoolee,lbachega,smidkiff,ychu}@purdue.edu

Abstract. This paper describes Ant, a debugging framework targeting
MPI parallel programs. The Ant framework statically analyzes programs,
marking code regions as being executed by all processes or executed by
only some of the processes. The analyzed program is then instrumented
with calls to an invariant violation monitoring and detection library. The
analysis allows regions to be instrumented based on whether all, or less
than all, processes execute the region. Ant's instrumentation strategy
allows sampled monitoring across processes in regions executed by all
processes. We present a case study using Ant with C-DIDUCE (a variant of DIDUCE for C) to find violations of value invariants in parallel
C/MPI programs. Ant's instrumentation strategy reduces the overhead
of monitoring by over 14 times with less impact on accuracy than a
scheme that simply distributes monitoring over all processes executing
the program.

Keywords: MPI, Parallel Program Debugging, Anomaly Detection,
DIDUCE.

1 Introduction

Bugs in serial programs cost the software industry billions of dollars in lost
productivity each year [1]. Sequential bugs, i.e., bugs not actually related to the
parallelization of a program, will continue to be a major problem in parallel
programs. Tools that identify potential sequential bugs will allow those bugs to
be fixed, and will save programmers from having to determine if the bug is a
sequential bug or a result of parallelization.

Many debugging tools require runtime monitoring of program points of interest. An important class of these tools is *invariant violation detection tools*,
which includes tools such as DIDUCE [2], C-DIDUCE [3] and AccMon [4][1] that,
in sequential programs, have runtime overheads of up to 20X, 1.21X and 3X,
respectively. A second class of debugging tools (e.g., [5–7]) look for statistical
variations in program behaviors between correct and incorrect runs, and can also

---

* This material is based upon work supported by the National Science Foundation
under Grant No. CCF-0916901.
[1] AccMon requires special hardware.

H. Kasahara and K. Kimura (Eds.): LCPC 2012, LNCS 7760, pp. 220–233, 2013.

have high runtime overheads. A naive port of these tools to parallel programs will have high overheads while executing on expensive parallel hardware.

This paper describes the Ant framework that allows these, and other tools that do not require all events of interest to be monitored, to efficiently and accurately target parallel MPI programs. Ant does this by solving two important problems. First, Ant allows the results gathered on many processes to be merged in a theoretically sound way that gives useful results. Second, Ant uses the inherent parallelism of the program being monitored to reduce the overhead of the debugging tool, while maintaining a high level of accuracy. We show the effectiveness of Ant using a case study involving C-DIDUCE [3], an implementation of DIDUCE [2] that targets C instead of Java programs.

DIDUCE, C-DIDUCE and the value invariant hypothesis. Statistical and invariance based debugging tools such as DIDUCE and C-DIDUCE assert a hypothesis that serves as the foundation of the tool. DIDUCE and C-DIDUCE assert the *value invariant hypothesis*, which states that a given variable takes on a small set of values during its lifetime, even with different input data, and rarely occurring deviations from this set of values indicate buggy or anomalous behavior. Detecting where these deviations occur aids in debugging. The literature on these and similar techniques (e.g., [3, 2, 4, 7, 8]) empirically validate the utility of the asserted hypotheses in sequential programs.

Correctly but naively extending a debugging tool to parallel environments. In our case study, the Ant framework asserts a parallel version of the value invariant hypothesis. Ant asserts that a value invariant holds across different input datasets, across similar processes executing the program, and across executions involving different numbers of processes. In Section 3.2, we formally show that the merging of the monitoring data gathered over many processes will yield the same result as if the data was gathered in a single sequential execution.

Empirical evidence gathered from our case study targeting C with MPI programs and C-DIDUCE shows the practicality of exploiting the parallel value invariant hypothesis with Ant. We use four MPI parallel benchmarks that have bugs injected into them. Each process performs *replicated* monitoring, that is, each process performs the monitoring required by C-DIDUCE as if it were an independent program, with the results of the individual processes' monitoring collected and merged. This monitoring provides effective detection of the injected bugs, as explained in Section 4.

Exploiting application parallelism for efficient monitoring. Using the replicated monitoring described above, C-DIDUCE and DIDUCE suffer high overheads in parallel programs just as they do in sequential programs. One way to reduce these overheads is to have each of the P processes executing the program monitor $\frac{1}{P}$ of the events. This performs a sampled monitoring by distributing the monitoring evenly across the P processes. We call this type of monitoring *distributed* monitoring. As we show in Section 4, distributed monitoring significantly reduces the monitoring overhead, but suffers from reduced accuracy in detecting anomalous events of interest. The inaccuracy results from each process only sampling $\frac{1}{P}$ events, even in program regions that are not executed by all P processes.

Ant takes a more intelligent approach that achieves low overhead similar to that of distributed monitoring, and accuracy similar to that of replicated monitoring. It does this by using a static, compile time analysis to divide the program into regions that are executed by all processes (*All-process Regions* or *ARs*) and regions that are not executed by all processes (*Not-All-process Regions* or *NARs*). In ARs, Ant acts like distributed monitoring and each process monitors $\frac{1}{P}$ of the accesses. In NARs, all processes monitor all accesses, as with replicated monitoring. We present experimental results showing that Ant's strategy achieves the best of both replicated and distributed monitoring: it has nearly the overhead reduction of distributed monitoring with accuracy that is close to replicated monitoring.

To summarize, this paper presents the following technical contributions:

- A distributed monitoring that exploits the application parallelism;
- A flexible framework that allows sequential debugging tools to be used with parallel programs;
- A case study showing the use of Ant and the C-DIDUCE [3] value invariant tool with parallel C/MPI programs;
- The uses of ARs and NARs to guide program instrumentation for debugging tools, and data showing that this leads to accurate monitoring with a low overhead.
- Experimental results showing the validity of the parallel value invariant hypothesis and the effectiveness of C-DIDUCE on parallel programs.

The rest of the paper is organized as follows. Section 2 provides an overview of the Ant framework and the compile time analysis used in Ant, and our instrumentation techniques based on this analysis. Section 3 describes a case study of our framework, and Section 4 presents an experimental evaluation of the case study. Section 5 discusses related work, and Section 6 provides our conclusions.

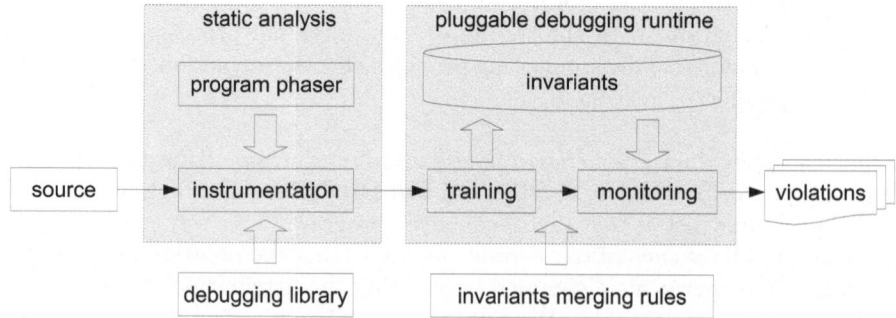

Fig. 1. Overview of the Ant Framework

2   The Ant Framework

The Ant framework, shown in Fig. 1, has two main components: (1) a static analysis component, whose input is a C/MPI program, and that identifies and instruments ARs and NARs, and (2) a debugging runtime. The compiler analysis and instrumentation is discussed in this section, and the use of an invariant violation detection and monitoring (runtime) technique is discussed in Section 3, when we discuss a case study using the C-DIDUCE value invariance debugging tool.

In this section, we describe the compile time analysis and instrumentation. The phase analysis marks the code regions as being *ARs* or *NARs*, and adjusts instrumentation strategies accordingly.

2.1   Region Demarcation Points (RDPs), ARs and NARs

We consider code to be in a NAR when it is control dependent on a branch whose conditional is a function of the process *rank* (i.e., process id). We call these conditional branches *region demarcation points* (RDPs). Ant's static analysis detects ARs and NARs by identifying RDPs, and this is done by following USE-DEF chains from the MPI_Comm_rank function calls. We are not interested in the value of the control expression or its variables, only that it is dependent on an MPI rank, and therefore that some processes may follow the true path from the conditional branch and others may not. All statements that are control dependent on the RDP are members of a NAR. We note that our analysis may be conservative – i.e., we may identify regions as NARs that are actually ARs, but the effect of this is to increase the monitoring overhead and (possibly) the accuracy.

Algorithm 2.1 describes the Ant static analysis for marking NARs and ARs of the input parallel program. First, RDPs are determined using the process id handles by traversing the control flow graph (lines 1 and 2). The data dependence of process id handles is considered in the gather_process_id_info function, so the handles data-dependent on the process rank are also added to the *pid_handles* set. Next, all of the statements in the program are checked to see if they are control dependent on the RDPs and marked as NAR or AR (lines 3 to 10). Finally, the callee procedures from NARs are iteratively marked as NARs (lines 11 to 16). The resulting program is ready for instrumentation as described in the following section.

Fig. 2 shows the time our benchmarks spend in ARs and NARs. The graph shows that programs spend the overwhelming part of their execution in ARs. This observation motivates our instrumentation strategy that provides much lower runtime monitoring cost and good accuracy in locating bugs.

2.2   RDP Guided Instrumentation

Our goal is to spread the monitoring across all processes when all processes are executing a region (i.e., are in an AR) and to ensure that all code is monitored when in a NAR. Thus, within a NAR, the instrumentation at a program point is

Algorithm 2.1 Ant Static Analysis for marking NARs and ARs

```
 1: pid_handles ← gather_process_id_info()
 2: RDPs ← gather_RDP_info(pid_handles, control_flow_graphs)
 3: for all statement in program do
 4:    pp ← get_control_dependent_point(statement)
 5:    if pp in RDPs then
 6:       mark statement as NAR
 7:    else
 8:       mark statement as AR
 9:    end if
10: end for
11: while change in NARs do
12:    for all callsite in NARs do
13:       procedure ← get_procedure(callsite)
14:       mark all statements in procedure as NAR
15:    end for
16: end while
```

replicated, i.e., performed by all processes, as shown in Fig. 3(a), with the instrumentation (i.e., the debug_lib_call) being executed by all processes. Within an AR, however, the instrumentation is *distributed* over the processes as shown in Fig. 3(b). In this case, the instrumented code is invoked every $\frac{1}{P}$ executions within a process, where P is the number of processes.

If the program point is in an AR but not in a loop, the guard expression controlling the execution of the instrumentation is *pid* == k, where k ∈ {0, ..., P − 1}. After being used to guard an instrumentation call, k is set to (k + 1) % P.

Although we provide a case study and implementation using C-DIDUCE, we believe that the framework can be used with at least two major classes of tools. The first class is *invariant violation detection* tools (e.g., [3, 2, 4, 8]), which look for violations of program invariants, such as what program location(s) normally

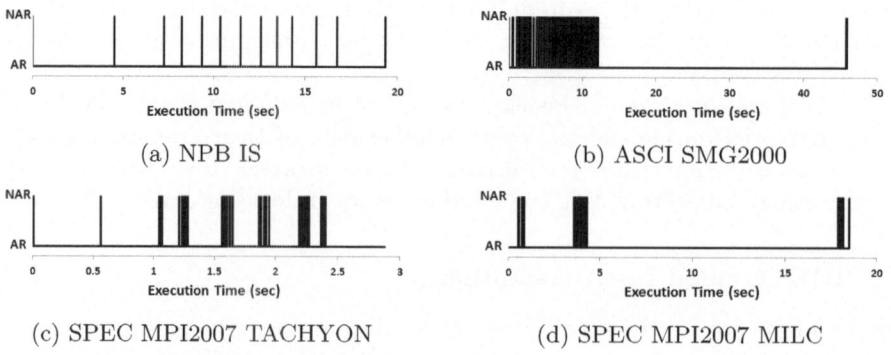

(a) NPB IS

(b) ASCI SMG2000

(c) SPEC MPI2007 TACHYON

(d) SPEC MPI2007 MILC

Fig. 2. Time spent in ARs and NARs during program execution

```
a1 = ...                          a1 = ...
debug_lib_call(a1);               if (process_rank == (i % num_procs))
...                                   debug_lib_call(a1);
```

(a) NARs   (b) ARs in a loop (loop index: i)

Fig. 3. Instrumentation example by different regions

access a memory location [4] and what values a variable normally has [3, 2]. The second class is tools that find statistical variations in program behaviors that are correlated to bugs (e.g., [5–7]). In both classes, Ant can reduce overheads compared to monitoring all accesses in all processes, with a minimal impact on precision, and offer similar overheads and improved precision relative to simply distributing the monitoring across processes.

3   Parallel Value Invariant Detection – A Case Study

We now present a case study of the Ant framework and its instrumentation technique using the C-DIDUCE [3] value invariant detection (VID) technique [2] adapted to parallel programs.

3.1   Overview of Value Invariant Detection (VID)

This paper uses C-DIDUCE [3], a C implementation of DIDUCE. The differences between DIDUCE and C-DIDUCE are because DIDUCE targets Java and C-DIDUCE targets C. Details of these differences can be found in [3]. Both perform a training run to determine an approximation to the set of all values seen by each reference in the program. DIDUCE associates each occurrence of a variable with the invariant $I = \langle M_t, V \rangle$, where V is the variables' initial value, and M_t is the value of an *invariant mask* after the t'th access. V is initialized to the variable value that is seen the first time some reference of the variable is executed, and M is initialized to be all 1's. Let w_t be the t-th value of V observed at the program point.

As each value w_t is observed, the test $(w_t \otimes V) \wedge M_t \neq 0$ is performed, where $\otimes$ is the bitwise XOR operation. If the test is true, the invariant is relaxed by updating the mask so that $M = M_{t+1} \leftarrow M_t \wedge \overline{(w_t \otimes V)}$. Intuitively, each update of the mask results in the mask having a value of '0' in bit positions where both a '0' and a '1' have been previously seen. A mask position containing a '1' indicates that all previous values only had a '1' in that position, or that all previous values only had a '0' in that position. Whether only a '0' or '1' value was seen is determined by inspecting the corresponding bit of V. Thus the test determines if the value w_t differs in one or more bits from all previously seen values, and if it does, the mask is relaxed to indicate this.

In a production run with a different input, values that are not in the (approximate) set of seen values are detected by applying the test above. However, not all invariant violations are treated equally. In particular, violations with values that are seen many times are treated as being less important than violations with values that occur only a few times. The intuition behind this is that values that are seen many times are more likely to be values that should have been in the invariant set. At the end of the run, the different violations are ranked, and a listing of violations, in rank order, is produced. As with other debugging and anomaly detection tools, the assumption is that lower ranked violations are less likely to correlate to a bug, and that a programmer debugging a program will examine the highly ranked violations, fix any indicated errors, and then either re-execute the program, or re-train and re-execute the program.

3.2 Extending VID to Parallel Programs

To adapt VID to parallel programs, we extend the value invariants hypothesis to parallel programs, as follows. First, we observe that a large part of the computation performed in a parallel program is identical regardless of the number of processes used to execute the program. Intuitively, this is true because given the same input the parallel and sequential versions of the program will return the same answers, disregarding numerical stability and round-off effects. Based on this observation, we allow training runs to use a smaller input on a small number of processes, and detection runs using larger inputs on a large number of processes. While significantly lowering the cost of training runs, it creates another problem: How do we form the approximations of the sets of invariant values that will be used by each of the P' processes on the detection run from the approximations formed by the P processes on the training runs? Consider the expression for the mask in $I = \langle M_t, V \rangle$ defined above. When the expression is monitored at time t, the mask value will be

$$M_t = \bigwedge_{i=1}^{t} \overline{(w_i \otimes V)} \wedge M_0 = \bigwedge_{i=1}^{t} \overline{(w_i \otimes V)},$$

since $M_0 \equiv 1$. It follows from the DeMorgan's laws and the definition of $\otimes$:

$$M_t = \bigwedge_{i=1}^{t} \overline{(w_i \otimes V)} = \bigwedge_{i=1}^{t} (\overline{w_i} \wedge V) \vee (w_i \wedge \overline{V})$$

$$= \bigwedge_{i=1}^{t} ((w_i \vee \overline{V}) \wedge (\overline{w_i} \vee V)) = \bigwedge_{i=1}^{t} (w_i \vee \overline{V}) \wedge \bigwedge_{i=1}^{t} (\overline{w_i} \vee V)$$

$$= (\overline{V} \vee \bigwedge_{i=1}^{t} w_i) \wedge (V \vee \bigwedge_{i=1}^{t} \overline{w_i})$$

Now, consider the invariant sets $I_k = \langle M_{k,t}, V_k \rangle$ and $I_j = \langle M_{j,t}, V_j \rangle$ of the same variable reference (i.e., the same program point) built in two different processes (p_k and p_j). We can merge both to form a single invariant set $I' = \langle M'_t, V_i \rangle$, with

$$M'_t = \left[\overline{V_k} \vee (\bigwedge_{i=1}^{t} w_{k,i} \wedge V_j \wedge \bigwedge_{i=1}^{t} w_{j,i}) \right] \wedge \left[V_k \vee (\bigwedge_{i=1}^{t} \overline{w_{k,i}} \wedge \overline{V_j} \wedge \bigwedge_{i=1}^{t} \overline{w_{j,i}}) \right],$$

and V_i equal to either V_k or V_j. We note that our I' is exactly the I' that would be formed if all dynamic references to the monitored variable at this program point, in all processes of the parallel program, had been used to form a single I, and the variable's value is not a function of the number of processes. Our formulation allows the approximate invariant set for each variable reference to independently collected during the parallel run, and then merged in time proportional to the static number of monitoring points in the program, as required by our parallel value invariance hypothesis.

3.3   Using C-DIDUCE with the Ant Framework

As described in Fig. 1, C-DIDUCE can be easily used with the Ant framework. For the static analysis, the debugging library information, such as the function names (and relevant parameters) for the invariant training/monitoring, needs to be provided. This information is used by the Ant framework when instrumenting the function calls. The initialization function information for C-DIDUCE is also required, therefore a runtime initialization call is inserted right after the MPI runtime initialization. This initialization sets the training/monitoring mode and allocates memory for the invariant data structures. On exiting the program, the invariant information is written to output files and the post-run tools merge the output files. In training mode, the output files contain the value invariant training data and are merged into one training file as described in the previous section. In monitoring mode, the output files contain the invariant violation information and this information is also merged into one violation list. The different debugging tools may require different rules for merging the output so tools implementing the merging rules are also required.

3.4   Scalability

Although C-DIDUCE with the Ant framework uses post-run analysis, it is scalable to a large number of processes and large data sets. In training mode, the number of records in each output file is at most the static number of invariant monitoring points. Merging these files requires a fixed number of set operations on each file as described in Section 3.2. Therefore, the execution time for merging training data is linear in the number of processes. In monitoring mode, the number of records in each output file is also at most the number of invariant monitoring points. Since C-DIDUCE only writes to output files when there are invariant violations in monitoring mode, the number of records in each file is typically less than the number of monitoring points. Merging these files requires a fixed number of comparisons based on the confidence drop, as described in the DIDUCE paper [2]. Therefore, the execution time for merging the invariant violation data is also linear in the number of processes. The larger data set does not affect the scalability of our post-run analysis within the Ant framework because the analysis depends on the number of invariant monitoring points, not the size of data set. Here, the larger data set size causes more updating or checking of the invariant at each program point at runtime but does not increase the amount of data being merged from the output files at post-runtime, nor, in the worst case, is the monitoring overhead higher than it would have been without our technique, and as shown in our experimental results, the overhead is, in practice, much less.

4   Experimental Results

In this section, we provide quantitative evidence of the effectiveness of Ant framework in reducing overheads and detecting buggy behavior with C-DIDUCE.

Table 1. Benchmark characteristics: "LOC" is lines of code; "Exe. size" is the executable size; "Inst." is the number of instrumentation points; "NARs" is the number of NAR code regions; "N.Procs." is the number of procedures with NARs/total procedures.

	Description	LOC	Exe. size	Inst.	NARs	N.Procs.
IS	Bucket Sorting	1.2K	680 KB	348	12	1/11
SMG2000	Semi. Multigrid Solver	22.7K	1.1 MB	7278	10	10/349
TACHYON	Parallel Ray Tracing	12.9K	890 KB	1732	22	17/413
MILC	Quantum Chromodynamics	15.8K	871 KB	3560	115	48/310

4.1   Implementation and Experimental Setup

Static analysis and instrumentation, described in Section 2, are implemented in the Cetus compiler [9]. All variable writes in the program and all variable reads of control expressions in the program are monitored. The benchmarks used in the DIDUCE and C-DIDUCE studies [3, 2] are sequential, and so we use the four benchmarks described in Table 1: NPB-IS [10], ASCI-SMG2000 [11], SPEC MPI2007-TACHYON and SPEC MPI2007-MILC [12].

The same kinds of bugs were injected as with the original DIDUCE and C-DIDUCE studies, and the bug types are the same as those found in the Siemens bug benchmarks [13]. Eight to eleven bugs were injected into each benchmark, with each bug injected into a different copy of the benchmark. The bugs are triggered by all processes that execute a path containing the bug.

Table 2 shows the types and the number of injected bugs in each benchmark. Bugs types are: *Value Mutation* which changes an assignment like a = x to a = x + c; *Loop Mutation* which changes loop bounds from i < mp to i < mp+1; *Control Mutation* mutates the operator of conditional expression in which changes an if statement condition from (a > b) to (a <= b). Bugs were injected into both NARs and ARs, and most bugs were placed into ARs.

We used machines with two quad core Intel Xeon 2.33GHz processors, 16 GB of memory, Linux 2.6.18 and the mpich2-1.0.8. The training run was done with 2 processes for all the benchmarks and the detection run was done with 16 processes for MILC and 32 processes for the other three benchmarks.

Table 2. The types and the number of injected bugs. "NAR LOC" is the number of lines of code in NARs; "NAR %" is the percentage of code in NARs; "T.Bugs" is the number of total bugs and the number by each type (V: value mutation/ L: loop mutation/ C: control mutation); "NAR Bugs" is the number of injected bugs in NARs; and "NAR Bug %" is the percent of bugs in NARs.

	NAR LOC	NAR %	T.Bugs(V/L/C)	NAR Bugs	NAR Bugs %
IS	126	10.5 %	8 (7 / 1 / 0)	1	12.5 %
SMG2000	373	1.6 %	10 (8 / 0 / 2)	1	10.0 %
TACHYON	576	4.0 %	11 (11 / 0 / 0)	1	9.1 %
MILC	2887	18.0 %	9 (4 / 0 / 5)	1	11.1 %

4.2   Performance of Optimized Parallel Value Invariant Detection

Fig. 4 compares C-DIDUCE monitoring overhead among replicated ("Replicated"), Ant's AR/NAR based monitoring ("Ant") and naive distributed ("Distributed") schemes for our benchmarks. The figure shows that there is significant overhead reduction going from Replicated to Ant and Distributed, with a reduction of 15X for NPB IS, 4X for ASCI SMG2000, 11X for SPECMPI TACHYON and 5X for SPECMPI MILC. The reason why the maximum overhead reduction for Distributed is less than the number of the processes is that Distributed monitoring itself incurs the overhead of checking the process rank at each monitoring point, as described in Section 2.2. The Ant and Distributed overheads are very similar (differing by 1.4% to 13%) and low, because the programs are usually executing ARs, as seen in Fig. 2. As discussed in the next section, accuracy is better with Ant than Distributed. Since Ant's monitoring is distributed in ARs, and analysis and instrumentation occur offline, our technique is inherently scalable with increasing process counts.

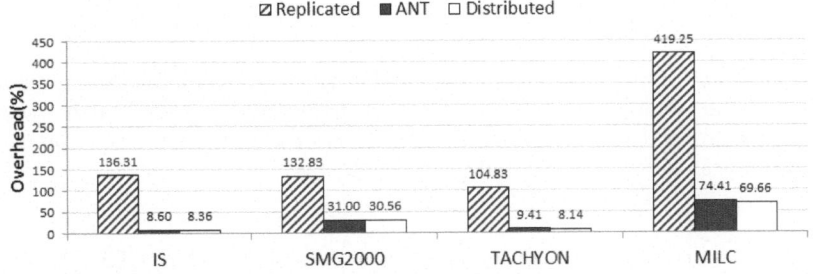

Fig. 4. The comparison of C-DIDUCE overhead against the execution time with no instrumentation

4.3   Accuracy of Optimized Parallel Value Invariant Detection

We now present experimental data showing the effectiveness of the three different
monitoring schemes in detecting the injected bugs.

Note that even with fully replicated monitoring, some bugs go undetected
because (1) they may not be executed by C-DIDUCE, or (2) they may not
appear as bugs because the statement is executed a small number of times and all
values appear equally valid, or the approximation (V and M_t) used by DIDUCE
misses outlier values. This happens with DIDUCE and C-DIDUCE in sequential
programs.

Training runs were done with the original, correct benchmarks using small
data sets. After training, each copy of a benchmark containing an injected bug
was run with the large data set under all three monitoring versions.

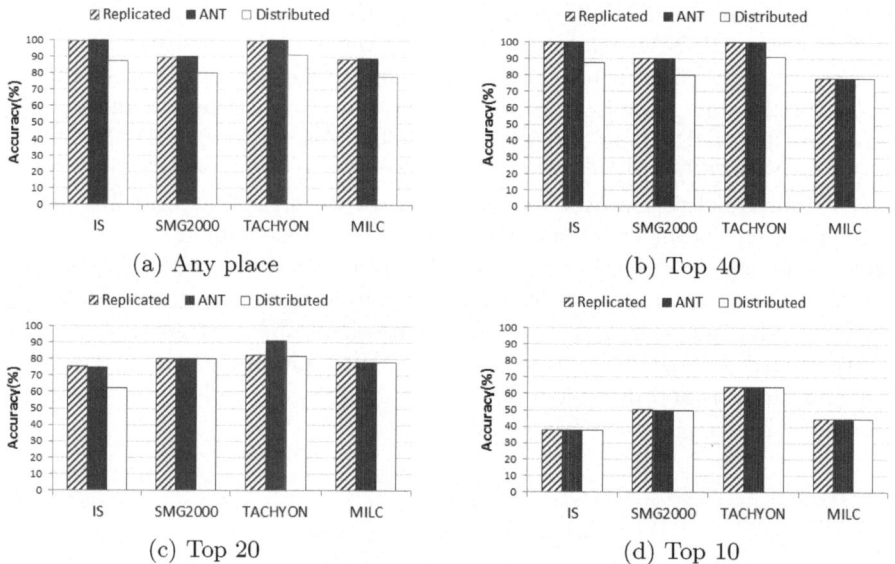

(a) Any place   (b) Top 40

(c) Top 20   (d) Top 10

Fig. 5. Accuracy of bug detection by the ranking in the violation list. Any place means
any rank in the violation list was considered as successful detection. Top 40 means the
ranking is within top 40 of violation list. Top 20 is within first 20 of violation list. Top
10 is within first 10.

Fig. 5 presents bug detection rates for each version of C-DIDUCE. A detection
rate of 100% means that all injected bugs are detected by C-DIDUCE. Because
DIDUCE and C-DIDUCE rank anomalies as to the likelihood of them being a
bug, we report the rates for bugs that occur in the top 10, 20, or 40 anomalies, or
that are detected anywhere. Note that Ant is nearly as accurate as Replicated,
despite having a much lower overhead, showing the effectiveness of the Ant
monitoring technique. Ant is also more accurate than Distributed because of Ant

monitoring all accesses in all processes within NARs, with the bugs found by Ant and not Distributed all being in NARs. Thus Ant uses a distributed scheme when it is safe to and otherwise uses a replicated scheme. With TACHYON in Fig. 5(c), Ant does better than Replicated because a program crash causes Ant to lose violation data which coincidentally causes an injected bug to be ranked higher.

4.4 Discussion

Our experimental results show that the distributed versions of C-DIDUCE increased the performance of the invariant detection by up to 15X while (unlike Distributed) maintaining almost the full accuracy of the expensive Replicated monitoring. We could further reduce the overhead of Ant's monitoring by using *clustering* of similarly behaving processes [14, 15] to determine the clusters within NARs, and distributing the monitoring across the processes within each cluster, in the same way Ant does with ARs. This will be particularly important for programs that spend more time in NARs, and this is the focus of ongoing research.

5 Related Work

Debugging Sequential Programs. There has been previous work focusing on the development of tools to aid the debugging of sequential programs, and we have mentioned some of them earlier. DIDUCE [2] introduces a debugging technique of value invariant violation detection. AccMon [4] discusses PC-invariant based debugging. Artemis [3] provides a debugging framework using context invariant to reduce the overhead of debugging tools. Other tools [6–8] describe debugging techniques using statistical variations in program behaviors between correct and incorrect runs. These tools are complementary to our work in that Ant framework is applicable to these tools. Unlike our work, these tools target sequential programs.

Debugging Parallel Programs. There are several previous works on debugging parallel programs. TotalView [16], Mantis [17], and Prism [18] support typical debugging methods such as setting breakpoints for step-by-step execution, specifying the processes or threads of interest, etc. Other similar work includes that of Stringhini et al. [19], Cheng et al. [20] and Wismuller et al. [21]. Ant differs from these tools in that Ant exploits the parallelism of the application to reduce the overhead of sequential debugging tools when used with parallel programs.

Process Clustering. Another research area looks for outliers in the behavior of processes in a cluster. These often use statistical techniques to find clusters of similarly behaving processes based on metrics such as communication patterns, volumes, stack traces, and so forth, and then look for outliers in terms of control flow behavior, or the previously mentioned metrics among the processes in a cluster. Work related to this includes that of Mirgorodskiy et al. [14], DMTracker [15], Arnold et al. [22, 23] and Hermes [24]. Ant framework is orthogonal to these approaches. It does *not* use statistical information to form clusters or find outliers within a cluster. Ant uses statically determined partitioning of regions to drive instrumentation for sequential bug-finding tools to improve the performance of the tools.

Static Analysis. Kamil, et al. [25] suggest a static analysis based on a concurrency graph to determine whether two statements can run concurrently. However, our conservative linear algorithms, as shown in Algorithm 2.1, is faster than their quadratic algorithm, and are effective enough for our debugging purpose as shown in experimental results.

6   Conclusions

We have presented the Ant debugging framework for MPI parallel programs, included its static AR/NAR detection analysis and instrumentation strategy. We presented a case study that extends to parallel programs with the C-DIDUCE debugging tool developed for sequential programs. More specifically, we have presented the design and implementation of parallel value invariant analysis and experimentally shown the validity of the parallel value invariant hypothesis and the effectiveness of C-DIDUCE on parallel programs. In the future, we plan to expand the Ant framework to target shared-memory parallel programs.

References

1. Software errors cost U.S. economy $59.5 billion annually, NIST News Release 2002-10 (2002)
2. Hangal, S., Lam, M.S.: Tracking down software bugs using automatic anomaly detection. In: Proceedings of the 24th International Conference on Software Engineering, pp. 291–301 (2002)
3. Fei, L., Midkiff, S.P.: Artemis: practical runtime monitoring of applications for execution anomalies. In: PLDI 2006: Proceedings of the 2006 ACM SIGPLAN Conference on Programming Language Design and Implementation, pp. 84–95. ACM Press, New York (2006)
4. Zhou, P., Liu, W., Fei, L., Lu, S., Qin, F., Zhou, Y., Midkiff, S., Torrellas, J.: AccMon: Automatically detecting memory-related bugs via program counter-based invariants. In: Proceedings of the 37th Annual IEEE/ACM International Symposium on Micro-architecture, MICRO 2004 (2004)
5. Liblit, B., Naik, M., Zheng, A.X., Aiken, A., Jordan, M.I.: Scalable statistical bug isolation. In: Proceedings of the ACM SIGPLAN 2005 Conference on Programming Language Design and Implementation (2005)
6. Liblit, B., Aiken, A., Zheng, A.X., Jordan, M.I.: Bug isolation via remote program sampling. In: Proceedings of the ACM SIGPLAN 2003 Conference on Programming Language Design and Implementation, pp. 141–154 (2003)
7. Liu, C., Yan, X., Fei, L., Han, J., Midkiff, S.P.: Sober: statistical model-based bug localization. In: ESEC/FSE-13: Proceedings of the 10th European Software Engineering Conference Held Jointly with 13th ACM SIGSOFT International Symposium on Foundations of Software Engineering, ACM Press (2005)

8. Ernst, M.D., Czeisler, A., Griswold, W.G., Notkin, D.: Quickly detecting relevant program invariants. In: Proceedings of the 22nd International Conference on Software Engineering, pp. 449–458 (2000)
9. The Cetus Project, http://cetus.ecn.purdue.edu
10. NAS Parallel Benchmarks, http://www.nas.nasa.gov/publications/npb.html
11. The ASCI Purple Benchmark, https://asc.llnl.gov/computing_resources/purple/archive/benchmarks/
12. SPEC MPI2007, http://www.spec.org/mpi2007/
13. Hutchins, M., Foster, H., Goradia, T., Ostrand, T.: Experiments of the effectiveness of dataflow- and controlflow-based test adequacy criteria. In: Proceedings of the 16th International Conference on Software Engineering, ICSE 1994, pp. 191–200. IEEE Computer Society Press, Los Alamitos (1994)
14. Alexander, V.: Mirgorodskiy, Naoya Maruyama, and Barton P. Miller. Problem diagnosis in large-scale computing environments. In: SC 2006: Proceedings of the 2006 ACM/IEEE Conference on Supercomputing, p. 88. ACM (2006)
15. Gao, Q., Qin, F., Panda, D.K.: DMTracker: finding bugs in large-scale parallel programs by detecting anomaly in data movements. In: SC 2007: Proceedings of the 2007 ACM/IEEE Conference on Supercomputing. ACM (2007)
16. TotalView, http://www.roguewave.com/products/totalview.aspx
17. Lumetta, S.S., Culler, D.E.: The Mantis parallel debugger. In: SPDT 1996: Proceedings of the SIGMETRICS Symposium on Parallel and Distributed Tools, pp. 118–126. ACM Press, New York (1996)
18. Sistare, S., Dorenkamp, E., Nevin, N., Loh, E.: MPI support in the Prism programming environment. In: Supercomputing 1999: Proceedings of the 1999 ACM/IEEE Conference on Supercomputing (CDROM), p. 22. ACM Press (1999)
19. Stringhini, D., Navaux, P., de Kergommeaux, J.C.: A selection mechanism to group processes in a parallel debugger. In: In Proceedings 2000 International Conference on Parallel and Distributed Processing Techniques and Applications (PDPTA 2000) (June 2000)
20. Cheng, D., Hood, R.: A portable debugger for parallel and distributed programs. In: Proceedings of Supercomputing 1994, pp. 723–732 (November 1994)
21. Wismuller, R., Oberhubera, M., Krammera, J., Hansenb, O.: Interactive debugging and performance analysis of massively parallel applications. Parallel Computing 22(3), 415–442 (1996)
22. Arnold, D.C., Ahn, D.H., de Supinski, B.R., Lee, G.L., Miller, B.P., Schulz, M.: Stack trace analysis for large scale debugging. In: International Parallel and Distributed Processing Symposium, p. 64 (2007)
23. Lee, G.L., Ahn, D.H., Arnold, D.C., de Supinski, B.R., Legendre, M., Miller, B.P., Schulz, M., Liblit, B.: Lessons learned at 208k: towards debugging millions of cores. In: SC 2008: Proceedings of the, ACM/IEEE Conference on Supercomputing, pp. 1–9. IEEE Press, Piscataway (2008)
24. Strom, R.E., Bacon, D.F., Goldberg, A.P., Lowry, A., Yellin, D.M., Yemini, S.A.: Hermes: a Language for Distributed Computing. Prentice-Hall, Inc., Upper Saddle River (1991)
25. Kamil, A., Yelick, K.: Concurrency Analysis for Parallel Programs with Textually Aligned Barriers. In: Ayguadé, E., Baumgartner, G., Ramanujam, J., Sadayappan, P. (eds.) LCPC 2005. LNCS, vol. 4339, pp. 185–199. Springer, Heidelberg (2006)

Compiler Automatic Discovery
of OmpSs Task Dependencies

Sara Royuela[1], Alejandro Duran[1,2], and Xavier Martorell[1]

[1] Barcelona Supercomputing Center
{sara.royuela,xavier.martorell}@bsc.es
[2] Intel Corporation
alejandro.duran@intel.com

Abstract. Dependence analysis is an essential step for many compiler optimizations, from simple loop transformations to automatic parallelization. Parallel programming models require specific dependence analyses that take into account multi-threaded execution. Furthermore, asynchronous parallelism introduced by OpenMP tasks has promoted the development of new dependency analysis techniques. In these terms, OmpSs parallel programming model extends OpenMP tasks with the definition of intertask dependencies. This extension allows runtime dependency detection, which potentially improves the performance when load balancing or locality rule the execution time. On the other side, the extension requires the user to figure out data-sharing attributes and the type of access to each data in all tasks in order to correctly specify the dependencies. We aim to enhance the programmability of OmpSs with a new methodology that enables the compiler to automatically determine the dependencies of OmpSs tasks, thus releasing users from the task of manually defining these dependencies. In this context, we have developed an algorithm based on the discovery of code concurrent to a task and liveness analysis. The algorithm first finds out all code concurrent with a given task. Then, it computes the data-sharing attributes of the variables appearing in the task. Finally, it analyzes the liveness properties of the task's shared variables. With this information, the algorithm figures out the proper dependencies of the task. We have implemented this algorithm in the Mercurium source-to-source compiler. We have tested the results with several benchmarks proving that the algorithm is able to correctly find a large number of dependency expressions.

1   Introduction

The use of parallel programming models is a vital element in the achievement of higher performance and better programmability, in short, greater productivity. OpenMP* has become the most used parallel programming model for shared memory systems by virtue its simplicity and scalability. Although the model already provides a stable and useful standard for the parallelization of structured loops and dense numerical applications, new research directions have appeared. One of them is the concept of *task*, which has grown as a result of the need of parallelizing applications with different characteristics (e.g., amount of load imbalance in loops, while-loop based, recursiveness, etc.).

H. Kasahara and K. Kimura (Eds.): LCPC 2012, LNCS 7760, pp. 234–248, 2013.
© Springer-Verlag Berlin Heidelberg 2013

OpenMP defines the `task` directive that represents an independent unit of work. Different units are synchronized with specific directives (`barrier` and `taskwait`), which ensure sequential consistency of the parallel program. However, these synchronizations restrict the run-time freedom to schedule tasks because they define the boundaries of the region where a task can be executed at compile-time. OmpSs is a parallel programming model that introduces the idea of asynchronous parallelism defining dependencies among tasks. Data-dependence clauses in an OmpSs `task` can be `in`, `out` or `inout`. This OpenMP extension increases the freedom of the run-time at the moment of scheduling a task: tasks are executed when there are available resources and all tasks they depend on have been executed. Nonetheless, the extension implies a sensitive loss of programmability as it requires the programmer to define the data-dependence attributes of the tasks. The process of analyzing the data flow of the different tasks can be difficult because of the uncertainty about the exact moment when the task will be executed and the potentially large number of variables that can be involved in this analysis.

Our main contributions in this paper are:

- An algorithm for the automatic discovery of data-dependence attributes of variables in OmpSs tasks. This algorithm improves the programmability regarding the definition of asynchronous parallelism, and thus, the productivity of the programming model. In order to define concurrent regions in the code and establish possible race conditions, the algorithm uses our previous work on the automatic discovery of data-sharing attributes of OpenMP tasks. After that, it computes the dependencies among tasks and reports to the user those variables that cannot be analyzed due to the lack of information at compile time.
- An implementation of the proposed algorithm in the Mercurium source-to-source compiler and proof of the algorithm benefits for a set of OmpSs task benchmarks. We compute the percentage of task expressions whose dependencies can be automatically determined.

2   Motivation and Related Work

Different parallel programming models have appeared as a response to the demand of increasingly productive systems. OpenMP [18] has become a *de facto* standard for shared-memory parallel programming because of its flexibility, programmability and portability. The latest specifications of OpenMP (from 3.0) have been conceived to handle dynamic generation of unstructured parallelism by defining of explicit `tasks`. The model allows the parallelization of program structures like while-loops and recursive functions, and reduces in most cases the load imbalance and the communication overhead. Each OpenMP task has a data-environment defined by data-sharing attributes. The allowed data-sharing clauses are `private`, `firstprivate` and `shared`. Nonetheless, the uncertainty introduced by OpenMP tasks regarding the precise moment when they are going to be executed requires the insertion of synchronization points to ensure the finalization of all tasks and establish some order in their execution.

However, this compile-time form of task synchronization can avoid the parallelization of tasks with no data conflicts. This is because frontiers between tasks are fixed in the input program. Hence, tasks which are in different *synchronized regions* (sections of code delimited by consecutive synchronization points) likely run concurrently and tasks in the same region run sequentially. OmpSs [10] is a parallel programming model based on OpenMP and StarSs [19] that extends OpenMP with the definition of asynchronous parallelism. The model implements data-dependence attributes for `tasks`. These attributes specify, for each task, the expressions containing `shared` variables that are dependent. The different data-dependence attributes allowed are:

input A task with an l-value as `input` dependence is eligible to run when all previous tasks with the same l-value as `output` dependence have finished its execution.

output A task with an l-value as `output` dependence is eligible to run when all previous tasks with the same l-value as `input` or `output` dependence have finished its execution.

inout A task with an l-value as `inout` dependence is considered as if it had an `input` and an `output` clauses evaluating for the same l-value.

A *Task Dependence Graph* (TDG) is generated at run-time using the expressions that appear in the dependence clauses. This graph represents an order in the tasks that cannot be broken to ensure sequential consistency of the parallel code. In Fig. 1 we depict the TDG corresponding to the code in Listing 1.1. Each instance of the task *foo* depends on the instance generated on the previous iteration because of the dependencies `input(A[i-1])` and `inout(A[i])`. The same happens to the instances of *bar* task, because of the dependencies `input(B[i-1])` and `inout(B[i])`. In addition, each instance of the task *bar* depends on the instance of the task *foo* created in the same iteration due to the dependencies `inout(B[i])` and `output(B[i])`, respectively.

Listing 1.1. OmpSs code sample showing dependencies among tasks

```
1 void compute ( int * A , int * B, int N ) {
2   for ( int i = 1 ; i < N; ++i ) {
3 #pragma omp task input(A[i −1]) \
4                     inout(A[i]) output(B[i])
5     foo ( &A[i −1], &A[i], &B[i] );
6
7 #pragma omp task input(B[i −1]) inout(B[i])
8     bar ( &B[i −1], &B[i] );
9   }
10 }
```

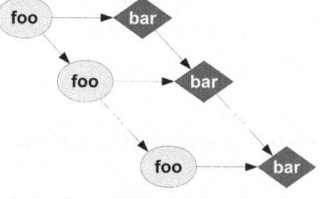

Fig. 1. Task Dependence Graph resultant from code in Listing 1.1

There are several data structures used to approach the dependence analysis. Two of the most common are mathematical equations and dependence graphs. Mathematical techniques are used by powerful methods such as the Polyhedral model based libraries [9]. Nonetheless, these methods are aimed for regular access patterns and it should be extended to represent the indeterminism of tasks. Therefore, we focus on graph based designs. The *Program Dependence Graph* (PDG), defined by Ferrante et al., [12] is an intermediate representation where both data and control dependencies are explicits. PDG differs from the Control Flow Graph (CFG) in that CFG enforces a fixed sequencing of operations whereas the PDG only determines necessary sequencing between operations, exposing potential parallelism. This representation has been proved to be useful in many different fields such as program vectorization [8], fault diagnosis [4], register allocation [17] and auto-parallelization [23].

It is important to differentiate methods generating the dependence graph statically at compile-time (e.g., auto-parallelizing compilers) and methods generating this graph dynamically at run-time (e.g., OmpSs TDG) because compile-time methods require the resolution of alias analysis at that moment. This is a hard and not always possible job. In the code shown in Listing 1.2 no auto-parallelization is possible because alias analysis for pointers a and b is not feasible at compile-time. Instead, a compiler implementing OmpSs auto-dependencies algorithm should be able to define two tasks as shown in Listing 1.3, where aliasing is solved at run-time.

Listing 1.2. Input code with room to improvement

```
1 void f ( int n, int * a, int * b ) {
2   for ( int i=0; i<n; ++i )
3     a[i] = i
4   for ( int i=0; i<n; ++i )
5     b[i] = i
6 }
```

Listing 1.3. Code improved with OmpSs

```
1 void f ( int n, int * a, int * b ) {
2 #pragma omp task output(a[0:n])
3   for ( int i=0; i<n; ++i )
4     a[i] = i
5 #pragma omp task output(b[0:n])
6   for ( int i=0; i<n; ++i )
7     b[i] = i
8 }
```

Even though we have proved graph based methods to be convenient to determine dependencies, the TDG mechanism used in OmpSs requires the user to manually define data-dependencies among tasks. This can be a difficult and therefore, an error-prone process because users must be capable of finding the variables that are shared and analyzing the kind of access to these variables in order to figure out the correct dependencies.

Many approaches have appeared in the last years to include dependence analysis in programming models that exploit task-level parallelism. Most of them are based on OpenMP, but there also exist some other parallel programming models, such as Jade [20] and Intel® Threading Building Blocks (Intel® TBB) [13]. However, these alternatives have certain disadvantages: Jade adds too much overhead since it tries to extract concurrency at run-time and TBB requires a thorough redesign of the program that differs greatly from the original version in style and size. Moreover, Kegel et al. [14] demonstrated that TBB does not produce performance benefits compared with other high-level parallel programming languages such as OpenMP.

Focusing on OpenMP extensions, different proposals have been presented in order to solve the dependence problem for task synchronization using dependence graphs created at compile-time. Larsen et al. [15] presented an extension of OpenMP that makes it possible to declare inter-task communication patterns. They introduce a new clause depends that, placed in specific points of the code where synchronizations are performed, can be used to declare dependencies with other tasks. The evaluation of the clause is done both at compile-time, for simple cases, and at run-time, in the remaining cases. They demonstrate that there is no performance degradation because of the increase of inter-task communication knowledge. Nonetheless, their work does not take array slicing into account and rather assume entire arrays to be shared. Furthermore, their syntax needs to explicitly determine the edges of the dependency graph (which tasks a task depends on) in addition to the variables involved in the dependence and the direction of the dependence. Thus, imposing an arduous and unreliable duty for programmers and compilers. Baudish et al. [7] presented a translation procedure from purely synchronous guarded actions generated by multi-threaded OpenMP-based C-code. They create an *Action Dependence Graph* (ADG) derived by a syntactic analysis of the read and write sets of all actions. Afterwards, they merge the actions in the ADG into different tasks depending on the dependencies found in the graph. Furthermore, they demonstrate how dependence analysis allows the reduction of the overhead introduced by synchronizations. However this is a very specific solution for codes coming from a synchronous language compiler and can only be used for such inputs.

A different OpenMP approach is the one presented by Altenfeld et al. [2]. They parallelize the MICRESS application using OpenMP tasks. The hot spot of the application is a solver for non-symmetric linear systems used during the calculation of stress on a micro-structure material grid. They build a TDG at run-time where a node represents a pair of grains that are connected in the grid and edges connect those nodes that cannot be executed in parallel. Then, they use different heuristics to obtain different colorings of the graph, each one representing a different parallel solution. They use k phases of task creation by the master thread over the k-coloring of each graph. In each phase, OpenMP tasks are created for one single color. They compare this scheduling method with a *first-come-first-serve* solution. The results show a lost of speed-up in the TDG version due to the time consumption of the coloring algorithm. Furthermore, their implementation is specific and limited to the MICRESS application.

The previous works demonstrate that the definition of dependencies among tasks can avoid unnecessary synchronizations. Nonetheless, all of them present some problems caused by the inherent constraints of their the methodology. On the one hand, compiler dependence techniques can be too conservative due to the lack of information at compile-time (exact control and data flow knowledge) that causes the compiler to take safe decisions during the analyses (aliasing, non-linear subscripts). On the other hand, some run-time techniques may need too many resources. Andersch et al. [3] evinced OmpSs to be a viable alternative to other established parallel programming models such as Pthreads by exploring the expressiveness of OmpSs and comparing its performance with Pthreads. Expressions in the dependence clauses can be easily evaluated at run-time, thus creating the TDG while executing without a significant loss of time [11]. However, users are required to analyze all data accesses in order to define the proper dependencies for each task. This is a tedious and potentially error-prone process. As an example, in Listing 1.4 we show a blocked algorithm that calculates the Cholesky decomposition using OmpSs. Fig. 2 shows the distribution of tasks that computes each position of the low triangle matrix for different block sizes (BS) (the left matrix shows the result for a BS of 2 and the right matrix shows the result for a BS of 3). Tasks T3 and T4 compute the elements in the diagonal of the matrix. Elements computed by tasks T1 and T5 depend on the value of the block size: these tasks compute the lower triangle matrix of size BS starting by the top left corner of the matrix, avoiding the elements in the diagonal. Tasks T2 and T6 compute all the rest lower triangle matrix.

We present a modification of our previous work for automatically determine the data-sharing attributes for OpenMP tasks [22]. We apply this modification instead to the automatic discovery of OmpSs task dependencies. This work differs from others in that the task dependency graph is computed at run-time together with the information of the dependence clauses. A task dependency does not relate a task with another task at compile-time. It is the run-time, when no aliasing problems exist, who evaluates the clauses and defines which tasks are dependents on each others. In order to automatically define the dependence clauses, first we need to know which tasks run concurrently, then determine possible race conditions, and finally perform liveness analysis.

Fig. 2. Cholesky matrix computation distributed by tasks

Listing 1.4. Left handed Cholesky in place implemented with OmpSs

```
1 /* Method that computes the Cholesky decomposition.
2  * @a in/out matrix which the decomposition is computed with.
3  * BS is the block size
4  * N is the number of rows/colums of a. */
5 void cholesky(float a[N][N]) {
6
7    /* Loops traversing the lower triangle matrix by rows */
8    for (int jj = 0; jj < N; jj += BS) {
9      for (int j = jj; j < MIN(N, jj+BS); j++) {
10
11 #pragma omp task in(a[j+1:jj+BS−1][0:j−1], a[j][0:j−1])   // T1
12                     inout(a[j+1:jj+BS−1][j])
13        for (int i = j+1; i < jj+BS; i++){
14          for (int k = 0; k < j; k++)
15            a[i][j] = a[i][j] − a[i][k] * a[j][k];
16
17 #pragma omp task in(a[jj+BS:N−1][0:j−1], a[j][0:j−1])      // T2
18                     inout(a[jj+BS:N−1][j])
19        for (int i = jj+BS; i < N; i++)
20          for (int k = 0; k < j; k++)
21            a[i][j] = a[i][j] − a[i][k] * a[j][k];
22
23 #pragma omp task in(a[j][0:j−1]) inout(a[j][j])           // T3
24        for (int k = 0; k < j; k++)
25          a[j][j] = a[j][j] − a[j][k] * a[j][k];
26
27 #pragma omp task inout(a[j][j])                           // T4
28        a[j][j] = sqrt(a[j][j]);
29
30 #pragma omp task in(a[j][j]) inout(a[j+1:jj+BS−1][j])     // T5
31        for (int i = j + 1; i < jj+BS; i++)
32          a[i][j] = a[i][j] / a[j][j];
33
34 #pragma omp task in(a[j][j]) inout(a[jj+BS:N−1][j])       // T6
35        for (int i = jj+BS; i < N; i++)
36          a[i][j] = a[i][j] / a[j][j];
37
38      }
39    }
40 }
```

3   Proposal

Following the same syntax introduced by Lin et al. [16], we implement a new keyword, AUTO_DEPS, for the clause `default`. The clause `default(AUTO_DEPS)` attached to an OmpSs task construct launches the automatic discovery of data-dependence attributes of a given task. We present an modification of our previous work [22] for the automatic discovery of data-sharing attributes in OpenMP tasks (auto-scoping from now on). Data dependencies among tasks can only occur for shared variables in a race situation. Thus, we use the auto-scoping method to define the sections of code that are concurrent with a task and then determine the data-sharing attributes of variables without explicitly determined attributes. We extend this method to handle, not only variables, but also references to sub-objects such as *array element reference* (`a[2]`), *array sections* (`a[1:5]`), *field references* (`a.b`) and *shaping expressions* (`[5][10]a`). Algorithm 1 shows a high-level description of the algorithm we present in this paper.

Algorithm 1. High-level description of the auto-dependence algorithm for OmpSs tasks

---

1. Define the regions of code that execute concurrently with a given task. As we defined in the auto-scoping algorithm, these regions are bounded by the immediately previous and next synchronization points of the task, and belong to:
   (a) Other tasks scheduled in the region described above.
   (b) Other instances of the task if scheduled within a loop or in a parallel region.
   (c) Code from the parent task between the task scheduling point and the synchronization of the task.
2. For all variables with implicitly determined data-sharing attributes, compute the correct data-sharing attribute.
3. For all expressions containing or being `shared` variables, determine the data-dependence expression depending on the liveness properties of the variables before and after the execution of the task.
4. For all variables that do not fit in the third step, return the data-sharing attribute computed during the second step.

The algorithm returns one of the following group for the expressions involved:

- PRIVATE: The variable is to be scoped as `private`.
- FIRSTPRIVATE: The variable is to be scoped as `firstprivate`.
- SHARED: The variable is `shared` but it does not cause a dependence.
- SHARED_OR_FIRSTPRIVATE: The variable can be scoped as either `shared` or `firstprivate` without altering the correctness of the results. It is an implementation decision to scope it as `shared` or `firstprivate`.
- INPUT: The expression contains/is a `shared` variable and it is to be determined as an `input` dependence.
- OUTPUT: The variable contains/is a `shared` variable and it is to be determined as an `output` dependence.
- INOUT: The variable contains/is a `shared` variable and it is to be determined as both `input` and `output` dependence.
- UNDEFINED: The algorithm is not able to determine the behavior of the variable.

The algorithm works under the hypothesis that the input code is correct and comes from an original sequential code that has been parallelized with OpenMP. Otherwise, the results of the algorithm may be incorrect. Algorithm 2 shows the computation of all dependence attributes of a task t.

Algorithm 2. Detailed description of the auto-dependence algorithm for OmpSs tasks

1. Apply steps 1, 2 and 3 of the auto-scoping Algorithm 1 to classify all variable v with implicit data-sharing appearing in t into one of the following groups: PRIVATE, FIRSTPRIVATE, SHARED, SHARED_OR_FIRSTPRIVATE (v cannot be a dependence because either v is dead after the *exit* of t or it is alive but only read in t and never used in any concurrent code), RACE (v can be a data race), UNDEFINED.

2. For all e, expression from v that has been classified as RACE (v itself or a sub-object of v if v is aggregate or array access), apply the following rules in order:

   (a) If the race condition occurs between one statement in t and some other statement concurrent with t, and belongs to t's parent task, then v must be privatized to avoid the race condition. We privatize v as follows:

   –If the first action on e within t is a read, then v must be FIRSTPRIVATE.

   –If the first action on e within t is a write, then v must be PRIVATE.

   (b) If the race condition occurs between a statement in t and some statement in t' (where t' is some other task or other instance of the same task t, that runs concurrently with t), then v is classified as SHARED.

3. For all e, expression formed from a SHARED variable v, apply the following rules in order (Liveness analysis for expressions is explained below):

   (a) If e is alive at the entry of the task (task scheduling point), then:

   –If e is used in the code executed concurrently with t by the parent task of t, no dependency exists, so v remains SHARED.

   –Otherwise, e is classified as INPUT.

   (b) If v is alive only at the exit of the task (task completion), then it is classified as OUTPUT.

   (c) If v is alive at the entry and at the exit of the task, then it is classified as INOUT.

Strengths and Weaknesses. The algorithm is perfectly accurate when the input code fulfill the hypotheses, meaning it never produces false positives and the reported results are always correct. Specific rules cover the cases when the algorithm cannot determine the data-sharing attribute of a variable. The undetermined variables are reported back to the user. The limitations of the auto-dependencies algorithm come from the limitations of the auto-scoping algorithm, which are:

- Tasks containing calls to functions the code of which is not accessible at compile time. All variables that may be involved in these functions cannot be scoped, therefore, data-dependence attributes cannot be computed. These variables can sole be global variables and address parameters of the unaccessible function.

- Regarding the implementation, the compiler may be unable to determine the sections of code that are concurrent with the task. In the cases, just the variables that are local to the function (including its parameters) where the task is scheduled can be automatically classified. All the rest are classified as UNDEFINED and reported to the user to be manually classified.

Liveness Analysis. Liveness analysis applied in this algorithm must consider access to subparts of a variable as it considers OmpSs. Data-dependence clauses can be applied to expressions such as *array element references, array sections* and *field references*. Consequently, we calculate the liveness of each array and aggregate subpart, and we post-process this information if necessary (The auto-scoping algorithm calculates *liveness* of variables but not subparts, because OpenMP only allows data-sharing attributes for variables. The auto-dependencies algorithm implements a second step that merges the *liveness* information of all the subparts of an object, obtaining a unique property per variable). We consider a whole object to be *alive* if any of its parts is *alive*, and we consider a whole object to be *dead* if all its parts are *dead*.

Example. Applying the auto-dependence algorithm to the code introduced in Listing 1.4, the compiler can determine all the data-dependence expressions, which are defined manually in the example, because they are local to the function that is defining the tasks. Consequently, step 1 will scope variable a as RACE for all tasks because all tasks are defined within a loop construct, and different concurrent tasks can access the same position of a at the same time. Step 2 will determine a as SHARED for all tasks because there is no race condition occurring between a task and its parent task. Finally, step 3 will analyze the expressions containing shared variables and its liveness. During this step, liveness information provides the sections of a that are accessed in each task and the dependence clauses for each section are produced.

4   Implementation

Mercurium [5] is a source-to-source research compiler with support for C/C++ and Fortran designed for fast prototyping. The main goal of Mercurium is to implement OpenMP and extensions to it. Nevertheless, it has been used to implement other programming models such as Cell Superscalar due to its extensibility. As we show in Fig. 3, Mercurium uses a plug-in architecture, where each plug-in is a compiler phase. These phases form a pipeline that transforms an input source into an output source, which is afterwards passed to a back-end compiler (e.g., gcc, nvcc). The front-end creates a common Internal Representation (IR) for C/C++ and Fortran. This IR is used by all phases, however, some phases can transform it causing next phases to work with a new version of the IR. We defined a new phase in the compiler that allows applying different analysis and high level optimizations. We implemented the auto-dependences algorithm 2 in this new phase, along with other analysis necessary for the automatic discovery of data-dependence clauses: *control flow analysis, use-definition chains, liveness analysis, induction variable analysis, loops analysis, reaching definitions, array analysis* and *auto-scoping*. All of them are both intra- and inter- thread, and intra- and inter- procedural for methods contained in the same file.

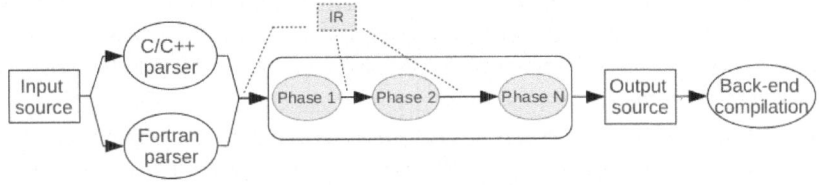

Fig. 3. Mercurium compiler phases pipeline

In Fig. 4 we show the flow chart for the analysis performed during the process of the automatic discovery of data-dependence clauses in OmpSs tasks. Each step is described in detail below.

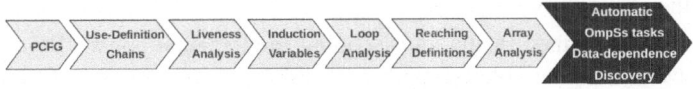

Fig. 4. Flow chart of Mercurium analyses used during the task data-dependence automatic discovery

1. We first build a *Parallel Control Flow Graph* (PCFG) [21] with specific support for OpenMP. In this graph, parallelism (`parallel` and `task` OpenMP constructs) is represented with special nodes expressing that more than one thread can execute concurrently the code contained in the node. Moreover, all implicit memory flushes and barriers are made explicit. Finally, task synchronizations are specified by special edges denoting the boundaries of a task execution. In Figs. 5 and 6 we show a task scheme example and the high-level representation of these tasks in the PCFG. We exemplify how `taskwait` constructs synchronize just the previous tasks that are scheduled by the encountered of the `taskwait` (the `taskwait` synchronizes `task A`, but not `task B`), whereas `barrier` constructs synchronize any previously scheduled task that has not yet been synchronized (`barrier` synchronizes, not only `task C` and `task D`, but also `task B`). Note how tasks are connected by dotted edges meaning synchronization points.

2. Considering the PCFG as the basis of the remaining analysis, we first calculate *use-definition chains*. This calculation determines, for each node in the PCFG, which objects or sub-objects are used before being defined and which objects are defined.

3. Afterwards, we calculate the *liveness* properties of the graph. This provides the sets of variables that are live at the entry and at the exit of each node in the graph. Once again, this is computed from inner nodes to outer nodes.

4. Then we apply an algorithm for the computation of *induction variables*. We have extended our previous implementation of this analysis in order to deal not only with *for* loops, but also with *while* and *do-while* loops. This analysis tags each PCFG loop node with information about the induction variables (IV), $< symbol, stride, type(\text{basic or derived}) >$, used in the iteration.

5. Taking into account the previous information about the IVs, we then perform *loops analysis*. This analysis allows us to determine the limits of the IVs creating, for each induction variable, a triplet of $< lowerbound, upperbound, stride >$. Information attached to the graph in the previous step is now extended with the new knowledge.

6. The next action is *reaching definitions* calculation. Basically, we want to know the value of induction variables and other potential array subscripts at any point of the PCFG. This analysis adds new information to each node in the graph in the form of tuples like $< symbol, value >$.

7. At this point, we are able to apply *array analysis* to determine which sections of an array are accessed at a given point. We use the same triplet notation used for IVs to define the array sections.

8. At this point, we apply the algorithm defined in Section 3 to define the *data-dependence clauses* of the tasks in the PCFG. This step will change the IR adding the new data-dependence clauses where necessary and will return an additional list with all the variables that have been classified as UNDEFINED, so the user can specify them manually.

As it was explained in the auto-scoping implementation, we have decided to further specify that variables scoped as SHARED_OR_FIRSTPRIVATE as follows:

- Scalar variables are defined as FIRSTPRIVATE because the cost of the privatization should be comparable to the cost of one access to a shared variable.
- Array and aggregate variables are defined as SHARED because it may be advantageous to privatize an array or an aggregate only in those cases where many positions of the array or many fields of the aggregate are accessed many times.

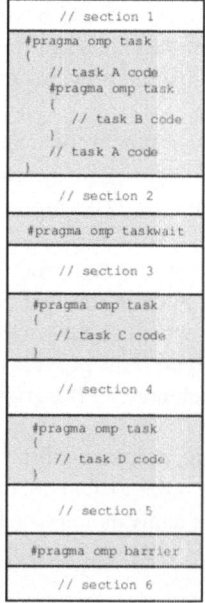

Fig. 5. Code scheme with tasks

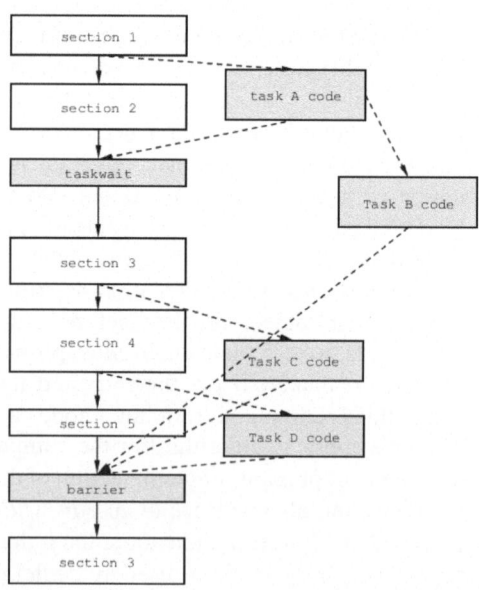

Fig. 6. Abstraction of the PCFG used during the auto-scoping showing the connections of the tasks in Fig. 5

Our implementation is limited regarding pointers because we do not perform alias analysis. In some cases when we cannot determine accesses to an aliased pointer, we are not able to define the dependence expression. These situations are reported to the user.

5 Evaluation

In order to test the proposed algorithm in terms of productivity, we have used the Barcelona OpenMP Task Suite [1] (BOTS) and some other benchmarks developed in the Barcelona Supercomputing Center [6]. In Table 1, we introduce the benchmarks used in our evaluation with a brief description of each algorithm. Table 2 describes the principal characteristics of each benchmark: the language of the source code, the number of lines and the number of tasks, whether or not they contain nested tasks and the method used in the functions where the tasks are defined (iterative, recursive or both).

Table 1. Short description of the benchmarks used in the evaluation

Benchmark	Description
Alignment	Dynamic programming algorithm that aligns sequences of proteins.
FFT	Spectral method that computes the Fast Fourier Transformation.
Fib	Recursive version of the Fibonacci numbers computation.
Health	Simulation method for a country health system.
Floorplan	Optimization algorithm for the optimal placement of cells in a floor plan.
NQueens	Search algorithm that finds solutions for the N Queens problem.
SparseLU	Linear algebra algorithm that computes the LU factorization of a sparse matrix.
Stencil	Stencil algorithm over a matrix structure.
Cholesky	Linear algebra algorithm that computes the Cholesky decomposition of a matrix.

Table 2. Summary of the benchmarks used in the evaluation

iter Stands for iterative methods
rec Stands for recursive methods

Benchmark	Source language	Lines count	#tasks	Nested tasks	Tasks inside omp...	Method
Alignment	C	694	1	no	for	iter
FFT	C	4859	41	yes	single	rec
Fib	C	45	2	yes	single	rec
Health	C	551	2	yes	single	iter & rec
Floorplan	C	344	1	yes	single	iter & rec
NQueens	C	405	1	yes	single	iter & rec
SparseLU	C	309	4	no	single/for	iter & rec
Stencil	C	218	1	no	-	iter
Cholesky	C	70	6	no	-	iter

We have run all these examples replacing in each task all data-dependence clauses by the new clause `default(AUTO_DEPS)`. In order to evaluate the programmability, we have calculated the number of expressions the compiler has been able to determine the data-dependence clause of. We do not take into account in our evaluation the variables that have been scoped as `UNDEF_SC` due to the limitations of the auto-scoping

algorithm, but only the variables that do not appear as dependencies (so they are classified as UNDEF_DEP during the auto-dependences algorithm) but they are. We show the
results in Table 3. For those benchmarks that no dependency clauses are needed, we do
not compute the ratio of success.

Overall, we see that our implementation is able to determine the 88% of dependence
expressions. Cases as *FFT* contain aliased pointers that avoid our implementation determining several dependence expressions. The compiler is able to report the user that
it may be an INPUT, OUTPUT or INOUT dependence in some objects, but it is not able
to determine the specific expression. Some other expressions classified as UNDEF_DEP
come from the fact that our loop analysis is not able to determine the section of an array
accessed within a loop. On the contrary, cases such as the *Cholesky* benchmark are easy
for the compiler because all loop boundaries are known, hence, the compiler is able to
determine the sections accessed of any array. For some examples, it is interesting to
compare the results of the auto-scoping with the results of the auto-dependences. For
instance, this is the case of the *Floorplan*, *Fib* or *Nqueens* benchmarks, where variables
that were privatized during the auto-scoping, are now defined as dependencies. In the
case of the *SparseLU*, we are able to compute the dependencies, but the lack of expressions analysis causes some results to appear in both the INPUT and the OUTPUT
groups, instead of appearing in an INOUT group.

Table 3. Mercurium automatic task dependence results for different benchmarks

IN Stands for input expressions
OUT Stands for output expressions
PRIV Stands for private variables
FIRSTPRIV Stands for firstprivate variables
UNDEF_SC Stands for variables for which auto-scoping cannot be computed
UNDEF_DEP Stands for variables for which auto-dependence cannot be computed

	Automatic classification						Reported to the user		
	PRIV	FIRSTPRIV	SHARED	IN	OUT	INOUT	UNDEF_SC	UNDEF_DEP	(%)success
Alignment	5	5	0	0	0	0	11	0	-
FFT	0	241	0	11	2	2	1	77	16.30%
Fib	0	4	0	0	2	0	0	0	100.00%
Health	0	3	0	0	0	0	1	0	-
Floorplan	2	5	0	1	0	2	5	0	100.00%
NQueens	0	5	0	1	0	0	0	0	100.00%
SparseLU	3	7	0	3	2	0	6	0	100.00%
Stencil	0	6	0	7	0	2	1	0	100.00%
Cholesky	0	16	0	26	3	20	0	0	100.00%

6   Conclusions and Future Work

In this paper we present a new algorithm that allows the automatic discovery of data-
dependence clauses for OmpSs tasks. Our main goal is to relieve the programmer
from the error-prone work of calculating manually both the data-sharing attributes (to
define the shared variables) and the data-dependence attributes (taking into account
only shared variables). We implement a new algorithm modifying our previous work

for the automatic scope of OpenMP task variables, which analyzes task synchronization points to define regions of code that run concurrently. We have also extended our analyses (use-definition chains, liveness analysis, induction variable, loop analysis and reaching definitions) in order to deal with sub-objects (array elements, array sections, shaping expressions and field references). We have defined a new clause `default(AUTO_DEPS)` that, along with OmpSs tasks, triggers the automatic discovery of such dependencies among tasks. We have used BOTS and other benchmarks to test the enhancement of programmability provided by this optimization and proved that the compiler is able to automatically determine the dependence attributes for a large amount of expressions. The expressions that cannot be automatically classified are reported to the user to proceed to the manual definition of the dependencies.

In the future we want to improve our implementation to cope with non-accessible function codes. To do so, we are considering to define in the compiler the behavior of the most common system functions such as dynamic memory management (allocation, release, etc.) or printing methods. We also want to take advantage of the common IR provided by Mercurium for C/C++ and Fortran and extend our analysis for Fortran. Furthermore, we want to implement basic compiler analysis such as constant propagation and transforming expressions to a canonical form, in order to make the implementation simpler and the dependence expressions more readable. With these improvements, we want to test our algorithm in other benchmarks. Additionally, we are thinking on applying this algorithm to other programming models based on task-level concurrency.

Acknowledgements. We would like to acknowledge the support of the European Commission through the ENCORE project (FP7-248647), and the support of the Spanish Ministry of Education (contracts TIN2007-60625, CSD2007-00050), and the Generalitat of Catalonia (contract 2009-SGR-980). Intel and TBB VTune are trademarks or registered trademarks of Intel Corporation or its subsidiaries in the United States and other countries. *Other brands and names are the property of their respective owners.

References

1. Duran, A., Teruel, X., Ferrer, R., Martorell, X., Ayguadé, E.: Barcelona OpenMP Tasks Suite: A Set of Benchmarks Targeting the Exploitation of Task Parallelism in OpenMP. In: 38th International Conference on Parallel Processing (ICPP 2009), Vienna, Austria, pp. 124–131. IEEE Computer Society (September 2009)
2. Altenfeld, R., Apel, M., an Mey, D., Böttger, B., Benke, S., Bischof, C.: Parallelising Computational Microstructure Simulations for Metallic Materials with OpenMP. In: Chapman, B.M., Gropp, W.D., Kumaran, K., Müller, M.S. (eds.) IWOMP 2011. LNCS, vol. 6665, pp. 1–11. Springer, Heidelberg (2011)
3. Andersch, M., Chi, C.C., Juurlink, B.H.H.: Programming parallel embedded and consumer applications in OpenMP superscalar. In: Ramanujam, J., Sadayappan, P. (eds.) PPoPP, pp. 281–282. ACM (2012)
4. Baah, G.K., Podgurski, A., Harrold, M.J.: The Probabilistic Program Dependence Graph and Its Application to Fault Diagnosis.. IEEE Transactions on Software Engineering 36(4), 528–545 (2010)
5. Barcelona Supercomputing Center. The NANOS Group Site: The Mercurium Compiler, http://nanos.ac.upc.edu/mcxx

6. Barcelona Supercomputing Center. Barcelona Supercomputing Center – Centro Nacional de Supercomputación (2011), http://www.bsc.es/
7. Baudisch, D., Brandt, J., Schneider, K.: Multithreaded code from synchronous programs: Extracting independent threads for OpenMP. In: DATE, pp. 949–952. IEEE (2010)
8. Baxter III, W., Bauer, H.R.: The Program Dependence Graph and Vectorization. In: PPL, pp. 1–11 (1989)
9. Bondhugula, U., Hartono, A., Ramanujam, J., Sadayappan, P.: A practical automatic polyhedral parallelizer and locality optimizer. In: Proceedings of the 2008 ACM SIGPLAN Conference on Programming Language Design and Implementation, PLDI 2008, pp. 101–113. ACM, New York (2008)
10. Duran, A., Ayguadé, E., Badia, R.M.: OmpSs: a Proposal for Programming Heterogeneous Multi-Core Architectures. PPL 21(2), 173–193 (2011)
11. Duran, A., Ferrer, R., Ayguadé, E., Badia, R.M., Labarta, J.: A Proposal to Extend the OpenMP Tasking Model with Dependent Tasks.. International Journal of Parallel Programming 37(3), 292–305 (2009)
12. Ferrante, J., Ottenstein, K.J., Warren, J.D.: The Program Dependence Graph and its Use in Optimization. In: Paul, M., Robinet, B. (eds.) Programming 1984. LNCS, vol. 167, pp. 125–132. Springer, Heidelberg (1984)
13. James: Intel® Threading Building Blocks. O'Reilly Media, Inc. (July 2007)
14. Kegel, P., Schellmann, M., Gorlatch, S.: Using OpenMP vs. Threading Building Blocks for Medical Imaging on Multi-cores. In: Sips, H., Epema, D., Lin, H.-X. (eds.) Euro-Par 2009. LNCS, vol. 5704, pp. 654–665. Springer, Heidelberg (2009)
15. Larsen, P., Karlsson, S., Madsen, J.: Identifying Inter-task Communication in Shared Memory Programming Models. In: Müller, M.S., de Supinski, B.R., Chapman, B.M. (eds.) IWOMP 2009. LNCS, vol. 5568, pp. 168–182. Springer, Heidelberg (2009)
16. Lin, Y., Terboven, C., an Mey, D., Copty, N.: Automatic Scoping of Variables in Parallel Regions of an OpenMP Program. In: Chapman, B.M. (ed.) WOMPAT 2004. LNCS, vol. 3349, pp. 83–97. Springer, Heidelberg (2005)
17. Norris, C., Pollock, L.L.: Register Allocation over the Program Dependence Graph.. In: PLDI, pp. 266–277 (1994)
18. OpenMP ARB. OpenMP Application Program Interface, v. 3.1 (September 2011), http://www.openmp.org
19. Planas, J., Badia, R.M., Ayguadé, E., Labarta, J.: Hierarchical Task-Based Programming With StarSs. International Journal of High Performance Computing Applications 23(3), 284–299 (2009)
20. Rinard, M.C., Scales, D.J., Lam, M.S.: A High-Level, Machine-Independent Language for Parallel Programming. IEEE Computer 26(6), 28–38 (1993)
21. Royuela, S.: Compiler Analysis and its Application to OmpSs. Master's thesis, Technical University of Catalonia, 1012
22. Royuela, S., Duran, A., Liao, C., Quinlan, D.J.: Auto-scoping for OpenMP Tasks. In: Chapman, B.M., Massaioli, F., Müller, M.S., Rorro, M. (eds.) IWOMP 2012. LNCS, vol. 7312, pp. 29–43. Springer, Heidelberg (2012)
23. Sarkar, V.: Automatic partitioning of a program dependence graph into parallel tasks. IBM Journal of Research and Development 35(5), 779–804 (1991)

Beyond Do Loops: Data Transfer Generation with Convex Array Regions

Serge Guelton[1], Mehdi Amini[2,3], and Béatrice Creusillet[3]

[1] Telecom Bretagne, Brest, France
`name.surname@telecom-bretagne.fr`
[2] MINES ParisTech/CRI, Fontainebleau, France
`name.surname@mines-paristech.fr`
[3] HPC-Project, Meudon, France
`name.surname@hpc-project.com`

Abstract. Automatic data transfer generation is a critical step for guided or automatic code generation for accelerators using distributed memories. Although good results have been achieved for loop nests, more complex control flows such as switches or while loops are generally not handled. This paper shows how to leverage the convex array regions abstraction to generate data transfers. The scope of this study ranges from inter-procedural analysis in simple loop nests with function calls, to inter-iteration data reuse optimization and arbitrary control flow in loop bodies. Generated transfers are approximated when an exact solution cannot be found. Array regions are also used to extend redundant load store elimination to array variables. The approach has been successfully applied to GPUs and domain-specific hardware accelerators.

Keywords: data transfers, convex array regions, redundant transfer elimination, GPU.

1   Introduction

The last decade has been showcased by the frequency wall limitation and the beginning of a computing era based on parallel computing. One of the solutions that emerges is based on the use of hardware accelerators, for instance Graphical Processing Units (GPUs). These are massively parallel pieces of hardware, usually plugged in a host computer using the PCI-Express bus, that can provide important performance improvements for data-parallel program.

The main drawback of these accelerators lies in their programming model. There are two major points: first the programmer has to exhibit in some way the huge amount of parallelism required to fulfill the accelerator capacity; second, since the accelerator is plugged in the system and embeds its own memory, the programmer has to explicitly manage Direct Memory Access (DMA) transfers between the main host memory and the accelerator memory.

The first point has been addressed in different ways using dedicated languages/libraries like Thrust [1], with directives over plain C or Fortran [13,26,19],

---

[1] `http://thrust.github.com/`

H. Kasahara and K. Kimura (Eds.): LCPC 2012, LNCS 7760, pp. 249–263, 2013.

or through automatic code parallelization [5,6,25]. The second point has been addressed using simplified input from the programmer [13,27,19], or automatically [4,24,1,26] using compilers.

This paper exposes how the array regions abstraction [12] can be used by a compiler to automatically compute memory transfers in presence of complex code patterns. Three examples are used throughout the paper to illustrate the approach: Listing 1.1 requires interprocedural array accesses analysis, and Listing 1.2 contains a while loop, for which the memory access pattern requires an approximated analysis.

This paper is organized as follows: array region analyses are first presented in Section 2; then Section 3 introduces the basis of *statement isolation*, a compiler pass that transforms a statement into a statement executed in a separate memory space. A redundant transfer elimination algorithm based on array regions is then introduced in Section 4 to optimize the generated data transfers. Finally, some applications are detailed in Section 5.

```
1  // R(src) = {src[φ₁] | i ≤ φ₁ ≤ i + k − 1}
   // W(dst) = {dst[φ₁] | φ₁ = i}
3  // R(m) = {m[φ₁] | 0 ≤ φ₁ ≤ k − 1}
   int kernel( int i, int n, int k, int src[n], int dst[n-k], int
5      m[k]) {
     int v=0;
7     for( int j = 0; j < k; ++j )
         v += src[ i + j ] * m[ j ];
9     dst[i]=v;
   }
11 void fir( int n, int k, int src[n], int dst[n-k], int m[k]) {
     for( int i = 0; i < n - k+ 1; ++i )
13       // R(src) = {src[φ₁] | i ≤ φ₁ ≤ i + k − 1, 0 ≤ i ≤ n − k}
         // R(m) = {m[φ₁] | 0 ≤ φ₁ ≤ k − 1}
15       // W(dst) = {dst[φ₁] | φ₁ = i}
         kernel(i, n, k, src, dst, m);
17 }
```

Listing 1.1. Array regions on a code with a function call

```
1  // R̄(randv) = {randv[φ₁] | (N−3)/4 ≤ φ₁ ≤ N/3}
   // W̄(a) = {a[φ₁] | (N−3)/4 ≤ φ₁ ≤ (5*N+9)/12}
3  void foo(int N, int a[N], int randv[N]) {
     int x=N/4,y=0;
5     while(x<=N/3) {
         a[x+y] = x+y;
7         if (randv[x-y]) x = x+2; else x++,y++;
     }
9  }
```

Listing 1.2. Array regions on a code with a while loop

2   Introducing Convex Array Regions

Convex array regions were first introduced by Triolet [23] with the initial purpose of summarizing the memory accesses performed on array element sets by
function calls. The concept was later generalized and formally defined for any
program statement by Creusillet [12,10] and implemented in the Paralléliseur
Interprocedural de Programmes Scientifiques (PIPS) compiler framework.

Informally, the READ (resp. WRITE) regions for a statement s are the set
of all scalar variables and array elements that are read (resp. written) during
the execution of s. This set generally depends on the values of some program
variables at the entry point of statement s: the READ regions are said to be a
function of the memory store σ preceding the statement execution, and they are
collectively denoted $\mathcal{R}(s,\sigma)$ (resp. $\mathcal{W}(s,\sigma)$ for the WRITE regions).

For instance the READ regions for the statement on line 6 in Figure 1.1 are
these:

$$\mathcal{R}(s,\sigma) = \{\{\mathtt{v}\}, \{\mathtt{i}\}, \{\mathtt{j}\}, \{\mathtt{src}(\phi_1) \mid \phi_1 = \sigma(\mathtt{i}) + \sigma(\mathtt{j})\}, \{\mathtt{m}(\phi_1) \mid \phi_1 = \sigma(\mathtt{j})\}\}$$

where ϕ_x is used to describe the constraints on the xth dimension of an array,
and where $\sigma(\mathtt{i})$ denotes the value of the program variable $\mathtt{i}$ in the memory
store σ. From this point, i is used instead of $\sigma(\mathtt{i})$ when there is no ambiguity.

The regions given above correspond to a very simple statement; however, they
can be computed for every level of compound statements. For instance, the READ
regions of the **for** loop on line 6 in the code in Figure 1.1 are these:

$$\mathcal{R}(s,\sigma) = \{\{\mathtt{v}\}, \{\mathtt{i}\}, \{\mathtt{src}(\phi_1) \mid i \leq \phi_1 \leq i + k - 1\}, \{\mathtt{m}(\phi_1) \mid 0 \leq \phi_1 \leq k - 1\}\}$$

However, computing exact sets is not always possible, either because the compiler
lacks information about the values of variables or the program control flow, or
because the regions cannot be exactly represented by a convex polyhedron. In
these cases, over-approximated convex sets (denoted $\overline{\mathcal{R}}$ and $\overline{\mathcal{W}}$) are computed.
In the following example, the approximation is due to the fact that the exact set
contains holes, and cannot be represented by a convex polyhedron:

$$\overline{\mathcal{W}}(\llbracket \mathtt{for(int\ i=0;\ i<n;\ i++)if\ (i\ !=\ 3)a[i]=0;} \rrbracket, \sigma) = \{\{\mathtt{n}\}, \{\mathtt{a}[\phi_0] \mid 0 \leq \phi_0 < n\}\}$$

whereas in the next example, the approximation is due to the fact that the
condition and its negation are nonlinear expressions that cannot be represented
exactly in our framework:

$$\overline{\mathcal{R}}(\llbracket \mathtt{if(a[i]>3)b[i]=1;\ else\ c[i]=1} \rrbracket, \sigma) =$$
$$\{\{\mathtt{i}\}, \{\mathtt{a}[\phi_0] \mid \phi_0 = i\}, \{\mathtt{b}[\phi_0] \mid \phi_0 = i\}, \{\mathtt{c}[\phi_0] \mid \phi_0 = i\}\}$$

Under-approximations (denoted $\underline{\mathcal{R}}$ and $\underline{\mathcal{W}}$) are required when computing region
differences (see [11] for more details on approximations when using the convex
polyhedron lattice).

READ and WRITE regions summarize the effects of statements and functions
upon array elements, but they do not take into account the flow of array element

values. For that purpose, IN and OUT regions have been introduced in [12] to take array kills into account, that is to say, redefinitions of individual array elements:

- IN regions contain the array elements whose values are *imported* by the considered statement, which means the elements that are read before being possibly redefined by another instruction of the statement.
- OUT regions contain the array elements defined by the considered statement, which are used afterwards in the program continuation. They are the *live* or *exported* array elements.

As for READ and WRITE regions, IN and OUT regions may be over- or under-approximated.

There is a strong analogy between the array regions of a statement and the memory used in this statement, at least from an external point of view, which means excluding its privately declared variables. Intuitively, the memory footprint of a statement can be obtained by counting the points in its associated array regions. In the same way, the READ (or IN) and WRITE (or OUT) regions can be used to compute the memory transfers required to execute this statement in a new memory space built from the original space. This analogy is analyzed and leveraged in this paper and especially in Section 3.

3   Communications Code Generation

This section introduces a new generic code transformation, called *statement isolation*. It turns a statement s into a new statement $\mathrm{Isol}(s)$ that shares no memory area with the remainder of the code, and is surrounded by the required memory transfers between the two memory spaces. In other words, if s is evaluated in a memory store σ, $\mathrm{Isol}(s)$ does not reference any element of σ. The generated memory transfers to and from the new memory space ensure the consistency and validity of the values used in the extended memory space during the execution of $\mathrm{Isol}(s)$ and once back to the original execution path.

This transformation assumes no aliasing between the different variables referenced by s, so that array regions of two different variables cannot overlap. It is applicable to any statement for which the array region can be computed, either exactly or approximately.

The transformation is formally described in [15]. To illustrate how the convex array regions are leveraged, the `while` loop in Figure 1.2 is used as an example. The exact and over-approximated array regions for this statement are as follows:

$$\mathcal{R} = \{\{\mathrm{x}\}, \{\mathrm{y}\}\} \qquad \overline{\mathcal{R}}(\mathrm{randv}) = \{\mathrm{randv}[\phi_1] \mid \frac{N-3}{4} \leq \phi_1 \leq \frac{N}{3}\}$$

$$\mathcal{W} = \{\{\mathrm{x}\}, \{\mathrm{y}\}\} \qquad \overline{\mathcal{W}}(\mathrm{a}) = \{\mathrm{a}[\phi_1] \mid \frac{N-3}{4} \leq \phi_1 \leq \frac{5*N+9}{12}\}$$

The basic idea is to turn each region into a newly allocated variable, large enough to hold the region, then to generate data transfers from the original variables to the new ones, and finally to perform the required copy from the new variables to the original ones. This results in the code shown in Figure 1.3, where isolated variables have been put in uppercase. Statements (3) and (5) correspond to the exact regions on scalar variables. Statements (2) and (4) correspond to the over-approximated regions on array variables. Statement (1) is used to ensure data consistency, as explained later.

Notice how `memcpy` system calls are used here to simulate data transfers, and, in particular, how the sizes of the transfers are constrained with respect to the array regions.

```
void foo(int N, int a[N], int randv[N]) {
  int x=0,y=0;
  int A[N/6], RANDV[(N-9)/12], X, Y;
  memcpy(A, a+(N-3)/4, N/6*sizeof(int));                  //(1)
  memcpy(RANDV, randv+(N-3)/4, (N-9)/12*sizeof(int));    //(2)
  memcpy(&X, &x, sizeof(x)); memcpy(&Y, &y, sizeof(y));//(3)
  while(X<=N/3) {
    A[X+Y-(N-3)/4] = X+Y;
    if (RANDV[X+Y-(N-3)/4]) X = X+2; else X++,Y++;
  }
  memcpy(a+(N-3)/4, A, N/6*sizeof(int));                  //(4)
  memcpy(&x, &X, sizeof(x)); memcpy(&y, &Y, sizeof(y));//(5)
}
```

Listing 1.3. Isolation of an irregular while loop using array region analysis

The benefits of using new variables to simulate the extended memory space and of relying on a regular function to simulate the DMA are twofold:

1. The generated code can be executed on a general-purpose processor. It makes it possible to verify and validate the result without the need of an accelerator or a simulator.
2. The generated code is independent of the hardware target: specializing its implementation for a given accelerator requires only a specific implementation of the memory transfer instructions (here `memcpy`).

Converting Convex Array Regions into Data Transfers. From this point on, the availability of data transfer operators that can transfer rectangular sub-parts of n-dimensional arrays to or from the accelerator is assumed. For instance,

```
size_t memcpy2d(void* dest, void* src,
                size_t dim1, size_t offset1, size_t count1,
                size_t dim2, size_t offset2, size_t count2);
```

copies from `src` to `dest` the rectangular zone between $(\text{offset1}, \text{offset2})$ and $(\text{offset1} + \text{count1}, \text{offset2} + \text{count2})$. `dim1` and `dim2` are the sizes of the memory areas pointed to by `src` and `dest` on the host memory, and are used to compute the addresses of the memory elements to transfer.

We show how convex array regions are used to generate calls to these operators. Let src be a n-dimensional variable, and $\{src[\phi_1]\ldots[\phi_n] \mid \psi(\phi_1,\ldots,\phi_n)\}$ be a convex region of this variable.

As native DMA instructions are very seldom capable of transferring anything other than a rectangular memory area, the rectangular hull, denoted $\lceil\cdot\rceil$, is first computed so that the region is expressed in the form

$$\{src[\phi_1]\ldots[\phi_n] \mid \alpha_1 \leq \phi_1 < \beta_1, \ldots, \alpha_n \leq \phi_n < \beta_n\}$$

This transformation can lead to a loss of accuracy and the region approximation can thus shift from *exact* to *may*. This shift is performed when the original region is not equal to its rectangular envelope.

The call to the transfer function can then be generated with $\mathtt{offset}k = \alpha_k$ and $\mathtt{count}k = \beta_n - \alpha_k$ for each k in $[1\ldots n]$.

For a statement s, the memory transfers from σ are generated using its read regions $(\mathcal{R}(s,\sigma))$: any array element read by s must have an up-to-date value in the extended memory space with respect to σ. Symmetrically, the memory transfers back to σ must include all updated values, represented by the written regions $(\mathcal{W}(s,\sigma'))$, where σ' is the memory state once s is executed from σ. [2]

However, if the written region is over-approximated, part of the values it contains may not have been updated by the execution of $\mathrm{Isol}(s)$. Therefore, to guarantee the consistency of the values transferred *back* to σ, they must first be correctly initialized during the transfer *from* σ. These observations lead to the following equations for the convex array regions transferred from and to σ, respectively denoted $Load(s,\sigma)$ and $Store(s,\sigma)$:

$$Store(s,\sigma) = \lceil \overline{\mathcal{W}}(s,\sigma) \rceil$$
$$Load(s,\sigma) = \lceil \overline{\mathcal{R}}(s,\sigma) \cup (Store(s,\sigma) - \underline{\mathcal{W}}(s,\sigma)) \rceil$$

$Load(s,\sigma)$ and $Store(s,\sigma)$ are rectangular regions by definition and can be converted into memory transfers, as detailed previously. The new variables with *ad-hoc* dimensions are declared and a substitution taking into account the shifts is performed on s to generate $\mathrm{Isol}(s)$.

Managing Variable Substitutions. For each variable v to be transferred according to $Load(s,\sigma)$, a new variable V is declared, which must contain enough space to hold the loaded region. For instance if v holds short integers and

$$Load(s,\sigma) = \{v[\phi_1][\phi_2] \mid \alpha_1 \leq \phi_1 < \beta_1, \alpha_2 \leq \phi_2 < \beta_2\}$$

then V will be declared as $\mathtt{short\ int}\ \mathtt{V}[\beta_1 - \alpha_1][\beta_2 - \alpha_2]$. The translation of an intraprocedural reference to v into a reference to V is straightforward as $\forall i,j,\ \mathtt{V}[i][j] = \mathtt{v}[i + \alpha_1][j + \alpha_2]$.

---

[2] Most of the time, variables used in the region description are not modified by the isolated statement and we can safely use $\mathcal{W}(s,\sigma)$. Otherwise, e.g. $\mathtt{a[i++]=1}$, methods detailed in [12] must be applied to express the region in the right memory store.

The combination of this variable substitution with convex array regions is what makes the isolate statement a powerful tool: all the complexity is hidden by the region abstraction.

For interprocedural translation, a new version of the called function is created using the following scheme: for each transferred variable passed as an actual parameter, and for each of its dimensions, an extra parameter is added to the call and to the new function, holding the value of the corresponding offset. These extra parameters are then used to perform the translation in the called function.

The output of the whole process applied to the outermost loop of the Finite Impulse Response (FIR) is illustrated in Figure 1.4, where a new KERNEL function with two extra parameters is now called instead of the original kernel function. These parameters hold the offsets between the original array variables src and m and the isolated ones SRC and M.

```
1  void fir(int n, int k, int src[n], int dst[n-k], int m[k]) {
     int N=n - k+ 1;
3    for( int i = 0; i < N; ++i ) {
       int DST[1],SRC[k],M[k];
5      memcpy(SRC, src+i, k*sizeof(int));
       memcpy(M, m+0, k*sizeof(int));
7      KERNEL(i, n, k, SRC, DST,M, i/*SRC*/, i/*DST*/, 0/*M*/);
       memcpy(dst, DST+0, 1*sizeof(int));
9    }
   }
```

Listing 1.4. Interprocedural isolation of the outermost loop of a Finite Impulse Response

The body of the new KERNEL function is given in Figure 1.5. The extra offset parameters are used to perform the translation on the array parameters. The same scheme applies for multidimensional arrays, with one offset per dimension.

```
   void KERNEL(int i, int n, int k, int SRC[k], int DST[1],
2        int M[k], int SRC_offset, int DST_offset, int M_offset) {
     int v=0;
4    for( int j = 0; j < k; ++j )
       v += SRC[i+j-SRC_offset]*M[j-M_offset];
6    DST[i-SRC_offset]=v;
   }
```

Listing 1.5. Isolated version of the kernel function of a Finite Impulse Response

4   Redundant Transfer Elimination

The *statement isolation* pass considers a statement independently of its context. However, it is sometimes possible to limit the volume of transferred data when considering the context, either through the elimination of redundant data transfers between isoalted statements, or through overlapping of transfers with computations.

This section informally describes an original contribution to the former using a step-by-step propagation of the memory transfers across the Control Flow Graph (CFG) of the host program. It has been more formally described with proofs in [14]. The main idea is to move *load* operations upward in the Hierarchical Control Flow Graph (HCFG) so that they are executed as soon as possible, while *store* operations are symmetrically moved so that they are executed as late as possible. Redundant load-store elimination is performed in the meantime.

In the following, we only consider optimization of mutliple isolated section during a sequential execution.

4.1   Interprocedural Propagation

When a *load* is performed at the entry point of a function, it may be interesting to move it at the call sites. However, this is valid only if the memory state before the call site is the same as the memory state at the function entry point, that is, if there is no write effect during the effective parameter evaluation. In that case, the *load* statement can be moved before the call sites, after backward translation from formal parameters to effective parameters.

Similarly, if the same *store* statement is found at each exit point of a function, it may be possible to move it past its call sites. Validity criteria include that the *store* statement depends only on formal parameters and that these parameters are not written by the function. If this the case, the *store* statement can be removed from the function call and added after each call site after backward translation of the formal parameters.

4.2   Combining Load and Store Elimination

In the meanwhile, the intraprocedural and interprocedural propagation of DMA may trigger other optimization opportunities. *Loads* and *stores* may for instance interact across loop iterations, when the loop body is surrounded by a load and a store; or when a kernel is called in a function to produce data immediately consumed by a kernel hosted in another function, and the DMA have been moved in the calling function.

The optimization then consists in removing *load* and *store* operations when they meet. This relies on the following property: considering that the statement denoted by "memcpy(a,b,10*sizeof(in))" is a DMA and its reciprocal is denoted by "memcpy(b,a,10*sizeof(in))", then in the sequence memcpy(a,b,10*sizeof(in));memcpy(b,a,10*sizeof(in)), the second call can be removed since it would not change the values already stored in a.

Figure 1.6, illustrates the result of the algorithm. It demonstrates the interprocedural elimination of data communications represented by the `memload` and `memstore` functions. These function calls are first moved outside of the loop, then outside of the `bar` function; finally, redundant *load*s are eliminated.

```
void bar(int i, int j[2], int k[2]) {
  while (i-->=0) {
    memload(k, j, sizeof(int)*2);
    k[0]++;
    memstore(j, k, sizeof(int)*2);
  }
}
void foo(int j[2], int k[2]) {
  bar(0, j, k);
  bar(1, j, k);
}
```

⇓

```
void bar(int i, int j[2], int k[2]) {
  while (i-->=0) k[0]++;
}
void foo(int j[2], int k[2]) {
  memload(k, j, sizeof(int)*2); // load moved before call
  bar(0, j, k);
  memstore(j, k, sizeof(int)*2);// redundant load
      eliminated
  bar(1, j, k);
  memstore(j, k, sizeof(int)*2);// store moved after call
}
```

Listing 1.6. Illustration of the redundant load store elimination algorithm

4.3 Optimizing a Tiled Loop Nest

Alias et al. have published an interesting study about fine grained optimization of communications in the context of Field Programmable Gate Array (FPGA) [1,2,3]. The fact that they target FPGAs changes some considerations on the memory size: FPGAs usually embed a very small memory compared to the many gigabytes available in a GPU board. The proposal from Alias et al. focuses on optimizing loads from Double Data Rate (DDR) in the context of a tiled loop nest, where the tiling is done such that tiles execute sequentially on the accelerator while the computation inside each tile can be parallelized.

While their work is based on the Quasi-Affine Selection Tree (QUAST) abstraction, this section shows how their algorithm can be used with the less expensive convex array region abstraction.

The classical scheme proposed to isolate kernels would exhibit full communications as shown in Figure 1.7. An inter-iteration analysis allows avoiding redundant communications and produces the code shown in Figure 1.8. The

```
for( int i = 0; i < N; ++i ) {
2  memcpy(M,m,k*sizeof(int));
   memcpy(&SRC[i],&src[i],k*sizeof(int));
4  kernel(i, n, k, SRC, DST, M);
   memcpy(&dst[i],&DST[i],1*sizeof(int));
6 }
```

Listing 1.7. Code for FIR function from figure 1.1 with naive communication scheme

```
for( int i = 0; i < N; ++i ) {
2  if(i==0) {
     memcpy(SRC,src,k*sizeof(int));
4    memcpy(M,m,k*sizeof(int));
   } else {
6    memcpy(&SRC[i+k-1],&src[i+k-1],1*sizeof(int));
   }
8  kernel(i, n, k, SRC, DST, m);
   memcpy(&dst[i],&DST[i],1*sizeof(int));
10 }
```

Listing 1.8. Code for FIR function with communication after the inter-iterations redundant elimination

inter-iteration analysis is performed on a do loop, but with the array regions. The code part to isolate is not bound by static control constraints.

The theorem proposed for exact sets in [1] is the following: [3]

Theorem 1.

$$Load(T) = \mathcal{R}(T) - \left(\mathcal{R}(t < T) \bigcup \mathcal{W}(t < T)\right) \qquad (1)$$
$$Store(T) = \mathcal{W}(T) - \mathcal{W}(t > T) \qquad (2)$$

where T represents a tile, $t < T$ represents the tiles scheduled for execution before the tile T, and $t > T$ represents the tiles scheduled for execution after T. The denotation $\mathcal{W}(t > T)$ corresponds to $\bigcup_{t>T} \mathcal{W}(t)$.

In Theorem 1, a difference exists for each loop between the first iteration, the last one, and the rest of the iteration set. Indeed, the first iteration cannot benefit from reuse from previously transferred data and has to transfer all needed data, while the last one has to schedule a transfer for all produced data. In other words, $\mathcal{R}(t < T)$ and $\mathcal{W}(t < T)$ are empty for the first iteration while $\mathcal{W}(t > T)$ is empty for the last iteration.

For instance, in the code presented in Figure 1.7, three cases are considered: $i = 0, 0 < i < N - 1$ and $i = N - 1$.

---

[3] Regions are supposed exact here; the equation can be adapted to under- and over-approximations.

Using the array region abstraction available in PIPS, a refinement can be carried out to compute each case, starting with the full region, adding the necessary constraints and performing a difference.

For example, the region computed by PIPS to represent the set of elements read for array src, is, for each tile (here corresponding to iteration i)

$$\mathcal{R}(i) = \{ \text{src}[\phi_1] \mid i \leq \phi_1 \leq i + k - 1,\ 0 \leq i < N \}$$

For each iteration i of the loop except the first one (here $i > 0$), the region of src that is read minus the elements read in all previous iterations $i' < i$ has to be processed; that is, $\bigcup_{i'} \mathcal{R}(i' < i)$.

$\mathcal{R}(i' < i)$ is built from $\mathcal{R}(i)$ by renaming i as i' and adding the constraint $0 \leq i' < i$ to the polyhedron:

$$\mathcal{R}(i' < i) = \{ \text{src}[\phi_1] \mid i' \leq \phi_1 \leq i' + k - 1,\ 0 \leq i' < i,\ 1 \leq i < N \}$$

i' is then eliminated to obtain $\bigcup_{i'} \mathcal{R}(i' < i)$:

$$\bigcup_{i'} \mathcal{R}(i' < i) = \{ \text{src}[\phi_1] \mid 0 \leq \phi_1 \leq i + k - 2,\ 1 \leq i < N \}$$

The result of the subtraction $\mathcal{R}(i > 0) - \bigcup_{i'} \mathcal{R}(i' < i)$ leads to following region:[4]

$$Load(i > 0) = \{ \text{src}[\phi_1] \mid \phi_1 = i + k - 1,\ 1 \leq i < N \}$$

This region is then exploited for generating the *loads* for all iterations but the first one. The resulting code after optimization is presented in Figure 1.8. While the naive version loads $i \times k \times 2$ elements, the optimized version exhibits loads only for $i + 2 \times k$ elements.

5   Applications

The transformations introduced in this article have been used as basic blocks in compilers targeting several different hardware, showing their versatility. They are partially listed here with references to more detailed paper about each work.

- the redundant load store elimination described in Section 4 has been used in [14] for vector instruction sets to optimize loads and stores between vector registers and the main memory. In that case data transfers were not generated by *statement isolation* but through vector instruction packing, leading to the code in Listing 1.9 for a vectorized scalar product. Redundant load store elimination leads to the optimized version in Listing 1.9.
- The communication generation for an image-processing accelerator, TER-APIX [8], described in [14] relies on the *statement isolation* from Section 3.

---

[4] As the write regions are empty for src, this corresponds to the loads.

```
for(i0 = 0; i0 <= 199; i0 += 4) {
  SIMD_LOAD_V4SF(vec20, &c[i0]);
  SIMD_LOAD_V4SF(vec10, &b[i0]);
  SIMD_MULPS(vec00, vec10, vec20);
  SIMD_STORE_V4SF(vec00, &pdata0[0]);
  SIMD_LOAD_V4SF(vec30, &RED0[0]);
  SIMD_ADDPS(vec30, vec30, vec00);
  SIMD_STORE_V4SF(vec30, &RED0[0]);
}
```

```
SIMD_LOAD_V4SF(vec30, &RED0[0]);
for(i0 = 0; i0 <= 199; i0 += 4) {
  SIMD_LOAD_V4SF(vec20, &c[i0]);
  SIMD_LOAD_V4SF(vec10, &b[i0]);
  SIMD_MULPS(vec00, vec10, vec20);
  SIMD_STORE_V4SF(vec00, &pdata0[0]);
  SIMD_ADDPS(vec30, vec30, vec00);
  SIMD_STORE_V4SF(vec30, &RED0[0]);
}
```

Listing 1.9. Body of a vectorized scalar product, before and after redundant load store elimination

- The SCALOPES project associated an asymmetric MP-SoC with cores dedicated to task scheduling, to a semi-automatic parallelization workflow. *Statement isolation* has been used to generate inter-tasks communications [24].
- SMECY is an innovative compilation tool-chain for embedded multi-core architectures. This on-going project [22] is another use case that exhibits how convex array regions are well suited to communication and mapping problems. In that case, *statement isolation* generates data transfers between different fields of a structure, showcasing that it does not support only arrays, but also imbrication of structure of arrays.
- The code generation for GPUs in Par4All [21] relies on *statement isolation* to efficiently manage communications. It relies on generic data transfers and kernel calls that can use a CUDA or OpenCL backend. A typical output is showcased in Listing 1.10.

```
P4A_copy_to_accel_2d(sizeof pt[0][0], 90, 99, 90, 99 ,0 ,0
    , pt ,*p4a_pt0);
P4A_copy_to_accel_1d(sizeof t[0], 20, 20, 0, t, *p4a_t0 );
p4a_launcher_run(*p4a_pt0, range, step, *p4a_t0, xmin, ymin
    );
P4A_copy_from_accel_2d( sizeof pt[0][0], 90, 99, 90, 99, 0,
    0, pt, *p4a_pt0);
```

Listing 1.10. Typical Par4All-generated DMA

All these architectures use a load-work-store paradigm, so the code transformations described in this paper can be used to generate or optimized generic data transfers, although they are rather different targets.

6 Related Works

The issue of generating memory transfers between a host processor and an attached accelerator has been studied at multiple occasions in the past.

Convex array regions were already used in the PIPS framework [9] for High Performance Fortran (HPF) code generation. We leverage this approach by decoupling analysis, transfer generation and transfer optimization.

In the same context, the Omega project [20] relied on the manipulation of sets of affine constraints over integer variables. Non-affine conditions and function calls were handled by *uninterpreted function symbols*, a technique described in [28] that does not provide the summarizing capability of interprocedural convex array regions.

Beyond HPF, in the field of embedded computing, other approaches based on memory layout detection and interaction with the memory access patterns have been proposed [16]. The code generation for transfer instructions depending on available communication models has been studied through the polyhedral model [17].

Recently, polyhedral techniques have been applied to generate data communications between a CPU and a GPU, as detailed in [6,18]. The benefit of using convex array regions over these approaches is their ability to retain some important information concerning data accesses even in non-affine situations, by gracefully degrading their accuracy.

An approach that shares some similarities with ours is described in [7]. This paper enhances classical polyhedral techniques to tackle `while` loops and arbitrary conditionnals, relying on over-approximation of the iteration domains through convex hulls. However, it does not propose any solution other than inlining to handle function calls.

7 Conclusion

Automatic code generation currently seems a good lasting option while heterogeneous architectural models are emerging at a sustainable pace, and as a single application may have to be executed on different numerous targets during its life cycle. In this context, efficiently managing data transfers between different memory spaces is a key issue, usually addressed by restricting the control flow of the application kernels.

In this paper, we introduce several techniques relying on the summarizing power of array region analyzes, to lift these barriers and broaden the input class of applications, without sacrificing the efficiency of the generated code.

These techniques have been implemented in the PIPS compiler infrastructure used by the Par4All tool. They have been successfully used to generate code for GPGPUs, vector processing units, domain-specific architectures, including heterogeneous architectures with task scheduling dedicated cores... Other targets are yet being considered such as multi-GPUs architectures. In addition, our approach could be adapted to directly manage memory hierarchies like software managed cache in GPUs.

Acknowledgments. This work has been supported by French National Research Agency (ANR) through the FREIA Project, the OpenGPU project, and the MediaGPU project. We are grateful to François Irigoin, Ronan Keryell, and Fabien Coelho for their valuable advices.

References

1. Alias, C., Darte, A., Plesco, A.: Program Analysis and Source-Level Communication Optimizations for High-Level Synthesis. Rapport de recherche RR-7648, INRIA (June 2011), http://hal.inria.fr/inria-00601822
2. Alias, C., Darte, A., Plesco, A.: Optimizing Remote Accesses for Offloaded Kernels: Application to High-Level Synthesis for FPGA. In: 2nd International Workshop on Polyhedral Compilation Techniques, Impact (January 2012)
3. Alias, C., Darte, A., Plesco, A.: Optimizing Remote Accesses for Offloaded Kernels: Application to High-level Synthesis for FPGA. In: Proceedings of the 17th ACM SIGPLAN Symposium on Principles and Practice of Parallel Programming, PPoPP, pp. 1–10. ACM, New York (2012)
4. Amini, M., Coelho, F., Irigoin, F., Keryell, R.: Static compilation analysis for host-accelerator communication optimization. In: International Workshop on Languages and Compilers for Parallel Computing, LCPC (September 2011)
5. Amini, M., Creusillet, B., Even, S., Keryell, R., Goubier, O., Guelton, S., McMahon, J.O., Pasquier, F.X., Péan, G., Villalon, P.: Par4All: From convex array regions to heterogeneous computing. In: 2nd International Workshop on Polyhedral Compilation Techniques, Impact (January 2012)
6. Baskaran, M.M., Ramanujam, J., Sadayappan, P.: Automatic C-to-CUDA Code Generation for Affine Programs. In: Gupta, R. (ed.) CC 2010. LNCS, vol. 6011, pp. 244–263. Springer, Heidelberg (2010)
7. Benabderrahmane, M.-W., Pouchet, L.-N., Cohen, A., Bastoul, C.: The Polyhedral Model Is More Widely Applicable Than You Think. In: Gupta, R. (ed.) CC 2010. LNCS, vol. 6011, pp. 283–303. Springer, Heidelberg (2010)
8. Bonnot, P., Lemonnier, F., Edelin, G., Gaillat, G., Ruch, O., Gauget, P.: Definition and SIMD implementation of a multi-processing architecture approach on FPGA. In: Design Automation and Test in Europe, DATE, pp. 610–615. IEEE Computer Society Press (2008)
9. Coelho, F.: Étude de la Compilation du High Performance Fortran. Ph.D. thesis, Université Paris VI (1993)
10. Creusillet, B.: Array Region Analyses and Applications. Ph.D. thesis, MINES ParisTech. (1996)
11. Creusillet, B., Irigoin, F.: Exact vs. Approximate Array Region Analyses. In: Sehr, D., Banerjee, U., Gelernter, D., Nicolau, A., Padua, D.A. (eds.) LCPC 1996. LNCS, vol. 1239, pp. 86–100. Springer, Heidelberg (1997)

12. Creusillet, B., Irigoin, F.: Interprocedural array region analyses. International Journal of Parallel Programming 24(6), 513–546 (1996)
13. Entreprise, C.: HMPP workbench, http://www.caps-entreprise.com/hmpp.html
14. Guelton, S.: Building Source-to-Source compilers for Heterogenous targets. Ph.D. thesis, Télécom Bretagne (2011)
15. Guelton, S.: Transformations for memory size and distribution. [14], chap. 6
16. Kandemir, M., Ramanujam, J., Irwin, M.J., Vijaykrishnan, N., Kadayif, I., Parikh, A.: A compiler-based approach for dynamically managing scratch-pad memories in embedded systems. In: Computer-Aided Design of Integrated Circuits and Systems, vol. 23, pp. 243–260. IEEE (February 2004)
17. Meister, B., Leung, A., Vasilache, N., Wohlford, D., Bastoul, C., Lethin, R.: Productivity via automatic code generation for PGAS platforms with the R-Stream compiler. In: Workshop on Asynchrony in the PGAS Programming Model, APGAS, Yorktown Heights, New York (June 2009)
18. Meister, B., Vasilache, N., Wohlford, D., Baskaran, M.M., Leung, A., Lethin, R.: R-Stream compiler. In: Padua, D.A. (ed.) Encyclopedia of Parallel Computing, pp. 1756–1765. Springer (2011)
19. NVIDIA, Cray, PGI, CAPS: The OpenACC Specification, version 1.0 (November 2011), http://www.openacc-standard.org/Downloads/OpenACC.1.0.pdf
20. Pugh, W.: The Omega test: a fast and practical integer programming algorithm for dependence analysis. In: Conference on Supercomputing, pp. 4–13. ACM, New York (1991)
21. Silkan: Par4All initiative for automatic parallelization (2010), http://www.par4all.org
22. Torquati, M., Vanneschi, M., Amini, M., Guelton, S., Keryell, R., Lanore, V., Pasquier, F.X., Barreteau, M., Barrère, R., Petrisor, C.T., Lenormand, É., Cantini, C., De Stefani, F.: An innovative compilation tool-chain for embedded multi-core architectures. In: Embedded World Conference (February 2012)
23. Triolet, R., Feautrier, P., Irigoin, F.: Direct parallelization of call statements. In: ACM SIGPLAN Symposium on Compiler Construction, pp. 176–185 (1986)
24. Ventroux, N., Sassolas, T., Guerre, A., Creusillet, B., Keryell, R.: SESAM/ Par4All: a tool for joint exploration of MPSoC architectures and dynamic dataflow code generation. In: Proceedings of the 2012 Workshop on Rapid Simulation and Performance Evaluation: Methods and Tools, RAPIDO, pp. 9–16. ACM, New York (2012)
25. Verdoolaege, S., Grosser, T.: Polyhedral Extraction Tool. In: 2nd International Workshop on Polyhedral Compilation Techniques, Impact (January 2012)
26. Wolfe, M.: Implementing the PGI accelerator model. In: Proceedings of the 3rd Workshop on General-Purpose Computation on Graphics Processing Units, GPGPU, pp. 43–50. ACM, New York (2010)
27. Wolfe, M.: Optimizing Data Movement in the PGI Accelerator Programming Model (February 2011), http://www.pgroup.com/lit/articles/insider/v3n1a1.htm
28. Wonnacott, D., Pugh, W.: Nonlinear array dependence analysis. In: Proceedings of the Third Workshop on Languages, Compilers and Run-Time Systems for Scalable Computers (1995)

Finish Accumulators: An Efficient Reduction Construct for Dynamic Task Parallelism

Jun Shirako, Vincent Cavé, Jisheng Zhao, and Vivek Sarkar

Department of Computer Science, Rice University
{shirako,vincent.cave,jisheng.zhao,vsarkar}@rice.edu

1   Introduction

Parallel reductions represent a common pattern for computing the aggregation of an associative and commutative operation, such as summation, across multiple pieces of data supplied by parallel tasks. In this poster, we introduce *finish accumulators*, a unified construct that supports predefined and user-defined parallel reductions for *dynamic task parallelism*. Finish accumulators are designed to be integrated into structured task parallelism constructs, such as the `async` and `finish` constructs found in the X10 and Habanero-Java (HJ) languages, so as to guarantee determinism for accumulation and to avoid any possible race conditions in referring to intermediate results. In contrast to lower-level reduction constructs such as atomic variables, the high-level semantics of finish accumulators allows for a wide range of implementations with different accumulation policies, *e.g.*, *eager*-computation vs. *lazy*-computation. The best implementation can thus be selected based on a given application and target platform. We have integrated finish accumulators into the Habanero-Java task parallel language, and used them for research and teaching. In addition to their higher-level semantics, experimental results demonstrate that our Java-based implementation of finish accumulators delivers comparable or better performance for computing reductions relative to Java's atomic variables and concurrent collections.

2   Programming Model

In our model, parallel tasks asynchronously transmit their data to finish accumulators with *put* operations and retrieve the results by *get* operations. A finish accumulator ac is accessible to sub-tasks if and only if ac is associated with a `finish` statement and the sub-tasks are created within the `finish` scope. To ensure an absence of races, `get` operations by sub-tasks return the value at the beginning of the associated `finish` scope and are not affected by `put` operations within the same `finish` scope. In the example in Figure 1, an accumulator ac is associated with the outer `finish` scope and hence accessible to T_1, T_2, and T_3 while the put operation by T_4 will throw an exception because T_4 does not belong to the associated `finish` scope and can happen both before and after the get operation by T_1.

H. Kasahara and K. Kimura (Eds.): LCPC 2012, LNCS 7760, pp. 264–265, 2013.

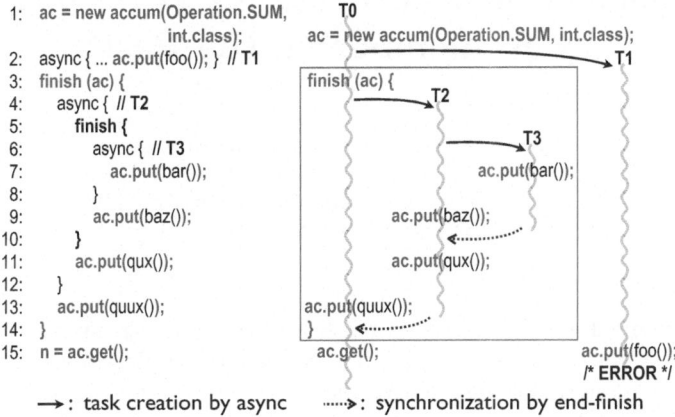

```
1:   ac = new accum(Operation.SUM,
                    int.class);
2:   async { ... ac.put(foo()); } // T1
3:   finish (ac) {
4:       async { // T2
5:           finish {
6:               async { // T3
7:                   ac.put(bar());
8:               }
9:               ac.put(baz());
10:          }
11:          ac.put(qux());
12:      }
13:      ac.put(quux());
14: }
15:  n = ac.get();
```

→: task creation by async   ⋯⋯▶: synchronization by end-finish

Fig. 1. Finish accumulator example with four tasks

3   Experimental Results

We summarize our experimental results on an 8-core (2 quad-cores) 2.4GHz Intel *Core i7* system and a 64-thread (8 cores × 8 threads/core) 1.2 GHz Sun *Ultra-SPARC T2* system using four applications with reductions. For finish accumulators, we used the Habanero-Java compiler and runtime with the work stealing scheduler. *JUC* represents pure Java versions that use the `java.util.concurrent` library — `AtomicInteger` for Nqueens and Fibonacci, `ReentrantLock` for Sudoku, and `ConcurrentHashMap` for WordCount. The *eager* and *lazy* cases refer to implementation variants of finish accumulators; *eager* is based on atomic operations analogous to the *JUC* version and *lazy* is a two-step approach that computes local reductions on each worker and then performs a global reduction at the `end-finish` synchronization point. We can see that *eager* has comparable or better performance than *JUC* except in the case of WordCount, where JUC benefits from the optimized `ConcurrentHashMap` implementation. However, *lazy* always shows the same or better performance compared to other two versions.

Table 1. Speedup related to lazy accumulators with 1 thread

	Core i7 with 8 cores				UltraSPARC T2 with 64 threads			
	Nqueens	Fibonacci	Sudoku	WordCount	Nqueens	Fibonacci	Sudoku	WordCount
JUC	2.28×	1.05×	5.69×	2.50×	1.87×	2.18×	12.69×	4.97×
Eager	2.25×	1.10×	6.08×	0.46×	13.41×	5.24×	12.65×	0.62×
Lazy	4.72×	2.20×	5.77×	5.54×	21.18×	23.91×	12.55×	5.10×

FlashbackSTM: Improving STM Performance by Remembering the Past*

Hugo Rito and João Cachopo

ESW/INESC-ID Lisboa/Instituto Superior Técnico
{hugo.rito,joao.cachopo}@ist.utl.pt

As multicore machines become pervasive, an ever growing number of programmers face the challenge of building highly parallel applications that take full advantage of modern parallel hardware architectures. Software Transactional Memory (STM) [3] is one promising abstraction to simplify this task because when using an STM programmers may ignore low-level synchronization details and simply specify which operations must execute atomically inside transactions. It is then the STM's responsibility to preserve the program's semantics, while maintaining as much parallelism and concurrency as possible.

Although STMs exhibit very good performance in read-dominated workloads, the same cannot be said about workloads in which transactions conflict very frequently. Each time a transaction conflicts it imposes a significant cost on the system, originating from the need to abort and redo the whole transaction.

In this work we propose the FlashbackSTM, an STM system that extends a lock-free STM—the JVSTM [1]—with the concept of memo-transactions. Unlike normal transactions, our new memo-transactions populate a per-transaction memoization [4] cache with information about their runtime behavior and use the information stored in the memo-cache to memoize reexecutions.

In the FlashbackSTM nested transactions never fail (closed nesting) and top-level transactions that fail to commit restart from the beginning. However, in the reexecution each nested memo-transaction searches the transaction's private memo-cache for a hit. If it is successful, the memo-transaction uses the information stored in the cache and proceeds to the commit phase without reexecuting. When the top-level transaction eventually commits with success, valid memoization information is added to a central memo-cache shared by all transactions.

To memoize transactions, the FlashbackSTM needs to recognize when it is about to execute a transaction with an outcome that is already known and, when that is the case, to replicate the behavior of that transaction without reexecuting it. Given that the behavior of a transaction may depend on the shared state of the application, each memo-entry stores not only the arguments supplied to the transaction but also the transaction's read-set, as proposed in [5].

This way, a memo-entry is valid if and only if both the arguments supplied to the atomic method and the arguments stored in the memo-cache match, and all the memory positions referenced in the cached read-set still hold the same value

---

* This work was supported by FCT (INESC-ID multiannual funding) through the PID-DAC Program funds and by the RuLAM project (PTDC/EIA-EIA/108240/2008).

H. Kasahara and K. Kimura (Eds.): LCPC 2012, LNCS 7760, pp. 266–267, 2013.

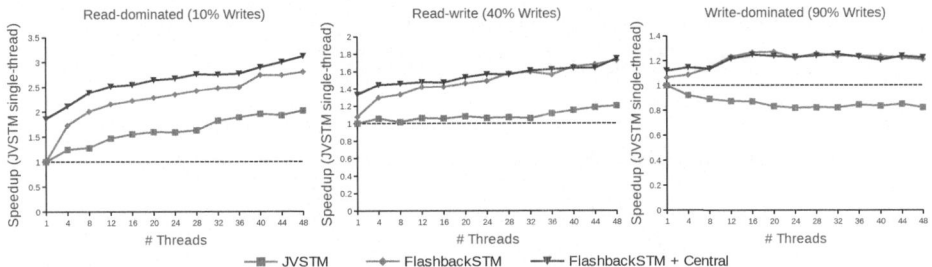

Fig. 1. Speedups for the STMBench7 benchmark and three distinct workloads

as when the read-set was stored in the memo-cache. Additionally, the memo-cache stores the transaction's result value and the transaction's write-set, which is applied to shared state if the transaction subsequently commits with success.

For our evaluation we considered the STMBench7 [2] benchmark. In Figure 1, we present the speedup of the benchmark with the JVSTM, the FlashbackSTM, and the FlashbackSTM with the central memo-cache, using as baseline the execution time of the benchmark with the JVSTM single thread for each workload.

As expected, FlashbackSTM behaves the best with read-dominated workloads, cutting the runtime of the benchmark to a third, scaling well up to 48 threads, and outperforming the JVSTM, which is highly optimized for read-intensive workloads. In the write-dominated workload, the results are not as impressive and FlashbackSTM improves the performance of the benchmark with 48 threads by 20% only. Nonetheless, we consider the write-dominated results quite promising, specially if we take into account that for the same workload JVSTM's performance only deteriorates as we increase the number of threads.

Furthermore, these results were obtained when we applied memoization to a single method of the benchmark that is called by less than 5% of all operations executed in our tests. For that reason, in the future, we intend to perform a more extensive profiling of the STMBench7 benchmark to find other methods where memoization can be used efficiently and better understand under which conditions memo-transactions are most beneficial.

References

1. Fernandes, S., Cachopo, J.: Lock-free and scalable multi-version software transactional memory. In: Proceedings of the 16th ACM Symposium on Principles and Practice of Parallel Programming, PPoPP 2011. ACM (2011)
2. Guerraoui, R., Kapalka, M., Vitek, J.: STMBench7: A benchmark for software transactional memory. SIGOPS Oper. Syst. Rev. 41, 315–324 (2007)
3. Herlihy, M., Moss, J.: Transactional memory: Architectural support for lock-free data structures. SIGARCH Comput. Archit. News 21, 289–300 (1993)
4. Michie, D.: Memo functions and machine learning. Nature 218(1), 19–22 (1968)
5. Rito, H., Cachopo, J.: Memoization of methods using software transactional memory to track internal state dependencies. In: Proceedings of the 8th International Conference on the Principles and Practice of Programming in Java, PPPJ 2010 (2010)

Kaira: Generating Parallel Libraries and Their Usage with Octave[*]

Stanislav Böhm, Marek Běhálek, and Ondřej Meca

Department of Computer Science FEI, IT4 Innovations
VŠB Technical University of Ostrava
Ostrava, Czech Republic
{stanislav.bohm,marek.behalek,ondrej.meca}@vsb.cz
http://verif.cs.vsb.cz/kaira/

We are developing a tool Kaira[1,2]. Our main development goal is to create a practically usable general-purpose high-level visual programming tool for the area of High Performance Computing (HPC), especially for distributed memory systems. We feel that there is a space for this research. Tools used by practitioners in this area are usually low-level ones (like Message Passing Interface – MPI) or domain specific tools.

Kaira is designed as a complete development environment, it includes: modelling, testing and debugging. The tool is released as open-source project under GPL licence. An important role in our project plays an abstract computational model. Semantics of our models are based on a formalism of *Coloured Petri Nets* (CPNs). CPNs are a high-level extension of Petri Nets (PNs), where tokens can carry values. PNs naturally capture parallel behaviour. They can serve also as a way how to think about algorithms, not only a way how to tell a computer what to do. PNs provide natural visual representations of models so we can straightforwardly provide visual editing of models and their simulations. Nevertheless, Kaira is not an automatic parallelization tool. A user has to specify a parallel behaviour explicitly, but it can be done in a form of a high level model. From such models, Kaira derives resulting applications with various implementation details. We do not want to visually program a complete application using CPNs. We want to focus on parallelisms and communication aspects only. Sequential parts of a program can be created in a "standard" programming language and integrated into visual models. The current implementation supports integration of codes written in C++. From such model, Kaira is able to generate a standalone parallel application. The resulting applications use MPI and pthreads as a parallel backend. These applications can be directly executed on HPC computers.

One of the new features of Kaira is the ability to generate parallel libraries from our models. More precisely we are able to generate standalone C++ libraries or C++ libraries with an interface to Octave[1]. A library interface is generated solely from Petri nets without need any additional C++ code. This

[*] The work was supported by: GAČR P202/11/0340, the European Regional Development Fund in the IT4Innovations Centre of Excellence project (CZ.1.05/1.1.00/02.0070) and Student project SP2012/127.
[1] http://www.gnu.org/software/octave/

H. Kasahara and K. Kimura (Eds.): LCPC 2012, LNCS 7760, pp. 268–269, 2013.

feature was implemented to allow quickly interchange time-consuming parts by parallel running functions without modifying the rest of a program. Optionally we can also generate Remote-Procedure-Call (RPC) interface where both client and server are generated. For example it allows to run Octave in a single instance on a laptop and run performance demanding pars of a program on HPC hardware in a form of MPI application. The whole chain of actions: how to get data from Octave, send them to a server, initiate MPI computation and return results back to Octave is automatically generated from our models.

To demonstrate the abilities of Kaira's Octave libraries we implemented a parallel computation of generalized inverse $\mathbf{K}^+$ of a block diagonal matrix $\mathbf{K}$ (for $\mathbf{K}^+$ holds $\mathbf{KK}^+\mathbf{K} = \mathbf{K}$). Using such block diagonal matrices, we are usually able to straightforwardly divide computations and perform them in parallel. For example in Total-FETI domain decomposition method it is one of the most time consuming operations. The Karia's model for this problem is in the Figure 1. More precisely in our example we compute $\mathbf{y} = \mathbf{K}^+\mathbf{x}$ using Cholesky decomposition ($\mathbf{L}^T\mathbf{L} = \mathbf{P}^T\mathbf{AP}$) and N is the number of blocks. From this model Kaira is able to produce a client-server application that use MPI and threads on a server side and offers Octave function on a client side.

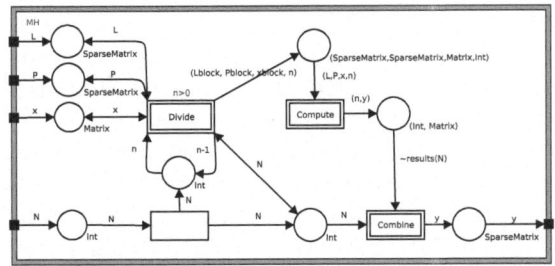

Fig. 1. Kaira's model solving $\mathbf{y} = \mathbf{K}^+\mathbf{x}$

To conclude, Kaira is able to produce parallel running libraries that can be used directly in C++ or Octave. Moreover it takes only few lines of C++ code and a simple Petri net model. Although if there is a space for various optimizations, we were able to get a relatively efficient parallel solution quickly and by iterative approach. Also we were able to get this solution without knowledge MPI or thread programming, which can be crucial for some Octave users.

References

1. Böhm, S., Běhálek, M., Garncarz, O.: Developing Parallel Applications Using Kaira. In: Snasel, V., Platos, J., El-Qawasmeh, E. (eds.) ICDIPC 2011, Part I. CCIS, vol. 188, pp. 237–251. Springer, Heidelberg (2011)
2. Běhálek, M., Böhm, S., Krömer, P., Šurkovský, M., Meca, O.: Parallelization of ant colony optimization algorithm using Kaira. In: 11th International Conference on Intelligent Systems Design and Applications (ISDA 2011), Cordoba, Spain (2011)

Language and Architecture Independent Software Thread-Level Speculation

Zhen Cao and Clark Verbrugge

School of Computer Science, McGill University
Montréal, Québec, Canada H3A 2A7
zhen.cao@mail.mcgill.ca, clump@cs.mcgill.ca

1 Introduction

Thread-level speculation (TLS) has historically been investigated in the context of novel hardware designs Chen and Olukotun, 2003, Steffan et al., 2005 Quiñones et al., 2005. Pure software designs to TLS, however, have relatively recently become of interest, trading increased overhead concerns for the potential of providing new and user-friendly approaches to extracting parallelism, and making use of commodity multiprocessors without the need for new hardware Pickett and Verbrugge, 2005, Oancea and Mycroft, 2008. Investigation of such approaches, however, tends to be hampered by the need for such systems to build on specific language or execution contexts with implicit source-level requirements, and lack of integration with a realistic compiler infrastructure.

As a flexible solution, in this paper we develop a software-based TLS system based on the popular LLVM compiler framework. Our design is fully integrated into the generic, language and machine-neutral LLVM intermediate representation (IR), allowing us to take advantage of the full gamut of input languages and output architectures supported by LLVM, as well as the variety of compiler optimizations built into the framework.

2 Design

The design involves changes to both front-end and back-end components. The former is needed as we use programmer-directed speculation. Annotations are added to the LLVM IR from user-specified *fork* and *join* points, a relatively minor change that allows our work to be easily ported to multiple language contexts. The back-end support consists of an LLVM speculator pass and a TLS runtime library, which is managed within the language neutral LLVM IR context.

The TLS runtime library has a global thread manager object to serve as interface between the library and the speculator pass. The thread manager manages for each CPU three objects maintaining thread status data, global buffering and local buffering of the speculative thread, avoiding dynamic memory allocation for efficiency. As we use *out-of-order speculation* in which there are at most one-pair of threads synchronizing, a neat feature is that the design and implementation is lock-free. We compile the runtime library into a bytecode library and link it with

H. Kasahara and K. Kimura (Eds.): LCPC 2012, LNCS 7760, pp. 270–272, 2013.

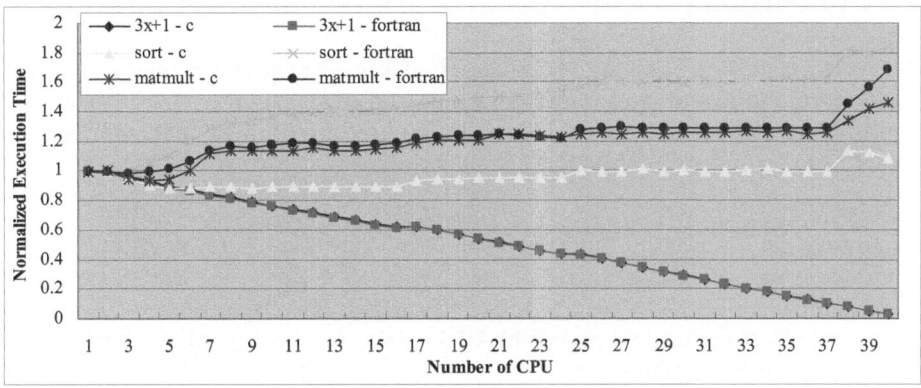

Fig. 1. Performance Results

the bytecode of the speculated source program, enabling it to be incorporated into subsequent LLVM optimization passes, including inlining of library function calls.

The speculator pass generates a TLS runtime library call to assign the ID of an available CPU to the speculative thread. Since LLVM does not allow branching directly to another function we construct a *speculation table* to redirect entry control flow, implemented as a switch instruction that jumps to either normal entry or to the speculation block depending on an input parameter. At the join point synchronization with the speculative thread is performed if necessary. Within the non-speculative thread this process is encapsulated by a library function, which returns true/false if the speculative thread commits/rollbacks. If true is returned control branches to a *synchronization table*, redirecting control flow to a synchronization block given the corresponding block counter.

We allow speculative threads to enter nested functions, which is non-trivial since the non-speculative parent thread needs to reconstruct equivalent stack frames, but stack frames are not available at the LLVM IR level. We track stack frames as the speculative thread descends into a call chain. The speculator pass generates a TLS library call to register a new frame for each nested function call, which is matched by another TLS library call to pop the frame up at return points. The non-speculative parent then generates a corresponding call chain, restoring frame data as it descends during synchronization, a process enabled by a library call inserted at the top of the non-speculative function.

3   Experimental Results

The TLS system is implemented on llvm 2.9 with llvm-gcc-4.2.2.9 front-end. The system is experimented on a 40-core Intel Xeon machine. We use a synthetic benchmark "$3x + 1$" problem as well as two realistic benchmarks: merge-sort and matrix multiplication. The performance results are illustrated in Figure 1.

4   Conclusions

Our work provides a basis for TLS research in a full-featured compiler framework that accommodates a wide variety of input and output contexts. Experimental results show that the system enables scalable speedup for ideal benchmarks, with potential for speedup in real-world applications.

References

[Chen and Olukotun, 2003]Chen, M.K., Olukotun, K.: The Jrpm system for dynamically parallelizing Java programs. In: ISCA 2003: Proceedings of the 30th Annual International Symposium on Computer Architecture, pp. 434–446 (2003)

[Oancea and Mycroft, 2008]Oancea, C.E., Mycroft, A.: Software thread-level speculation: an optimistic library implementation. In: IWMSE 2008: Proceedings of the 1st International Workshop on Multicore Software Engineering, pp. 23–32 (2008)

[Pickett and Verbrugge, 2005]Pickett, C.J., Verbrugge, C.: SableSpMT: a software framework for analysing speculative multithreading in Java. In: PASTE 2005: ACM SIGPLAN-SIGSOFT Workshop on Program Analysis for Software Tools and Engineering (PASTE 2005) (2005)

[Quiñones et al., 2005]Quiñones, C.G., Madriles, C., Sánchez, J., Marcuello, P., González, A., Tullsen, D.M.: Mitosis compiler: an infrastructure for speculative threading based on pre-computation slices. In: PLDI 2005: Proceedings of the 2005 ACM SIGPLAN Conference on Programming Language Design and Implementation, pp. 269–279 (2005)

[Steffan et al., 2005]Steffan, J.G., Colohan, C., Zhai, A., Mowry, T.C.: The STAMPede approach to thread-level speculation. ACM Transactions on Computer Systems (TOCS) 23(3), 253–300 (2005)

Abstractions for Defining Semi-Regular Grids Orthogonally from Stencils

Andrew Stone and Michelle Mills Strout

Colorado State University
{stonea,mstrout}@cs.colostate.edu

In various applications including atmospheric and ocean simulation programs, stencil computations occur on grids where sub-domains of the grid are regular (e.g., can be stored in an array) but boundaries between sub-domains connect in an irregular fashion. We call this class of grids *semi-regular*. Implementations of stencils on semi-regular grids often have grid-structure details tangled with the stencil computation code. This tangling of details requires programmers to have full knowledge of the current grid structure to make changes to the stencil computations and makes changing the grid structure extremely expensive. Existing libraries and tools [1–7] for stencil computations have not focused on this class of grid, focusing instead on purely regular or irregular grids. In this poster we introduce abstractions for the class of semi-regular grids and describe the GridLib library where we have implemented these abstractions. These abstractions enable a separation of grid, algorithm, and parallelization for semi-regular grids.

Semi-regular grids appear in Earth simulation applications such as the Parallel Ocean Program (POP), Global Cloud Resolving Model (GCRM), and the Flow-Following Finite-Volume Icosahedral Model (FIM). Examples of semi-regular grids include the lat/lon, torus, dipole [8], tripole [9], icosahedral [10], and cubed-sphere [11] grids. Different grids have different advantages: for example, the tripole grid is specialized for ocean simulation programs, cells in the icosahedral grid are evenly sized, etc. These grids consist of sets of regular subdomains and data for these subdomains is stored in arrays (as opposed to graph data-structures). With the array representation neighbors are accessed during stencil computations directly rather than indirectly through adjacency lists. When the stencil does not perform enough computation to hide the indirect access, the locality direct access offers will improve performance. However, the performance benefit is not without a cost: the array representation requires specialized code be implemented to handle nodes lying along subdomain boundaries. For example, in the icosahedral grid, specialized code is needed to communicate data between arrays and to handle points that represent the north and south poles. Such specialized code obfuscates the stencil algorithm code and is replicated for each stencil.

To address these issues, GridWeaver introduces a border mapping abstraction to specify connectivity around subgrid borders. The border mapping abstraction maps sets of points in a halo around a subgrid to sets of points in a (potentially) different subgrid. With this abstraction we are able to specify connectivity

H. Kasahara and K. Kimura (Eds.): LCPC 2012, LNCS 7760, pp. 273–274, 2013.

patterns commonly seen in semi-regular grids such as periodic boundaries, adjacent subgrids, and folded borders. To address communication GridLib automatically calculates a communication plan object. Communication plans specify what communication must occur to fill halo cells for blocks of locally distributed data. GridWeaver also includes abstractions for conducting stencil computations, conducting reduction operations, and distributing data.

These abstractions enable a separation of specification between the connectivity of, the algorithm, and parallelization concerns. This separation improves code clarity and simplifies code maitenance.

References

1. Colella, P., Graves, D.T., Keen, N.D., Ligocki, T.J., Martin, D.F., Mccorquodale, P.W., Modiano, D., Schwartz, P.O., Sternberg, T.D., Straalen, B.V.: Chombo Software Package for AMR Applications: Design Document. Technical report, Lawrence Berkeley National Laboratory (2009)
2. Kamil, S., Chan, C., Williams, S., Oliker, L., Shalf, J., Howison, M., Bethel, E.W.: A generalized framework for auto-tuning stencil computations. In: Proceedings of the Cray User Group Conference (2009)
3. Unat, D., Cai, X., Baden, S.B.: Mint: realizing cuda performance in 3d stencil methods with annotated c. In: Proceedings of the International Conference on Supercomputing, ICS 2011, pp. 214–224. ACM, New York (2011)
4. Christen, M., Schenk, O., Burkhart, H.: Automatic code generation and tuning for stencil kernels on modern shared memory architectures. Comput. Sci. 26, 205–210 (2011)
5. Maruyama, N., Nomura, T., Sato, K., Matsuoka, S.: Physis: an implicitly parallel programming model for stencil computations on large-scale gpu-accelerated supercomputers. In: Proceedings of 2011 International Conference for High Performance Computing, Networking, Storage and Analysis, SC 2011, pp. 11:1–11:12. ACM, New York (2011)
6. Giles, M.B., Mudalige, G.R., Sharif, Z., Markall, G., Kelly, P.H.J.: Performance Analysis and Optimization of the OP2 Framework on Many-Core Architectures. The Computer Journal 55(2), 168–180 (2011)
7. DeVito, Z., Joubert, N., Palacios, F., Oakley, S., Medina, M., Barrientos, M., Elsen, E., Ham, F., Aiken, A., Duraisamy, K., Darve, E., Alonso, J., Hanrahan, P.: Liszt: a domain specific language for building portable mesh-based pde solvers. In: Proceedings of 2011 International Conference for High Performance Computing, Networking, Storage and Analysis, SC 2011, pp. 9:1–9:12. ACM, New York (2011)
8. Smith, R.D., Kortas, S.: Curvilinear coordinates for global ocean models. Technical report, Los Alamos National Laboratory, LA-UR-95-1146 (1995)
9. Murray, R.J.: Explicit Generation of Orthogonal Grids for Ocean Models. Journal of Computational Physics 126(2), 251–273 (1996)
10. Tomita, H., Tsugawa, M., Satoh, M., Goto, K.: Shallow Water Model on a Modified Icosahedral Geodesic Grid by Using Spring Dynamics. Journal of Computational Physics 174(2), 579–613 (2001)
11. Sadourny, R.: Conservative Finite-Difference Approximations of the Primitive Equations on Quasi-Uniform Spherical Grids. Monthly Weather Review 100(2), 136–144 (1972)

Author Index